W9-ANP-822

GLOBALIZATION AND
THE HUMANITIES

Hong Kong University Press thanks Xu Bing for writing the Press's name in his Square
Word Calligraphy for the covers of its books. For further information, see p. iv.

For Art, my son

May his world be grounded in liberty for more

GLOBALIZATION AND
THE HUMANITIES

Edited by David Leiwei Li

香港大學出版社
HONG KONG UNIVERSITY PRESS

Hong Kong University Press
14/F Hing Wai Centre
7 Tin Wan Praya Road
Aberdeen
Hong Kong

© Hong Kong University Press 2004

ISBN 962 209 653 0 (hardback)
ISBN 962 209 654 9 (paperback)

Secure On-line Ordering
http://www.hkupress.org

British Library Cataloguing-in-Publication Data
A catalogue record for this book is available from the British Library.

Printed and bound by Liang Yu Printing Factory Ltd., in Hong Kong, China

Hong Kong University Press is honoured that Xu Bing, whose art explores the complex themes of language across cultures, has written the Press's name in his Square Word Calligraphy. This signals our commitment to cross-cultural thinking and the distinctive nature of our English-language books published in China.

"At first glance, Square Word Calligraphy appears to be nothing more unusual than Chinese characters, but in fact it is a new way of rendering English words in the format of a square so they resemble Chinese characters. Chinese viewers expect to be able to read Square Word Calligraphy but cannot. Western viewers, however are surprised to find they can read it. Delight erupts when meaning is unexpectedly revealed."

— Britta Erickson, *The Art of Xu Bing*

Contents

Acknowledgements

This collection of essays originated in a University of Oregon symposium, *The Prospects and Problems of Globalization*, in June of 2000. I thank the Collins Fund, the English Department, and the Oregon Humanities Center at the University of Oregon for their generous funding of the symposium. Gratitude is also due to George Rowe, the editor of *Comparative Literature* for the permission to reprint the following chapters originally appeared in a special issue of *CL* that I guest edited (53.4 [Fall 2001]):

Chapter 1
Masao Miyoshi, "Turn to the Planet: Literature, Diversity and Totality."

Chapter 2
Alison M. Jaggar, "Is Globalization Good for Women?"

Chapter 3
R. Radhakrishnan, "Globalization, Desire, and the Politics of Representation."

Chapter 5
Román de la Campa, "Latin, Latino, American: Split States and Global Imaginaries."

Chapter 6
Rob Wilson, "Doing Cultural Studies Inside APEC: Literature, Cultural Identity, and Global/Local Dynamics in the American Pacific."

Chapter 11
Bruce Robbins, "'Very Busy Just Now': Globalization and Harriedness in Ishiguro's *The Unconsoled.*"

Introduction:
Globalization and the Humanities

David Leiwei Li

I

The phenomenon that comes to be known as "globalization" is both complex and contradictory. Some trace it to the dawn of human civilization while others locate its origin in recent history. Some talk about it as a practical reality while others consider it yet a figment of imagination. Regardless of its contentious meaning and amorphous contour, globalization has registered as much in popular consciousness as it does in academic discourse. We shall approach the concept in its many contemporary manifestations, especially its ramification in the humanities. In economic terms, globalization signifies a worldwide domination of free-market capitalism with its local accommodations and resistances. In political terms, it speaks to the changing nature of the nation-state, the emergence of non-governmental organizations and electronic public spheres as these new entities negotiate with border-transcending capital for the governance of peoples and the sustenance of their interests. In cultural terms, globalization signals an individual's inevitable mediation with the regime of commodification and consumption that both universalizes desires and particularizes traditions. Overall, globalization seems to exemplify the proliferation of compressing and distancing mechanisms that transform our experience of time and space as well as of one another. Thus, David Harvey regards globalization as "time-space compression"; that is, an extraordinary speed-up of social life on a global scale together with the shrinkage of physical space through technology and the reduction of time to the perpetual and schizophrenic present (240). Accordingly, globalization is viewed as an instance of "time-space distanciation," in which both local and distant social institutions and incidents have become mutually dependent and equally formative. In the words of Anthony Giddens, it is "the intensification of worldwide social relations which link distant localities in such a way that local happenings are shaped by events occurring miles away and vice versa" (64). Nowhere could one find a more telling example of such intensified processes of planetary interaction, of "the *stretching* of social, political and economic activities across frontiers" and "on a continuum with the local, national and regional" than September 11 (Held et al. 15, original emphasis).

Manhattan is not an island, and the Manichaen claims of transcendent good and evil, of freedom versus fundamentalism, be they from the center or the periphery of world power, seem misleading representations of our global condition. Here, I find Michael Hardt's and Antonio Negri's comments especially relevant:

> It is more accurate and more useful to understand the various fundamentalism[s] not as the re-creation of a premodern world, but rather as a powerful refusal of the contemporary historical passage in course . . . one could argue that postmodern discourses appeal primarily to the winners of globalization and fundamentalist discourses to the losers. In other words, the current global tendencies toward increased mobility, indeterminacy, and hybridity are experienced by some as a kind of liberation but by others as an exacerbation of their suffering. (146, 150)

Fundamentalisms are not geopolitically or culturally exclusive; they cannot be circumscribed within national boundaries or coded solely in civilizational terms. The medieval guises in which fundamentalisms appear are modern articulations of authoritarianism — whether they are of Christian, Muslim, Hindu, or Confucian origin. Even in an Islamic world that seems to radically encapsulate the problematic of globalization now, we behold the coexistence of secular Muslims and sacrosanct Muslims, of people who can readily access the market, mass education, and mass media, and of people who cannot afford to eat at McDonald's, whose only option of education is the madrasa, and only dream of salvation, mecca. There is far much history to be lived before global capitalism can hope to fulfil Francis Fukuyama's prediction of "the end of history" wherein all prior forms of historical contradiction will purportedly be resolved. Indeed, there is so much of what Samuel Huntington calls "the clash of civilizations", occurring both within and without civilizations, that our humanity seems under siege.

If the humanities comes into being at a point when Europe dominates the world system, how does it reconstitute the world of knowledge after the political decolonization of Asia and Africa and the apparent neocolonization of the globe by late capital? If the humanities has evolved as historical reactions to theist orders, how does it approach that part of our humanity still steeped in a submission to religious precepts, hierarchical conceptions of social order, and resistance to secularism? If the humanities are social technologies that engineer autonomous individuals in modernity and sovereign subjects of the nation-state, what is its *raison d'être* in today's world where finance capital and televisual media crisscross national borders in the inculcation of global consumers? If the humanities recapitulates Enlightenment ideals — culturally non-specific yearnings for universal peace, prosperity, equality and justice — how does it address the persistence of poverty that global capital has simultaneously alleviated and exacerbated? How does it deal with violence that originates from the experience of extreme powerlessness and exclusion, in order to encourage discussion of variant conceptions of the common good and the shared practice of human rights?

Though not explicitly framed in this manner, the restructuring of the canon with which the humanities in the US has been preoccupied for the past three decades appears to reflect these concerns. Contemporary globalization, as Fredrick Buell has it, is a kind of "deep sea change that is reshaping not only quotidian lives, familiar institutions, and local cultures but also ongoing attempts to present them in fields ranging from sociology, history, economics, art, and literature to science itself" (6). The many heated theoretical and methodological debates in humanistic study should therefore be properly understood in light of the enhanced awareness of the world and the attempt to negotiate new global relationships. If geopolitical globalization yields "a decentered set of subnational and supranational interactions — from capital transfers and population movements to the transmission of information," its cultural manifestation is evident in ways the world has been representationally reorganized in the academic specialities, into new areas, new subjects, and new disciplines. As such decentering "challenges the existing nation states to reformulate their cultural identities for a more complexly interconnected era," it enables the shifting of disciplinary boundaries in the humanities and the production of "hybrid interdisciplinarity" (ibid. 7, 11).

Buell's affirmation of this disciplinary decentering is for Bill Readings a source of anxiety. It is not that Readings harbors any nostalgia for the supposed sovereignty of national identity. But the decoupling of the nation-state and the modern notion of culture has meant for him a critical absence of political agency through which the traditional subject of the humanities is produced. "Since the nation-state is no longer the primary instance of the reproduction of global capitals," Readings contends, "'culture' — as the symbolic and political counterpart to the project of integration pursued by the nation-state — has lost its purchase" (12). In the apparent collapse of this nation and culture integrity, the transnational capitalist system now offers people a "non-ideological belonging: a corporate identity in which they participate only at the price of becoming operatives" (48). While Buell is hopeful that the register and recognition of cultural difference in the intertwined strains of world history provides meaningful channels to think about a shared planetary destiny, Readings is afraid that "the international and interdisciplinary flexibility" — which arises in the decline of the nation-state and the wake of its cultural hegemony — may not be a better alternative, especially if it is envisaged merely to meet the demands of the global market (49). Neither the progressive appeal to multiculturalism nor the conservative defense of the masterpieces is adequate for Readings, whose distaste for the Enlightenment narrative of truth and autonomy seems extended to the work on cultural capital.

One may agree with Readings that Pierre Bourdieu's analyses indeed proceed by presuming "the single, closed game is the game of national culture" (107). But to dismiss on this ground alone Bourdieu's insight on the very process the Enlightenment ideal of widening social access for the common people has been betrayed in the actual unequal distribution of cultural capital seems myopic. It is especially so in view of Readings's own ethical commitment: his, not unlike Bourdieu's, is a commitment against imperial sovereignty and a commitment to justice. Such justice is envisioned through a notion of the subject that is by necessity incomplete. "The singularity of the 'I' or the 'you' is," in Readings words, "caught up in the network of obligations that the individual cannot master" (185). This incomplete individual whose existence is forever indebted to the endless web of local and global relationships thus entails that "the political as an instance of community" "does not establish an autonomous collective subject who is authorized to say 'we' and to terrorize those who do not, or cannot, speak in that 'we'" (188). By positing social bond as a necessity of sharing and proposing a world community whose obligation to its members are infinite, Readings wishes to transcend "the capitalist logic of general substitutability (the cash-nexus)" which is for him "the logic of the restricted or closed economy" underlying the nation-state as a geocultural formation (ibid.).

Philosophically persuasive, Readings's vision of an inherently open global community of non-finite obligations suffers from a lack of material specification, just as Bourdieu's democratic impulse is paled by restricting the universal to the national. Evocative of such familiar topics on globalization and the humanities as the tension between nationalism and cosmopolitanism, the local and the global (Wilson and Dissanayake, Nussbaum and Cohen, Jameson and Miyoshi, and Cheah and Robbins), Readings's utopian community is however liable to become an alibi through which the fervent call for obligations could evaporate in thin air. Though weakened, the nation-state remains a vital institution where the exercise of obligations of the kind that Readings theorize can find its feasible fulfillment. One thinks of children of illegal immigrant laborers and maids in California and wonders why the state or the States are not obligated to educate them. One also thinks of electronic engineers trained in India and working in the Silicon Valley and wonders why the jobs and wealth they create here should not be shared in their original homeland. These are just examples in which the "ethic probity" of a mutually dependent global community Readings envisions may wed well Bourdieu's insistence on the more equitable distribution of capital, cultural or otherwise, which is no longer confined to national communities (192).

Instead of accepting his conclusion to abandon "that legitimating metanarrative" of the Enlightenment, we should not let the imperfect realization of its promises blind us from fully appreciating the significance of the nation-state both as an historical institution and an inspiring trope of democratic covenant (ibid.). Not only does it remain a site where the metaclaims of equality present tangible checks on the march of neoliberal capital and its gospel of deregulation and privatization, the nation-state continues to signify a sense of the communal whose democratic principle and potential, more importantly, are capable of being "transvaluated" and rearticulated in other forms (ibid., 179). Readings's critique of the autonomous subject and advocacy of interdependency should help us recognize the radical disparity of the haves and the have-nots in our world, and reckon with the obscene concentration of wealth and power in the hands of a few nations, corporations, and individuals. His suggestion on the inexhaustible social bond should help us imagine democratic covenants and systems of distribution that are infinitely more equitable, capacious, and just. It should encourage us to accomplish what the cultural and ideological apparatus of the nation-state has so far failed — rescuing the humanities, to resonate with Readings, from the ruins.

II

This volume is a collective academic enterprise that frames recent debates and developments in the humanities in a salient globalization paradigm. The divergent contributions here share the premise that the drastic transformation in world economy and international politics since the end of the Cold War is accompanied by concurrent efforts in the humanities to question the validity of a nation-bound conception of culture. The questionings evidence at once a desire to comprehend the ever-changing conflicts and consolidations of an emergent planetary culture and the will to affect the course of its evolution through representation. Against "the tyranny of the market" (Bourdieu), which naturalizes in barely disguised neo-Darwinian terms both the aggregation of power for the increasingly few and the disintegration of social bond, we are committed to an egalitarian model of global distributive justice and determined to cultivate a cosmopolitan communal consciousness.[1] The humanities seems an appropriate arena wherein an alternative form of globalization based on universal human rights can be imagined to counter the hegemony of neoliberal privatization and deregulation. It is also an arena where the exercise of intellectual agency can effect possible change in the enhancement of public education and the reproduction of cultural capital, especially for the world's deprived.

This book is divided into two parts. Part I, "Field Imaginaries," investigates the changing nature of the nation-state with a particular emphasis on the transformation of the disciplines and areas of humanistic inquiry. Part II, "Virtual Worlds and Emergent Sensibilities," calls attention to the radical impact by the technologies of capital on everyday life, on the way one positions oneself and relates to another in a changing social universe. The geopolitical and disciplinary dimensions thus converse with the communicative and individual aspects of globalization both to provide new perspectives on the perennial concern of the communal in the humanities and to rehearse more democratic orders of representation.

The geopolitical form has its inseparable aesthetic alter ego; otherwise, one cannot really comprehend the methodological challenges and reconstitution of legitimate subject matter that dominate the humanities in recent decades. Speaking from the vantage points of disciplines and areas, postcolonial, ethnic, regional and transnational studies, with their overlapping domains and shifting boundaries, the contributors in Part I, "Field Imaginaries," accomplish two significant tasks. On the one hand, they historicize the process in which the centrality of the nation-state in the humanities has been transformed. On the other hand, they offer a refreshing take of such altered state without being unduly enthusiastic about the bliss of uprooted and unbounded knowledge production. Just as nationalism and globalism coexist and compete in the province of international politics, academic subjects continue to reside in the uneven negotiation of residual institutional structures and emergent intellectual inquiries.

For Masao Miyoshi, Alison Jaggar, and R. Radhakrishnan, the gaping gaps in global wealth and power prompt an imperative centering of inequality as the most essential category of ethical inquiry. The weakening of the nation-state is considered a general weakening of its political commitment to the common people. In contrast to the critique of the universal that fuels much insightful revisions in the past, and the rhetoric of celebratory difference, still prevalent in certain corners of the academic left, we witness here a concerted progressive voice at once attuned to discrepant social realities and appealing to a dialogical conception of global justice. Their analyses contradict the presumption of nation-states' demise, as their prognosis demands the articulation of a symbiotic humanity.

To inaugurate this imaginative "Turn to the Planet," Miyoshi calls our attention to the end of the cold war, when the ascendancy of neoliberalism in the macro sphere of global political economy parallels the spread of desocialized individualism in the micro sphere of the self. The gospel of privatization has the pernicious effect not only of polarizing the rich and the poor of the world, but also infiltrating the psychic makeup of the individual who is now likely to regard predatory "self-interest" and "optimal waste" as the rational norm of daily life. Under this condition, Miyoshi questions the reigning logic of difference and warns against the hair-splitting breakup of group identity. Instead of advocating a recuperation of the nation-state, he endeavors to "restore the sense of totality to the academic and intellectual world," both professionally and politically. Such a task entails the rejection of neoliberal globalization's exclusionism and the discovery of an all-inclusive totality that will nurture our common bonds to the planet, our custodial responsibility to it, and our duty to work out a sustainable economy that will "reduce consumption without cutting employment." The creative domain of literature and literary studies, Miyoshi believes, is where the "ideal of planetarianism" acquires its most persuasive power, making possible its translation into political viability.

Such planetarianism must be located in an axis of common goods — among them, "peace, prosperity, and democracy" — and worked through the figure of "women," according to Alison Jaggar. Confronting globalization in unambiguous ethical terms, "Is Globalization Good for Women?" seems to have linked Miyoshi's vision of an egalitarian totality with *Is Multiculturalism Bad for Women?* (Okin et al.), which productively teases out the odds of simultaneously affirming group-specific identity and a universal ideal of equality. If globalization in its dominant neoliberal form signifies the accelerating integration of a single global market and the destruction of welfare, it is, Jaggar argues, bad for the majority of the world's women. In its feminist re-vision, however, globalization could be liberating for humanity. Jaggar reinserts the concepts of justice and rights to dissect neoliberalism's promise of "peace, prosperity, and democracy." The end of the Cold War has not delivered the peace dividends once imagined. Instead, increasing militarism exhausts resources for health, education, and social services, exacerbates the subjugation of civilian populations, pollutes the environment and degrades women. Economic inequality is increasing not only between the North and South but also within them, with women of color and women in the South bearing disproportionately the brunt of low wages, uncertain employment, poor working conditions, and sexual exploitation. In an argument reminiscent of Amartya Sen's *Development as Freedom*, Jaggar addresses issues of economic and political redistribution and self-determination, and proposes an alternative "globalization from below." She envisions a feminist transnational alliance that would be able to expand the abstract yet implicitly male norms of "civil and political rights" to include "entitlements to education, to work and to a standard of living adequate for the health and well-being of self and family." Because women are vastly over-represented in the world's poor, "a concern for guaranteeing women's human rights" represents an alternative to neoliberal globalization and could go far in promoting a world of true social good for everyone.

If Jaggar opts for feminist NGOs (Non-Governmental Organizations) to fight against the concentration of power in the few First-World societies, R. Radhakrishnan emphasizes the ubiquity of agency and sovereignty for

Third-World nation-states. "Globalization, Desire, and the Politics of Representation" exposes neoliberal globalization as a regime of uneven development through which dominant nationalisms dismantle their subaltern counterparts. Because of their historical achievement of full sovereignty, the developed nations now claim an ethico-political authority insisting both on the deconstruction of Third-World nationalisms and the realization of a new world order on behalf of the rest. Although this clearly constitutes a problem of political representation on the planetary stage, a model of "techno-globality" has been introduced to dematerialize the agency of sovereignty and citizenship in weaker nation-states while promote a pseudo-form of network inclusiveness that disguises the naked power of the dominant nation-states.

Working through such figures as Said, Spivak, Charterjee, Ashis Nandy and Amitav Ghosh, Radhakrishnan imagines a world that hinges on "the value of human relationality" and the universality of "suffering," the latter of which, not incidentally, also informs Paul Gilroy's recent argument for cosmopolitan political coalitions beyond the color line. Here, Radhakrishnan intriguingly correlates the need to balance political power between nation-states with the need for a redistribution of desire. If the dominant desire pivots on "the objectification of the other," "real desire" of the type he proposes "derives from a radical 'lack' that impoverishes every ego that would seek to sign for plenitude in its own name." This model of reciprocal transcendence, not dissimilar to Readings' concept of the inexhaustible social, should give guidance to a new global imaginary. It would encourage an understanding of cultural and civilizational incompleteness and the need for relational bonding among existing nation-states and peoples. Until we submit it to this dialogical mix of "self-centered perceptions and other-centered perceptions," he contends, globalization is but domination in another name.

Like Miyoshi, Paul Jay premises his argument on the state of disciplinary disintegration. He views "fragmentation" as inherent to literary history and refuses to grant coherence to the humanistic disciplines once dominated by Eurocentrism. However, he is conscious of a disciplinary struggle between postcolonial studies and the more recent globalization studies. Jay concedes that postcolonial studies are primarily the work of Third-World intellectuals rooted in the experience of political decolonization and nation-building, while globalization studies seem largely the product of Western intellectuals grounded in complex theories of postnational structures and cultures. However, to see the latter as a threat to the former is for him to register a historical break that assigns "postcolonialism" to "the rise of modernity and the epoch of nationalism" and "globalization" to a "postmodern and postnational" phenomenon. A more helpful conception, Jay contends, lies in the continuum of colonization and decolonization, understanding both as integral historical processes that culminate in globalization.

Having emphasized on this continuity, Jay nevertheless resonates with R. Radhakrishnan in noting that neoliberal globalization threatens the economic and cultural autonomy of nation-states, especially the emergent ones. The question he poses then is this: "How can globalization studies contribute to the project of postcolonial studies when globalization itself is now a central threat to the postcolonial nation-state?" Elaborating on Ania Loomba's position in *Colonialism/Postcolonialism*, Jay works against both the commodification of hybridity and the fetishization of purity by emphasizing the traveling nature of culture and the historical co-production of the indigenous and the foreign. With this critical caution, he performs a reading of Arundhati Roy, Zadie Smith, Mohsin Hamid, and Salman Rushidie and shows the potential of approaching texts in a transnational framework that simultaneously attends to the catastrophic and the congenial effects of contemporary globalization.

If Jay's transnational imaginary entails a traveling trajectory, Roman de la Campa's "Latin, Latino, and American" situates this trajectory in the convergence and collision between a hemispheric construction of the Americas and the animate republican fictions of the United States. Such deeply established academic disciplines as American and Latin American Studies, in his view, owe their constitution to civilization/barbarism, Anglo/Latin, North/South divisions. To start, de la Campa zeroes in on the Latino population in the US, linking its migratory shifts and permanent diaspora with the motions of global capital and the concept of "split states." A split state captures for him a severed entity, the condition of remittance economy and the process of re-territorialization that not only applies to states whose paths to modernity come under stress but also suggests a postnational symptom full of cultural, economic, and political possibilities. With its internal plurality — Cubans and Puerto Ricans on the East Coast and Mexicans on the West — Latino America blurs civilizational models and unsettles the North and South divide. With its hemispherical scope, the Latino-Latina category also demands comparative examinations of Latino and Latin American studies. To the extent that their racial profile includes African, Amerindian, and Asian ancestries historically excluded from the melting pot equation, to the extent that a prevalent bilingualism and biculturalism characterizes their cultural identity, and to the extent that their music crosses over both English and Spanish markets, Latino Americans appear to figure new ways of imagining the Americas as well as multicultural redefinitions of the state. At the same time, however, de la Campa cautions against the media construction of consumer citizenship and calls upon academic intellectuals to respond critically to this undercurrent of neoliberal globalization.

A similar counter-hegemonic impulse underlies Rob Wilson's critique of the "Asia/Pacific" construct. "Doing Cultural Studies Inside APEC (Asia Pacific Economic Cooperation)" reveals how global/local dynamics expresses itself in regionalization. The yoking of Asia to the Pacific evidences the power of transnational economies not only in remaking the material world but reorganizing it discursively. The tactics of APEC are for Wilson exemplary of the interests of global capital. Imagined into a consensus-like shape, APEC would "fuse disparate units, from city-states, superpowers, and Third-World entities" into a "teleological optimism" and mandatory "free market capitalism." This cheery vision of Asian Pacific economic cooperation, while disrupting older Orientalist binaries of formal colonialism, conceals the depth of North/South imbalances and suppresses historical complexities. Discontent with but not dismissive of this articulation, Wilson sees an opportunity for a contestatory mode of "critical regionalism" to emerge. If the transnational commitments of APEC indicate the geopolitical ungluing of nation-states and the imagining of an Asia/Pacific community, cultural studies will have to transcend its residual attachment to "traditional disciplines (e.g. English) or large area studies formations (e.g. Asian Studies)." A critical Asian Pacific regionalism must be localized to bring out its full contradictory social meaning, and to do so demands "border-crossing, conceptual outreach, nomadic linkages, and interdisciplinary originality." Citing Bamboo Ridge's creative endeavors and the critical work done at the English department of the University of Hawaii, Manoa, Wilson substantiates his theoretical proposal with exemplary practices of a "counter-national localism."

Sympathetic with arguments against the container models of national culture, Brook Thomas, however, alerts us to the benefits of cross-examining the globalized notion of multiculturalism in the specific geopolitical institutions of its promulgation. A comparative analysis of multiculturalism in the United States, Canada, Australia, and New Zealand, "(The) Nation-State Matters," demonstrates how the history of settlement and the particularity of state formations shape the relative distinction of the four modes of multicultural practice. The careful construction of such a dialogical genealogy and the critical attention to the variations in the federal systems help bring out not only the categorical dangers of reifying racial groups, for example, Asians or Caucasians, but also contestations among visible and invisible minorities, immigrants and indigenes. More significantly, it challenges the prevalent theories that inform much of our thinking about multiculturalism and globalization. For the former, Thomas notes how appropriations of continental theory in the US often lapse into a conflation of French and American state systems, resulting in a "distorted analysis of [historical] conditions." For the latter, he deplores the premature claim of late capital's global reign and endeavors to retain "nation-states" as "one possible site of resistance to the unrestrained flow of capital." Together, Thomas convinces us how the nation-state is able to halt neoliberal globalization and why it continues to matter.

III

If Part I, "Field Imaginaries," exemplifies a complex charting of the changing humanities in response to the dense traffic between the global and the national, Part II consists of case studies that concentrate more on the prospects and problems engendered by new technologies in communication, transportation, and international business that affect the way we imagine the communal and sustain the individual. The decline of the literary and the national is first approached with an eye towards the cyberspace, which not only typifies the velocity and density of global transactions today but also makes available unprecedented modes of sociality and textuality. If print capitalism has cultivated, as Benedict Anderson's famous thesis goes, the "imagined community" of the nation, does the advent of the internet deliver an "electronic commonwealth" on a transnational scale (Abramson et al.)? In what way does the electronic media strengthen or threaten existing territorial powers and in what way does it secure or loosen the formation of community and subjectivity as we know them? How the emergence of cyberspace, which for many heralds an era of digital capitalism, redefines social groups, reorganizes political energies, and reshapes individual identities thus constitute the analytical core of the three essays on "Virtual Worlds."

Against a considerable body of theoretical literature enthusiastic about the decentralized architecture of the web and its possibilities for borderless planetary politics, Allen Chun and Jia-lu Cheng's study of "the growth of internet communities in Taiwan" stresses the importance of "local institutional forces" in determining the net's global reach. Chun and Cheng cite the crucial role of the Taiwanese government in the development of the net and treat such development as part of a state policy that deliberately democratizes politics and liberalizes economy to "localize the nation" for the changing global realities. Instead of transcending the traditional real, the contour of cyber communities resembles a disorderly overlap of an "extended private and public." Such communities are not to be equated with the conventional conception of the "public sphere." They constitute for Chun and Cheng the "liminal social," a space that encourages participation of groups whose minor status in society has meant an overall foreclosure to the dominant media and forum. Aside from democratic access through democratic dissemination of information, this liminal social, however, runs the risk of being submerged in its discursive subaltern state and failing to have its "countertalk" translated and transformed into political opposition in the traditional public sphere. Chun and Cheng worry that the medium of cyberspace, rather than "presenting itself as an expanded political public as envisaged by critical theory," may instead "open a back door to the public sphere."

Chun and Cheng's sober assessment that the cyber space, instead of being a liberating alternative, may indeed become a space of retreat from the traditional public sphere is paralleled by Liu Kang's concern that the power of global capitalism may seriously undermine the promise of the internet for egalitarian social consciousness. There appears a cross-strait critical consensus on the separate yet inseparable evolution of cyber communities in the divided transnational Chinese states. In "Internet in China," Liu anchors his analysis first on the arrival of the new press that trespasses state-owned and commercially-oriented local presses, second on the mushrooming of public forum (chat rooms) on politics and culture, and third on the revival of the literary via e-publication. Though generally sanguine about its pluralizing and decentralizing role in undermining censorship, Liu underscores the fact that the new media also "poses formidable problems": whether the internet political forum will lead to a "democratic sphere" in China or a "nursery of social antagonism" remains uncertain.

What is certain and distinctive about internet in China is its proliferation of e-fiction sites that in turn drives the boom in conventional publishing and cultural production. Here Liu takes note of the contradictory ideologies at work. On the one hand, Chinese urban youth culture converges with America's young entrepreneurial technocrat — *Xin xin ren lei*, or the "New, New Humanity" (a Taiwanese coinage soon popularized on the mainland) meeting *the Yettie* (Sam Sifton), as it were, in their shared pursuit of self-pleasing lifestyles. On the other hand, one hears the insurgent voice of the Chinese New Left in such an experimental play as *Che Guevara,* summoning the spirit of Argentine guerrilla leader against China's turn to capitalism and materialism. The Internet in China finally exemplifies for Liu a "deterritorialized" arena in which "new forms of domination and exclusion" continue to contend with "forces for democracy and justice."

Struggles for democracy present particular challenges when subjects of such struggle are dispersed between nation-states. In a situation where the institutions of the home country are unavailable and that of the host country seem unfamiliar, does the internet become a convenient channel for deterritorialized politics or does it represent the displacement of politics all together? Sangita Gopal's "Home Pages" provides a complex reworking of this question. She first points out the often-neglected equivalence between migration within and immigration across national boundaries that contemporary globalization has brought about. Internal motions of people and instantaneity of cyber communication, she argues, have come to destabilize the conventional conception of immigrant subjectivity, at once blurring the categories of "immigrant" and "native" and reconfiguring the "digital diaspora" through new forms of consumption. While recognizing the role of websites and portals in suturing new immigrant subjectivity, easing alienation, and collapsing the distance between "neighbors" and "foreigners," Gopal also realizes that ontologies enabled by cyber commerce eliminate the political potential associated with the construction of "netizen" (Poster 101). In this light, the Indian immigrant's resort to cyber communication is symptomatic of the questionable status of his/her body in accessing the American body politic. On the other hand, if the new Indian immigrant cyber subject is "a blueprint for the global subject," such a subject will have "nothing at stake except its own nodality, its identity becom[ing] the sum of its passwords and interfaces" in the commercial universe. Here one hears in Gopal the unmistakable echo of Chun and Cheng, Liu Kang, Miyoshi and Radhakrishnan, as well as Bill Readings, in their concerted caution against the disembodiment and dissolution of political agency. Finally, these localized takes on global interconnectivity not only challenge the inherent openness and democracy frequently associated with the cyber media but also crystallize the ideological ramifications of cyber mediation for politics, commerce, and personal commitments.

Cybernetic virtual worlds are only a node of "the electronically networked economy," the latest "capitalistic mode of production [that] shapes social relationships over the entire planet" (Castells 504, 502). Besides being a global mode of economic production, network capitalism is becoming a hegemonic form of culture. As such, it comes to transform what Raymond Williams terms "the structures of feeling" once lodged within the relative stability of the nation-state, the school system, and the family with their institutional distinctiveness and autonomy. Under the duress of transnational financial flows that infiltrate at once national borders and personal psyches, however, "Emergent Sensibilities" arise. The delineation of such sensibilities is the task of the last couple of essays, both readings of texts intended to tease out the human consequences of globalization as well as the possibilities of individual and institutional choice. Granted that globalization represents, in Fredric Jameson's enigmatic phrase, "the becoming cultural of the economic, and the becoming economic of the cultural" (Jameson and Miyoshi 60), does this integration of culture and capital leave room of resistance against the type of "network society" that Manuel Castells seems to have presented as a *fait accompli* ?[2] At the heart of the readings is an attempt to articulate available cultural resources both to counter the neoliberal logic of flexible capital and profit motif and cultivate cosmopolitan feelings and subject formations based on the values of equality and democracy.

The pace of planetary capitalism is punctured by what Bruce Robbins felicitously terms "everyday harriedness," a global "time deficit" that collapses the conventional boundaries of work and home, national allegiance and international commitments. A reading of Kazuo Ishiguro's *Unconsoled*, "Very Busy Just Now" illustrates the ambivalence of everyday harriedness. It pursues the serious implications of this global time crunch for the psychological and social reorganization of space and the project of "refashioning ethics to suit our transnational condition." Both professionalism and cosmopolitanism, as the domain of work and the domain of the international, respectively, seem pitted against the domain of the family, a postmodern remnant of a pre-industrial formation that is asked to stand in for all the values of bonding and belonging. Though against the "eroticizing of expertise" and the kind of "professional affectivity" that "substitutes recruitment for reproduction," Robbins declines to valorize ideological privatism and insists on generating sympathies and solidarities beyond the traditional family. Drawing from the creative vitality of *Unconsoled*, he proposes that the novel's premise of "time/space compression" also "includes a utopian foretaste of unearthly temporal abundance." When properly harnessed, it should energize our effort to reinvent the public at the level of the personal, undercut the gendered divide between work and family, and finally lead us towards a "broader and more inclusive civility."

Like Robbins's, my own contribution is preoccupied with the question of ethical living when local frames of reference are being incontrovertibly intertwined with global circuits of commodity and desire production. "Concentricity, Teleology, and Reflexive Modernity in Edward Yang's *Yi Yi*" interprets the director's most recent film to date against an oeuvre that tracks clairvoyantly the effects and affects of the Taiwanese economic miracle. The film's deployment of narrative and arrangement of imagery, beyond the representation of a society's meteoric rise on the global stage, I argue, form a productive conversation with the various theories of the modern, whether pre-, post, "multiple," "singular," "alternative" or "reflexive" (Eisenstadt et al., Jameson 2002, Gaonkar et al., and Beck et al.). Unique to this modern of East Asian variety is its radical temporal and spatial disruption. On the one hand, this modern is characterized by an extreme condensation of historical experience — the transition and transformation from the agrarian, to the industrial, to the postindustrial — within a single generation what takes European societies centuries to complete. On the other hand, it is marked by the precipitous removal of boundaries and the incredible feeling of openness. How the protagonists of *Yi Yi* or the players of the "silicon island" negotiate their radically condensed and abruptly decentered existence is the focus of Yang's movie, which at once captures the free and fragmenting flows of global capital and cultivates a cosmopolitan agency that deliberately locates the individual within the concentric communal and the perpetuity of humanity.

Yang's privileging of an ethic of relationality is resonant of Jaggar's conception of the "good," Miyoshi's "ideal of planetarianism," Robbins's notion of "inclusive civility," and Radhakrishnan's model of "reciprocal transcendence," just to name a few voices in this critical chorus on globalization and the humanities. Against the tyranny of the market and the violence of unilateral militarism, ours are among the voices of resistance that endeavor to open up dialogues on how we want to live together as a global community. It is my hope that this anthology will help us puzzle out, however minusculy, the predicament of our interdependent planetary culture. It shall help us garner the imaginative energy of writers, critics, artists and scholars to engender ways of thinking and means of creating conditions that will warrant the equal, just, and environmentally sound flourishing of our humanity.[3]

Part I

Field Imaginaries

1

Turn to the Planet:
Literature, Diversity, and Totality

Masao Miyoshi

LITERARY STUDIES IN 1983

In 1983, I was in Seoul to present a paper. The occasion was a conference on East Asian literature, a topic not too different from the one assigned to me for another event last year in the same city. This seventeen-year interval may not seem to be a long time in a normal phase of history. Between 1715 and 1732, for example, or even between 1918 and 1935, the change was certainly not trifling, but still the sense of continuity was quite strong. The difference between 1983 and 2000, however, is so immense that we can barely grasp the magnitude of the changes and transformations that occurred between these years, and in fact the phrase "a normal phase of history" is itself beginning to lose meaning. It looks as if we are heading toward a future where the pace of change will accelerate to such an extent that the trace of history may be erased as time hurries along through our everyday life. In this chapter, I'd like to recall the ideas that were crucial, or that I considered crucial at that 1983 conference, and then set those ideas against what seems crucial now and reflect on the intervening events. Such a comparison might also reveal what has survived unchanged and suggest what may remain intact in the future. I will discuss the changes and continuities both inside and outside what has been known as "literature."

By the beginning of the 1980s, the impact of Edward Said's *Orientalism*, published in 1978, had spread far beyond its immediate range of the Middle East and colonial history. His Nietzschean and Foucauldian message on the genealogy of the concepts of power and learning had become generalized in the discourse of modern history. As everyone knows, *Orientalism* radically challenged the orthodoxy in disciplines like history, anthropology, geography, and sociology, as well as literary criticism. Many branches of the humanities and social sciences had been formed during the colonial period with unexamined assumptions about the centrality of European and North American civilization, and intellectuals emerging in the just liberated former colonized world found in Said's criticism something both revolutionary and fundamental for mapping the history and geography of the future. The term "Orientalism" was added to the vocabulary of many languages as a name for the hegemonic ideology of domination. This was to be the beginning of a new paradigm for equality and the open mind. In the context of the dominant practice of the Eurocentric formulation of knowledge, however, the anti-Orientalist criticism was looked on as a disturbing challenge. To the academic establishment, it was a movement of rebellion and resistance — at least at the initial stage.

The East Asian field (where I have been more than an occasional sojourner) has long been organized from the colonial perspective, and thus Said's criticism was not accepted at once, especially by established scholars. Critical categories transferred from European literature to East Asian literature — without scrutiny as to their applicability — were still very much in use at the beginning of the 1980s. Genre, form, structure, periodicity (such as "modernity" and "modernization"), intentionality, affect, authorship, originality, audience, textuality, media, plot, character, tonality, the idea of "literature" itself, and many other fundamental literary and cultural notions — as well as the terms used in describing and analyzing European literature(s) and culture(s) — were more or less randomly chosen as approximations. Even at the 1983 conference in Seoul, there were sharp divisions and disagreements among the panelists on the merit of the newly proposed transvaluation.

As I reread my contribution, "Against the Native Grain: Reading the Japanese Novel in America," I am reminded of several events both personal and critical that took place around that time. I came to know Edward Said well; while he was finishing the final manuscript of *Orientalism* at the Center for Advanced Study in the Behavioral Sciences at Stanford, I was in Berkeley writing my book *As We Saw Them*, published in 1979. I am not comparing my book to Said's here: mine is a modest analysis of a cultural encounter, narrativized and ironic, whereas *Orientalism* is theoretical and oppositional, that is, both philosophical and political. I was stunned by the force of his opposition, which fundamentally challenged the liberal tenet, from which I had not quite been able to extricate myself despite my deepening disillusionment with academic intellectualism and liberalism. Said's position was different from Foucault's in refusing to universalize power and neutralize justice. It made a deeper impact on me, furthermore, as I joined him in various programs concerning the Palestinian struggle for survival against Israel, including visits to the West Bank and Tunis at his invitation in the 1980s. To the extent that I agreed with him on the matter of power and resistance, I was fully prepared to follow Said in viewing Japanese literature vis-à-vis Eurocentricity. Of course, I think I had attempted a similar project of transvaluation with *As We Saw Them* — as the title implied with its ironic coevality of "we" and "them" — except that mine was not fired with the resistance and opposition in which Said was unavoidably and passionately engaged. The contribution I made at the 1983 Seoul conference was in a way my first explicit statement as an act of resistance, a resistance which has lasted to this day under changing circumstances.

In 1983 my interest was far more literary than it is now. The problems I saw in the novel were within a literary context and in literary terms, although these problems and terms nearly always referred to external historical developments. I chose prose narrative fiction as the crucial focus of comparison and confrontation among cultures of the world. Poetry and drama trace back to antiquity everywhere before diverse economic and industrial developments sundered the world into haves and have-nots, while the "novel," or rather prose narrative fiction — of considerable length, printed and mass-circulated, describing the actions and events of the ordinary people — emerged after industrialization and colonialism widened the gap between rich and poor.[1] As I saw it, the prose fiction form reveals this history far more clearly than do poetry and drama, enabling me to avoid cultural and literary essentialism. However, if we place the prose narrative forms of various countries within the one category of the novel, we are likely to overlook different formal features inscribed by the historical variants in development and power. Difference, in this view, was the way to illumination.

In the 1983 paper, I discussed the modern Japanese narrative form *shosetsu* as having features that refuse to be classified under the headings that hold for the Western novel. Just to take one instance, because of the "aspect" — the temporal grammatical category of the Japanese language, where the perfect and imperfect are used rather than past, present, and future tenses as in English — the narrative sequence of the *shosetsu* tends to be coeval rather than consequential, discouraging the causal linking of narrative elements. Here, the preterit or the historical past tense — "the ideal instrument for every construction of a world . . . the unreal time of cosmogonies, myths, History and Novel," according to Roland Barthes — is not available (*Writing Degree Zero* 30–31). The *shosetsu* thus tends to be paratactic instead of syntactic, resulting in weakened and loosened — or freer and open-ended — plotting. Similarly, the absence of Japanese genesis and apocalypse myths has led to the rejection of a clear beginning and, more important, a clear ending or resolution in Japanese prose narratives. These narratives may often continue on and on, at times refusing the possibility of closure altogether.

This difference between the novel and the *shosetsu* at their high modernist/modernizing stages — from the late nineteenth century to the mid twentieth — might be explained by the marked residual oral features in the *shosetsu*, even though it is no longer an oral performance but a printed narrative just like any novel. While the modern novel is marked by invention, particularistic landscape, revision, analysis, spatiality, distance, comprehension, expansion, massive length, sculpturesque textual autonomy, and depth and interiority in characterization, the oral narrative is characterized by memory, formulas, repetition, display, temporality, proximity and intimacy, insularity, ritualism, episodic brevity and fragmentation, contextual communality, and social roles/relations of characters. Literacy requires the infrastructure of printing, distribution, leisure, and wealth, whereas orality depends on village or other communal space and physical places where the reciter and audience can assemble together. Such intimate sites have either vanished or been replaced by mechanical reproductions, such as radio or television, in the literate industrial societies. Literacy might thus be considered a central cultural marker of capitalist, metropolitan, colonial societies; orality, in contrast, seems tied to agricultural, peripheral, colonized societies.

I hasten to add that I do not mean to differentiate literacy and orality as being capable and incapable, respectively, of analytic and abstract speculation, as do Jack Goody and Ian Watt, or as being pacific and innocent on the one hand and violent and aggressive on the other, as argued by Levi-Strauss and Walter Ong. Nor do I agree with Jacques Derrida, Brian Street, and Roger Chartier, who insist that orality and literacy are ultimately indistinguishable. A given society as a whole is always endowed with a mixture of orality and literacy (and here I agree with Derrida, Street, and Chartier), but the two *activities* are distinguishable in the manner and circumstance of communication. Furthermore, metropolitan societies and peripheral societies make different use of literacy. However, orality does not evolve into literacy along the axis of progress, nor is orality prelapsarian innocence doomed by literacy. They are two different speech acts, which variously develop in the manifold conditions of history. The qualitative superiority or inferiority of the two is meaningless, as are the relative merits of the novel and *shosetsu* forms.

All this I argued in order to prove that the critical terms that were the products of one form did not fit the other. This, in retrospect, was my attempt to liberate the *shosetsu* and other peripheral narrative forms such as the Chinese, Arab, or Urdu narratives from metropolitan literary domination. I liked to indulge myself by fantasying that, as a written text, the novel — begun in the West nearly simultaneously with the commencement of colonialism — was fit for distribution over great distances and thus particularly suitable, unlike the oral recitation, for the writer in the metropolis to send out to the colonies far away — just like an emissary or a command from the colonial office to viceroys or governors in the far-flung corners of the world. I was convinced that the novel was inescapably colonialist — even with an anti-colonialist theme. However, the oppositional force wished to attribute to the *shosetsu* form had to be considerably curtailed because of Japan's peculiar place in the history of colonialism. It is indisputable, on the one hand, that Japan has been faced with Euro-American hegemony and adventurism since the mid-nineteenth century. Although military occupation was highly unlikely, the economic and political containment of Japan by the US and European powers was as comprehensive as that of any other Asian nation. Even more importantly, Euro-American cultural indifference to Japan was both disturbing and incomprehensible to its intellectuals in the early twentieth century, who were thoroughly familiar with proclamations of Enlightenment universalism. By the 1930s, Kuki Shuzo, Tanabe Hajime, Miki Kiyoshi, and other Japanese writers had sought out Heidegger, Husserl, and Jaspers, and when they found that the German philosophers were both ignorant about and indifferent to their country their disappointment was profound. Their construction of a nationalist philosophical system that eventually served as an apologia for Japan's aggression can be traced to such an experience of Eurocentricity. On the other hand, Japan was the first non-Western country to develop modern imperialism. Taking to heart the advice given by Bismarck and other Western leaders, the Japanese oligarchy and militarists quickly employed *real politik* and the instrumentality of colonialism for their own industrial development. After victory against imperial China and Russia around the turn of the century, Japan's swagger over its intra-Asian domination was unmistakable in the *shosetsu* of the time, not only thematically, but also in the narrative forms with which the writers of the time were beginning to experiment.

Said was able to extend the idea of Orientalism to include political oppression and thereby to take an uncompromisingly anti-Orientalist position in dealing with the questions of Palestine and Islamic countries. My own liberationist revisionism concerning the West and the Rest, however, had to be seriously qualified. I had to focus on both the West *and* Japan, that is, on the forces of oppression wherever they may have originated. And the fact that I presented the paper near the former colonial governor's headquarters in Seoul no doubt intensified the need to revise my Saidian anti-Orientalism, without, of course, forgetting Euro-American oppression in the process. All this was eighteen years ago.

YEAR 2001: DISCIPLINE ON THE WANE

To switch to the year 2001, the kind of literary exercise I have just described is no longer current in the literary critical scene in the United States and in many other countries. First, the sort of grammatical/formal analysis of literary products seems to interest very few scholars now, according to the programs of conferences and meetings and the books and journals being published. The idea of literature as composed of autonomous formal inventions survives largely within the guarded walls of a few traditionalist enclaves. Gone also is the argument concerning the interrelationships of power among nation-states and national literatures. In fact, the idea of the nation-state is itself very much in decline, not in literary studies alone, of course, but in intellectual discourse as a whole. If colonialism is talked about, it is often in terms of the era after the colonial rule, within the boundary of so-called *"post*colonial" discourse. Colonialism in this view is safely detached from today's state of affairs. Said's name has been replaced by Homi Bhabha's, Stuart Hall's, and Arjun Appadurai's, a changeover signifying the replacement of political economy by culture as a central paradigm. The structure of political-economic oppression is now explained as a hybrid cultural program in which the subalterns powerfully affect the oppressors' culture as they struggle for survival. With this transformation of the political-economical into the cultural, moreover, the suffering of the oppressed is de-emphasized. While colonialism has not as yet been converted into a benign civilizing act, history is certainly now looked upon with more leniency and latitude.

As for the decline in literature in general, one can at once point to the waning of canonic writers and works, established and mainstream scholars, conventional genres, and national literary history. White male masters first began to be replaced by female writers. Nearly at the same time, minority writers — male and female — emerged as a new dominant, but female minority writers took center stage. Over the last decade, fiction as a whole has lost its allure for the general public — except perhaps for pulp romances — and interest in foreign cultures, especially European literatures and languages, has begun to disappear. One of the simplest indicators of this radical change is in the recent figures in enrollment, recruitment, and placement at the undergraduate, graduate, and faculty levels in the humanities. The numbers of those enrolled in Russian, Italian, French, and German literatures and languages are down — conspicuously among undergraduates, but in graduate programs as well. A sharp decline is evident in the interest in literary studies as a whole. Far fewer undergraduates take courses in literature or major in it, which means fewer jobs for PhDs and fewer graduate students and seminars. Among the few enrolled in literature courses are social and natural science majors who want to have some "fun" in their college life — not a trivial development, since these are likely to be the students who constitute the main clientele of literary studies. There are faculty members, especially in the East Coast colleges, who are still active in specialized research in literary studies, but their classrooms are less crowded now, and fewer copies of their publications circulate.

Even among the disciplines on the wane, however, all is not lost. There are brisk departments, sections, and sectors even amidst the general decline. To begin with the most obvious, "theories" seem to have supplanted imaginative works such as the novel, poetry, and drama as the objects of study. Students and young scholars are too impatient to read an infinite number of texts that, as they see them, are mere materials for analytic statements. Skipping over novels, poems, plays, or historical documents, young — and older — scholars prefer ready-made summaries, abstractions, and analyses that are presumably provided by theorists as the end products of arduous examinations of primary documents. Novels and poems — at least the bygone works — are no longer being read with unmediated pleasure, an activity which strikes many ambitious scholars as indulgent and inefficient. Theories are to the point and, supposedly, endowed with universal and productive applications. Thus, theories are discussed with enthusiasm. In scholarly publications and graduate seminars, and increasingly also in undergraduate lectures, a knowledge of imaginative texts is no longer presumed; or rather, the students' ignorance is a given. Theories that were born out of a desire for universalism and systematization to redress prejudicial distortion and exclusion are now as commodified as Hollywood films or designer clothes. So what is the theory to theorize? What is the subject?

Today's theories abstract and construct systems of meanings rooted in the interrelationship of social groups: ethnic identities (minoritarian studies such as African-American, Hispanic American, Asian-American, etc.), gender studies (gay, lesbian, queer, and a variety of feminist studies), postcolonial studies (hegemonic/subaltern, diasporan, etc.), local/regional studies, and popular-culture studies, with emphases on the dominated and marginalized. The nation-state is much too totalizing and patriarchal a notion, and in current literary practice it is nearly always divided and subdivided into smaller units. Thus, for instance, the Association of American Studies is no longer about the US as represented by the hegemonic white male elites, that is, "traditional" history and society; rather it has virtually become a scholarly association devoted to the studies of ethnic minorities, a change suggesting contestations over the subject of history. Under the circumstances, the idea of totality is unsurprisingly taboo, avoided, distrusted, and ignored. Totality and universality, in this view, inevitably suggest repression and exclusion. The new social agenda is to recognize and insist on individual varieties, incommensurable differences. Such a development toward the principle of "difference," that is, multiculturalism, is no doubt salutary as long as it rejects the logic of concentrated power and authority instanced by univocal pretensions to world hegemony, Eurocentricity, American imperialism, dictatorship, elitism, racism, patriarchy, and any other totalizing and normalizing institutionality. Multiculturalism is propelled by the democratic impulse for equality and liberation. Before further discussing this democracy of dispersal in literary and cultural scholarship, however, I would like to examine the historical process by which such a change has been enabled since the early 1980s, the time of the earlier International Conference on East Asian Literature in Seoul.

THE SPIRIT OF SUVS

To resume the discussion where I left off, Said's criticism was no doubt liberationist, and it gradually gained momentum in the 1980s, even in the generally conservative East Asian field. One development in the 1980s, however, slightly altered the course of anti-Orientalism, particularly in the Japan field. By then the net effects of the devastatingly wasteful US adventurism in the 1960s and 1970s were beginning to become visible. The US trade imbalance was looming larger every year, and Japan was, as it still is, accumulating a huge trade surplus. In order to curb Japanese exports to the United States, the US formed the 1985 Plaza Agreement, which doubled the exchange rate of yen against the dollar. However, this strategy failed. By cutting the cost of labor and the margin of profit, Japan's industry increased its world market share throughout the 1980s. Consequently, the mood of protectionism intensified in the US, and Japan was portrayed as America's greatest menace, threatening to leap from the world's second largest economy to the leader in the twenty-first century. Inside Japan, the sense of confidence and arrogance grew as the unaccustomed affluence replaced the humiliating poverty of the years around WWII. The Japanese real estate industry began, very foolishly in retrospect, to buy up American lands and buildings, driving Americans to a frenzy of patriotism. At that time Ezra Vogel of Harvard wrote *Japan as Number One*, ostensibly to warn smug Americans, but perhaps also to flatter Japanese industry in the hope of serving as its chief apologist — for a fee. While US protectionism sought to stir up ugly patriotism, Japan's counterpatriotism was nearly as disturbing. Once again, my criticism of US hegemony had to be tempered by a stricture on Japan's own insular nationalism.

Alongside Japan-US international relations, there were three interconnected and far greater developments emerging in the context of the entire world in the 1980s and 1990s, which have fundamentally altered all national and international relations: first, the ascendancy of the so-called neo-liberal economy; second, the end of the cold war; and, finally, the spread of desocialized individualism, or self-interest and self-indulgence, as the rational choice in everyday life. These developments, which can be categorized under the rubric of "globalization," have each also played a profound role in altering the course of literary studies, or even the humanities as a whole — a point I will discuss more fully later on. First, neo-liberalism. After the elections of Margaret Thatcher in 1979 and Ronald Reagan in 1980, the UK and US accelerated the policy of privatization: denationalization and deregulation of industries, austerity programs, tax cuts on behalf of corporations and the wealthy, and various anti-labor measures. Business took steps to restructure the production process to make industry more efficient and profitable, presumably to survive the intensifying competition from Japan and emergent economies. In addition to increasing productivity by downsizing, corporations transferred production, capital, and market overseas. That is, they found cheap labor abroad, and by the use of robotics and digital technology blocked the labor movements as well as lowered wages. When they needed skilled labor from abroad, on the other hand, they demanded and usually received cooperation from both home and host governments. They also transferred their operations to places where corporate taxes were lower and environmental or human rights regulations were looser, extracting concessions not only from foreign governments but also from their own municipal, state, and federal governments. Corporations thus curbed the regulatory power of the states, but made use of them whenever it was to their advantage. Despite the conservative propaganda, the US did not end subsidies, but simply transferred them from the indigent to the wealthy and corporate. Such developments were a harbinger of the soon-to-arrive post-cold war economic order, which placed multinational and transnational corporate interest at the center stage of state policy.

Throughout the cold war the state was able to support corporations through direct military procurement that amounted to a huge proportion of the national economy (see my "A Borderless World?"). In the world after 1990, where the rationale of the security state system was reduced to a defense against a handful of ramshackle rogue states, direct subsidies to corporations of vast sums in the name of defense became difficult to justify. The new situation required a new narrative. Hence, the state insisted that there was actually no peace; that local, civil, and tribal wars were chaotic and unpredictable, and so even more hazardous to the United States than the cold war; that religious and cultural conflicts were bound to break out; that the United States and other industrial nations must remain rich and strong to defend civilization; and that corporate wealth best brings prosperity to the general population. The ideology of neo-liberalism was thus incubated. Left alone, corporations in service and manufacture are presumably at their most productive. Deregulation lowers the price and benefits consumers. Huge corporations are the most efficient and thus most beneficial to the public. Self-dependence not only strengthens the moral fiber of citizens, but also promotes production. Public programs are wasteful and corrupt. While all such presumptions are more believed than documented, taken together, they help create an economic order that not only concentrates wealth and power among the few, but also protects the center against any future challenge from the fringes.

The end of the cold war was certainly not unrelated to such an economic development. Unable to keep up with the joined forces of Western capital, the Soviet Union and its satellite states collapsed around 1990. What the end of the cold war brought about was twofold: the unchallenged neo-liberal economic paradigm in the world and the realignment of the Third-World nations. First, the structure of the modern nation-state that had long constituted the basis for capitalism, colonialism, and social organization was abruptly found to be superfluous and out of date. While the East-West rivalry lasted, the state needed the cohesiveness of a people as a reliable military resource for protection or aggression; likewise, the rich in control of the state needed people as a dependable source of labor for greater accumulation of their wealth. The state, in short, needed the nation. Once the cold war was over and the world became a potentially seamless economic field, however, the huge multinational corporations could transfer their capital, labor, technology, factory, market, and products to any place as long as it was more efficient and profitable, as we have already seen. For corporations the national boundary was often an impediment; they needed the freedom to range over an unbounded space.

Second, during the cold war both the Western and Eastern blocs were rivals in forming alliances with Third-World countries. One remembers the US State Department strategies and CIA operations in Africa, the Middle East, Southeast Asia, the Far East, and South America. To keep countries on their side, they chose whatever means available and expedient — foreign aid, propaganda, bribes, covert violence, manipulated elections, or the dispatch of marines, naval fleets, bombers and missiles. That is, as long as the cold war lasted, the impoverished non-aligned countries could manipulate the US and the Soviet to receive some handouts. Although most of the billions of dollars poured out in these years merely served to enrich dictators like Mobutu Sese Seco, Marcos, Suharto, the Saudi or Kuwait sultans, and General Pinochet — the list was endless, just as the transgression and ineptitude of the State Department and CIA were infinite — some money did reach the poor in these areas. With the end of the cold war, however, even this meager beneficence stopped nearly everywhere except for the odd couple of Israel and Egypt. Private corporations have no interest in helping the poor: they are under fiduciary obligations to make profits. They would consider it their duty to write off sub-Sahara Africa as unprofitable and therefore useless and absent. Even when some 25% of the youth in these countries are dying of AIDS, the pharmaceutical companies will not make drugs affordable to them.[2] Less than two percent of the world's capital now flows through the sub-Sahara Africa — with the exception of the Union of South Africa. Genocide draws no attention when private corporations perpetrate it.

The gap between the rich and poor has existed throughout history, but the proportion of the difference was far smaller between nations, as has already been mentioned. In 1999 the per capita GDP of the richest, Switzerland, and the poorest, Myanmar, were $43,060 and $100, a ratio of 430 to 1 (*Economist* 40). And this discrepancy is not as sharp as that between the annual income of the average CEO and the blue-collar worker in the United States, a ratio of 475 to 1 as of spring 2000 (Phillips). The point here is not just the immensity of the unequal distribution of wealth itself, nor the continuing growth of the gap, although they are both important enough. Rather, it is that the gap between the few super rich and the vast majority of humanity separates them as if they had nothing in common. That is, the rich of the world have more to share with each other across national borders, or even across the East-West or North-South divide, than with most of their fellow citizens. The world is sectioned into nations and nationalities only for those who cannot afford to move or travel beyond their home countries. For the rich, the world is indeed transnational and deterritorialized.[3]

What is most important to world trade now is not the flow of manufactured goods, but of speculative currencies, bonds, and derivatives — to the tune of one trillion dollars or more a day. With digital technology, the transfer of financial capital is easy, fast, and cheap. Although it is theoretically possible to keep track of all financial transactions, there is no mechanism as of now for any state, or its central bank, or any international organization, to control, or even monitor, such an immense transnational flow (Castells). As the nation-state becomes increasingly dysfunctional, those in charge of mapping the world economy are also discarding various social constructions invented for nurturing unified nation-states.

The third recent development — not a clearly definable event, but no less perceptible and pervasive than the neo-liberal economy and the end of the cold war — is that the drive for winning has spread far beyond the corporate organization and into our personal life. Neo-liberalism or globalization is not just an operational policy of corporations and governments. The legitimation of private profit over and above public good is based on a belief in competition as the fundamental human condition, and triumph as the ultimate goal of life. Those in need of help are held in contempt as inept, lazy, and superfluous, while the entrepreneurial "winners" are held in awe as capable, quick, and intelligent. Wealth and power are considered natural rewards for such strengths; poverty and marginalization, on the other hand, are the just desserts of the failures. In a situation such as this, self-interest is not only something one needs to protect from encroachment and exploitation by others, but also a guiding principle to be aggressively pursued for its own sake and with a matter-of-fact disregard for others. Opportunism is encouraged as a mark of flexibility and intelligence. The intensifying concentration of wealth and power is both a cause and effect of such social-psychological development.

A pervasive acceptance of consumerism is also both a cause and effect of neoliberalism. Without vast and rapid consumption, the capitalist economy would just collapse. And most economists never question economic expansion as a fundamental social need. Consumption is now considered indispensable to the increase of production. Consumption for the sake of consumption via built-in obsolescence and insatiable desire — optimal waste, really — is calmly accepted and integrated by the public into everybody's daily life. The ecological consequences of untrammeled waste are vaguely felt, and some environmental protection is certainly discussed or even enforced. But it has so far not received serious consideration in economic terms — like most other public needs and programs. Without being nostalgic, one can readily recall that merely a few decades ago frugality even among the rich was seen as decent and commonplace and conspicuous consumption as crude and exceptional. Since then, social behaviors have changed immensely in most industrial countries. Among the wealthiest, everything must be big, new, and priceless. Even the moderately rich must aspire to flamboyant exhibition. The spirit of SUVs infiltrates all areas of everyday life — from architecture, to urban planning, to "life-style." Ostentatious displays are no longer frowned upon by tribal surveillance. Unrestrained and unregulated by any tradition or authority, self-indulgence is now nearly an unembarrassed mark of success. Furthermore, the behaviors of the affluent, unlike in earlier days, have not so far aroused resentment among those who cannot afford them. The poor are happily persuaded that consumerism will soon become accessible to them. They are willing to wait in their dream and desire. Unless the few protests that broke out recently in cities such as Seattle, Washington, DC, Prague, and Davos manage to gather force, the world economy seems steaming ahead in its current course toward — no one knows where.[4]

TOWARD AN INCLUSIVE TOTALITY

Global neo-liberalism is powerfully altering fundamental assumptions within literary studies as well. Earlier in the second half of the twentieth century, the logic of difference was a strategy of liberation. The rejection of the nation-state as totalizing similarly implies the existence of more particularistic social units. In an immigrant and multiracial country such as the United States or Australia, multiculturalism is an obvious consensual choice, each group, minority or majority, demanding its own autonomous and independent, that is, incommensurable space. Without doubt, multiculturalism is preferable to the monoculturalist oppression of minorities by the dominant group. The logic of difference, however, paradoxically poses three internal difficulties that are likely to perpetuate a condition of exclusion and neglect for minorities.

First, insofar as each group's incommensurability means total uniqueness, the affairs of any given group are a matter that does not — or should not — concern the member of any other group. If this principle of noninterference is practiced resolutely, the minority — presumably less resourceful — groups must be left alone to shift for themselves. The majority group then has neither accountability to nor responsibility for the minority groups. Second, the problem of totality does not vanish when a nation is divided into ethnic or gender groups. Each group of course constitutes a totality that is smaller, but nonetheless as controlling and demanding as that of the nation. Consider, for instance, the minority called Asian American? Shouldn't that general and abstract entity be broken down into Chinese-American, Korean-American, Vietnamese-American, and many other sub-groups? And among Chinese-Americans, are the mainland Chinese to be considered in the same category as the Taiwanese? The Hong-Kong Chinese? Overseas Chinese? Chinese Women? Gays? Lesbians? Queers? Where does the logic of difference stop? Doesn't a particular individual remain as unrepresented within such categories as does a citizen of a totalized nation?

Third, among the three main categories of difference (race, gender, and class), class is distinct from the other two in that class has no reason to retain its identity if liberated, whereas race and gender have no reason to lose theirs. Race and gender can thus be viewed as more "authentic" identities than class, since class aspires to erase itself. In the identity politics that has consumed literary studies in recent years, this distinction among the three categories is tacitly assumed — with the result that class is seldom mentioned, unlike ethnicity and gender. Quite obviously, the ruling class welcomes this silence. For this reason alone, transnational corporatism has warmly embraced multiculturalism. Diversity at this juncture is a favored public policy, not a subversive program.

If every literary and cultural system is incommensurable, the idea of "comparative" literature is an oxymoron. Incomparables cannot be compared. In fact, very little serious work is being done now in the area of comparing national or regional literatures. Such efforts are being supplanted by studies of the inner workings of a culture or literature, which presumably are different from those of another. Power, however, is nearly always introduced as the constitutive factor — effectively casting every ethnic or gender minority in a more or less similar light, the light, for instance, of victimology.

The problem with the logic of difference is not just classificatory. In asserting autonomy and independence, each group rejects commonality with others and demands a certain internal cohesiveness. This need for solidarity is — functionally, at least — as disciplinarian as any national demand for loyalty and patriotism. And where does the authority of each group originate? How is the right to power and representation legitimized? Even parliamentary democracy will have to be rejected here, since elective representation requires the definition of an electorate, a totality. The minority leadership in this sense is likely to be based on self-proclamation, opening a way to opportunism and confusion. If sectionalism and secession are freely allowed, on the other hand, the social structure of a minority group will collapse into atomism. (That literary discourse can also be splintered by a similar kind of factionalism has recently been pointed out by Nina Auerback in "Acrimony" and K. Anthony Appiah in "Battle of the Bien-Pensant.") Such a situation in fact only encourages the usurpation of power by an opportunist within the group who knows how to represent the atomized multiplicity by manipulating sympathy, loyalty, and celebrity. Such a situation also clearly benefits the leaders of the dominant group, who can pursue their own interests with no regard for the minorities, just as they had always done before the days of liberation.

The disintegration of not just comparative literature, but literary studies as a whole, may be already under way. If our fractured groups are engrossed in their self-interests, outsiders have good reason to feel repulsed by them. The general public wants to understand its place in the "globalized" world, and there is a deep concern with the waste-based economy. And yet those who have traditionally intervened in such issues are preoccupied with their internecine struggles conducted in a language of their own. The public is excluded and unwanted as long as it refuses to learn the jargon of partisans and to become partisan. And as we have already seen, the public seems increasingly to look elsewhere for cultural interpretation and criticism. Literary productions — novels, plays, and poetry — are at present still alive, but they are no longer closely connected with the critical and analytic segments of the university.

The global economy, on the other hand, is having a profound impact on today's university, as I have described in "Ivory Tower in Escrow." The corporatized university is preoccupied with the market force, most conspicuously around information technology (IT) and bio-engineering. Outside of applied sciences, basic research — now called "curiosity research" — is visibly being ignored. Technology transfer has become the urgent agenda for administrators and managers of both business and academia. Thus learning is rapidly being transformed into intellectual property, and the free exchange of information into commerce. As "globalization" thus goes ahead full-speed, literary scholars remain absorbed in joyless self-isolation and futile in-fights. Under such circumstances, literary studies have little chance of competition, or even survival, within the walls of the university itself.

My interest here is, however, not in the recuperation or resuscitation of my professional specialization. Rather, I am concerned with restoring a sense of totality to the academic and intellectual world, both intellectually and politically. By now we know that particularity without totality is nonsense, deadening, and useless. Literary and cultural critics must look out at the world and interconnect all the workings of political economy and artistic and cultural productions. We must keep reminding ourselves that the "global" economy is not global at all, but an exclusionist economy. We must discover the sense of true totality that includes everyone in the world.

For this purpose, the return to the nation-state probably will not work any more. The old power structure has proven a failure much too often in the past two centuries of its history. Perhaps we need a new organization, one that is truly global and inclusive of all. There is one such core site for organizing such an inclusiveness, though entirely negative at present: the future of the global environment. For the first time in human history, one single commonality involves all those living on the planet: environmental deterioration as a result of the human consumption of natural resources. Whether rich or poor, in the East or the West, progressive or conservative, religious or atheist, none of us can escape from the all-involving process of air pollution, ozone layer depletion, ocean contamination, toxic accumulation, and global warming. Of course, the rich will try to stay as far away as possible from the pollution, but even they cannot remain protected for long. We can start from this realization of total commonality as we map out our world and engage in research and scholarship. Literature and literary studies now have one basis and goal: to nurture our common bonds to the planet — to replace the imaginaries of exclusionist familialism, communitarianism, nationhood, ethnic culture, regionalism, "globalization," or even humanism, with the ideal of planetarianism. Once we accept this planet-based totality, we might for once agree in humility to devise a way to share with all the rest our only true public space and resources.

What form this research on the preservation of the planet will take is not at all clear now, of course. It must combine environmental engineering with economics, political science, and cultural studies so that scholars in all fields may first work out the idea of an economy that will reduce consumption without cutting employment. The reduction of waste in the First World must be simultaneous with the increase of consumption in much of the Third World. They will have to devise a way to train and integrate the unused labor forces of the Third World to equalize wealth. By far the most difficult task in this project is how to invent a way to persuade, not advertise, culturally as well as politically, that there is no other future for any of us. Either through schools and universities, NGOs, UN-affiliated organizations, media, or residues of the state apparatus, we must curb our material dream and build a future that we will all share with an unprecedented commonality. For such a future we need to reimagine our common and universal culture, as we have never done in human history.

Of course, we may very well fail in this attempt. But if we do, we will not be there to see it. And perhaps we deserve to perish. On the other hand, faced with the fate of universally inescapable destruction and nullification, we may yet finally find a way to confront it together and to find a way to coexist with all others. There is at least that much promise of hope, the only hope we have been allowed to entertain together with everybody else on this planet.

2

Is Globalization Good for Women?

Alison M. Jaggar

Is globalization good for women? The answer to this question obviously depends on what one means by "globalization" and by "good" and which "women" one has in mind. After explaining briefly what I mean by "globalization" and "good" and indicating which women I have in mind, I intend to argue that globalization, as we currently know it, is not good for most women. However, I'll suggest that the badness of the present situation is not due to globalization as such, but rather to its specific neoliberal mode of organization. I'll identify some of the questions that globalization urgently raises for political philosophy and end by sketching one vision of an alternative form of globalization that could be very good for women — as well as for children and men.

TERMS OF DISCUSSION

What is globalization?

The term "globalization" is currently used to refer to the rapidly accelerating integration of many local and national economies into a single global market, regulated by the World Trade Organization, and to the political and cultural corollaries of this process. These developments, taken together, raise profound new questions for the humanities in general and for political philosophy in particular. Globalization in the broadest sense is nothing new. Intercontinental travel and trade, and the mixing of cultures and populations are as old as humankind; after all, the foremothers and forefathers of everyone of us walked originally out of Africa. The contemporary form of globalization did not appear *de novo* in 1989, with the collapse of so-called communism. It did not even originate in 1945 at Bretton Woods, New Hampshire, where the major institutions to administer the global economy were established, including the International Monetary Fund (the IMF), the World Bank, and the General Agreement on Tariffs and Trade (GATT), which was the precursor to the World Trade Organization (WTO). Rather than being an unprecedented phenomenon, contemporary globalization may be seen as the culmination of long-term developments that have shaped the modern world. Specifically, for the last half millennium intercontinental trade and population migrations have mostly been connected with the pursuit of new resources and markets for the emerging capitalist economies of Western Europe and North America.

European colonization and expansion may be taken as beginning with the onslaught on the Americas in 1492 and as continuing with the colonization of India, Africa, Australasia, Oceania and much of Asia. History tells of the rise and fall of many great empires, but the greatest empires of all came to exist only in the nineteenth and twentieth centuries. In 1815, Britain and France together controlled over one third of the Earth's surface, and by 1878 they controlled over two thirds. By 1914, Britain, France and the United States together controlled 85% of the Earth's surface. It was primarily in consequence of European and US expansion that the world became — and remains — a single interconnected system. European and US colonialism profoundly shaped the world we inhabit today. It produced the neoliberal philosophy that provides the rules for the war game currently known as "globalization," and it landscaped the highly uneven terrain on which that game is played.

Neoliberalism is the name given to the version of liberal political theory that currently dominates the discourse of globalization. Neoliberalism assumes that material acquisition is the normal aim of human life, and it holds that the primary function of government is to make the world safe and predictable for the participants in a market economy. Although its name suggests that it is a new variety of liberalism, neoliberalism in fact marks a retreat from the liberal social democracy of the years following World War II back toward the non-redistributive laissez-faire liberalism of the seventeenth and eighteenth centuries. It is characterized by the following features.

1. Under the mantra of "free trade," neoliberalism promotes the unobstructed flow of traded goods through eliminating import and export quotas and tariffs. It also abandons restrictions on the flow of capital. However, not only does it not require the free flow of labor, the third crucial factor of production, but it also actively seeks to control that flow. Although immigration from poorer to wealthier countries is currently at record levels, much of it is achieved in the teeth of draconian border controls that often cost would-be immigrants their lives. This lopsided interpretation of "free trade" enables business owners to move production to areas of the world where costs are lowest, perhaps due to lower wages, fewer occupational safety and health requirements, or fewer environmental restrictions, while simultaneously regulating the movement of workers wishing to pursue higher wages.

2. Global neoliberalism attempts to bring all economically exploitable resources into private ownership. Public services are turned into profit-making enterprises, and natural resources such as minerals, forests, water and land are opened up for commercial exploitation in the global market.

3. Neoliberalism is hostile to the regulation of such aspects of social life as wages, working conditions and environmental protections. Indeed, legislation intended to protect workers, consumers, or the environment may be challenged as an unfair barrier to trade. In the neoliberal global market, weak labor, consumer, or environmental standards may well become part of a country's "competitive advantage."

4. Finally, neoliberalism presses governments to abandon the social welfare responsibilities they have assumed over the twentieth century, such as providing allowances for housing, health care, education, disability and unemployment. Social programs, such as the Canadian health-care system, may even be challenged as de facto government subsidies to industry. "Defense and security" are among the very few government expenditures excluded from being judged "subsidies."

Many people have come to equate "globalization" with its current neoliberal incarnation, and they regard the costs of this system as inevitable consequences of modernization and progress. This perception discourages attempts to question the justice of neoliberal globalization or to envision alternatives to it. However, I believe that the most urgent task currently confronting political philosophy is to assess the justice of neoliberal globalization and to stimulate debate on possible alternatives.

What is "good"?

The term "globalization" evokes one venerable answer to an ancient philosophical question, the nature of the good life. This answer is the culminating vision of European Enlightenment philosophy — which in turn reflects an ancient Christian dream. It is the dream of the entire human species governed by universal law within a world order characterized by unity of purpose, shared concern, mutual responsibility, and common security. Its advocates promise that global neoliberalism will fulfill this dream by promoting the following goods:

1. *Peace.* Economic interdependence will make war unthinkable and so usher in an unprecedented era of world peace.
2. *Prosperity and social justice.* Expanded trade and economic competition will ensure the optimal allocation of scarce resources and increased economic efficiency, to the mutual benefit of all. Each region will produce what it is best suited for, according to its so-called "comparative advantage," and the rewards of individuals and countries will be proportionate to their contribution to the global market.
3. *Democracy.* Because trade liberalization requires expanded communications and freedom of movement, it will be accompanied by increased democracy.
4. *Environmental protection.* Increased world competition will encourage the elimination of waste and the efficient use of resources. Environmental resources will be conserved, and coordinated action will be undertaken to deal with transnational environmental problems such as acid rain and global warming.
5. *The end of racism and ethnocentrism.* Increased global interdependence and the consequent mixing of populations and cultures will undermine racism and ethnocentrism, thus realizing the ideal of a universal humanity.
6. *Women.* Neoliberal globalization will undermine local forms of patriarchal power, enabling women to become full participants in politics and the economy.

Who are women?

The deceptively simple question "Who are women?" has provoked many heated debates in recent feminist theory. In an effort to counter earlier generalizations about "women" that were false and exclusionary, contemporary feminists have been particularly concerned to argue that women have no essence. By this, they mean that no necessary and sufficient conditions exist for being a woman; no significant characteristics can be found that are attributable to all and only women. Feminists now insist that it is necessary to be constantly mindful of divisions among women, such as those of nationality, age, class, ethnicity, marital status, sexuality, religion — divisions that typically demarcate a status that is privileged from one that is stigmatized. Since no essential or typical or generic woman exists, broad generalizations about "women" must always be scrutinized because of the danger that they will exclude or marginalize some women. My interest is especially in women who are on the less privileged side of the various divides, in both the global North and the global South.[1]

I intend to argue that neoliberal globalization, despite its glowing promises, is helping to create a reality that is precisely the opposite of its promoters' rhetoric. Rather than experiencing an era of universal peace, the neoliberal world is ravaged by innumerable wars, many undeclared, and by high levels of militarism; many societies also face civil unrest and forms of institutional violence that are serious enough to be described as ethnic or class war. Not by coincidence, the same world is characterized by a rapidly widening gulf between rich and poor, both within and among nations. Thus, rather than bringing universal prosperity, neoliberal globalization is creating unprecedented wealth for a relative few and poverty and destitution for millions, even billions, of people. Increasing numbers of countries have adopted the outer forms of democracy as a cover for political authoritarianism and corruption, and the environment is being destroyed at an ever-accelerating rate. Finally, the neoliberal world is marked by the violent eruption of ethnic and racial hatreds and even genocide.

Peace, prosperity, democracy, environmental conservation and the elimination of racism and ethnocentrism are all overtly gender-neutral ideals, but each of them is also a distinctively women's issue. Because all known societies are structured by gendered value systems, which assign unequal status and privilege to men and women, as well as to whatever is culturally considered masculine and feminine, most — if not all — social issues carry meanings and consequences for women that are somewhat different from those they carry for men. To the extent that global neoliberalism undermines women's special interests in peace, prosperity, democracy, environmental health, and the abolition of racism and ethnocentrism, it is a system hostile or antagonistic to women.

Although neoliberal globalization is making the lives of many women better, it is making the lives of even more women worse. The lives of many of the world's poorest and most marginalized women in both the global South and the global North are deteriorating relative to the lives of better-off women and of men, and even deteriorating absolutely. In the next section I sketch some distinct ways in which the lives of many women have been affected by war, economic inequality and political authoritarianism; for reasons of space, I omit discussion of the distinct ways in which women are harmed by environmental destruction and by racism, ethnocentrism and xenophobia.

NEOLIBERAL GLOBALIZATION IN PRACTICE

War

Although the United States is sometimes said to have enjoyed more than half a century of peace, this statement ignores the numerous limited, undeclared, and proxy wars in which it has been involved during the last half of the twentieth century. These military activities did not diminish with the end of the cold war; recent highly visible examples include the Persian Gulf War at the beginning of the 1990s and the bombing of Kosovo in former Yugoslavia at the end of the same decade. In 1992, there were thirty-four wars worldwide, a new peak in the annual number of wars for the twentieth century. If "war" is defined to include civil war, then wars have occurred on every continent in the 1990s. Many of these have been associated with the advent of global neoliberalism, as indigenous people have resisted the exploitation of their land and resources by multinational corporations.

Despite the end of the cold war, military spending remains at high levels around the world, with the exception of a more than fifty per cent decline in Eastern Europe and the former Soviet republics. The United States continues to be the largest military spender in the world, accounting for almost half of global defense outlays, and continues to produce nuclear weapons. Since the Persian Gulf War in 1991, it has also become the world's top arms exporter; US arms exports well exceed the total arms exports of all other arms exporting countries combined. In most countries, the hoped-for "peace dividend" from the end of the cold war has not materialized. In the United States, a far larger proportion of income tax revenues are spent on the military than are spent on education, housing, job training and the environment combined. Worldwide, over half the nations of the world still provide higher budgets for their militaries than for their countries' health needs, and some devote more funds to military programs than to education and health combined.

With the advent of neoliberal globalization, military production has been used less for national defense and increasingly for the domestic repression of popular movements, many of which protest the activities of multinational corporations. Military training is increasingly devoted toward the subjugation of civilian populations, including the suppression of trade union protests and strikes. Human rights, as well as environmental and indigenous groups, are often labelled subversive and suppressed by militaries or paramilitaries and death squads, with the reformers who survive being forced into exile.

Women, especially poor women, bear a disproportionately heavy share of the burdens imposed by war and militarism. This is partly because an ever-increasing proportion of the casualties of war is comprised of civilians rather than soldiers. In World War I, twenty percent of the casualties were civilians; in World War II, that percentage more than doubled (to fifty percent). Seventy percent of the casualties in the Vietnam War were civilians, and about ninety percent of the casualties of today's wars are estimated to be civilians. The combatants in war are predominantly male, but the vulnerable civilians are predominantly, though not exclusively, women (and children). They are also Southern women, since most casualties of recent wars have occurred in the global South. In fact, women (and children) constitute eighty percent of the millions of refugees dislocated by war.

Military production is highly profitable for wealthy Northern investors, who certainly include some women. It also creates jobs both for the Northern middle class, who work in research and development, and for relatively uneducated people, who enlist in the military or work producing weapons. However women, especially poor women, receive far fewer benefits than men from the job opportunities created in the North by military production, both because they are largely excluded from the fields of scientific and technical research and because many of the US military's clerical and administrative tasks, mostly done by women, have been shifted to private contractors. More significantly, poor women in both the global North and South suffer disproportionately when tax revenues are allocated to the military rather than to social services, because women's primary childcare responsibilities often force them to rely more heavily than men on social services such as housing, health care, and education. High military spending diverts resources from more productive uses and leads to low total output and personal consumption in most regions of the world. Poor women in the global South have paid an especially high price for militarism, which has starved health, sanitation, education, and sustainable food cultivation and created a continuing dependence of the South on the North for maintaining and operating sophisticated weaponry. Militarism has been a major cause of Southern debt, making Southern countries vulnerable to onerous loan conditions that have imposed especially heavy burdens on women.

Militarism is also the world's major polluter of the environment, from which women suffer disproportionately, and it promotes cultural values that instrumentalize or degrade women. For instance, militarist governments often endorse masculinist ideologies that define men as warriors, promoting a culture of violence that spills over into violence against women on the streets and in the home. Meanwhile, women are defined as mothers of the nation; high birthrates are promoted and women's paid employment is discouraged. Women's sexuality is regarded as a national resource, their sexual autonomy is controlled, and they are expected to provide sexual services for warrior heroes. Simultaneously, women's sexuality is seen as a weak link in the national armor, and the mass media may promote an image of women as weak, corrupting and corruptible. In the 1990s, these ideas have combined to rationalize the use of rape as a systematic weapon of war, most notably in former Yugoslavia.

Prosperity

Viewed in one light, the world has indeed experienced unprecedented prosperity over the last fifty years, and especially over the last decade. The US stock market has reached record highs, despite financial collapses in Asia and Latin America; GNPs are high in many nations; tourism is one of the world's largest industries; young people drive around in sport utility vehicles talking on mobile phones. But although many people are better off than ever before, prosperity is limited to certain regions of the world and to certain groups within those regions. At the same time, poverty is increasing relatively and often absolutely as a result of massive and growing economic inequalities. These are occurring within most countries, especially among economic classes and regions, and they are also increasing among countries, as the East/West political system has given way to the North/South economic system, in which the North is vastly more wealthy than the South. Because of these inter- and intra-national inequalities, abundance for the (relatively) few is matched by poverty and even destitution for the many in the global economy. Neoliberal globalization has created many enormous winners but many more huge losers, and women are disproportionately represented among the losers.

The United Nations Annual Development Report for 1999 asserted that the gap between the world's rich and poor had reached "grotesque" proportions. In 1960, the countries with the wealthiest fifth of the world's population had per capita incomes 30 times that of the poorest fifth; by 1990, the ratio had doubled to 60 to one; by 1997, it stood at 74 to one. By 1997, the richest 20 percent had captured 86 percent of the world's income, while the poorest 20 percent had a mere one percent. For many — perhaps most — poor people in the world, neoliberal globalization has resulted in their material conditions of life deteriorating not only relative to the more affluent but also absolutely. In more than eighty countries, per capita incomes are lower than they were a decade ago; in sub-Saharan Africa and some other least developed countries, per capita incomes are lower than they were in 1970. In developing countries, nearly 1.3 billion people do not have access to clean water, 1 in 7 primary age schoolchildren are not in school, 840 million people are malnourished, and an estimated 1.3 billion people live on incomes of less that $1 per day. Meanwhile, the assets of the 200 richest people in 1998 were more than the total income of 41 percent of all the world's people.

Economic inequality is increasing not only between the global North and South but also within them. In June 2000, for instance, the US Federal Reserve reported that the net worth of the richest one percent of US households rose from 30 percent of the nation's wealth in 1992 to 34 percent in 1998. Meanwhile, the share of the national wealth held by the bottom 90 percent of US households fell from 33 percent in 1992 to 31 percent in 1998. The median inflation-adjusted earnings of the average US worker were 3.1 percent lower in 1997 than in 1989, and the poorest 20 percent of US citizens were making less in real terms at the end of the nineties than in 1977. One in 100 Americans was homeless at least temporarily in the year 2000.

Women in the global North, especially women of color, are disproportionately impoverished by the economic inequality resulting from "free" trade, which has resulted in many hitherto well-paid jobs being moved from the global North to low-wage areas in the global South. These jobs have been replaced in the North by so-called "McJobs" — "casual," contingency or part-time positions (often in the service sector), which are typically low-paid and lack health or retirement benefits. Although the reduction in the real hourly wage since the 1970s affects all low-paid workers in the United States, it especially affects women and, among women, especially women of color, because they disproportionately hold lowpaid jobs. The US Census Bureau recently reported that the earnings gap between men and women widened for the second consecutive year in 1999.

In the erstwhile Second World, elites are benefiting from the privatization and exploitation of hitherto publicly owned resources, but the dismantling of welfare states and consequent cuts in health services, education, and childcare has undermined the quality of life for most people. In 7 out of 18 East European countries, life expectancy was lower in 1995 than in 1989 (falling as much as five years since 1987), and enrollment in kindergarten had declined dramatically. Women have suffered disproportionately from the massive unemployment following the collapse of the socialist economies and the decline of social services. They have been pushed out of high-income and comparatively high-status positions in areas such as public management or universities, and many highly educated women have been forced to turn to prostitution, street-vending, or begging.

Comparable inequalities exist within what used to be called the Third World, even though some countries, especially those on the Pacific Rim, have prospered so much from the transfer of many industries that they are now thought of as societies in transition, newly industrializing countries or NICs. Gross domestic products have grown in other parts of the global South as a result of the mechanization of agriculture and the development of cash crop export economies, and some women are definitely among the beneficiaries of these changes, especially women in the families of Southern elites. Overall, however, women are disproportionately represented among the Southern losers from global neoliberalism. Pre-existing patriarchal social structures tend to limit women's direct access to any new wealth entering Southern economies as a result of economic globalization; women may access wealth through marriage, but often they are not in positions from which they can profit directly from the economic changes. For instance, women's responsibility for children makes it harder for women than for men to move to where the new paid jobs are located.

Greater efforts recently have been made to include Southern women in development, which is generally assumed to be a benevolent process of economic growth. Helping women participate in this process has been generally interpreted as helping them to gain a money income, and such efforts have increased Southern women's participation in the cash economy. However, the results of these efforts have not been unambiguously "good" for women; at best, they have been mixed.

To gain a money income, women have to produce something to sell in the market, and what most women have to sell is their labor. Women have become the new industrial proletariat in export-based industries, especially in much of Asia, where governments tempt multinational corporate investment with gendered stereotypes of Asian women workers as tractable, hard-working, dexterous — and sexy. Within these industries, wages and working conditions are often very poor, and harassment by bosses and managers is endemic. Again, the result is contradictory: the power of the women's fathers is reduced, but the women are superexploited by foreign corporations with the collusion of their own governments. As employees, they often experience a type of labor control that is almost feudal in its requirements of subservience and dependence. Thus, the global assembly line could be seen as allowing some Southern women to exchange one master for another.

Many women in the global South work not in the formal economy but in the informal economy, a kind of shadow economy not reflected in official records. Its workers typically do not pay taxes, and their jobs are unregulated by health and safety standards. It is characterized by low wages or incomes, uncertain employment, and poor working conditions. Women predominate in the informal economy, which covers a wide range of income generating activities, including declining handicrafts, small-scale retail trade, petty food production, street vending, domestic work, and prostitution. It also includes home-based putting-out systems and contract work. Women are often forced into the informal economy because they are driven off the land by the expansion of export agriculture, especially in South America and South East Asia. Those who remain in the countryside rather than migrating to the shanty towns that encircle most major Third-World cities are often forced into casual, contingent labor. Landless women from the poorest households are more likely to predominate as seasonal, casual, and temporary laborers at lower wages than their male counterparts.

Neoliberal globalization has increased the sexualization of all women, partly via a multibillion dollar pornography industry, and many women have been drawn into some aspect of sex work. In some parts of Asia and the Caribbean, sex tourism is a mainstay of local economies. Sex work includes, but is not limited to, servicing the workers in large plantations, servicing representatives of transnational corporations, servicing troops around military bases, and servicing UN troops and workers. Prostitution is certainly not a new phenomenon, but global neoliberalism has encouraged it in several ways. Most obviously, it has disrupted traditional communities and displaced and impoverished many women, who see few other options for a livelihood. In addition, nineteenth-century colonialism created images of the "exotic" "native" women, whose sexuality was defined as highly attractive and fascinating, yet related to the supposed natural primitiveness of the "other" cultural group. Today, media in Europe and North America still portray brown or black women as tantalizing erotic subjects, while in non-European countries white women are exoticized and eroticized. In consequence, a vastly expanded global sex trade results in millions of women being employed as sex workers outside their countries of origin.

The most obviously gendered feature of neoliberalism is its worldwide cutbacks in social programs. These cutbacks have affected women's economic status even more adversely than men's, because women's responsibility for caring for children and other family members makes them more reliant on such programs. In the global South, cuts in public health services have contributed to a rise in maternal mortality; in the global North, making hospitals more "efficient" has involved discharging patients earlier — to be cared for at home by female family members. Reductions in social services have forced women to create survival strategies for their families by absorbing these reductions with their own unpaid labor. The effect of these strategies has been felt especially in the global South, where more work for women has resulted in higher school dropout rates for girls. In addition, the introduction of school fees in many Southern countries has made education unavailable to poorer children and especially to girls. Less education and longer hours of domestic work obviously contribute to women's impoverishment by making it harder for them to attain well-paying jobs.

The feminization of poverty was a term coined originally to describe the situation of women in the United States, but the phenomenon has now become global, and its scale is increasing. The United Nations reports that women now comprise 70 percent of the world's 1.3 billion poor. Women's poverty in both North and South is linked with disturbing statistics on children's nutritional status, mortality and health. In many Southern countries, including Zimbabwe, Zambia, Nicaragua, Chile and Jamaica, the number of children who die before the age of one or five has risen sharply after decades of falling numbers.

Democracy

The spread of global neoliberalism has been accompanied by the establishment of formal democracy in many countries, especially in the erstwhile Third World, where a number of dictatorships have been ended, and in Eastern Europe, where so-called communist forms of government have been overthrown. Democracy has been encouraged in these regions by formal guarantees for freedom of thought, speech, press and association, and by the establishment of multiple political parties. However, the institutionalization of formal democracy has not resulted in increased political influence for women, especially for poor women and especially at the levels of designing global structures and policies. In the world of neoliberal globalization, democracy has a white man's face.

Although women's representation among heads of government and in national legislatures has always been lower than men's, the spread of neoliberal globalization in the early 1990s was accompanied in many places by a dramatic fall in women's governmental participation. Most dramatic was the decrease in women's representation in the national legislatures of Eastern Europe and the former Soviet Union, which was as high as 29 percent in the 1980s, but dropped to 7 percent in 1994. Women's participation in national legislatures is now rising again in Eastern Europe and elsewhere, but at the same time the importance of national legislatures is decreasing. Neoliberal globalization has undermined the sovereignty of many nations, especially the poorer ones, and is increasingly concentrating political power in the hands of a few wealthy nations, powerful investors, and global financial institutions. At this level, the influence of women, especially poor women, is minimal.

The neoliberal abandonment of fixed currency exchange rates and of controls on currency transfer de facto undermines the sovereignty of all countries because it enables powerful investors to cause a financial crisis by withdrawing billions of dollars into and out of national financial markets literally in a nanosecond. Thus, such investors can veto the democratically determined policies of supposedly sovereign nations simply by withdrawing their money.

More formal limits on the sovereignty of many nations occurred in the 1980s, when international lending institutions imposed neoliberal policies of structural adjustment on debtor nations in the then Third World as conditions of borrowing money or of rescheduling existing debts. Although the governments of the debtor nations formally agreed to these conditions, their agreement was often coerced by their history. Their countries had often been impoverished by centuries of colonization, which had drained them of massive resources and wealth, destroyed their economic self-sufficiency, and left them dependent on the metropolis for manufactured goods and for training indigenous professional and skilled workers. In order to end their economically disadvantageous position as suppliers of raw materials, such countries were virtually forced to borrow. In addition, many debts were assumed by autocratic rulers, who were supported by wealthy First-World countries as a bulwark against popular insurgencies regarded as "communist," and they often used borrowed funds to subvert local democracy through the military repression of their own populations.

The birth of the World Trade Organization in 1995 created a supranational organization whose rules supersede the national laws of its signatory nations on issues of trade. The WTO, which establishes the rules for global trade and functions as a sort of international court for adjudicating trade disputes, construes trade matters so broadly that they include not only tariff barriers but also many matters of ethics and public policy. For instance, the rules of the WTO challenge the European Union's bans on bovine growth hormone, on furs from countries that still use leghold traps, and on cosmetics tested on animals. Because the WTO regards ethical and health standards only as barriers to trade, it prevents countries from making their own decisions on ethics and food safety. The WTO is formally democratic in that each of its 142 plus member countries has one representative or delegate, who participates in negotiations over trade rules, but democracy within the WTO is limited in practice in many ways. Wealthy countries have far more influence than poor ones, and numerous meetings are restricted to the G-7 group, the most powerful member countries, excluding the less powerful even when decisions directly affect them.

Despite the fact that sovereign states are the only official members of the institutions administering the global economy, critics also charge that the current system of neoliberal globalization is dominated unofficially by transnational or multinational corporations, who "rent" governments to bring cases before the WTO. Because the budgets of many multinational corporations are far larger than those of many nominally sovereign states, it is easy for these corporations to influence the definitions and interpretations of the rules of the global economy by lobbying, bribing, and threatening governments or government officials. In addition, the WTO's dispute resolution system allows challenges to the standards and regulations adopted by federal, state, provincial and local governments to protect human, animal or plant life. If the standard in one country is higher than that in another, the higher standard can be challenged as a "technical" or "non-tariff" barrier to trade. Cases are heard before a tribunal of "trade experts," generally lawyers, who are required to make their ruling with a presumption in favor of free trade, and the burden is on governments to justify any restrictions on this. The dispute resolution system permits no amicus briefs, no observers, no public record of the deliberations, and no appeals. Thus, whether or not health, safety and environmental standards are "science-based" and so acceptable is determined by panels of experts, unelected and unaccountable, who have the power to overturn legislation and regulation adopted by elected bodies.

The present organization of the global economy undermines democracy by rendering the sovereignty of poor nations increasingly meaningless and further excluding the poorest and most vulnerable people across the world. Many women, who are disproportionately represented among the poorest and most vulnerable of all, are effectively disenfranchised. The virtual absence even of privileged women from the decision-making processes of such bodies as the World Bank, the International Monetary Fund, and the World Trade Organization reflects the minimal influence exercised by women at the highest levels of global politics.

Poor women's lack of influence at the global level is not compensated by increased influence at the lower levels of politics, despite the new neoliberal emphasis on civil society and despite the fact that poor women have often been leaders in community activism. With the advent of global neoliberalism, an increasing proportion of so-called development assistance from richer to poorer countries has become channeled through nongovernmental organizations rather than through the governments of the recipient countries. Whereas neoliberals justify this change as avoiding official bureaucracy and corruption and as empowering grassroots women, critics argue that addressing social problems through private rather than public channels undermines democracy by depoliticizing the poor. Involvement in "self-help" micro-projects encourages poor women to exhaust their scare energies in developing ad hoc services or products for the informal economy, rather than mobilizing as citizens to demand that the state utilize their tax monies for the provision of public services. Some critics argue that foreign-funded NGOs are a new form of colonialism because they create dependence on nonelected overseas funders and their locally appointed officials, undermining the development of social programs administered by elected officials accountable to local people. Thus, even though NGOs create programs that involve and serve women, their mission of providing services privately tacitly acquiesces in the state's shedding of its public responsibilities. Even though they use the language of inclusion, empowerment and grass-roots democracy, NGOs often undermine the social citizenship entitlements of poor women.

Envisioning Alternatives to Neoliberal Globalization

Contemporary neoliberal globalization is characterized by the massive consolidation of wealth in a relatively few hands, by radically unequal access to and control over material resources, information and communications, by the centralization of political power and absence of democratic accountability, by environmental destruction, and by virulent racism and ethnocentrism. Its rhetoric of equality and participation masks a reality of domination and marginalization for most of the world's women. However, just as we once distinguished perfect markets from existing markets and socialist ideals from various so-called socialisms, so we must now distinguish the existing neoliberal incarnation of globalization from its possible alternative forms. The questions raised by globalization are simultaneously deeply philosophical and of immediate public concern. They include, though certainly are not limited to, the following.

What are peace and security?

Is peace simply an absence of conflict between sovereign states that have formally declared war on each other or the absence of sectors of local populations armed to seize state power? How should we think about economic embargoes, especially when nations differ so enormously in their ability to impose such embargoes and in their vulnerability to them? How should we think about judicial institutions that rationalize incarcerating large sections of local populations for nonviolent crimes motivated by poverty? Is a country secure when it is "protected" by a "missile defense shield" built at the expense of social infrastructure? Is the world at peace when it is policed by one or a few powerful nations that arrogate to themselves the right to determine when international law has been violated and what "punishment" is appropriate for alleged violations? Is the world at peace when a hundred million women are "missing" and when those girls and women who remain are subjected to infanticide, the systematic withholding of food, medical care and education, and gender-based battery, rape, mutilation, and even murder? What are real peace and security and what are their preconditions?

What is prosperity?

How can we redefine goods to include more than commodities, and wealth to mean more than material consumption? How can we measure prosperity in a way that is sensitive both to the quality of life and to inequalities in access to material resources? Is trade "free" in any meaningful sense when poor nations have no alternative to participating in an economic system in which they become ever poorer? When is trade "fair," and what is equality of opportunity among states? Can any sense be made of the notion of "natural" resources, when things like fossil fuels, sunny climates, coral beaches or strategic locations become resources only within larger systems of production and meaning? How can we determine what a country's "own" resources are, when every country is what it has been made over the course of human history? If countries' resources are unequal, what might justify global redistribution? Do racialized groups or nations that have expropriated or exploited others in the past now owe reparations, and, if so, how should these be determined? How should the notion of economic "efficiency" be understood? How does the ideal of fair trade mesh with other values such as democracy, autonomy, empowerment, community, responsibility and environmental quality? How can we rethink the concept of economic restructuring?

What is democracy?

Which groups are entitled to self-determination, and what does self-determination mean? How can democracy be institutionalized at global, regional, national and local levels? How can nations that are radically unequal economically share equally in the governance of a global economy? How can ideals of global democracy be related to older ideals of national self-determination and sovereignty? In a global democracy, how should we rethink the notions of membership, belonging, and citizenship? What function do borders have in a global democracy, and what entitles people to a right of abode? What claims do global citizens have to control the allocation of local resources, and what claims do local citizens have on global resources? How can we create institutions responsive to the needs of the dispossessed, the excluded and the stigmatized? How can democracy be established in households and families?

What is a healthy environment?

What ideals or principles should guide human interaction with the nonhuman environment, given that this environment is always changing and that every change benefits some individuals, groups or species at the expense of others? How can we ensure that human impacts on the nonhuman environment do not benefit human groups that are already wealthy and powerful at the expense of those who are already poor and weak? How can we ensure that present appropriations of environmental resources meet Locke's condition of leaving "as much and as good" for generations yet to come?

Racial/ethnic diversity

Are groups that have suffered past injury entitled to compensation? Is the existence of universal norms compatible with respect for the integrity of cultures and traditions? Can human equality be combined with appreciation for cultural difference?

What is good for women?

Although none of the above questions mentions women explicitly, their formulation owes much to feminist thinking, which has shown that women cannot thrive in the absence of genuine peace, prosperity, democracy, a healthy environment, and respect for cultural tradition. Women have begun to reconceptualize these ideals in grassroots discussions all over the world, but the issues are too complex to be pursued here. Instead, I conclude with a single example of transnational feminist organizing that provides one alternative to the dominant neoliberal model of globalization.

"WOMEN'S RIGHTS ARE HUMAN RIGHTS:" AN EXAMPLE OF GLOBALIZATION FROM BELOW

The concept of rights emerged from European Enlightenment, and it has always been somewhat controversial. Nineteenth-century utilitarians worried that rights talk lacked solid grounding, and Jeremy Bentham famously called rights "nonsense on stilts." Marxists have often charged that rights talk tends to rationalize class privilege because of its historical connection with private property and because rights advocates have often focused on establishing formal rights while ignoring the availability of real opportunities to exercise them. Third-World anti-colonialists have challenged rights as a form of Western cultural imperialism, used against non-Western communities and destructive of cultural traditions. Even though the concept of rights has been extremely useful historically to Western feminism, some recent Western feminists have contended that rights reflect a masculine morality of "justice," as opposed to a supposedly more feminine morality of care. Finally, some Third-World feminists have complained that rights are a legalistic concept hardly useful to those without the means to seek legal redress for violations of their rights. For these and other reasons, many critics have contended that "rights talk" is so infected by its bourgeois, masculine, and Western origins that it is incapable of articulating a viable challenge to local manifestations of male dominance, let alone to a world order that is deeply antagonistic to women.

Despite these criticisms of the concept of rights, however, a worldwide grassroots activist movement has taken up the slogan "women's rights are human rights." This movement has used the concept of rights to challenge many abuses of women previously unrecognized as rights violations, including direct assaults on women's bodily integrity.[2] So far, the women's human rights movement has been most successful in addressing women's "first generation" civil and political rights. These protect such rights as liberty, freedom of thought, opinion, conscience and religion, and political participation, and are often construed as protecting individuals primarily from their governments. However, a new focus on women's "second generation" rights, which include entitlements to education, to work, and to a standard of living adequate for the health and well-being of self and family, is increasingly being used to challenge many aspects of neoliberal globalization. Indeed, by showing that the more blatant abuses of women often spring directly from their economic vulnerability, feminists have tacitly if not explicitly implicated neoliberal globalization in many violations of women's "first generation" rights. For instance, they have observed that the worldwide preference for boys over girls, and the consequent neglect, abuse and even infanticide of girls, is rooted in economic structures rather than laws. The 1993 Vienna Declaration and Program of Action highlighted the connections between women's economic vulnerability and their murder, torture, sexual coercion and abuse.

In revealing how abuses of women's human rights have often been neglected, excused or denied, the women's human rights movement has demonstrated that previous understandings of human rights have taken the paradigmatic human to be male. Sometimes abuses of women's rights have been seen as "normal," "natural," or "inevitable" because women have been viewed as "other," inherently different from men. At other times, substantive equality for women has been equated with formal equality, because women have been seen as just the same as men, and their distinct histories and situations have been denied. Either way, human rights have been interpreted on an implicitly masculine model. Women's human rights activists are now moving from trying to include women in "men's" rights to challenging the covert masculine norm concealed in traditional understandings of so-called human rights. For instance, they are pointing out that violations of women's human rights are typically carried out by non-state as well as state actors — often by male family members — and that they occur in the private as well as the public sphere. Thus, they argue that the definition of state sanctioned repression should be expanded to include acceptance of family forms in which brides are sold and in which fathers and husbands exert strict control over women's sexuality, dress, speech, and movement. Similarly, slavery should be redefined to include forced domestic labor and prostitution. The definitions of war crimes should be expanded to include systematic rape and sexual torture. Conceptions of genocide should be expanded to include female infanticide, the systematic withholding of food, medical care and education from girls, and the battery, starvation, mutilation, and even murder of women.

The movement for women's human rights provides one indication of how globalization could work to benefit women. This human rights movement is, after all, a transnational movement, inconceivable outside a wider context of globalization. International conferences (such as in Mexico City in 1975) brought together local activists and made it possible for them to create mailing lists and eventually global networks. In preparation for the UN conference in Beijing in 1995, many regional meetings were held that produced deeper understanding of local conditions — partly by setting them in a global context. The global context helped local activists to see a variety of phenomena — rape and domestic battery in the US and Europe, genital cutting in Africa, sexual slavery in Europe and Asia, dowry death in India, and the torture and rape of political prisoners in Latin America — as examples of violence against women. Rather than being an idea imposed from above, the idea that women's rights are human rights emerged from grassroots activism and illustrates how feminist reconceptualizations of "universal" rights are compatible with wide local diversity in interpretation and action. The idea of women's rights as human rights allowed women across the world to forge common bonds and provides an example of "globalization from below."

Feminist transformations of pre-existing understandings of rights have implications that go beyond the lives of women "only." For instance, by revealing the link between violations of women's first generation rights and the denial of their second generation rights, feminists have shown that human rights are indivisible rather than separable from each other, and this recognition of the indivisibility of rights certainly has applications to other economically vulnerable groups. More broadly, the movement for women's human rights reveals how women's equality is inseparable from other aspects of social progress. When inequalities are increasing among classes, regions, racialized and ethnic groups, and among nations, it is impossible to obtain sustainable improvements in women's economic and social position because women are represented in all these groups, and when inequality exists women always suffer disproportionately. Conversely, however, it is impossible to alleviate these superficially ungendered inequalities without greater equity for and participation by women and therefore without addressing specifically gendered forms of inequality.

In challenging the false, male-biased humanism of older conceptions of human rights, the women's human rights movement implicitly suggests that the normative human be imagined as female rather than male. Such a re-imagining has far-reaching consequences, because women are vastly over-represented among the poor and illiterate of the world, and they are certainly those most vulnerable to oppressive systems of power. A concern for guaranteeing women's human rights could inspire alternatives to the neoliberal model of globalization and go far toward promoting a world of prosperity, peace, environmental protection, democracy, and respect for racial/ethnic diversity, that is, a world in which all women could flourish.

3

Globalization, Desire, and the Politics of Representation

Rajagopalan Radhakrishnan

What is the attraction of globality, and why is its rhetoric so seductively irresistible? What is the nature of its authority? Let me begin by suggesting that the triumphalism of globality has to do with the fact that it seems to emanate from reality itself even as it speaks persuasively for that reality. As a *fait accompli*, globality presents itself both as reality and as a representation of that reality, all within a unified temporality. It is as though the very essence of reality were global, and, therefore, any attempt at interrogating globality would be nothing short of discrediting reality itself. But how did reality get globalized so absolutely and normatively, and by what process did the space between reality and representation get closed up and claimed in the name of globality? Part of my purpose in this essay is to put some pressure, historical as well as theoretical, on the ideological structuration of globality, and to examine how such a profoundly uneven and relational category gets spoken for as though it were a thing, an essence, an incontrovertible property of reality itself. Consequently my focus in the following discussion will be on the tensions between globality as perspective and globality as content, globality as uni-polar and globality as multi-polar, and globality as process and globality as realized vision and product.

Fredric Jameson begins his essay "Notes on Globalization as a Philosophical Issue" with a schematic account of the phenomenon of globalization:

> Four positions on our topic seem logically available. The first affirms the opinion that there is no such thing as globalization (there are still the nation-states and the national situations; nothing is new under the sun).

The second also affirms that globalization is nothing new; there has always been globalization and it suffices to leaf through a book like Eric Woolf's *Europe and the People without History* to see that as far back as the neolithic trade routes have been global in their scope, with Polynesian artifacts deposited in Africa and Asian potsherds as far afield as the New World.

Then I suppose one should add two more: one that affirms the relationship between globalization and that world market which is the ultimate horizon of capitalism, only to add that the current world networks are only different in degree and not in kind; while a fourth affirmation (which I have found more interesting than the other three) posits some new, or third, multinational stage of capitalism, of which globalization is an intrinsic feature and which we now largely tend, whether we like it or not, to associate with that thing called postmodernity. (54)

I do not intend to examine all four scenarios or offer an opinion on the classification itself. My focus will be on the "first position," which, according to Jameson, asserts that as long as nations and nation-states continue to exist and exert hegemonic influence on geopolitical circumstances, globality and globalization are at best an ideological illusion. I would like to suggest on the contrary that there is indeed no contradiction between the logic of globalization and the self-interest of dominant nationalisms and nation-states. Just as notions of trans- and inter-nationalism are posited not on the basis of any critical negation of and/or divestment from the ideology of nationalism, but rather on the basis of a supranationalism that holds on to and consolidates the privileges and prerogatives of dominant nationalism, so, too, globalization extends the regime of uneven development between developed and developing nations (see Balibar and Wallerstein). Noam Chomsky drives this point home with great polemical verve:

Putting the details aside, it seems fairly clear that one reason for the sharp divide between today's first and third worlds is that much of the latter was subjected to "experiments" that rammed free market down their throats, whereas today's developed countries were able to resist such measures.

That brings us to another feature of modern history that is hard to miss, in this case at the ideological level. Free market doctrine comes in two varieties. The first is the official doctrine that is taught to and by the educated classes and imposed on the defenseless. The second is what we might call "really existing free market doctrine": For thee, but not for me, except for temporary advantage: I need the protection of the nanny state,

but you must learn responsibility under the harsh regimen of "tough love."
("Free Trade and Free Market" 361)

Rather than posit globality and nationalism as adversarial projects, I maintain that globalization takes the form of the dismantling of subaltern nationalisms by developed nationalisms. Globality and globalization are the Darwinian manifesto of the survival of the fittest: the strong nations will survive "naturally," for it is in their destiny to survive as nameless and unmarked nations, whereas weak nations will inevitably be weeded out because of their unsatisfactory performance as nation-states. In other words, the strong nations will have earned the ethicopolitical authority to deconstruct the sovereignty of Third-World national rights precisely because these fully developed nations have succeeded in actualizing this form of sovereignty. The developing nations, on the other hand, will be blamed for their inability to secure this sovereignty on their own behalf, and, furthermore, they will be blamed and penalized if they raise the flag of subaltern national sovereignty in revolt against the standard of dominant national sovereignty. Globality is indeed the name of that ideological structuration that seeks once and for all to realize "the world" as a worthy trophy to be held aloft by some nation-states on behalf of all.

If postmodern globality implies radical divestment from the politics of nationalism, such a divestment has different implications for Third-World nationalisms. When I use the term "postmodern" here, I refer to the "anti-representational" strand of thought within the vast and heterogeneous repertoire of postmodernism. Within the context of the developed world, the movement from modernity to postmodernity is macropolitically continuous and "conservative," whereas in the context of the underdeveloped world, whose very claim to citizenship in the modern world is the phenomenon of "underdevelopment" (see Gupta), the movement towards a postmodern economy of meaning is disruptive. In the case of the developed nations the capacity for going global enhances the capacity for self-representation as powerful nation-states, whereas in the case of the underdeveloped nations globalization attenuates and eviscerates national sovereignty. Within the global postmodern space of advanced capitalism, what is problematized is not the representative and representational space of nationalism as such or the legitimacy of representation *qua* representation, but the ethico-political rights of postcolonial peoples to realize themselves as sovereign nation-states. Successful and dominant nationalisms are rewarded, while subaltern and emerging nationalisms are penalized for wanting the very things that dominant nationalisms have successfully monopolized merely by getting there first. Nowhere is this hideous double standard more visible than in the case of nuclear power, as developing countries with potential or demonstrated nuclear capacity are criminalized as "rogue states" without any recognition of the fact that this "roguery" was initiated in the first place by the superpowers (see Bidwai and Vinaik). It is as if a mighty criminal arrogated to him/herself the authority of the cop on the basis of her/his prior and therefore norm-setting entry into the realm of criminality and transgression. Nuclear capability and the CTBT (the Comprehensive Test Ban Treaty) is not, however, my present concern. Rather, I am concerned with the status of representation as it inheres in the nation and the nation-state. As I have been maintaining all along, global capital as motored by postmodernist epistemology authorizes the belief that the flow of capital in and by itself identifies people's interests the world over and speaks for them nonideologically. Such an assumption is as theoretically inept as it is counterfactual. Indeed, even under the premise of transnational and border-busting globality, protectionism and industrial and economic policy are well in place. But protectionism practiced by powerful nation-states is not named as such, whereas subaltern protectionism is immediately demonized as rabid nationalism. If the nation form is dismantled in the postcolonial context, who then will speak for the peoples of the Third World: Capital, NAFTA, WTO, or the president of the USA?

Let us take a quick look at the opposition to the WTO talks in Seattle and the IMF. As has been noted by many writers and analysts, this opposition has created many strange coalitions in the face of a common woe.[1] To summarize these accounts somewhat schematically, there is the so-called ideological opposition between multinational and transnational corporations, on the one hand, and the sovereignty of nation-states, on the other. There is also the opposition between a border-busting capital and a nationally administered labor pool. Multinationals and transnationals, it is argued, undermine the sovereignty of nation-states because their only allegiance is to themselves, not to the ideological politics of nationalism. However, this argument — as lucid and persuasive as it may sound — fails to make the all-important distinction between actualized (and dominant) super-nationalisms and emergent nationalisms. Just as by its very definition nationalism empowers division and not relational or empathic solidarity, just as nationalism is posited on the fundamental assumption that there are good nationalisms (Us) and bad nationalisms (Them), so, too, these transnational configurations reassert the supra-national power of dominant nationalisms, thus making their nationalist ideologies transparent and invisible, and necessitate an ongoing inferiorization of emergent nationalisms. Take the simple instance of the loss of jobs, which are not categorized as "human" jobs but as American or Canadian or Mexican or Indian jobs. The leaders of the free world evince no embarrassment as they protect and represent their labor, their people power, their right to a fair share of global employment opportunities. It is inevitable that they do so, but they might as well do it with ideological candor, instead of parading their recidivism into mercantilism as a vigorous advocacy of free trade. It is obvious that First-World national governments become interventionist when the ideology of free trade suddenly turns inimical to their own economic interests. When was the last time that an American president showed concern or altered foreign trade policy in response to dire job losses in Mexico or in the Philippines? But, on the other hand, when the Mexican peso tumbles, American politicians are eager to help the Mexican economy so that America and American workers will not pay the price. In the unequal relationship between Mexico and the US, not only must Mexico deliver the impossible goal of living up to US expectations, but it must also prepare itself to be demonized and castigated for ineptness should it fail. In a similar fashion, World Bank and IMF interventions in the economies of the Third World have been undertaken in the name of a world system that represents the interests of the dominant economies. The motivation here is neither benevolence nor altruism, but an egocentric concern that the weaker economies should be maintained in a state of systemic viability that is compatible with the growth patterns and objectives of the G7 — even if such a form of viability endangers sustainable development within those poor and underdeveloped economies. And that is why most IMF and World Bank prescriptions for Third-World ills take the form of fundamental structural changes and redefinitions of priorities. The logic runs thus: be viable for us (the system) so that you can be viable for yourself. If there are genuine priority clashes, or if, for example, the local and national economic well-being of Indonesia requires strategic protection from rapacious foreign investment, these issues are quickly dismissed as incompatible with the avant-gardism of a developmental globality that unflinchingly invests in the underdeveloped world with the intention of maintaining it in eternal dependence and heteronomy. Within such a vision of dominant globality, the weaker economies are condemned to fantasies they can never actualize and to teleologies over which they have no direct agential control. Thus, the ideology of dominant globality plays out a duplicitous ideological game: on the one hand, it insists that the entire world should think uni-polar — that is, that the rest of the world should look like, resemble, emulate, and follow the Western lead; on the other, it requires that non-Western peoples remain forever the other. They cannot and should never be allowed to become us or like us, but they should bond with us like an indigent and hapless relative in need who pathetically solicits our help; in this way the chasm of an unbridgeable and unactualizable desire remains always in place. When others behave like us, they become a threat, so they need to be contained within a sanctimonious rhetoric of pedagogy that ensures their perpetual discipleship or apprenticeship. We are virtuous and immaculate in what we do, but they are flawed and roguish in their repetition of our deeds. To sum up, globality shores up dominance and continues the anthropological fantasy of maintaining the other in intimate and yet exotic followership.

This in a nutshell is the lie of globalization: though the official blurbs maintain that the reality of globality transcends the sovereignty of nation-states, in fact and in effect the world invoked by globality remains structured according to a hierarchy in which subaltern nations are chronically engaged in the project of theatricalizing themselves as eternal laggards and "catcher uppers." The users of what Partha Chatterjee has called the "derivative discourse" are paralyzed as the objects of derivative discourse, and, as a result of this paralysis, the political agency of Third-World nations is effortlessly subsumed by the ideology of a post-representational globality. Globality, as it confronts the underdeveloped countries, marks the space of incommensurability where the inter- and the intra-national modes of organization and community historicize their mutual a-synchrony. Within the figurality of the postcolonial nation-state, for whom does the nation-state speak, and to whom is its rhetoric addressed? Does the addressee influence, perhaps even constitute, the legitimacy of the rhetoric, or is the rhetoric ideologized without reference to an addressee? Moreover, how is the internal addressee different from the one without? How does the temporality of the nation-state form create insides and outsides? When the head of a nation-state speaks and therefore the nation speaks too, is the nation addressing its own people, or is it addressing other sister and brother nations with whom it enjoys ideological and morphological contemporaneity? Within such a Janus-faced figurality, where is the point of balance — or homeostasis, if you will — between exteriority and interiority? When Jawaharlal Nehru made that memorable speech marking the birth of *India as a nation*, was he addressing the Indian people who henceforth would fill the interiority of India, or was he addressing the national peoples and national heads of states of the world, saying, "here we are in your ranks now: equal and contemporary." Within such an unavoidable double consciousness (I say unavoidable, since baptism by nationalism necessitates such an entry into the world of inter-nations), what are the safeguards against the sacrificing of "interiority" to the superior and prestigious demands of exteriority?[2] Third-World nationalism, much more than Western nationalism, is in constant danger of capitulating its "being for itself" in deference to the demands of "being for the other" — here, the demands of a global internationalism. Therefore, unless nationalisms are destabilized the world over and a genuine alternative is found to replace the imagined community of nation-states, the Third World would do well to focus on issues of representation, rather than place implicit trust in the post-representational flows of globality.[3]

If the discourse of representation operates on the principle that sovereignty needs to be produced on behalf of a people and their determinate and historically specific interests, the global network model assumes rather glibly that political issues of representation will be automatically taken care of in the name of capital and uncontrolled economic opportunism. Whereas the politics of representation does not attempt to exorcize the mediatory distance between the experiential and the political, the techno-global model attempts to "get real" by presuming to take the place of the real in the name of its own seductive immanence. Whereas the model of representation insists that the "political" can only be produced through a process of ideological interpellation, the techno-global model sells itself as the home of the political imaginary, thus severing all connection with the alterity of the ideological call.[4] The enticing aspect about technoglobality, particularly during these times of a general disillusionment with matters political and ideological, is that it promotes the belief that the political inheres in the model in a thoroughly transparent and trans-ideological manner. Reality matters, not the political; if anything, politics mars, disfigures and polemicizes reality — that is the manifesto of techno-globality. This message sells since it makes the promise that the political does not have to be produced any more and that a certain way of "phenomenologizing" the real will indeed take the place of the real. The narcissistic imaginary of techno-globality, in not allowing the awkwardness of a jagged and contested "hors-texte," intends to celebrate its own immanent interiority as a form of experiential plenitude. In consonance with such a celebration of immanence, the techno-global model inculcates in its members a sense of inclusion that is in fact a facile substitute for the concept of agential citizenship. If inclusiveness has been the agonizing issue that all political movements and revolutions have faced, the techno-global revolution makes of inclusiveness a pseudo-problem by suggesting that the network is indeed God's formal answer to the problem of "unconnectedness." Get on the network and *ipso facto* you are included, valorized, and politicized. The power and the persuasiveness of the network model is its ability to create space without ideological location or situatedness. In a sense, this could be termed the ultimate aestheticization of the political. No other phrase captures this tendency better than the phrase "global village" — a phrase that looks back to the history of the village only to dehistoricize it in the context of techno-globality.

In a recent interview in *The Nation*, Noam Chomsky responded to the question, "Can the master's house be dismantled by the master's tools?" by suggesting that chipping away at the system is a real and critical alternative to despair and apathy (28–30). Chomsky's suggestion is not unlike Chatterjee's notion of "the derivative discourse," or Ranajit Guha's concept of "the small voice of history." Derivative discourses and the small voices of history are incapable of achieving systematicity on their own behalf. The best they can do to authorize their own sense of agency is to chip away, to "signify" their intentions on a pre-existing and often alien text. These political actors are incapable of writing their own scripts; they can at best "turn the pages" of the dominant script in a certain way, as suggested by Derrida. Is this enough? Is anything else possible other than "a war of position" a la Gramsci? As we try to evaluate the possibilities of "signifying" and "chipping away," it would be worthwhile to consider critically the nature and the phenomenology of tools in general. What are tools, and what is the nature of their inherence in specific ideologies, isms, and worldviews? Are tools a kind of methodology definitively anchored in the theories and the epistemologies that gave rise to them, or are they detachable in a purely pragmatic and opportunistic interest? To what extent are tools faithful to their origins? Finally, does any body or group really "own" tools except in a purely functional and instrumental way? There are two related issues here: one is, to use Ralph Ellison's suggestive phrasing from *Invisible Man*, the thinker-tinker relationship (7) or, in Marxist terminology, the theory-praxis relationship; the other is the issue of achievable agency.

In regard to the relationship between tools and those using them, the postcolonial situation presents itself as a complex and interesting instance. If both modernity and nationalism are historicized as a derivative discourse in the Third World, how can the derivative discourse be owned agentially (as against just being assimilated or instrumentalized) by the non-West? How bad and crippling a stigma is "derivativeness," and is there any way of redemption over and beyond it? Can derivativeness be negated, or is there a way of working through and beyond derivativeness into a realm of originality and one's own-ness? To avail of Partha Chatterjee's compelling insight again, can anything be done at all at the level of the political that can erase the mark of epistemological derivativeness? Or to use Néstor Gárcia Canclini's terminology (see *Hybrid Cultures*), is it enough that non-Western cultures choose to enter and exit modernity in their own way and in accordance with their own needs and priorities? Why privilege epistemology to such an extent that it begins to underestimate the power of the political? Is it really necessary for the Third World to come up with its own organic and integral epistemology as a precondition for a successful resistance to Eurocentrism? Where and how should the Third World signify its valence both as "something in itself" and as a form of difference from the paradigm of Euro-American modernity? The postcolonial predicament can be summed up thus: how can political unification be achieved on the basis of double-consciousness?

If we look to Edward Said, two possibilities emerge: traveling theory and the possibilities of contrapuntal meaning.[5] The moment theory travels, its origins are immediately de-sacralized, relativized, and rendered contingent upon the realities and circumstances to which it moves. A theory "born" in the West can become a tool of resistance in the non-West. Hybridized, heterogenized, mimicked and shot through with difference, metropolitan theory is submitted to a process (to conflate Spivak with Said) of catachresis, as a result of which every metropolitan articulation is simultaneously realized as a postcolonial articulation.[6] And yet, all of these strategies remain micropolitical and/or signifying practices, that is, strategies of ex-orbitation and supplementation incapable of formulating their own autonomous teleology. In their attempts to realize themselves as radical and interventionary perspectives these strategies are still caught up, in a reactive mode, with the canonicity of the given metropolitan text. Instead of signifying on an "alien" text, should they not be signifying on their own texts? But then, on the other hand, doesn't the very nature of "signifying" turn inside out the proper differentiation between "one's own" and "the other's"?

In his moving essay "Towards a Third World Utopia," Ashis Nandy makes a concerted effort at realizing the Third World both as perspective and as the possibility of a different vision and content. To quote Nandy: "Thus, no utopia can be without an implicit or explicit theory of suffering. This is especially so in the peripheries of the world, euphemistically called the third world" (21). Nandy goes on to say that "to have a meaningful life in the minds of men, such a utopia must start with the issue of man-made suffering, which has given the third world both its name and uniqueness" (*Traditions* 21). Nandy affirms that his essay is "guided by the belief that the only way the third world can transcend the sloganeering of its well-wishers is, first, by becoming a collective representation of the victims of man-made suffering everywhere in the world and in all past times; second, by internalizing or owning up to the outside forces of oppression and then coping with them as inner vectors; and third, by recognizing the oppressed or marginalized selves of the first and the second worlds as civilizational allies in the battle against institutionalized suffering" (21). Nandy's essay dares to use the much-maligned term *utopia* with theoretical rigor and ethico-political conviction. It enacts a creative tension between the desired place-less-ness of utopia and the perspectival specificity of the location from which utopia is being visualized. A similar move is made by Amitav Ghosh in his novel *The Shadow Lines*, about which I will have more to say below. Another feature of Nandy's contribution is that it boldly espouses "content" as the basis on which Third-World utopias may be differentiated from other utopias. However, the content term that Nandy chooses is not "development," "progress," "emancipation," or "industrialization"; the key word for him is "suffering." And with that word Nandy strikes unequivocally an ethical register (see also Sen). Rather than invoke the pathos inherent in suffering, Nandy seeks to ground suffering as a powerful intra- and inter- subjective and cognitive category. Unlike technological and developmental/positivist utopianism that seeks to negate suffering, consolidate gains already made on the basis of a zero-sum, winner-take-all model, and thereby perpetuate the terrain of imbalance and inequity (see Guinier), Nandy's utopianism is directed at the human conscience in all its inter- and intra- civilizational complexity. In conceptualizing suffering as that perspectival category from which utopia is to be envisioned, Nandy opens up a vital relationship between self-centered imaginings and other-oriented commitments (cf. Madan). In endowing epistemology with an authority that is coevally but differentially ethical, Nandy in effect limits and renders the self-centered economy of the abidingly vulnerable to the ubiquitous demands of alterity. Two points need to be made to differentiate Nandy's conceptualization of suffering from pathos-based and/or victim-centered articulations of suffering. First, in Nandy's discourse, suffering is realized simultaneously as experiential and proactively agential; and out of suffering comes critical knowledge which in turn empowers the voice of suffering to make its own cognitive epistemological intervention by envisioning its own utopia rather than accept an assigned position within amelioratory schemes proposed by the dominant discourse. Secondly, suffering, though exemplified in a certain way by the Third World, is a universal and omni-locational phenomenon that cuts across rigid and overdetermined self-other oppositions. No one or no one position has a monopoly on suffering, and, furthermore, no one should partcipate in what Angela Davis has memorably termed, "an olympics of suffering." Suffering as such demands exotopic and translocal modes of understanding and diagnosis (see Bakhtin). Unlike the call of dominance that incites mindless emulation on the part of the slave to desire the place of the master (see Zizek and Butler), the empathy that suffering generates makes possible a decentered mode of cognition that is deconstructive of the politics of binarity, of normative insides and outsides.

It is only on the basis of such an epistemology of suffering that the Third-World perspective on utopia can be actualized as a perspective of persuasion. Not unlike the project of ethicizing subalternity that liberates "subaltern as perspective" from subaltern as merely teleological (see Das), Nandy's rhetoric of advocacy seeks to realize the Third-World perspective as the ethics of the permanent revolution. Just as it is the objective of subalternity as perspective not to get rid of subalternity as ethico-political force and category, it is Nandy's objective to keep alive "suffering" as a point of view even as he attempts to coordinate a global project to eradicate suffering in all its protean manifestations. It is in this spirit that Nandy's rhetoric on behalf of the Third World — and, therefore, the entire world — seeks to "transcend the sloganeering of its well-wishers." It is vital to notice that the crucial trope here is that of transcendence — a transcendence of the merely political and the opportunistic in the name of a multilateral, universal, ethical accountability. In an ironic way, Nandy questions the process of disingenuous politicization that reduces a thoughtful response to suffering into merely sloganeering and shibboleth-making. For not only is sloganeering superficial and un-self-reflexive, it is also sanctimoniously self-righteous. Nandy thus implicitly critiques both a vulgar and axiomatic insiderism that assumes that the Third World is recognizable through ideological posturings of defensive and paranoid rectitude, and a tendency to treat the Third World as a ghettoizable zone rather than as a universalizable perspective with the potential for a translocal jurisdiction through transformative powers of persuasion. Nandy's discourse deconstructs the putative opposition between past and present, between the West and the Rest, in order to galvanize ethical accountability as a persuasive universal imperative. Just as Said would insist that ethico-political projects need to be imagined across and beyond existing asymmetries and that generalizations need to made audaciously precisely when they seem least probable, Nandy too enlists the First, what used to be the Second, and the Third World as civilizational allies in the fight against institutional suffering. For Nandy insides and outsides are never given as absolute a priori points of and for orientation, but are indeed constituted and produced as transactional functions of inter- and intra- historical and civilizational influence and dialogue. Just as he argued in *The Intimate Enemy* that colonialism inflicts deep wounds both on the colonizer and the colonized, here, too, Nandy tries to imagine therapeutic spaces of reciprocal rehabilitation. It is precisely by avowing the ubiquitous nature of oppression and suffering and by acknowledging ongoing collusions between so-called insides and outsides in the perpetuation of oppression and suffering that a utopian transcendence may be imagined in a multilateral mode.

Nandy offers us three assumptions on which his aspirations are based: 1) no civilization has a monopoly over good or right ethics; 2) the purpose of any civilization is critically to alter its own self-awareness, and 3) any utopian imagination is unavoidably caught up in the contradictions and imperfections of its own particular historical situation. To put it in Nandy's words, "imperfect societies produce imperfect remedies of their imperfections" (22). And it is this last assumption that I wish to elaborate in the context of the current euphoric drive towards globalization. My point is that techno-capital driven blueprints for globalization are in fact tacit and ideologically disavowed utopian blueprints as well: globalization as a natural panacea for all human ills. As I have already stated at the very beginning of this essay, it is only by delinking the ethico-political and the ideological from the economic, and the theoretical-critical from the descriptive, and the politics of representation from simulacral phenomenology, that the rhetoric of globalization has been able to conceal the fact that globalization is intended as a utopian resolution of the problems of the world: a utopia sans politics, ethics, or ideological content. It has become possible, thanks to techno-capital, to embody utopia as a form of seductive immanence, of the here-and-now, and bracket away once and for all questions of representation and ideological perspectivism. In a post-communist, post-socialist world where "politics" and "ideology" are dirty words, techno-capital has become the undisputed motor of history and decides descriptively "what is to be done." The difference between an ethically inflected utopianism and the utopianism of techno-capital is that the latter, blessed with historical amnesia, can afford to be un-self-reflexive regarding its own practices and assumptions, as well as its rootedness in an imperfect world. In denying the necessary dialectical tension within the far from perfect perspective from which utopia is being imagined — that is, in being brashly positivist as against being deconstructive or hermeneutic — the dream of globalization ossifies or degenerates into the literalism of a fulfilled utopia.[7] The point of view that authorizes the utopian vision is dramatically purged, to use Foucault's language, of its own unreasonable history and geneaology. The ruse of techno-capital is that it creates an illusion that its perspective is already immaculately endowed with the semantic content of the utopia-to-be. Instead of utopia as multilaterally imagined and as an ongoing radical difference from itself, we now entertain utopia as the unipolar uniperspectival valorization of the temporality of "techno-capital." If the creation of violent dystopias during times when marxism-communism degenerated into Stalinist statism had to do with the brutalization of the present in the name of the future and the violation of the ethics of the means in the name of the ends of politics, the current rhetoric of utopian globalization offers a somewhat different scenario. Having discovered that the means will always defer, complicate, and re-route the authority of the ends, the current globalist discourse, in all its spectacular implosive brilliance, creates the magical impression that the realm of the means has been exorcized altogether. The "means" are the magical body of the Real. The networks, the flows, the border busting, the trashing of national sovereignties are not means towards a specific end; they are instead phenomena that are part of the Real, now mediatized and made available as pure and formal expressivity across the international division of labor.

What sense does the world make and from what point of view? How is it that point of view is both transcended and preserved as it were in its cognitive access to the alterity of the world as real? If all that we are talking about is point of view and its sublation through transcendence, how is one to distinguish and adjudicate among the legitimacies of different points of view? On what criteria is one point of view deemed invasive, colonizing of reality, and preemptive of other perspectives on the real, and another point of view recognized as generous and solicitous of reality on behalf of every perspectival desire and longing? Amitav Ghosh raises this question with memorable brilliance in *The Shadow Lines*: "One could never know anything except through desire, real desire, which was not the same thing as greed or lust: a pure, painful and primitive desire, a longing for everything that was not in oneself, a torment of the leash, that carried one beyond the limits of one's mind to other times and other places, and even, if one was lucky, to a place where there was no border between oneself and one's image in the mirror" (29). Before I undertake an analysis of this statement, it might be useful to add that this novel begins with the following definition of the value of human relationality and connectedness: "I could not bring myself to believe that their worth in my eyes could be reduced to something as arbitrary and unimportant as a blood relationship" (3). If going global means acknowledging a certain connectedness, what is the basis for such a connectedness? The narrator in the novel asserts unambiguously that the order of affiliation is of greater significance than the merely given but arbitrarily consecrated order of filiation. Filiation is arbitrary whereas affiliation is the result of agential choice and elaboration. Blood relationships tend to be tautologous, banal, repressive, and even racist through a militant exclusivity that gets naturalized in the name of natalism/nativism. Throughout the novel, Ghosh denaturalizes and makes ambiguous the ontological status of blood and its putative capacity to build and cement solidarities such as nationhood. Is blood, to echo Derrida's famous reading of Levi Strauss, nature or culture? If blood is what unites all of humanity, then all human beings are one large oceanic and undifferentiated family.[8] Blood is indisputably coextensive with all human life. But, on the other hand, blood does not get ideologized as national blood unless and until it is shed in a certain cause, within the structure of a certain antagonism: blood against blood in denominational fury — bloodshed passionately for one group and in hatred of another, both bloods divided but semanticized as "official and national bloods" in the service of the cause that pits blood against blood, nation against nation. It is in the historical reality of being spilt that blood becomes meaningful as a filiative category and construct. When the English and the French are at war as nations, they demonstrate themselves as national-universals at the very moment when the national-ness of each repudiates the universal in the other. (It is of course undeniably true that the shedding of blood by colonized peoples in their struggle against colonialism is of a different ethico-political order than the blood shed between two "equal nations"; my point rather is that the necessary "shedding of blood" is ritualistically sacralized as the foundation of a collective and yet exclusionary identity.) It is this undecidability of blood as it straddles the filiative and the affiliative orders that has rendered all nationalisms a scandal. Within the aporetic figurality of nationalism affiliative bonds created in historical and secular struggle become valorized as a form of filiation and then naturalized. Such a naturalization militarizes borders and inaugurates a politics of immurement that guarantees that there will be perpetual outsiders. But what would it take to value affiliation radically so that solidarities and recognitions will always take place in an open space rather than within exclusionary regimes? The first passage I quoted from *The Shadow Lines* provides a possible answer.

What is "real desire" that is "painful and primitive" (a dangerous anthropological term being used positively by a Third-World writer and intellectual), and how is it to be known apart from lust and greed? What is the object of real desire and what is the object of lust? How is the alterity of the Real honored by real desire, but traduced by lust? "The longing for everything that is not in oneself" — isn't that a kind of exoticism/orientalism that finds in the other, by way of a prescription for the incompleteness of the self, the mystique that will cure and complete the lack in one's self? Didn't colonialist desire dress up its determinate lack as universal and symbolic Lack and thereby justify its appetitive objectification of "the colony?" Didn't colonialist desire find itself narcissistically in the very lack that was nothing but the object of the colonial gaze? In what way is the postcolonial, Third-World desire for loss of self anything other than a mimetic recuperation of the anthropological impulse? Within the dyadic structure of desire and lack, which term fixes the other so that the desire-lack game can be set in motion? Within this dyadic game, can the gaze be returned, its direction reversed, so that the roles become mutually reversible? If the desire of man fixes woman as "his" lack, and the desire of the West fixes the East as "its" lack, can woman and the East realize man and the West as their respective "lacks"? (see Yegenoglu). How can reciprocity of the gaze be achieved without the objective alterity of a third term? Transactions between self and other need to take place simultaneously on two registers: one, where the self is negotiating with the alterity of the world; and two, where different selves are negotiating with one another as one another's self and other. Both registers are getting played out at the same time with implications for each other.

How is the alterity of the world as Real invoked differently by the subaltern gaze and the dominant gaze? I would like to suggest that the very alterity of the world-as-real is neither a given, nor is it single. It is only within the specificity of an epistemological model or gaze that the alterity of the Object is announced and recognized. And, since there are several perspectival gazes oriented to the Object, there are as many alterities as Object as there are gazes. It is in this sense that one asks: what is the subaltern world like compared to the dominant world, even though there is only one subtending reality that relates the subaltern to the dominant. The ability of each gaze or perspective to realize the alterity (the symbolic authority) of the Object is perennially interrupted by the perspectivism of every other gaze, each engaged in realizing its own symbolic authority. The very alterity of the world-as-real is pluriform and contested, and the eventual "worlding" of the world depends on the extent to which the different gazes negotiate with each other on the basis of the strength of their symbolic currency. It is both a matter of contestation and persuasion. On the register of the political, the subaltern political imaginary has to produce its own symbolic authority in opposition to and with the intention of unseating the symbolic authority of the dominant discourse.[9] On the ethical register of persuasion, however, the subaltern task is that of convincing the dominant discourse that in a world of shifting significations, it is wiser, truer, freer, and more just to relate to the world-as-real on the basis of the subaltern symbolic than on the basis of the dominant symbolic, that the subaltern representation of the Real is more valuable and worthwhile for all concerned than the dominant representation.[10] The difference as well as the distance between "what the world looks like" and "what the world should look like," — the difference between the actual and the ideal, the "is" and "the ought to be" — is best expressed as a function of ongoing multilateral transactions among perspectives committed to the task of reciprocal transcendence in the name of the One World in the making.

To put all this in the context of the politics of globalization, it matters from whose perspective the world is being realized as One. It also matters in what or whose currency the world is being "worlded" and within the symbolics of whose language the pros and cons of globalization are being discussed. As I have been trying to argue by way of Ghosh's novel, there are good and bad instances of transcendence. "Eating the Other" (Hooks) is certainly not an example of ethical transcendence. A lusty or greedy transcendence would involve one point of view establishing a binding and normative relationship

with the Real on behalf of all perspectives. It is a logic whereby I say that I
don't have the responsibility of proving the benevolence and the legitimacy
of my god so long as I have the ability and the power to desecrate or
destabilize the authority of your god. What makes my perspective axiomatic
and universally binding is not the justice or the fairness of its vision but its
power to destroy or depoliticize other perspectives. The lust of the dominant
desire is posited on the objectification of the other and the nihilation of the
right to pleasure of the other. It is through this process of nihilation that the
dominant participant names his/her desire as the Real of the encounter, and
his/her lack as the semantic body of the Real. The Other in this experiential
nexus ceases to have the right to name the experience and interpret it. The
ultimate trope of such an encounter is of course rape, where the other is
both implicated and silenced in the dominant self 's experience. But I still
haven't answered the key question: how is real desire different from lust?
How does the economy of real transcendence create a balance between
what is lost and what is gained, and who is gaining and who is losing? For
starters, real desire is non-egocentric and derives from the notion of a radical
"lack" that impoverishes every ego that would seek to sign for plenitude in
its own name. Transcendence is intended as a qualitative movement that
both acknowledges the specificity of the location that inaugurates the
transcendence and marks that very location or state of being as one to be
left behind. At the other end of the arc of transcendence is the other as
activated and eroticized by the desire of the self. Is the other as self violated
by the desire of the self undertaking transcendence? Why should the "other
self" be available for transcendence at all unless the transcendence is mutually
effected? I do not mind being the object or terminus of your transcendence
so long as you consent to being the object and terminus of mine. It is only
within such a context of reciprocal transcendence and the ethical obligation
that it entails that the question of freedom can even begin to get posed
contrapuntally against the reality of objectification. Are relationships
unthinkable outside the law of mutual objectification? Is freedom conceivable
as a proactive project undertaken in multiple solidarities rather than as a
game of mutual negations and objectifications? In other words, can you and
I ground our freedom in the universality of the One rather than make freedom
the function of the formula "my freedom is in my right to objectify you and
yours in your right to objectify me." As I have been trying to argue, the issue
of freedom as a transcendental function among and between perspectives
can only be part of a more basic accountability to the alterity of the big O:

the alterity of the One World as Real that is perennially both pre-given and available for realization by the heterogeneity of multiple perspectives.

To return then to the dynamics of transcendence as proposed by Amitav Ghosh: one of the chief preoccupations in that novel is how to realize a critical and mutually transformative relationship between "mirrors" and "windows." Under what conditions do mirrors that reflect the self back to itself become windows that open out to the others outside, and when do windows that provide a vision "outside" for the self become surfaces of self-recognition?[11] And indeed, if such a transformation is possible, what would be the nature of globality that would underlie such a possibility? If the world has indeed gone global, within such a cartography is it possible, say, for a village in India to look at itself in the mirror and as a result see the metropolitan reality of Paris? When London looks through the window at Lagos, as a result does it see a critical reflection of itself? The reasons for transcendence that Ghosh offers us are similar to Nandy's reasons: because no one culture or civilization is complete in itself, the only way to deal with incompleteness is to radically "dialogize" possibilities of knowledge and cognition, that is, in-mix self-centered perceptions with other-oriented perceptions to actualize a different world, script a different historiography. Wonderful as all this sounds in a utopian vein, a cautionary note needs to be sounded. Who is seeking completion and who is undertaking the pilgrimage of losing self in the other? Even given the unavoidable incompleteness of any civilization, are some incomplete civilizations more dominant and deemed less incomplete than others? To put it more concretely, in a world structured hierarchically between East and West, developing and developed nations, is the longing of the West for completion from the East somehow considered not as drastic as the longing of the East for completion by the West? Let us say, and here I am using fairly stereotypical characterizations just to make a point, the West is looking to the East for spiritual enhancement and enrichment and the East is looking to the West for technological advancement. Which of these two needs for completion would be considered more dire? In a world-historical situation where materialism and technology are valorized more than spirituality and matters "interior," it is inevitable that oriental dependency would position itself in a weaker position within the global structure.

There is a further problem with the ontology of the transcendence model, considered in a utopian framework. What is the nature of the tension between the egocentric "one" seeking transcendence and the pre-personal One without whom transcendence loses all meaning? Between the initial egocentric "one" that is the protagonist of transcendence (the Indian one, the American one, the Somalian one, the female one, the ethnic one, etc.) and the figurality of transcendence there lies a gap, and it is worthwhile to ensure that the project of transcendence does not become a mere act of surrender to a dominant discourse. This danger is particularly endemic in the context of postcolonial transcendence, as envisioned by Ghosh, since postcolonial realities can never be sure that they have succeeded in persuading the metropolis to play the same game that they are interested in playing. In other words, unless the ethical imperative honored by both parties is the same, there is every possibility that transcendence might have the effect of depolitizing postcolonial interest and agency. This dangerous possibility can easily be understood in the context of a game where one jumps and the other catches: what if the other, midway through the game, sensing superior control, intends differently and chooses not to catch? Within the symbolic alterity of the utopian horizon, there must be some way of making sure that no one participating political imaginary suddenly decides to own the horizon in its own name and thereby claim that its mirror be unilaterally legitimated as the window for all. The commitment to the utopian horizon has to find a way to keep the space of the Real open so that the globality of the world does not become just another name for Westernization or Americanization. The problem, both theoretical and methodological, with utopian spatiality is that of coordination and synchronization: how to deal simultaneously with the here and now and the long haul. How to think into reality the qualitative place-less-ness of utopia as a function and consequence of a critical thinking-through of the problems of the here and now? How to entertain passionately and postpone in rigorous critique the utopian horizon in the name of present history? In Ghosh's terms, how to go beyond "the shadow lines" of nationally demarcated identity regimes not by denying the historical reality of the shadow lines but rather by working deconstructively through the lines so that their authority may be rendered insubstantial, substance-less, and shadowy? If utopia is the imaginary multilateral answer to the problem of unequal perspectives and uneven temporalities, then such a resolution, to be legitimate, has to work its way through the agonistic field of perspectivism, redress wrongs and injustices en route, and not make a clean break from the politics of perspectives. Ghosh offers us the practice of what a character in his novel calls, "imagining with precision." Though all realities are imagined or invented and not natural, it is important that people invent their own realities rather than dwell passively and reactively in realities invented by others. The point here is that it is a good thing to be othered in general by the process of epistemology, but within such a general alienation, there is still a place for political agency.[12] But the real and intricate challenge is how to imagine one's reality not in egocentric isolation, but relationally with other imaginings. One of the cardinal points that Ghosh makes through his inventive and transgressive reading of cartography is that places in the world that are considered far and remote from one another are in fact closer to one another than places considered to be in close proximity. And often, a place in another nation is closer to one's location than a fellow-location within one's own country. It is in the context of a creative and diasporan rethinking of the politics of proximity and distance that Ghosh uses the phrase "imagine with precision." The phrase dramatizes a valuable tension between the freedom to be different, heterogeneous, non-normative, and subjective, as realized in the word "imagine," and the rigor invoked by the term "precision," which denotes a certain representational fidelity as well as accountability. Here, by precision, Ghosh does not mean the facticity of empiricism, or the propositional rectitude of positivism, or the egocentric drive towards self-adequation; in Ghosh's text, precision does not inhere in any one location. Precision is a thoroughly exotopic and ekstatic concept whereby the correctness of any one location can be determined only with reference to the precision with which it invokes its relationship to all other locations, and thereby the correctness of every other location. Precision operates as a form of global accountability as well as connectedness that functions as the ethical *a priori* that sanctions the attempt of every location to name and understand itself. Precision becomes the ethic as well as the narrative aesthetic whereby the story of every self is committed not to violate the story of the other. Precision is honored as that radical alterity without which the narrative of humanity degenerates into the history of warring nations, militarized boundaries, and homes that reek with hatred of the other. It may not be a bad idea to submit globality to such imaginative precision.

4

Globalization and the Postcolonial Condition

Paul Jay

We live in an age increasingly dominated by the phenomenon of globalization. While the publication in June, 2000 of Thomas L. Friedman's *The Lexus and the Olive Tree* brought the significance of economic and cultural globalization home to a wide public audience, it was old news in an age in which everything from food, music, identity, culture, film, the economy and politics had "gone global." This was especially true inside the academy, where papers, conferences, and books on globalization have proliferated with increasing rapidity since the mid-1980's.[1] Indeed, by the time Friedman had published his book, the study of globalization had already migrated from departments of economy and political science through sociology departments and cultural studies programs into the field of literary studies.[2] What started out as a sub-field dedicated to tracking the rise of an increasingly global network of economic relations dominated by transnational corporations has steadily evolved into a globalized field of cultural studies, as scholars and critics in a range of disciplines in the humanities and social science have come to recognize that commodities, currencies, and cultures are inseparable, that the globalization of economies brings with it the globalization of cultures, and that, indeed, it is nearly impossible to figure out where economic globalization stops and cultural globalization begins.

Harvard University Press published one of the more important academic books on globalization well before the appearance of *The Lexus and the Olive Tree*, Bill Readings' *The University in Ruins* (1998). Readings develops a trenchant analysis of the impact globalization has had on the North American university, focusing on how the demise of the nation-state has been affecting the humanities in general, and literary studies in particular. He reminds us that the rise of the modern university is intimately connected to the evolution of the modern nation-state, that the needs of nationalism and the operations of the university were deeply connected from the outset. In Readings' view, the modern university, which evolved under Humboldt at the University of Berlin and was later adopted in the United States (7), always had a "national cultural mission" (3), in part because the modern idea of "culture" and the modern idea of the nation developed in close relation to one another (12), so much so that the "University ... has historically been the primary institution of national culture in the modern nation-state" (12).

In Readings' view, however, globalization is very quickly putting an end to all this. With the contemporary shift from national economies to a global one, the proliferation of electronic media able to transmit information instantaneously while ignoring national boundaries, and with the power of transnational corporations eclipsing those of the nation-state, the university is undergoing in Readings' view a profound reorientation. "The University," he writes, "is becoming a different kind of institution, one that is no longer linked to the destiny of the nation-state by virtue of its role as a producer, protector, and inculcator of an idea of national culture" (3). Because "the process of economic globalization brings with it the relative decline of the nation-state" the University is undergoing a fundamental reorientation away from serving the needs of the nation-state toward serving the needs of transnational capital (3).

This change is having a particularly striking impact on the humanities. The modern university grew out of the values of the Enlightenment and was committed to the cultivation of character, an aesthetic education, and the development in its students of the capacity for philosophical critique. The central role of philosophy in this enterprise, and the later importance of a literary education as formulated by Matthew Arnold, who saw literature as central to his programmatic effort to provide culture to England as a bulwark against a rising working class, underscore the important role the humanities played in the modern university. "The current crisis of the university in the West" in the age of globalization, therefore, "proceeds from a fundamental shift in its social role and internal systems, one which means that the centrality of the traditional humanistic disciplines to the life of the University is no longer assured" (3).

Readings' analysis is important in helping us to understand how external forces related to the contemporary history of globalization have contributed to intellectual fragmentation in the academy, weakened the humanities, and led to a proliferation of what appears to be largely uncoordinated efforts to create new sub-disciplines and reorganize traditional curricula and programs. Clearly, the unprecedented explosion of theorizing about literary language, interpretation, textuality, authorship and reading since the late 1960s has played an important role in overturning conventional approaches to literary study in the classroom, in criticism, and in the curriculum. But nothing has quite had the kind of transformative effect on literary studies that globalization has had. This effect, we can now see, has all but undone the traditional Eurocentrism of literary studies in the West. As Edward Said has recently put it, "economic and political globalization ... since the end of the cold war ... has been the enveloping context in which literary studies are undertaken" (66):

> The gradual emergence in the humanities of confused and fragmented paradigms of research, such as those available through the new fields of postcolonial, ethnic, and other particularistic or identity-based study, reflects the eclipse of the old authoritative, Eurocentric models and the new ascendancy of a globalized, postmodern consciousness from which, as Benita Parry and others have argued, the gravity of history has been excised. (66)

As this quote makes clear, Said is less than sanguine about these developments. Like Readings, he takes the "deterioration of the position of the humanities" in the university to be a direct result of the "catastrophic effects of the global situation" (66). The end of Eurocentrism, in his view, has simply left us with a hodge-podge of critical approaches rooted in identity politics and shorn of a historical consciousness. In our rush to celebrate a "purely academic version of multiculturalism with which many people in the real world of ethnic division, conflict and chauvinism would find it difficult to identify," we miss paying attention to "sites of resistance to the terrible negative effects of globalization" (66). The worst of these effects for Said, beyond even the poverty and political divisions that attend globalization, is the "dominance of the United States as the only superpower left" (66). This dominance, of course, carries over into the realm of academic politics, for those of us who have worried about the extent to which global studies simply represents the re-colonization of "Other" literatures by Western academics are, in effect, concerned that transnational literary studies is coming to be dominated by a single superpower. From this point of view, globalization simply represents the return of Western colonization as postnational literary studies hitches itself to the globalization bandwagon and begins to subjugate the literature of the "Other" to its own paradigms. In this scenario, Eurocentrism is simply repackaged as globalization.

But are things really this bad? Is globalization itself simply the newest and most efficient agent of capitalist exploitation yet developed by the West, a process that relentlessly homogenizes and Westernizes the cultures it entangles in its net? Is the attention we pay in the academy to literatures and cultures formerly excluded by Eurocentrism corrupted by its association with a commitment to difference, diversity and multiculturalism that has already been cunningly co-opted by capitalism? And must we, along with Said, think of postcolonial studies, gender studies, the study of "ethnic" literatures and other approaches that grow out of identity politics as hopelessly compromised and fragmenting?

I don't think so. In the first place, there is nothing new about "fragmentation" in literary studies. Fragmentation actually has a long history in literary studies and is integral to its development. Whether we consider the steady fragmentation in English of the so-called "canon" from British, to British and American texts, and, more recently, "global English," or, its transformation from texts authored by white men to texts authored by women and minority writers, or whether we consider the historical proliferation of critical approaches ranging from philology, historicism, the New Criticism, structuralism, deconstruction, feminism, the *New* Historicism, postcolonialism, eco-criticism, etc., we see a discipline that has been constantly fragmenting and then reforming itself. In literary studies, as in most other academic disciplines, "coherence" and "fragmentation" are co-dependent. Coherence comes as a benefit of fragmentation. It isn't an alternative to it.

I think that in this light we need to be careful not to set up a historical view of literary studies in which a monolithic and coherent Eurocentrism remained dominant until postmodern fragmentation set in, a fragmentation specifically linked to the debilitating effects of globalization. This historical narrative is much too simplistic. Although literary studies in the West has been, as Said points out, dominated by Eurocentrism, disciplinary coherence within this framework broke down and re-organized itself with remarkable regularity during the whole of the twentieth century.[3] The current shift in literary studies, which Said and a host of other contemporary critics across the ideological spectrum, characterize as a new kind of fragmentation, simply represents another instance in which one form of coherence gives way to another as the discipline continues to evolve.[4] Earlier instances of this so-called fragmentation often occurred along narrow lines related primarily to methodology (philological, rhetorical, formalist, historical, Structuralist, poststructuralist, etc.) whereas recent forms of fragmentation are related more to political and social movements (Marxism, feminism, gay and lesbian studies, postcolonial studies, African American studies, and now, globalization studies). The current shift — if that is what we are witnessing — from a postcolonial to a global perspective, then, is consistent with the way the discipline of literary studies has developed over the whole course of the twentieth century.

This shift does, however, raise a number of pressing questions we need to explore: What kind of *historical* relation is there between postcolonialism and globalization? What impact will the increasing attention to what we call global culture have on our study of colonial cultures, postcolonial cultures and national identities? What kind of disciplinary relationship will develop between globalization studies and postcolonial studies? And finally, are the forms of personal and cultural hybridity produced by globalization destabilizing and to be lamented, or are they inevitable and potentially liberating? In what follows, I want to explore each of these questions in more detail.

One of the paradoxes of globalization, which in its current form challenges the power and autonomy of the nation-state, is that as a historical phenomenon it thrived on its complicity with an expanding nation-state. Immanuel Wallerstein's well-known formulation of "the modern world system," for example, which to an important degree paved the way for more comprehensive theories about globalization, is based on the idea that nation-state economies facilitated the development of a world economic system. Western nation-states, in particular, characterized by voracious economic development, strong governmental structures, and a powerful sense of national identity, controlled the developing global economy for their own benefit.[5] However, the rise of the multi-national corporation, and later, the internet, has transformed Wallerstein's world system by decentering the role of the nation-state. Indeed, more and more, Wallerstein's world system, tied as it is to the dominance of the modern nation-state, looks like the last phase of an age in eclipse, since under globalization the nation-state is being undermined by transnational forces that threaten its traditional power to regulate subjectivity and determine what constitutes cultural belonging.

While Wallerstein's world system was fundamentally an economic one, globalization is now recognized as a broadly *cultural* phenomenon. This shift from world system theory to the study of globalization involves a move away from the narrow study of global economic exchange to a more generalized study of transnational cultural exchange. While globalization started out as a disciplinary sub-field of economy and political science departments, it has become increasingly populated by sociologists, cultural theorists, and professors of English. It has developed by continually rethinking the relationship between economies, cultures, commodities and social behavior, and by focusing carefully on how systems of commodity exchange are also systems of cultural exchange.[6]

This shift away from a world system focus on the organizing power and autonomy of the nation-state toward globalization theory's focus on the reorganization of social formations, political alliances, and cultural identity and power along transnational lines, has profound implications for how we think about the organization of literary studies. The old Eurocentric model of literary studies, of course, was nationalist through and through, and so was demonstrably connected to what Wallerstein called a modern world system. Indeed, the organization of departments and curricula along national lines is a vestige of the organizing power of the very concept of the nation-state and is deeply connected to the kind of Eurocentrism Said discusses. In the United States, for example, literary studies have been structured like a political map, the borders of which have neatly duplicated those between modern nation-states ("English," "French," Spanish," "Italian," "German," etc.).

Of course these nationalist and largely Eurocentric paradigms for organizing literary studies were called into question by postcolonial studies well before the advent of globalization studies. Viewed together at this particular moment, postcolonialism and globalization seem to offer two distinct approaches to the transnational study of literature and culture. Postcolonial literary studies, of course, is rooted to a significant degree in the work of postcolonial intellectuals and writers, and is grounded in the political and social experience of political decolonization and nation-building, while globalization studies are primarily the product of Western intellectuals and are grounded in a complex of disciplinary theories focusing on *postnational* structures and cultures. Whether measured in terms of the background and experiences of scholars in the two fields, or in terms of the disciplinary interests, politics, and paradigms they invoke, it is not at all clear that there is the basis for developing a working relationship between postcolonial studies and globalization studies. Indeed, in Said's view, globalization looks like a direct *threat* to the postcolonial condition and its study.

As I noted earlier, in order to deal with these questions we have to consider the relationship between globalization and postcolonialism as historical phenomena. It seems to me that there are two different ways of looking at this relationship. The first would be to mark a clear historical distinction between the two, based on an understanding that while globalization is a *postnational* phenomenon, postcolonialism is linked to modernity and the long epoch of the nation-state. The second, however, would insist on a fundamental *connection* between postcolonialism and globalization, one based on an understanding that *both* colonialism and postcolonialism are integral to the very history of globalization. The first view would separate postcolonialism and globalization historically, connecting postcolonialism to the rise of modernity and the epoch of nationalism, while seeing globalization as fundamentally postnational and postmodern. While the second view recognizes that postcolonialism marks a *break* in the history of colonialism and the exercise of colonial power, it insists that postcolonialism belongs nevertheless to the late history of the nation-state. From this point of view, postcolonialism marks a break *in* the history of the nation-state, but not a break *from* that history.

The second point of view rejects the idea that globalization is simply a contemporary, or postmodern, phenomenon. It insists that globalization actually has a long history, and that the whole arch of European imperial expansion, colonization, decolonization, and the establishment of postcolonial states figures prominently in that history.[7] Instead of drawing a clear line between the modern age of the nation-state and the postmodern emergence of a transnational, global economic and cultural system, this point of view sees globalization as a long historical process unfolding in ever accelerating phases. To be sure, in the earlier phases of globalization, the nation-state linked colonization and capitalism together in the interests of its own expansion, but in its more recent phase multi-national corporations and the mass media have begun to challenge the power of the nation-state. Such observations from this point of view do not undermine the basic argument that colonialism, postcolonialism, and globalization are historically linked in important ways. They simply suggest how the long history of globalization might be written.

The first point of view sees postcolonialism and globalization as largely at odds with one another, and so does not suggest a very productive context for thinking about how the two approaches to transnational literary studies they inform can be reconciled. From this point of view, the postcolonial state is relegated to the fading epoch of modernity, while the structures and cultures of globalization are associated with postmodernity and with a future in which the nation-state plays an increasingly peripheral role. The second view is more helpful than the first, recognizing as it does that the histories of colonization, decolonization, and postcolonialism are part of the long history of globalization. This view productively connects the two by questioning the whole idea of a historical break separating postcolonialism from globalization. Indeed, it suggests that there will be some level of continuity between the issues taken up by both postcolonial and global literatures.

Of course, once we recognize this link we still must confront the fact that the forces of economic and cultural globalization have been, at the very least, a double-edged sword for postcolonial nations and the cultures they seek to sustain. While in the first phase of globalization the nation-state harnesses colonization with capital development in the interests of its own expansion, in its later phases multi-national corporations and the mass media begin to outpace its power.[8] The first stage suggests a historical epoch in which the formerly colonized achieve a measure of power and autonomy through the creation of a postcolonial nation-state. The forces of globalization represent something of an ironic moment for such a state. One irony, as Ania Loomba points out in her discussion of the work of Benedict Anderson, is that the nation-state is based on a European, colonial model, so that "anti-colonial nationalism," as represented by the emergence of the postcolonial nation-state, "is itself made possible and shaped by European political and intellectual history" (189). The structure that colonizes becomes, ironically, the vehicle of liberation. A second irony, as Loomba points out, is that at the very moment of the postcolonial state's constitution, the power and autonomy of the nation-state itself get called into question by transnational forces that threaten its demise. Worse yet, economic globalization demands participation in a transnational economic system that threatens the economy, the autonomy, and the cultural identity of all nation-states, especially newly emergent ones. The paradox here is painfully clear. Economic development seems tied to investment in the global economy, but that economy also brings with it a homogenizing, Westernizing cultural force threatening the cultural autonomy and identity of the nation-state. That force seems poised to take control of the very economy it might liberate.

How do postcolonial nations, and others seeking to preserve their cultural character, participate in the global system while protecting the autonomy and character of their national cultures? Opting out of the global economy all together doesn't seem to be a very viable option, yet the dangers of globalization as outlined by Said are clear. This quandary underscores the main challenge of constructing a working relationship between postcolonialism and globalization. On the one hand, it is not that difficult to see how colonization, decolonization, and postcolonialism are part of the larger history of globalization, a fact that implies the two processes or epochs can be studied in interconnected ways. But how can globalization studies contribute to the project of postcolonial studies when globalization itself is now a central threat to the postcolonial nation-state? There are other seeming contradictions as well. After all, isn't postcolonialism grounded in resistance to, and autonomy from the kind of colonization the forces of globalization seem to represent? Doesn't globalization, as a historical, political, economic and cultural force, threaten the distinct political structures and cultural identities of nation-states deeply committed to the process of recovering and enriching forms of cultural expression nearly obliterated by colonization? Isn't globalization a radically homogenizing force, one that inexorably spreads Western foods, fashions, music, patterns of consumption, and values wherever capital expansion and the media go, laying waste to local forms of identity and cultural expression? And worse, don't academic globalization studies represent the return of the repressed, the colonizing machinery of critical paradigms that in their most benign forms assimilate Otherness to Western disciplinary forms, and in their more insidious ones, as Ania Loomba has put it, celebrate globalization "as the producer of a new and 'liberating' hybridity or multiculturalism, terms that now circulate to ratify the mish-mash of cultures generated by the near unipolar domination of the Western, particularly United States, media machine?" (256).

These are hard questions to answer, especially for Western academics deeply interested in postcolonial literatures and cultures yet also fascinated by the processes of globalization and the hybrid cultural forms it is creating. We can begin to deal with them, however, by acknowledging that there ought to be two sides to Loomba's warning. We *do* need to guard against making a fetish of hybridity and multiculturalism when it simply represents a "mish-mash" of homogenized Western cultural forms and patterns of consumption, and we *do* need to be wary of celebrating the liberating effects of this "mish-mash" when it may be obliterating deep-felt and long-standing forms of cultural behavior. However, no matter where we come from, or what our cultural roots, we also need to guard against insisting that whole regions of the world, and their sometimes impoverished populations, must preserve their traditional cultural characters and resist accommodation with a global economy and the cultural changes it brings simply because we enjoy the richness and diversity their ways of dressing, eating, making music and living off the land represent (as if these cultures exist for the West as a kind of museum or living diorama). Of course, it is nearly impossible to question this impulse without seeming to side with Western, capitalist forces of exploitation and sameness, but I think we need to find a way to try. There has to be a more complicated, nuanced, and carefully thought-through position on the relationship between postcolonialism and globalization than the polar ones suggested by Loomba, that is, between the position that sees all forms of cultural hybridity or cultural experimentation and transformation as simply the evil result of globalization, and the position that unthinkingly celebrates hybridity and multiculturalism as paths to liberation from the paralyzing effects of cultural fundamentalisms wherever they may be. The first position makes a fetish of purity and stasis, ignoring the fact that cultures all over the world have always evolved syncretically in the context of complicated interactions with one another, and it plays down the extent to which people subject to contemporary Western cultural forms translate and appropriate them in complex ways. The second position runs the risk of making a fetish of syncretism and hybridity for its own sake, as if culture only liberates when it renounces rigid traditions and embraces syncretism and change. It can represent too enthusiastic an embrace of globalization without a recognition of the price it exacts all over the globe.[9]

It seems to me that transnational literary studies, whether it presents itself as postcolonial or global, has to begin with a recognition that cultures have always traveled and changed, that the effects of globalization, dramatic as they are, only represent in an accelerated form something that has always taken place: the inexorable change that occurs through intercultural contact, as uneven as the forms it takes may be. Sometimes that change has violent and tragic results stemming from conquest and the exercise of brute force. Sometimes it comes in the contexts of trade and commodity exchange, which often creates deeply institutionalized forms of economic oppression but can also facilitate fascinating forms of cultural improvisation in terms of social behavior or the production of anything from food to fashion, music and literature.[10] But it has always happened, and it is hard to find a place on the globe where what we might want to celebrate as local or indigenous culture is either local or indigenous. This is certainly the case with respect to the geographical areas central to my own recent work on transnational literatures in English: the Caribbean, South Asia, and the border zone of US/Hispanic America. One would be hard pressed to identify cultural forms that are "indigenous" in any of these regions. Culture and identity in these areas are the complex result of the long history of what we now call globalization. There are, lamentably, no "indigenous" Caribbeans in anything like the strict sense of the word. The literatures of the Caribbean are therefore deeply engaged with the complex interaction of native, African, Asian and colonial populations and cultures, all of which have contributed to the creation of a radically syncretic set of Caribbean populations.[11] The Indian sub-continent, where so much new literature in English has its roots, was swept by Greek, Persian and Islamic conquests that forged a deeply hybrid cultural mix in what became modern India, Pakistan, and Bangladesh well before the establishment of the East India Company and the British Raj. And of course the border regions of the US Southwest are characterized by a dizzying mix of native, Hispanic, and African populations and cultures (from Florida and New Orleans all the way to Southern California) that make the whole notion of the indigenous obsolete.

Understanding that globalization is not a contemporary phenomenon, but that it has a long history incorporating the epochs of colonization, decolonization, and postcolonialism, should help us deal with the complexity of cultural production in these regions without taking recourse to either of the polar positions I just reviewed. Globalization provides a historical framework through which we can analyze more carefully forms of political colonization and cultural syncretism created by the long global history of cross-cultural contact, and how they have directed the struggle of both "indigenous" and diasporic populations to develop forms of political and economic autonomy. Perhaps more importantly, this framework suggests a context in which the literatures of postcolonialism and globalization can be studied in relationship to one another. Indeed, if we accept the idea that globalization has a long history encompassing the various epochs of colonization, decolonization, and postcolonialism in all their historical complexity, it becomes difficult to draw clear distinctions between postcolonial literature and literature engaged more specifically with the contemporary effects of globalization.

This certainly seems to be the case with an increasing range of contemporary global fiction in English. On their surface, many of these texts seem to be less interested in postcoloniality than globalization, a fact that suggests the emergence of something we might be tempted to call globalization literature. I have in mind novels such as Arundhati Roy's *The God of Small Things*, Zadie Smith's *White Teeth*, Mohsin Hamid's *Moth Smoke*, Salman Rushdie's *The Ground Beneath Her Feet*, and the fiction of Meera Syal. These novels demonstrate only a minimal interest, if any at all, in the history of colonization and decolonization, or in the contemporary plight of the postcolonial nation-state. Roy's novel, though it is set in contemporary India (in the state of Kerala), engages the cultural legacy of the British Raj, and is profoundly critical of communist party rule in Kerala, is much less interested in India as a postcolonial nation than it is in the effects of globalization. Likewise, while Zadie Smith's *White Teeth* deals in a sustained way with the challenges Britain's mixed population poses to the whole question of "Englishness," it too deals more fundamentally with the kind of contemporary effects of globalization critics like Arjun Appadurai have focused on: migration, the media, and the role of the imagination in creating a diasporic, postnational identity.[12] And Hamid's *Moth Smoke* all but ignores dealing with contemporary Pakistan in the context of colonialism, decolonization and the problems that attend the postcolonial nation to focus almost exclusively on the disruptive effects the global economy has had on urban, Westernized Pakistanis.

While it is tempting to use these differences as a point of departure for drawing some clear distinctions between postcolonial literature and the literature of globalization, such distinctions do not really hold up to close scrutiny. Why? There are two principal reasons. In the first place, "postcolonial" fiction has to be defined quite narrowly in order to exclude the work of Roy, Smith and Hamid. While it is true that none of them deal specifically with the history of colonization and decolonization because they are more interested in the contemporary effects of globalization, in each of these books globalization is itself folded into the history of postcoloniality so that the historical effects of globalization are linked inextricably with the historical condition we call "postcolonial." They underscore the fact that the history of globalization is not separate from but rather *encompasses* the history of colonization, decolonization, and postcolonialism. In the second place, each of these novels deals with a range of issues — identity and its relationship to ethnicity and culture, the challenges of developing a cohesive sense of social belonging among disparate populations, the effects on local communities of global economic and commodity flows — that are demonstrably the concern of postcolonial fiction as well. We would have to take, then, a rather strict-constructionist approach in defining postcolonial fiction (a specific, sustained, and explicitly political engagement with colonial rule, the history of decolonization, and the practical difficulties of developing a postcolonial nation-state) in order to draw a firm distinction between postcolonial fiction and "global" fiction.

The continuity I have been discussing between colonization and decolonization, on the one hand, and the processes of globalization, on the other, can be made concrete if we take a more extended look at *The God of Small Things*. As I have already indicated, Roy's novel, beyond the deep (and controversial) cynicism of its treatment of communist rule in Kerala, has little to say about India as a nation-state, postcolonial or otherwise. *The God of Small Things*, rather, is about the transgression of boundaries (caste lines, "love laws," etc.), the debilitating effects of "Anglophilia," and the contemporary effects global culture and the global economy are having in Kerala. Paying scant attention to the political history of colonization and to the national political scene, all of this gets played out in Roy's novel within the narrow, claustrophobic confines of a family romance. The novel, Roy has insisted, is "not about history but biology and transgression."[13]

Roy's title seems to bear out this claim. The God of "small things" in her novel is associated with "personal despair" and "personal turmoil," while the God of "Big Things" is associated with history and the "public turmoil of a nation" (20). For many of the characters, personal despair results from transgressing what the narrator, Rahel, calls the "love laws ... laws that lay down who should be loved and how" (31). The terror her family experiences results from an uncanny confluence of events related to the transgressions of these laws, principally by Rahel's mother's love for the untouchable, Velutha, her Aunt's agonizing desire for a Priest, Father Mulligan, and the complex web of relationships Rahel and her brother, Estha, have with their British step-sister, Sophie Mol, and with their mother's lover, Velutha. However, the distinction between the personal and the historical gets complicated at the very outset of the novel. At the end of the first chapter, as Rahel ruminates over the cause of her family's tragedy, she is tempted to say it all began with a small thing, the arrival for a visit of their step-sister, for this triggered a series of events that led to catastrophe. It turns out, however, that "to say that it all began when Sophie Mol came to Ayemenem is only one way of looking at it":

Equally, it could be argued that it actually began thousands of years ago. Long before the Marxists came. Before the British took Malabar, before the Dutch Ascendency, before Vasco da Gama arrived, before the Zamorin's conquest of Calicut. Before three purple-robed Syrian bishops murdered by the Portuguese were found floating in the sea ... It could be argued that it began long before Christianity arrived in a boat and seeped into Kerala like tea from a teabag.

That it really began in the days when the Love Laws were made. The laws that lay down who should be loved, and how.

And how much. (32–3)

This other way of looking at the roots of her family's terror links the realm of small (personal) things in the novel with the realm of big (historical) things. By stressing how forms of purely biological attraction have long been regulated in India by religious and political institutions, and by conjuring up the long colonial history of India as the context for emphasizing the durability of these regulations, Roy implicitly questions the very distinction between the personal and the historical her title seems founded on.

Although in this passage the family's terror is traced back through the institutional and social history of religious proscriptions that long predate British colonial rule, that terror, personal and thus categorized in the novel as a "small thing," *is* linked later to the history of British colonialism and thus to "big things." This is done through Roy's manipulation of a place she calls the "History House." This house, in Rahel's childhood a ruin standing in the middle of an abandoned rubber tree estate, was once owned by an "Englishman who had 'gone native,' " a man she refers to as "Ayemenem's own Kurtz" and who she links explicitly to the "Heart of Darkness" (51). Much later in the novel, this house, linked as it is to the history of colonialism, turns out to be the very spot where the family's personal terror comes to a head. In making the History House both the representative site of British colonial terror *and* the site of the family's personal terror, Roy explicitly links the "big things" and the "small things" in her novel and historicizes them in relationship to the long global history of colonialism in India.

However, in one of the more important twists in the novel, the family is "trapped outside their own history" by being "Anglophiles" (51).

Chacko [their uncle] told the twins that, though he hated to admit it, they were all Anglophiles. They were a *family* of Anglophiles. Pointed in the wrong direction, trapped outside their own history and unable to retrace their steps because their footprints had been swept away. He explained to them that history was like an old house at night. With all the lamps lit. And ancestors whispering inside.

"To understand history," Chacko said, "we have to go inside and listen to what they're saying. And look at the books and the pictures on the wall. And smell the smells."

" ... But we can't go in," Chacko explained, "because we've been locked out. And when we look in through the windows, all we see are shadows. ... [O]ur minds have been invaded by a war. A war that we have won and lost. ... A war that has made us adore our conquerors and despise ourselves." (51–52)

In passages like these the terror Rahel's family experiences, personal though it may be, is linked to the history of British colonization. Where early on we are invited to mark a difference between the private and the public in the distinction between the God of Big Things and the God of Small Things, Roy methodically works to undercut that distinction so that the book ends up dramatizing the extent to which the "big things," grounded in history and the nation, and the "small things" grounded in personal and familial life, are inextricably interrelated. Elsewhere in the book, Roy connects the family's alienation from its own history and identity under colonial rule to the more contemporary forces of globalization. Indeed, Roy historicizes globalization in her book so that it not only incorporates both contemporary forms and the history of British colonialism, but also the successive series of conquests in the Indian continent that run back through the Dutch, the Persians, the Muslims and the Indo-Aryans to Alexander the Great.

As I noted earlier, the novel's treatment of contemporary globalization is even more prominent than its treatment of British colonialism. Early in the book Roy weaves a pointed critique of globalization into her description of Estha's walks around Ayemenem (he has returned in the early 1990s as an adult):

Some days he walked along the banks of the river that smelled of shit and pesticides bought with World Bank loans. Most of the fish had died. The ones that survived suffered from fin-rot and had broken out in boils.

Other days he walked down the road. Past the new, freshly baked, iced, Gulf-money houses built by nurses, masons, wire-benders and bank clerks, who worked hard and unhappily in faraway places. (14)

The material devastation brought to Ayemenem by globalization is complemented by Roy's description of "Foreign Returnees" at Cochin airport, Indians whose exposure to the cultures and commodities of the West has profoundly alienated them from India:

> And there they were, the Foreign Returnees, in wash'n'wear suits and rainbow sunglasses. With an end to grinding poverty in their Aristocrat suitcases. With cement roofs for their thatched houses, and geysers for their parents' bathrooms. ... Maxis and high heels. Puff sleeves and lipstick. Mixy-grinders and automatic flashes for their cameras. ... With love and a lick of shame that their families who had come to meet them were so ... so ... gawkish. *Look at the way they dressed! Surely they had more suitable airport wear! Why did Malayalees have such awful teeth?*
>
> And the airport itself! More like the local bus depot! The bird-shit on the building! Oh the spitstains on the kangaroos!
>
> *Oho! Going to the dogs India is.* (134)

These extended descriptions of how globalization has affected Ayemenem's waterways and those in Kerala who have been living abroad help reinforce Roy's treatment of how British colonialism and the effects of globalization have transformed Rahel's family. Perhaps Roy's most pointed treatment in this regard comes when she describes the impact globalization has had on the life of Rahel's aunt, Baby Kochamma. Unable to overcome the love laws that kept her from Father Mulligan, Baby Kochamma transfers all her energy to the "fierce, bitter" cultivation of an ornamental garden (26). After "more than half a century of relentless, pernickety attention," however, Baby Kochamma has abandoned her garden, seduced by satellite television. Now, instead of tending her garden, "she presided over the world in her drawing room on satellite TV":

> It wasn't something that happened gradually. It happened overnight. Blondes, wars, famines, football, sex, music, coups d'état – they all arrived on the same train. They unpacked together ... now whole wars, famines, picturesque massacres and Bill Clinton could be summoned up like servants. And so, while her ornamental garden wilted and dried, Baby Kochamma followed American NBA league games, one-day cricket and all the Grand Slam tennis tournaments. On weekdays she watched *The Bold and the Beautiful* and *Santa Barbara*. ... She enjoyed the WWF *Wrestling Mania* shows, where Hulk Hogan and Mr. Perfect, whose necks were wider than their heads, wore spangled Lycra leggings and beat each

other up brutally. ... Her old fears of the Revolution and the Marxist-Leninist menace had been rekindled by new television worries about the growing numbers of desperate and dispossessed people. She viewed ethnic cleansing, famine and genocide as direct threats to her furniture. (27–29)

The worst fears of globalization's critics are telescoped into this short passage. The material world of Baby Kochamma's garden, a place linked to home and the local, and the work she did with her own hands, is replaced by the electronic world of global television, a world paradoxically compelling for its being so alien, one in which American sporting events and soap operas mix so seamlessly with ghastly reports of dispossession, famine, massacres, and genocide, that it seems difficult telling them all apart. They are all done up in a manner simultaneously horrifying and "picturesque." Her own localized fears have not been eased by what she sees on television. They have been *replaced* by what she sees on television. Global culture brought to her through the auspices of CNN is both menacing and self-alienating. Her addiction to television seems to mark her dispossession by global culture.[14]

The God of Small Things is in many ways a work of *postnational* fiction, since in its relentless focus on the present it pays relatively little attention to the details of British colonization and the status of India as a postcolonial nation-state. If we were to define postcolonial literature narrowly in terms of its engagement with the idea of the nation and the practical political challenges of constructing a viable nation-state, Roy's novel would seem only marginally a work of postcolonial fiction. Moreover, given its preoccupation with examining the effects of globalization on her characters, the novel's postnational orientation suggests it belongs to a new species of post-post-colonial fiction, what I earlier termed the literature of globalization. However, the novel itself tends to undermine any useful historical distinction we might want to make between the postcolonial condition and globalization, since in her text Roy demonstrates that the postcolonial condition is itself produced as part of the history of globalization. This is why the novel requires a reading sensitive both to its critique of globalization *and* the extent to which that critique relates to Roy's examination of the contemporary condition of postcoloniality.

Where Roy's treatment of globalization focuses on the "catastrophic" effects we saw Said highlight, and while its approach to Anglophilia tends to reinforce Loomba's skepticism about the so-called "liberating" effects of "hybridity or multiculturalism," other recent novels have taken a very different approach to the effects of globalization. Vikram Chandra's *Red Earth and Pouring Rain*, for example, even more explicitly than Roy's novel, places the British colonization of India in the context of a globalized history of conquests running from Alexander the Great through Indo-Aryan and Islamic invasions right through the British Raj, and it charts as well the impact of US culture on contemporary India. However, Chandra's aim is less to isolate the contemporary effects of globalization and label them "catastrophic" than to insist on the utter banality of cross-cultural conquest and the forms of hybridization it has facilitated. In the epic sweep of Indian history conjured up in his novel there is no "India" that can plausibly be said to pre-date the kind of multicultural "mish-mash" Loomba insists is a contemporary product of Western media. In Chandra's historical India "newcomers and the old ones collided and metamorphosed into a thing wholly new and unutterably old," creating a world of "great harmony" that "bursts into being as differentiation," a paradoxical world in which harmony "is visible only by becoming non-unity," where "diversity, every part of it, is sacred, because it is one" (111–2). This world is the complex historical product of Indo-Aryan invasions and migrations into the Indus valley and the development and codification of Hinduism and the caste system (1600–1000 BC), the evolution of tribes into city-states, the evolving division along color lines between Aryans and Dravidians (1000–450 BC), the conquest of parts of India by Alexander the Great (327 BC), the founding of the Maurya dynasty and the routing of the Greeks and rise of Rajput power in the north (320–184 BC), the arrival of Muslim armies from the north in 712, successive raids between 712–1525 by Turks, Afghans and Persians, culminating in the establishment of the Mughal Empire, and finally, the arrival in India of the British and the solidification of their domination with the collapse in 1857 of the so-called Sepoy Mutiny.[15]

Chandra's narrative moves back and forth between historical sections that focus on the rise to power of the British in India in the decades leading up to the Sepoy Mutiny and sections set in the early 1990s, in California, that focus on a young Indian student named Abhay and the impact globalization has had on his sense of cultural identity. This structure has the effect of linking Abhay's contemporary diasporic experiences with the history of British colonization and the effects *it* has on the identity of the book's other central character, Sanjay Parasher. Abhay and Sanjay share the role of narrator in *Red Earth and Pouring Rain*, and by the end of the novel their disparate experiences with colonization and the West become the vehicle for Chandra's exploration of how the long history of globalization perpetually conjures new hybrid identities.

This fact is sustained with particular force in the story of Sanjay. His mother becomes pregnant by eating a mysterious laddoo (a kind of doughnut) which has been produced, touched and otherwise handled by a mongrel group including Indian mystics and British soldiers of fortune. Although he eventually helps lead the forces which mutiny against the British in 1857, Sanjay's mystical paternity keeps him fascinated with the English, and in particular with their language and poetry. By the end of the novel, Sanjay has come to accept Englishness as part of his mixed identity, one that is grounded in the long history of hybridity Chandra is at pains to chronicle in the novel. This acceptance is at odds with the plight of other characters he is close to, particularly his friend Chotta, who asks Sanjay:

> Do you know who we are? ... [T]here is a new species on this earth. It is not this or that, it belongs not here or there, it is nothing. In the beginning, when we were born, Sanjay, we were just what we were, the sons of our mothers and fathers, but now we are something else. ... [A] new animal: chi-chi, half-and-half, black and white. Do you know what this means, black-and-white? ... We are this new thing that nobody wants, Sanjay. (455–6)

Chotta struggles under an old principle of order linked to clear and distinct divisions, what Chandra characterizes earlier in the novel as the "most fundamental of definitive statements" about the world: "I and you, us and them, what I am and what I am not, white and black" (111). Indeed, this principle of fixed and immutable divisions is the one that begins to be displaced by the idea that "there is a unity ... of this and not this, and this great harmony, this oneness, this Brahman, bursts into being as differentiation ... visible only by becoming non-unity" (112). This might be simply dismissed as Chandra's send-up of mystical double-speak if not for the fact that the whole force of his novel is focused on Sanjay's difficult acceptance of his hybrid identity. By the end of the novel, in London, Sanjay explains to a British detective that he is not the British subject named "Jones" he had earlier passed himself off as, but Sanjay Parasher:

> "Not Jones?"
> "My name is Parasher."
> "You're not English?"

"I am. But I am Indian."
"How can you be English if you're an Indian?"
"It is precisely because I'm an Indian that I'm English." (505)

Sanjay's insistence on being English *and* Indian suggests how far we are from the Anglophilia that plagued Chacko and his family in *The God of Small Things*. Indeed, the love laws Roy's characters suffer from are flouted in *Red Earth and Pouring Rain*. Sanjay's best friend, Sikander, who is like a brother to him, is the child of a Scottish father and Indian mother, and sexual relations between Indians and Anglos in the book are nearly routine. As youngsters, Chotta and Sanjay follow a friend's father to a house of prostitution. When the children are found out by the woman the father has had sex with, she tells them that

> They all come here, Brahmins and Rajputs and Company men. Here, touch-this-and-don't-touch-that and untouchability and your caste and my people and I-can't-eat-your-food is all forgotten; this is the place that the saints sang about, little men. Here, anybody can touch anybody else, nothing happens. (210)

This scene puts the world of division between castes and untouchables, and between Indian and British, in a context in which miscegenation and the production of hybrid subjectivities and cultural practices is the norm. Beneath the violent surface of caste, ethnic, religious and cultural difference evoked by the novel is a world of transgression and syncretism that preoccupies virtually all of the characters in Chandra's book, Indian and Anglo. Hybridity in the novel is not so much celebrated as simply taken as a given. The position of cultural difference and purity, most often ascribed in the novel to the British, is openly mocked by Chandra.[16]

Like Roy, Chandra draws a clear connection between the history of colonization and decolonization, the postcolonial condition, and contemporary forms of globalization. He does this through his treatment of Abhay, whose life is permeated by the pull of Western culture through his experiences with film, advertising, literature, and most importantly of all, an old Sears catalogue:

> You know when I got obsessed with America? ... From somewhere or other there showed up in our house a nineteen-sixty-seven Sears catalog ... [I] started to go through it page by page. I started with the men's wear, with all the blond, blue-eyed guys wearing checkered shirts tapering to

their bodies. Then the men's underwear, then the women's dresses, then the women's underwear, then the whole family groups, the mothers and daughters wearing the same dress and same bell-shaped hair, then the garden tools ... amazing and unbelievable, drivable grass cutters ... But best of all, at the back, saved for last, whole working and usable and immaculate swimming pools! Swimming pools you could order though the mail ... so that your pretty daughters, your crewcutted sons, your bloody stunning wife could paddle and float gently under the best sun in this best of all worlds. I mean it felt as if the top of my seven-year-old head had come off, that I had seen heaven, no not that exactly, but that this, this in front of me was what life must be. (361–2)

Chandra conjures up in this passage both the flow of commodities and the bland, homogeneous Western "lifestyle" most often associated with globalization. But where for Baby Kochamma in *The God of Small Things* the flood of Western products through her television has an anaesthetizing effect, for Abhay the effect is electrifying. Confronting the abundance of American commodities and the eerie symmetry of its families is for Abhay the beginning of journey taking him away from the grip of British colonialism into a complex and challenging encounter with the forces of globalization. Sanjay's nineteenth-century fascination with Englishness has its late twentieth-century correlation in Abhay's fascination with America, and the shift neatly marks the transition from India's experience with colonization to its experience with globalization. When Abhay later becomes a film student at Pomona College it sets the stage for his own coming to terms with an identity profoundly marked by Westernization and globalization.

Both Roy's novel and Chandra's, then, draw links between colonization, the postcolonial condition, and globalization. In *The God of Small Things* it seems only the slightest shift to move from Chacko's Anglophilia, a legacy of colonialism, to Baby Kochamma's being anesthetized by global Western television, a fate that links her to other victims of the global economy in the novel such as the Kathakali dancers. Likewise, in *Red Earth and Pouring Rain* Chandra plots his complicated novel to draw an important line running from Sanjay's fascination with the colonial British to Abhay's fascination with the cultural products of a global economy. Chandra's tendency to treat transcultural contact in a way that make its complex processes part of the normal scheme of historical development, his stress on Sanjay's acceptance of his bicultural identity, and his focus on Abhay's attempt to absorb Western culture in a way he can begin to reconcile with his own Indian identity all mark a contrast with Roy's blanket criticism of globalization. Where Roy tends to underscore the negative effects of globalization and hybridity Said and Loomba focus on, Chandra historicizes globalization and is interested, like Appadurai, in the transformative possibilities of the global imaginary.

Both novels dramatize the difficulty of drawing clear distinctions between the literatures of globalization and postcolonialism. Together they suggest that we cannot discuss postcolonial literature in isolation from the phenomenon of globalization, and conversely, that it is impossible to study globalization without dealing with the complex history of colonialism and postcolonialism. From this point of view, globalization studies is not so much a threat to postcolonial studies as it is an addition to it, a historical perspective on transnational relations that ought to expand the purview of postcolonial studies. As we have seen in my brief discussions of Roy and Chandra, the discourses of postcolonialism and globalization can be employed together in forging a contemporary approach to the study of transnational literatures and cultures that attends both to the negative effects of globalization and hybridization Said, Loomba and Roy call attention to *and* the more positive and potentially liberating ones Appadurai and Chandra highlight.

As the grip of Eurocentrism continues to give way in literary studies and we develop approaches to the study of literature in a transnational context we ought, as Said warns, to avoid a curriculum reflecting a fragmented range of "particularistic" or "identity-based" choices under the umbrella of "a globalized, postmodern consciousness from which ... the gravity of history has been excised." However, I have been arguing that we ought to connect transnational literary studies to the phenomenon of globalization precisely because it *does* focus on the gravity of history. If we analyze historically forms of personal and cultural hybridity as they have developed under the auspices of economic, military, religious and cultural globalization, we can avoid recycling the banal academic version of multiculturalism Said and Loomba rightly point out would be unrecognizable in the real world of ethnic conflicts. In order to accomplish this kind of analysis, we ought to fold our contemporary interest in globalization and hybridity into a deeper historical understanding of how forms of globalization have structured our personal, social, cultural and political identities for centuries.

5

Latin, Latino, American:
Split States and Global Imaginaries

Román de la Campa

Ours may be an age of disbelief, but America's hold on the universal imaginary seems to have withstood the test of time. As a distant moment of discovery, a hemispheric marker, or the naming of a powerful modern nation, America's claims to unique transcendental dimensions continue to seem natural — if not necessary — to peoples, nations, and academic traditions. These outlines are only disturbed when the concept is asked to suit a plurality that rests beyond these ritualized references, when America's fate as a field of differences comes into full view, for then there is hardly any consensus as to what it might or could mean. To think simultaneously of Guatemala, Argentina, Haiti and the United States as part of the same territory, for example, immediately brings an arresting challenge to bear on the idea of America, almost to a point of silence, even among those otherwise engaged in studying it. At that dramatic moment it becomes crucial to remember that the invention of America has always been an arbitrary exercise in location, a site not far from the lines of utopia and nostalgia.[1]

Attempts to configure or define American landscapes have varied considerably through the centuries. Colonial powers, republican schemes, and individual pursuits have all left their mark. Yet, despite their number and disparity, they all seem to share a proclivity for cartographical errors and mythological tales — New World, El Dorado, The Mayflower, and Caliban perhaps being the most dramatic. Systematic efforts to validate essential differences among the Americas occurred throughout the eighteenth and nineteenth centuries, but they only managed to demarcate a game of inflexible oppositions that still animates fables of identity and republican fictions. Civilization/barbarism, Anglo/Latin, North/South, capitalism/one-man-rule — thus went the familiar cartography that followed these civilizing impulses. Further migratory and cultural shifts across the Americas in the past few decades appear to have yielded new iterations of the same tendency: coordinates such as postmodernity/subalternity, civil society/chaos, global order/ungovernable cultures. Deeply established academic disciplines, among them US American and Latin American studies, owe their constitution to such divisions.[2] It remains an open question whether new metaphors and unexpected narratives can still claim these territories, or whether new constructs and unexpected subjects will aid in the blurring of these imaginary lines.[3]

American myths are abundant and prone to constant revision. The history of the North/South divide undoubtedly provides a key set of examples. One would be that of a continental mission inspired by providence — a myth that has long sustained national identity in the United States. To this America, thoroughly steeped in other narratives pertaining to language, race and work ethic, correspond various Latin American retorts that have mainly survived in the realm of cultural and artistic imagination, though they still sometimes imbue political rhetoric. Simón Bolivar's ambition to unite the South as one republic in the nineteenth century immediately comes to mind, even though it ultimately encountered insurmountable obstacles. *Ariel*, an essay published in 1900 by José Enrique Rodó, called for a less utilitarian, more aesthetically balanced rendition of the North American model, thereby striking a chord among Latin American intellectuals whose sense of regional identity no longer came primarily from Bolivarian unification projects, or from opposition to the lingering Spanish colonial rule in the Caribbean, but rather from the modernist verve of a cultural critique aimed at the United States, particularly after the Spanish-American War of 1898. A few years earlier, José Martí, a great modernist as well, had taken amore direct route to his lifelong critique of the United States. His essay "Our America" sought to contest the cultural and linguistic destiny of America as a signifier. It could be said that his utopia contained much more poetic symbolism than political specificity, and that his high-brow modern aesthetic obstructed a much needed emphasis on modernization programs, but it introduced nonetheless a radically new American compass in which indigenous and African-American cultures claimed a seat alongside those of European ancestry.

Such blueprints have sustained the Latin American imaginary for nearly a century, particularly through philosophical and literary debates that take for granted the North/South divide. Cultural modernity and modern state formation lay at the heart of these contentions, with the United States serving as marker for the finished product and Latin America as the failed or unfinished version, notwithstanding the internal diversity of both constructs. Much lies in the balance of how one approaches this complex cluster of issues and their implicit models. Within literature, these contradictory motifs have often assumed an organic whole, as evidenced in artful essays like Octavio Paz's *The Labyrinth Of Solitude* (1953), which sought to depict the history of the Mexican national character and its indigenous history as a tragic enigma behind which stood the failure of the state, a web of contradictory historical discourses without any possible resolution except as an artistic form which the Latin American modern aesthetic translated into a universal value.

The links between literariness and subjectivity took a more disjunctive turn with the fiction of Jorge Luis Borges around the mid-century mark, but the same constellation of motifs can still be traced through the magic realist constructs that fueled the area's novelistic boom at least until the 1970s, and perhaps beyond. This literary tradition, an object of veneration for most of the twentieth century, now claims the attention of deconstruction, often anxiously so, as if the latter's conditions of possibilities could only be found in the former's web of influence.[4] One should note in this regard that the poststructuralist cycle, much of it elaborated through research universities in the United States, has no doubt contributed various critiques of the modern aesthetic in Latin America and opened new lines of inquiry, among which feminism has made pivotal contributions.[5] But this paradigm must also sort out the perplexing effects of unexpected events on our understanding of the Americas as a whole, such as the end of the cold war, the termination of alternative paths to modernity inspired by revolutionary socialism, the end of ideology claims by global capital, and, perhaps most critical of all, the advent of techno-mediatic culture.[6] In the case of Latin Americanism, or for that matter US Americanism, one must also consider another unanticipated element of crucial importance: the expansion of the Latino population in the United States, its political and cultural dimensions, as well as its potential for critical thinking about the Americas.

Most critics concede that globalization and postmodern constructs impact different nations differently, but it seems fair to say that beyond that broad generality few critical paradigms take such complications to heart. Imagining the other's nation as one's own may be an inevitable byproduct of cultural analysis and area studies. Sifting through these events and their impact on theory has been a difficult and challenging task, as one can plainly see in Derrida's *Specters of Marx*, as well as the more recent *Empire* by Michael Hardt and Antonio Negri. The early lessons of literary deconstruction must also now contemplate questions posed by postcolonial, subaltern, and cultural studies that don't respond to neat modern/postmodern divides, nor to the old Anglo/Latin splits of the American imaginary.[7] Even if one takes a skeptical view of these new critical modes, it seems undeniable that they underscore the pressures brought to bear on academic disciplines by global capital and its migratory shifts.

LATINOS AND SPLIT STATES

The postmodern critiques of the Latin American state that generally issue from literary studies continue to harp on the most easily recognizable modern narratives, often reiterating old modeling tendencies and neglecting the impact of global pressures that foreshadow a new cartography of the Americas.[8] These include new state formations and perhaps even different ways of reading literary texts. After all, the example of Derrida's suggestive re-reading of Shakespeare, as well as Negri's and Hardt's poignant re-articulation of Renaissance thought, could not fail to yield new vistas for other aesthetic traditions, including those of Latin America. In any event, the Latin American state now proffers a radical re-territorialization process driven by widely different impulses, such as narcoguerrillas, maquiladoras, indigenous subalternity, sexual industries and postsocialism. The concept of split states also comes into play as a meaningful new category, given that more than half the Latin American nations now have in the United States permanent diasporas, whose dollar remittances constitute a leading item in their former nation's economies. A split state implies a permanently severed entity, a loss in many respects; but perhaps it could also suggest a postnational symptom that has many possibilities and applies to more than just states whose paths to modernity came under stress or failed to materialize altogether.

In that context it seems particularly important to situate US Latinos within the historical blueprints of American imaginaries, given that their unsuspected gaze upon America often cuts through the customary North/South divide. It is equally important to ponder what their suddenly acknowledged presence throughout the Americas portends for the future of these territories, Anglo, Latin, and otherwise. The bare facts on Latinos generally involve their growing numbers and political value, although one could argue that the cultural and economic ramifications are far more important. It is estimated that there are between 30 and 40 million Latinos in the United States, a deceiving statistic in many ways, since it masks many racial, economic, and cultural histories, and often conflates people born of Latin American and Caribbean ancestry with those of direct Spanish-European background. Their presence now engenders a $30 billion a year economy from consumer products advertised in Spanish in the United States, although not all of this population speaks Spanish, nor are all of the products advertised in Spanish purchased by them. The representation of Latinos in both the democratic and republican parties is also increasing, and in return both parties are paying close attention to the Latino vote, often through linguistic symbolism. The 2000 presidential campaign revealed an interest in speaking Spanish on the part of the candidates of both parties, Al Gore and George W. Bush. For the first time in current US history, weekly national press conferences are being broadcast in a language other than English.

The term "Latino" often generates unending and unsatisfying debates. Some prefer to employ the "Hispanic" designator, perhaps to invoke greater proximity to Spanish language and culture. Reasons abound for the use of one term or the other, or both, but the details of that discussion could lead us far from what concerns me here: the ontological plurality that comes from deriving an identity from more than one American imaginary, an aspect that has specific importance for all Latino groups, regardless of national, racial, or ethnic origin. This plurality can lead to different types of negotiation with language, culture, and even national bearings. It is not, therefore, a simple reference to a bilingual or bicultural condition, nor a call for a new twist in the melting-pot process of assimilation formerly bound to the history of European immigrants in the United States. It is rather a recognition of an unusual and persistent duality, nurtured by the constant flow of capital — human, symbolic, and financial — between the Americas. In that sense the Latino presence unsettles the civilizational models discussed earlier, be they of northern or southern provenance.

The implicit opacity of the Latino category may well constitute one of its most salient features, but, then again, one must begin by recognizing that a bit of equivocation is already present in its morphological relation with the term "Latin America," given that the latter carries within it a history of multiple referents, imaginaries, and imprecisions. Beyond its French connotations, "Latin America" conveys an American otherness that was always relational. It aimed to distinguish itself first from colonial Spain, then from US expansionism, and at times from both simultaneously. As suggested earlier, the "Latin" in Latin America has often performed as a signifier in search for differences between cartographic errors, foundational narratives and geopolitical pressures. Since these circumstances pertain not only to the Spanish American realm, but also to Brazil, and by implication, to the multilingual Caribbean, an even larger ambiguity comes into play that has often turned Latin America into a metaphor for America's other, a motif very much present in the area's literature and revolutionary movements.

The presence of Latinos or Hispanics in the United States has a long history dating to the eighteenth century, but it is barely studied in Latin America, at least until recently, when many governments suddenly awakened to their split-state predicament. In the United States that history is usually divided according to East and West Coast demographic patterns. Even today many academic disciplines continue to acknowledge Latinos only to the degree that their most visible communities demand it. It is customary, for example, to cite the Cuban and Puerto Rican presence in the East Coast since the end of the nineteenth century, a moment that features the Spanish-American War and its aftermath, which left Puerto Rico under the direct control of the United States and Cuba occupied for a number of years. Ever since that moment, perhaps a foundational false start, the East Coast has come to know, and expect, many other migratory moments from the Hispanic Caribbean. The West Coast story has been much more difficult to assemble and tell. It involves the history of territories occupied by nearly all the Western and Southwestern United States, which Mexico ultimately had to relinquish in 1848, as well as the intricate history of migrations between these two nations since that time. Even less is generally said of the indigenous cultures displaced from their territories and fundamentally ignored by both the Mexican and US national configurations.

By the middle of the twentieth century, waves of manual laborers from various Latin American countries, most from Mexico and the Hispanic Caribbean, began to migrate to major cities in the United States. No one suspected then that such a trail of anonymous masses would ultimately betray a political and economic interdependency amongst the nations involved, nor that global pressures would later intensify these flows into a full-fledged diaspora across the hemisphere. These early, or historical, Latinos appeared in literature in the form of the Nuyorican (Puerto Rican New Yorker) and the Chicano (Mexican-American). But it was mainly through cinema and theater (*West Side Story* in 1961 and *ZootSuit* in 1978) that they first gained national attention. Both portrayals, however, were bound by the pre-existing stereotypes of these groups as problem or delinquent youths in New York and Los Angeles. Perhaps because of the important time lag between them, *West Side Story*, a highly applauded Broadway fantasy, only managed to enhance that negative casting, while Luis Leal's *Zoot Suit* attempted to critique it. However, the latter's success on the West Coast never materialized in New York.

As one would expect, such deeply ingrained Latino stories found other representations. Flashy antecedents to Chicano youth called *Pachucos* radiated a distinctive style that early observers like Octavio Paz could never quite forget. As the renowned Mexican writer tells it in *The Labyrinth of Solitude*, upon meeting a group of them in the streets of Los Angeles in the early 1940s, he suddenly felt as if his own sense of national identity had been blinded by their presence (57). Far, also, from the simplistic gang representation in *West Side Story*, or from recent Broadway renditions such as Paul Simon's *Capeman*, is the complex narrative of the Nuyorican subject, which one could read in the early poetry of Miguel Algarín, founder of the Nuyorican Poet's Café in New York City. His narrative poems invite us to a world of characters, caught between New York and Puerto Rico, who nonetheless breathe a futuristic ontology, an unexpectedly refreshing sense of belonging nowhere, except in the verbal agility and poetic movement we have come to expect from border artists.[9]

Nuyoricans and Chicanos of the 1950s were not yet Hispanics or Latinos, but rather forgotten or disdained populations by both sides of their cultural duality, embodiments of a doubly negative sense of being: neither Puerto Ricans or Mexicans, nor Americans. Nationless multitudes, they fled to farming fields or to the industrial steel belt, just as the black population of the southern US did before them, in time forging enclaves known for their cultural vibrancy in Harlem, Detroit, Chicago, and Los Angeles.[10] As for Latin America, it had not yet discovered this side of its mirror image. Leading artists and intellectuals, like Octavio Paz, only had a disturbing intuition of its presence in the United States. The renowned literary prizes of the Cuban institution Casa de las Américas, for example, did not include Chicano literature amongst its categories until the 1980s, and always kept Nuyorican literature as a subgenre of the Puerto Rican corpus. In time, it would have to resolve how to regard the literary production of Cuban-Americans.

Cuba joins this phase of the Latino mapping after 1959, albeit in a somewhat oblique sense. Earlier examples of Cuban migration have their own significance: the tobacco industry attracted Cuban workers to the US South at the end of the nineteenth century, and the music business drew them to New York during the first half of the twentieth. Baseball also contributed a constant trickle, but 1959 marks the moment of no return as far as the history of Cuban masses coming to the United States for good. That early wave of Cubans was starkly different from those coming from Puerto Rico and Mexico; it constituted a wealthy class which left its country *en masse*, fleeing Castro's socialist rule. Their exodus turned into a political card in the cold war and, as such, was favored with economic and political benefits that no other migratory group has ever received in the United States. The economic success of professional Cubans, many of them children of Spaniards, ultimately transformed Miami's destiny. For various decades it was held together by an exile identity caught in the nostalgic promise of a triumphant return to the island.[11]

It could be argued, however, that Cuban-American identity assumes a bit of plurality in the 1980s and 1990s, about the same time the Cuban revolutionary regime discovers a void in its socialist imaginary. Massive waves of Cuban boaters and rafters from different racial and economic backgrounds arrived in Miami during those decades. Miami's Cuban other seemed to surface from these unexpected events, while the revolution's hold on the popular imaginary, which had cultivated a national path to modernity with the aid of socialist ideals, lost a good deal of its promise amongst the masses. The two Cubas were coming together in ways neither side had been able to foresee. Equally important, a new generation of Cuban-Americans born or raised in the United States came of age, many of whom had never known Cuba first hand. Outwardly, adherence to the old guard's ideological hold remained, but, inwardly, a shift could be seen in literary and artistic manifestations among younger Cubans.[12] Their sense of belonging to a plural American constellation began to respond to cultural rather than strictly political negotiations. Moreover, the dramatic surge in the population of Latinos and Latin Americans in Miami and various parts of Florida during the late 1990s introduced a more international flavor to the Cuban enclave.

If the arrival of Cubans reshaped Miami's history from the 1960s to the 1980s, the most recent chapters of that city's history are reshaping the Cuban imaginary, not only in the exile community, but in the split island nation as well. Hundreds of thousands of Latin Americans have taken up residence in

South Florida, many of them from Central American nations caught in twenty years of guerilla and counterguerilla wars. Latino internal migration followed in response to various stimuli: new economic possibilities in Central and South Florida, particularly after Disneyworld, Miami's advent as Latin American international metropolis, and the growing anti-Latino sentiment in other parts of the country. Large numbers of Brazilians, Colombians, Venezuelans and Argentinians have also arrived for various political and economic reasons. Needless to say, this is but one example of unprecedented population shifts with parallel histories in Los Angeles, Denver, New York and Chicago. Together they have contributed to the transformation of urban US America. Perhaps more importantly, this flow of human capital spells a postnational condition of broader ramifications.[13]

Opaque though it remains, the Latino-Latina category nonetheless yields many as yet undigested chapters in the history of the Americas that refuse to fit into national schemas or disciplinary paradigms. Moreover, its expanding hemispheric scope calls for new categories of analysis capable of gauging the uncertain terrain of new transnational migratory waves, new urban configurations, and the imaginaries of plural ontologies. Yet, this work must proceed without forgetting the importance, as well as the limits, of specific minority groups that were once the exclusive narrative of Latino history. Latino and Latin American studies may now require a closer look at each other's shifting boundaries, but historically the two have had quite separate histories. Academic traditions in the United States, always reluctantly implicit in the study of Latinos as a racialized minority, now awaken to the full spectrum of the Americas within its own soil.[14]

POST-MELTING POT AMERICA

The melting pot concept, perhaps the key narrative of US Americanism, propounds that the paths to the national family remain always open provided one abides by various implicit tenets, among them an English-only definition of the nation. The question of race, always present but never quite articulated, often gets submerged or confused with ethnicity, at least as it applies to various populations of European origin. Groups once considered races — Irish, Jews, and Italians, for example — in time became one of many ethnicities within the American family. The same cannot be said, however, for African Americans, American Indians, and to a considerable degree Asians and

Latinos, even after the latter master English. Race doesn't slip into ethnicity as easily in these cases. But it is the black/white divide that has always set the internal boundaries of the melting pot concept. More importantly, it has done so by applying a strict line of demarcation that turns anyone with one drop of black African blood into a non-white, and hence black, person.

To the extent that Latinos comprise a population of multiple races, cultures, and languages, their future in the American imaginary remains uncertain. It seems important to note, however, that their multiracial profile includes the three ancestries that have been historically excluded from the melting pot equation: African, Amerindian and Asian. This observation does not aim to suggest a celebration of putative "mestizo" identity formations in Latin America, which contain their own contradictions and forms of racism, nor any other form of exclusion or inclusion solely resting on race. My interest lies rather in the cultural complication of racial types, since black, white, and Asian Latinos don't necessarily define their cultural identity primarily according to racial or even ethnic characteristics. In that sense, to cast Latino demographic growth in competitive terms with African Americans, or any other group, seems counterproductive and misleading. One might instead consider that amongst Latinos racial markers seem secondary to cultural affinities, and, as such, they might contribute to a critique of a deeply rooted binary of essentialized whiteness and blackness.

The languages of critical theory, in the humanities as well as the social sciences, often stumble when attempting to account for this post-melting-pot period of American history.[15] New ethnic enclaves in the United States (Asian, West Indian, as well as Hispanic or Latino) respond to migratory pressures that have rendered meaningless many of the legal, psychological and literary categories that define one's sense of belonging to a nation. Today's Latino, for example, must speak more Spanish than ten or fifteen years ago. Newly arriving Latin Americans, on the other hand, find a US Latino culture that precedes them, largely articulated in English. Communities and neighborhoods can change from Latino to Latin American in a matter of decades, often blurring the lines between the two. Latin and Anglo-American literatures, another example, can no longer ignore the wealth of an in-between culture for which English may have become a linguistic home, but whose cultural references and tonalities require interpreters skilled in Spanish language and Latin American cultures. This sort of border crossing — perhaps most prevalent in music — causes considerable grief among "disciplinary nationalists," be they Latin or Anglo American or, for that matter, Latino.

The nexus between language, race and Americanism finds a dramatic register in Richard Rodriguez's memoirs on growing up on the West Coast as a Mexican American. His books are filled with ecstasy about learning English and becoming American, as well as contradictory feelings about Spanish and his Mexican father. This is particularly true of his first memoir *Hunger of Memory* (1982), in which he assigns Spanish to the secondary, forgettable, role of a private language, filled with sorrowful memories of a Spanish Catholicism that contrasts so much with the cheerful, futuristic, protestant American culture he so admires. His sense of rebirth through English and Americanism allowed him to leave behind a world of Spanish he identified with a static paternal influence. But Rodriguez was too bound to his childhood traumas in that book to foresee the growing importance of Spanish language and culture that would take place in the United States during the 1980s and 1990s. Moreover, he remained dismissive of the cross-back insight that came with subsequent times — the thought that he can return to Spanish without losing his English, in short, that he can perform in more than one language, or one nation, for that matter.

Rodriguez's second book of memoirs charts a somewhat different route on the interrelationship between language, literature and national identity. Although *Days of Obligation* (1992) is still somewhat possessed by the author's need to censure ethnic politics, he lets it be known, playfully, that he hardly seems to know anything about Mexico, or Latin America and its literature, or other topics he is now being asked, and paid, to write about by credit card companies, lucrative magazines, news shows, and other enterprises that are active agents in the constantly changing nature of the American character. His second memoir can thus be read as a rather coy critique of his first. It remains to be seen if *Days of Obligation* finds as many fervent readers in high school and college English departments as *Hunger of Memory*, but it certainly charts new paths for Rodriguez, as some of his irony is now turned toward himself. It is particularly amusing to see how his brush with the land of his father spelled new contradictions for him.

Although Rodriguez remains a Victorian reader at heart, his writing is inching closer to experimental narration, particularly as he flirts with Latin American and postcolonial literary topics that sell well. The result is a highly ironic and wickedly equivocal attempt to write about contemporary Latin America and Latino-California themes with a nineteenth-century American sensibility that is itself inspired by fine British literature. One cannot help but notice that a crossover aesthetic has found its way to Richard Rodriguez, and he in turn seems to have discovered a new America in which he can be a Latino writer after all. I am inclined to believe that the literary vigor of his second book seduced the ethnic fears of his first. The same could be said of *Brown*, his third and most recent collection of autobiographical essays.

The growing Latin American awareness of the Latino construct also deserves attention, even if the constant migration across American border zones makes it hard to demarcate where Latino USA begins and Latin America ends, or vice versa. Latin America now watches Spanish language television packaged in the United States with Latino perspectives and sensibilities, even if these broadcasts often portray a white, upper class image of Latinos hardly commensurate with the majority of those living in the United States, or with the audience intended for those shows. This is particularly evident in news telecasts such as *Primer Impacto*, or even the more lighthearted programs such as *Cristina* and *Sábado Gigante*. Conversely, the influx of Latin Americans into the United States impacts the Latino condition by calling for closer contact with Latin American nations and greater levels of Spanish competence. The crossover effect in music also affects other forms of artistic representation and identity formations. Moreover, it doesn't just move in the direction of English; it also requires the capacity to cross back into Spanish markets, symbols, and signs, as evident in the careers of Christina Aguilera, Jennifer Lopez, Ricky Martin, and many others. This is the insight that Richard Rodriguez lacked in *Hunger of Memory*, but one which is perhaps quite prevalent in both *Days of Obligation* as well as *Brown*.

The lines of demarcation between Latino USA and Latin America have also blurred beyond border zones. It is quite possible to find a wider representation of Latin Americans alongside Latinos in the streets of New York, Miami, Chicago, or Los Angeles than in many Latin American capitals. Then again, one isn't altogether sure when a resident Latin American in the United States becomes a Latino, or when a Latino re-energizes his or her Latin American provenance. Both return to their nations of origin at some point, as visitors, or in periods of oscillation. There they discover that they have changed and that they are perceived differently. Slang, attitudes, and perhaps even a bit of the local accent may require renewal. But this "loss," natural for anyone away from his other homeland, isn't simply the result of absence, or from having gained some American English; it is also a result of intense interaction with other Latin Americans and Latinos in the United States. For Latinos to feel "other" as they become Americanized seems logical, but to also discover a sense of plurality within the Spanish and Latin American cultures found in the United States presents a unique phenomenon, most prevalent in border cities, but also quite evident in major capitals.

How does one approach these new ways of imagining the Americas within, as well as between, nations? The idea of a permanent Latin American/ Latino diaspora with more than one language, one culture, and one national identity once seemed to correspond only to Puerto Rico, a nation officially divided at the moment of birth in 1898. Of course, Mexican history has always contained a vast unofficial diaspora dating back a half century earlier, a story that remained repressed by both sides of its border until very recently. Today, the number of nations with analogous histories has multiplied considerably. It includes Cuba, the Dominican Republic, Colombia, Ecuador, and several Central American countries. The list grows if one thinks of nations whose leading classes feel psychologically closer to Miami, New York and Los Angeles than to their own capitals. Internal pressures have also created intense forms of dispersal in Latin America. New and highly intense indigenous demands for a multinational redefinition of the state abound, as do treaties for free trade that attempt to fashion new regional alliances, and neoliberal economies that force massive evacuation from the countryside. These breaks are, in every sense of the word, beyond the reach of the nostalgia of the old nationalisms, or of the literary critique of the modern aesthetic.

AESTHETICS AND NEW CITIZENRY

Any new conceptualization of the Americas will likely entail a more detailed look at culture industries whose main product today revolves around the manufacture of desire through television production and computer technologies. This impulse has succeeded in fusing the culture of marketing with the realm of performativity, creating a new epistemic niche in direct competition with universities and other institutions for the best creative talents. As such, this constitutes a deeply contradictory element, since it bridges the culture of globalization and academic production precisely at the time that schools are becoming secondary agents of education — indeed, at a moment in which mass media service industries have managed to bring the acquisition of practical knowledge and training closer to the interests of corporations. It all points to an intricate nexus that links citizenship with consumption, thereby comprising new forms of distributing and packaging the symbolic capital necessary to enter middle class status.

It remains unclear, however, whether critical discourses can respond to this challenge. Cultural studies and deconstruction have yet to do so convincingly. To say that identity critique, multi-temporality, and multiculturalism have been made tangible in nearly all parts of the world only confirms the commonplace, celebratory side of postmodernism and cultural studies. Indeterminacy, in this case a global condition, requires a conceptual proximity to entanglements such as split-states, modern de-articulation, permanent diasporas, postnational imaginaries, and the intensive realm of consumer subjectivity.[16] Most of the Americas belong to this space: societies caught in discursive gaps between neo-liberal capitalism and post-socialism. The focus on Latinos, one of various key groups, provides an important index of this problematic where least expected, within the US itself.

The aesthetics of imaging — television, videos, advertisements, the internet, performative arts, and other media constructions of consumer citizenship — clearly exact a totally new relationship with academic intellectuals. The space once known as "the street" now breaks into the fold with a new force and legitimacy, no longer just an intruder that overturns the high-low cultural divide. The place of the researcher, or intermediary, becomes irremediably more public and ultimately more anxious, because capitalism itself demands it. This perhaps explains Harold Bloom's vehement attempt to revive the specific hierarchy of values implicit in literary studies: "There is nothing so essential to the Western Canon as its principles of selectivity, which are elitist only to the extent that they are founded upon severely artistic criteria. [...] One breaks into the canon only by aesthetic strength, which is constituted primarily of an amalgam: mastery of figurative language, originality, cognitive power, knowledge, exuberance of diction" (22, 29). There are many reasons to celebrate great literature and to wonder, along with Bloom, whether contemporary culture has prematurely abandoned aesthetic qualities that might prove indispensable for the postmodern age. However, today's students and consumers don't necessarily lack expressive exuberance and metaphoric idioms, some of which could qualify as "severely artistic." One immediately thinks of the visual excess in various forms of imaging, the oral exuberance of rap music, or the performativity invoked by the bodily movement of salsa music. Some will dismiss this contemporary "anthology," others will claim it has no relevance, but few will deny its existence altogether. As for wisdom and cognitive power, it seems pertinent to recall that great art has always been suspicious of such categories, for knowledge always invokes a discourse of truth and power immediately claimed by philosophy, history, and, most of all, ideology.

How, then, does one bridge the growing gaps between academic disciplines, their object of study, and new phenomena? Some might allege that it can't be done, given that objects of knowledge are necessarily by-products of disciplinary thinking, and that the latter have been dissolved by the twin forces of deconstruction and global reordering. Others prefer to look upon universities as places of resistance from which to reclaim disciplinary order. A third position might insist on a new approach in which critical theory explores a new role within, not outside, the growing nexus of cultural markets and the arts. Bloom, it would seem, wants to regain the value of great Western literature as reservoir of exemplary articulations of human experiences and to market his anthology to a reading public anxious about the demise of printed culture. But his proposal goes beyond that, since it includes non-European authors, including some Latin American greats difficult to categorize strictly in terms of West or non-West. His object of study thus shifts somewhat to the uncertain global scene, albeit in English only. Literary values would therefore be saved as translatable matter through the lingua franca of globalization, even if it means risking their most precious claim to artistry: uniqueness as texts in their own language, the site where "exuberance of diction" truly reveals itself. Equally important, they would be saved only to the extent that they conform to a singularly defined hermeneutic tradition that claims to speak in the name of humanity.

The work of Richard Rorty, perhaps the most prominent figure in current neo-pragmatic philosophy, provides another important instance of the confrontation between postmodern theories, the old lettered order, and the globalizing cultural dispersion. He understands, first, that Derridian deconstruction and Foucauldian meta-narrative critique should be seen as the continuation rather than the rupture of the Western hermeneutic tradition. He adds that these theoretical paradigms only make sense within the realm of literature, philosophy, and the fine arts. The trouble for the humanities, he argues, only arises when these modes of critique are deployed in popular culture or politics, because these fields tend to take their liberatory impulse too seriously, as if one could engender new utopias from deconstruction, or preserve the social radicalism of modern meta-narratives through their critique.

Rorty insists that postmodernity has a natural milieu beyond which it should not reach, and that it ought not to impose itself on others; rather, it should strive to consolidate communities which he calls "Postmodern Bourgeois Democracies of the North Atlantic," such as the United States, parts of Europe, and Canada (197–202). Only these nations correspond to the postmodern model in as much as they have managed to bring citizenship to the highest level known to history, an unsurpassed realm of individuation, satisfactions, opinions, lifestyles, and self-management. The citizens of these communities, like their philosophers, would thus live postmodernity as an internal dialogue that need not strive to attain universality because their national cultures have already reached what anyone could possibly imagine as universal. From this perspective, postmodern critiques need only attend to immanent movements within US American and European traditions, or conceive themselves as reflective explorations amongst postmodern democracies.

Rorty's reading may seem highly *sui generis*, but his call for a nationalist enclosure of postmodern philosophy should surprise no one. It registers an already familiar list of concerns that lay at the very heart of academic knowledge production: the active role of deconstruction in the dispersal of humanistic disciplines, the looming importance of marketing in academic endeavors, and the growing heterogeneity within the nation, more conflictive by the minute. One can see here, as well as in Bloom's construct, a poignant index of the uncertain future of national mythologies. Both register a breach that they hope to correct with an expanded Western aesthetic or a North American postmodern republic, but their disciplinary purview remains quite distant from the discursive exigencies of new subjects, be they women, ethnic minorities, gays, or not-so-new subjects such as laborers, now forgotten by both global capitalism and state socialism. Both also seem equally averse to exploring the nexus of marketing and imaging that now shapes, albeit contradictorily, the private ambitions of all subjects in all republics, including those with the most resources.

These pressures continue to startle academic structures, at times leading to surprising but revealing proposals that must somehow redraw the boundaries of the universal within national frameworks, be they linguistic, philosophical, or literary. Western, North-Atlantic, or universal, each imaginary must now field unprecedented tensions, not only migration waves that disturb the national identity like never before, but, what is more important, the techno-mediatic performance industry, which has proven capable of designing a rich anthology of multicultural products on its own. Another important contributor to the turbulent conceptual space after 1989 has been the decline of official socialism and Third Worldism, a topic outside the purview of Bloom and Rorty, yet one that is intimately related to their field of concerns. The implicit utopia of Western postmodernity may have been challenged by the cultural order of global economies, but it is equally important to note that the teleological project inspired by Third World modern narratives has lost even more prestige, as evident in Latin America and other areas once demarcated as such. This has led either to deep disenchantment or muted resistance amongst artists and intellectuals who continue to have a stake in imagining the world, even if, or precisely because, they live and work in states with compromised modernities.

Constructs such as Latinos must continuously unfold from such gaps and crevices in the current production of knowledge, sometimes explicitly, sometimes implicitly. It is not, however, just a question of Latinos, but rather of Americans, or more specifically, of the Americas, a hemisphere whose North-South relations have dramatically changed without warning or compass. The task seems to call forth a simultaneous examination of a multiplicity of elements — nation, genre, ontology, imaging, marketing, language, race — most likely within the purview of many disciplines, but clearly beyond the exhaustive reach of any one of them, even those with highly developed ways of absorbing difference immanently.[17] New insights will obviously be needed for differential approaches to cultures and nations with divergent or discomforting modernities. But perhaps the most one can say about this mapping of unsuspected encounters across nations, languages, and cultures in the Americas is that it can only proceed with a full awareness that the task will likely uncover mirrors bound to reflect the researcher's own unguarded gaze.

6
Doing Cultural Studies Inside APEC: Literature, Cultural Identity, and Global/ Local Dynamics in the American Pacific

Rob Wilson

This chapter offers a critical genealogy of US imperial dynamics in the Pacific by examining the discursive tactics of the Asia Pacific Economic Cooperation (APEC) and the emerging hegemony of transnational capital in the region. It tracks the dynamics of globalization and movements towards localization under which "Asia-Pacific" is being constructed into a postcolonial, if not postnational, identity as a coherent region of teleological belonging. The chapter invokes literary and cultural producers in order to force upon "Asia/ Pacific" a critical awareness of its own regional unevenness, alternative possibility, spatial contestation, and desublimated otherness. "Asia/Pacific" can thus become a critical signifier for a cultural and literary studies (inside APEC, as it were) in which opposition, location, indigeneity, and an alternative discursive framing of the region can be articulated.

Gathering a range of energies and possibilities under its neo-hybrid banner, "Asia Pacific" is used these days in all kinds of enchanting ways. We can speak of "Asia-Pacific cuisine" — it's a hit at gourmet restaurants of creolized invention like Roy's in Hawai'i Kai, Omei in Santa Cruz, and Indigo in Chinatown of Honolulu, and it shows up on menus at the Lai Lai Sheraton in Taipei and the Hyatt Regency in Seoul. There is likewise a mushrooming array of new *Asia-Pacific* art magazines, architectural symposia, fashion and interior design spreads, and literary journals that cash in on the mysterious allure of this sign. This popular usage bespeaks a postmodern utopia of post-orientalist consumption: the multiplex styles of "Asia" and "the Pacific" promise to meet and fuse in an expressive synergy called *Asia-Pacific*, and little harm will be done except to purists of cultural borders, nation-mongers, or diehard pre-modernists who refuse to dream in the late-capitalist future over the world's biggest ocean.

More than stylistic promise or commercial slogan, "Asia-Pacific" also serves as a political-economic signifier to bespeak and mediate the border-crossing expansionism — if not will to transnational community — emerging in this "borderless" region. This trope of Asia yoked to Pacific is used to mobilize the cash-driven transfusion and to drive the megatrends of *transnationalizing* economies in the region, which, without such a user-friendly geopolitical signifier, does not yet exist in anything like a coherent geopolitical or cultural framework. In such a discursive framework, our everyday spaces and lives inside the creativity and chaos of the Pacific are being shaped, coded, and reorganized under this "Asia-Pacific" banner. This cheery vision of regional coherence and geopolitical unity demands critical and global/local interrogation. What I want to do in this US-situated analysis is to expose the hegemonic vision of the Asia Pacific Economic Cooperation by looking at discrepancies of identity, uneven locality, and struggle in the region (in inside/outside places like Hawai'i and Taiwan). At the same time, I want to explore the possibility (for transnational literary and cultural studies) of developing a more globally and locally situated Asian Pacific Cultural Studies bent upon dealing with these very tensions and uneven dynamics of "contested localized knowledges" spreading across Asia/Pacific.[1]

Formed in Australia in 1989 and still adding economies and members in the new millennium, APEC serves as the most powerful shape this desire for regional coherence, shared teleology, and hegemonic unity (as tied to some implicit narrative of a post-communist co-prosperity sphere) now takes in the Asia-Pacific region.[2] As early as the 1960s, Japanese economists, speaking in international forums at the East-West Center in Hawai'i and other such sites in Australia, had formulated big visions of "economic and cultural cooperation." Not to be outflanked, Australian and American policy planners in the region cultivated these broad cultural and market links to Asia, pushing towards and shaping what came to be called "the Pacific Rim." Such postwar geopolitical alliances, from 1965 to 1990, helped forge APEC into existence as what a political economist of Korean and United States geopolitics, Bruce Cumings, warily calls a "capitalist archipelago" (25).

Now that United States policies regarding the region seem to be disoriented and decentered and the East-West Center is threatened with federal extinction an "Asia-Pacific Center for Security Studies" has opened, with substantial multinational funding, in Honolulu — to invoke one local example of institutional and conceptual instability in the region. In attempting to articulate some kind of post-cold war rationale for the East-West Center in order to defend it from Republican budget cuts, Hawai'i's Democratic Senator Daniel Akaka declared that this postwar center of cross-cultural knowledge production was "one of the most respected and authoritative institutions dedicated to promoting international cooperation throughout Asia and the Pacific." We should note the shift to an unstable, micropolitical vocabulary here: this new disjunctive signifier of "Asia" and the "Pacific" threatens to unhinge more residually imperialist "East-West" binary visions of governance and cold war teleology in the region. At the same time, in a document called *Joint Vision 2020*, Pentagon policy planners (reorienting the focus from West to East) have endorsed a shift of US military might from Europe to Asia, which (in the words of a *Honolulu Advertiser* editorial endorsing this geopolitical refiguring of global power) recognizes that "the center of gravity of American strategic interests has moved to the Asia-Pacific region" (A8).

The era of East-West orientalist binaries resulting from formal colonialism may be over, but the problems of North/South imbalances and economic injustice multiply on the international front: to invoke the specter of Karl Marx commenting on the emerging formations of market globalization in a London interview of 1871, "Let us sum it all up in a word. The working classes [note his use of the plural term "classes"] remain poor amid the increase of wealth, wretched among the increase of luxury" (Silvester 59).[3] Linking North America and Mexico to the export-driven dragons of East Asia, Tokyo, and the Pacific ex-settler states of Australia and New Zealand, APEC has been formed to ease trade barriers and to liberalize markets in the region in a consensus-like, patchy, culture-conscious, quasi-systematic way called "Open Regionalism." At this point of transnational emergence, although the dollar, yen, chabols, and nuclear weapons refuse casual governance, APEC gathers diverse "economies" for regional forums and policy prodding: Australia, Brunei, Canada, Chile, mainland China, Hong Kong, Indonesia, Japan, Malaysia, Mexico, New Zealand, Papua New Guinea, the Philippines, Singapore, South Korea, Taiwan, Thailand, the United States and others.[4]

If we wondered what "Asia Pacific" means and what cultural-political ingredients are (for now) to be included in its provenance, this is *one* way of defining the will to regional/cultural/postnational unity. The non-threatening term used to describe these diverse APEC players — so many loose "economies" linked around and within the Pacific Ocean — suggests a de facto way of overriding international problems and bypassing internal political tensions in such a market-driven forum. Imagined into consensus-like shape by some user-friendly trope of transoceanic Pacific "community" from Asia and the Pacific, APEC would fuse disparate units small and large, from city-states, superpowers, and Third-World entities, into a vision of regional coherence, teleological optimism, and regional "cooperation." This trope of "Asia-Pacific" is premised upon some uneven commitment to the mandates of free-market capitalism, a rather inchoate sense of shared Asia-Pacific cultural heritage, and the allure of a "Pacific Century" destiny. Civilizational strategy, looming crisis, and pragmatic necessity are making strange trans-Pacific bedfellows. As US Trade Representative Richard Fisher told the House Committee on International relations, when the 21-member Asia-Pacific Economic Cooperation gathered for its "post-crisis" forum in New Zealand in 1999, "APEC's role in helping shape the policies and attitudes that respond to the [global financial] crisis through reform, rather than a renewed turn toward nationalism and protection, will be crucial" (*Korea Herald* 1).

Under the post-orientalist umbrella of "Asia-Pacific," the complex "Chinese" polities of Taiwan, Hong Kong, Singapore, and mainland China can talk. The White Rim meets, as it were, its imperial-era others in the symbolic space of equivalency and "economic cooperation." Big and small are gathered to assume some symbolic equivalence around the bargaining table, diverse "Rim" players smiling in colorful Asian-Pacific shirts at the same Kodak photo sessions. This kind of Pacific regionality assumes some post-political cultural bonds, or at least a flow of underlying geographical and cultural linkages that will allow networking, linking, and downloading across the diverse polities and civilizational powers of Asia-Pacific.

As this trope of APEC community would have it, colonial history, world wars, and cold war trauma may now be washed away in the magical waters of this New Pacific. The American banker accused of murder in the Stephen King-based movie *Shawshank Redemption* (1994) dreams of just such a post-political Pacific. He longs to escape from the Maine prison where he is serving a life sentence to a little blue hotel by the Pacific, where he can forget the brutal humiliations, capitalist crimes, and hellish degradation of the body he has been through: "*This ocean*, as the Mexicans say, *it has no memory.*" Trauma and war riddle modern history, but the Pacific Ocean still elicits dreams of a more cooperative and communal future: "Everything flows toward the Pacific, no time for anything to sink, all is swept along" (Duras, *The Lover* 22).

To invoke the transnational-driven optimism of political economist Kenichi Ohmae as he theorizes the makings of a trilateral but "borderless" regional order, "Nation-states are eroding as economic actors, [and] region-states [like Taiwan, Guang-dong and Singapore] are taking shape" (125), region states which now recognize that their primary linkages are with the global economy. To survive, Ohmae says, these entities of borderless transnational interface must "put global logic first" in order to retool their industry and reshape their conceptual and social geography to fit the contours of this new transnational regionality. In Ohmae's trilateral (Japan/USA/Europe) arrangement of the "borderless economy" emerging to meet the mandates of globalized production, it is the "regionstate," not the nation-state, that becomes the primary agent of political-economic change. Regionalism as such mediates between the global drive towards transnationalization and the waning power of nation-states to control such crossborder flows.[5]

APEC, at least in today's vision of the Pacific as "metageographical" region, is the most broadly circulated framework for this large-scale restructuring move towards securing more open borders and regional inter-linkage.[6] *Globalize or die* is one crude way to put the transnational mandate for making local polities and doing cultural studies in the region. As Ackbar Abbas, a cultural critic of capitalist cultural deformations and globalization of the local in Hong Kong, has remarked, "We have cultural studies because we do not know what or where culture is" anymore inside such regions and sites.[7]

While sophisticated in the ways of global capitalism, APEC's vision of the "Asia-Pacific" is culturally and politically naive, ignoring, bypassing or just plain suppressing the cultural complexities and historical issues within the region in order to form this new identity. This kind of uncritical regionalism can be as dangerous as nationalist interpolation, even if it is taking place at a higher (and more sublimated) level, for the absent others against which APEC is forging its identity (such as the economies and cultures of Southeast Asia and the Pacific Islands) are silenced and bypassed, if not oppressed. The assumption of some Asia-Pacific regional unity is, after all, the invention and construct of the more prosperous globalizing powers who stand to benefit most by the borderless circulation of peoples, goods, and symbols within its *economistic* framework. As Masao Miyoshi has pointed out in his jeremiad-like critique of transnationalization as a new multicultural form of colonizing the local, the discourse of APEC expresses the vision of the transnational culture/class who "now have and will continue to have disproportionate income and freedom with which to master the new global spatiality" (70). Globalization of the local into some higher-level regional configuration has become the seeming mandate of the transnational cultural critic/class tracking in supple ways the uneven transcultural cash and sign flows, as the news reeks of identity politics, racial violence, ethnic strife, religious antagonism, gender suppression, not to mention structural imbalances of labor and profit along the "global assembly line" from New Jersey and South Korea to Manila and Saipan.

As a multicultural global fate, the "Asia-Pacific" imagined in more trenchantly localized senses by authors as diverse as Melville and Epeli Hau'ofa, Maxine Hong Kingston and Patricia Grace, Haunani-Kay Trask and Li Ang, John Dominis Holt and Vilsoni Hereniko, Kenzaburo Oe and Lois-Ann Yamanaka remains a riddle and a maze, a rim and a charm, a struggle and a curse, both dream and slime, an ocean with ancient contents and cyborg-like futures all cast into one strange global/local poetic. Although it may seem offensive or just plain irrelevant to bring together so many diverse metaphors and cultural constructions under the same frame, "Asia-Pacific," later in this chapter I sketch a provisional rationale for doing so in a more critical way than an APEC-like regionalism now allows. For this *post-national* or transnational commitment of APEC's vision of "Asia-Pacific" unity and global/local fusion reveals the future, I think, in which cultural and literary studies will take place in and across the Pacific. As a result, we must come to terms with this reconfigured cultural situation in which nations and localities are coming unglued at both local and global levels.

I bring up these vulgar *extra-literary* matters of globalization and location haunting APEC's "imagined community" of transnational unity and regional forms because one of my contentions is that if there is to be an Asia-Pacific Cultural Studies worthy of its peoples, symbolic heritages, and cultures, then one of the tasks for such a poetics is to challenge and critique these economistic master formations and discourses of the Pacific region. Cultural criticism needs to frame and locate such stories and master-tropes within history, pushing to unmask such global visions/representations of "the Asia Pacific" as a coherent, unified, user-friendly, anti-socialist, and evenly enriched region where the culture of global capitalism will come home to roost. Correspondingly, wherever it is to be located or housed — on the borders of traditional disciplines (like English) or larger area studies formations (like Asian Studies) — an "Asian-Pacific Cultural Studies" needs to nurture, support, and teach the literatures and narratives of those less powerful and subordinated in the region, whose complex claims upon the *Pacific* (many of whose contemporary works are written not in indigenous languages but in World English) and *Asia* (which was not and will never be a *single* "Orient") have too long been tokenized or ignored in the interests of settler peoples and *their* nation-states.

While contemporary cultural studies provides genealogies and critiques of dominant cultural forms and social frameworks of locality and national identity, propped up as they often are by national literary canons and the spread of academic discourses like that of "postcoloniality," it can also dialectically juxtapose these competing traditions and put them in critical dialogue in the present rather than keeping them held apart and quietist, confined to the past — Pacific Studies over there, English Department over here, Asian Studies back over there with Taoism and the Book of Tea. The invention of a critical "Asia-Pacific"-based poetics demands border-crossing, conceptual outreach, nomadic linkages, and interdisciplinary originality; its birth at this moment is mired in cultural politics and the global political economy. More needs to be done to intervene creatively as well in contexts and genres — media events, international forums, daily journalism and so on — that dominate the airwaves with APEC-like stories and Pacific Rising images. We need to begin articulating a "critical regionalism" in the Asia-Pacific region, one respectful of Asian and Pacific heritages, diasporas, and communities, but wary of hegemonic designs articulated upon these diverse localities and social groupings. The meaning of "Asia-Pacific" has to be struggled for and defined in specific cultural locations and institutional settings, for *internal* definitions of the "Asia-Pacific" will mean different things to different peoples, rival nations, racial and gender groupings, and hegemonic class agents. Global dreams of the Pacific region must be situated and *localized* to bring out their full contradictory social meaning, bringing them down to earth and cultural politics, placing such master-narratives of the local and small in their social communities, nearer to what Maxine Hong Kingston calls "those little stories of Chinese culture you learn from your mother," or what Kenzaburo Oe termed, "the myth of my own village."

In the Polynesian, Micronesia, and Melanesian islands alone, some 1200 languages, Albert Wendt is fond of saying, riddle and criss-cross the region into myriad unique communities and symbol systems. Cultural purity is no longer possible. Incommensurability reigns between cultures, between little stories and big. The English language itself has been in the Pacific for over two hundred years — not to mention the structuring narratives and moral binaries of light and dark from the *King James Bible* — and serves as the primary language for the Pacific literary emergence that is now taking place via writers like Wendt, Patricia Grace, Russell Soaba, Keri Hulme, Richard Hamasaki (alias "Red Flea" of nuclear protest) and Haunani-Kay Trask. "Wansalwara," a Papuan New Guinea pidgin term for "those who share the same salt water," is one Pacific writer's way of fusing by-water such various cultural groups and micropolitical islands across what Epeli Hau'ofa has called "Our Sea of Islands." The "postcolonial" Pacific, so-called within the dominant academic discourse, remains a contradiction-ridden maze.

These Pacific islands of rooted peoples and outreaching diasporas provide, after all, the land and language-ground for the indigenous peoples whose stories and symbols structured the Pacific before Euro-American disruptions and the mandates of economic modernity took over. Epeli Hau'ofa, a satirist of postcolonial elites and Pacific dependency patterns in *Tales of the Tikongs* and *Kisses in the Nederends*, has begun to reclaim indigenous modes of imagining Pacific space and Pacific time in his polemical essay (inspired by oceans and volcanoes as well as the indigenous people of the Hawaiian islands) "Our Sea of Islands," which counters economistic and demeaning social-science portraits of the Pacific islands as small, dry, and resource-poor places without hope.

In "Our Sea of Islands," Epeli Hau'ofa evokes a proud and civilizational vision of "Oceania" as a sublime Native Pacific space filled with navigational linkages, diasporic flows, native technologies and arts, and a rich oral heritage of legends, chants, myths, and stories of communal and self-empowerment. Undaunted by the flow of "deadly serious discourses" on "the nature of the Pacific Century [and] the Asia/Pacific co-prosperity sphere," Hau'ofa invokes the counter-ecology of this other indigenous Pacific and challenges neo-colonial dependency patterns with this *big* vision, *Oceania*:

> Oceania is vast, Oceania is expanding, Oceania is hospitable and generous, Oceania is humanity rising from the depths of brine and regions of fire deeper still. Oceania is us. We are the sea, we are the ocean, we must wake up to this ancient truth and together use it to overturn all hegemonic views that aim ultimately to confine us again, physically and psychologically, in the tiny spaces which we have resisted accepting as our sole appointed place, and from which we have recently liberated ourselves. We must not allow anyone to belittle us again, and take away our freedom. (98)

Any "Asia-Pacific" regional vision worthy of credibility needs to come to terms with this *aboriginal* "Pacific" complexity and history: it cannot do so by simply ignoring or repressing these peoples and their histories — by telling the same story of late capitalist weather spreading evenly across the huge region.

Unfortunately, there is as yet *no* "Asian-Pacific Cultural Studies" to deal with these transformations of place and purpose in any adequate or critical way. As we enter this era of amplified globalization and the spread of capitalist culture as popular norm, a new kind of "cosmopolitan" knowledge is called for, tracing unevenness, conscious of global/local discrepancies and movements, and theorizing interrelationships in the "single space economy" of global capital. As Fredric Jameson has pointed out (building on the "national-popular" thrust of Gramscian critical theory as situated intervention), the developing field of "Cultural Studies," in its British and American adaptations from Birmingham to Urbana, remains too narrowly tied to a NATO-based vision of global geopolitics, an American version of internationalization, and all too oblivious of issues and emergences in the Asia-Pacific (47). Still, this outburst of post-Birmingham Cultural Studies, as it globally proliferates and trenchantly localizes in differing national and regional contexts, has begun to answer the call for cultural situation and critical vision of the contemporary with positioned wariness, flexible languages, and decentered codes. We have seen the proliferation of "schizoid" global/local dialectics and non-binary explanations to map the uneven, fragmentary, and nomadic flux of capitalist culture across borders.

Still, it goes without saying that "Asia-Pacific Cultural Studies" does *not* yet have the density of purpose and grounded situation of vision, nor the institutional commitment and funding, that it already has in political-economic spheres. The struggle for definition, critical mass, and direction is important; as Arif Dirlik has written of the contemporary Asia-Pacific, "Definitions of the Pacific are part of the very struggle over the Pacific that they seek to describe" (3).[8] Metaphors matter and can materialize into compelling social forms and transformed pedagogies: an Asia-Pacific Cultural Studies, complexly located and richly linked, can help change the shape of canons and alter the historical imagination given the strange new power of the "Pacific Rising."

We are entering a brave new world, as Stuart Hall has noted, of "ascending and declining nationalisms" (25). The disoriented Western European nation-state described in Hall's mapping of transnational and diasporic flows is being undone simultaneously "above" and "below" its cherished structures of modernity by transnational relations and local ("ethnic") identities making contradictory claims upon time, place, and community ("The Local and the Global" 27).[9]

Cultural studies, in such emerging situations of globalization, needs to develop tools of relational "allegory" that can preserve "the differences of each historically situated and embedded experience, all the while drawing a [global/local/national] relation between those experiences" (Ross 672).

The United States, as I will discuss via an examination of Hawai'i as site of Asia/Pacific contradictions, has become a fungible, porous, and unstable entity of global/local deformation during these decades of heightened globalization at the capitalist core. In places driven by "Asian-Pacific" dynamics, like Taiwan and Hawai'i, regional forms are reconfiguring into counter-national and subnational longings *at the same time*, refiguring the national imaginary into something more transnational and indigenous/local in theme, as I have claimed. The local knowledge needed to get by these days requires a complex, expanding and fluid sense of globalization as a contemporary fate in the localities of the Asia-Pacific region.

In the 1980s my own sense of "globalization" as an everyday fate was amplified and had much to do with how I understood the claims of "the local," meaning a discourse of localization that was posited against the century-long hegemony of mainland US culture and its impact upon Hawai'i — something that intensified and thickened the Asian-Pacific commitment to place, community, history, location, and the languages and cultures under threat from forces of modern homogenization. This *Bamboo Ridge* discourse of "the local" was linked, at least in my own mind, with the claims for place-bound localism being enunciated in the late 1970s in the UK — by Kenneth Frampton as a counter-modernist postmodernism, or by Raymond Williams as a communal and class-based "bond to place" under threat from new (weirdly offshore, off ground, hard to locate and contest) structures of transnationalization. The emerging claim of Hawaiian nationalism gathering weight and socio-political efficacy in the 1980s was another and stronger form of this *counter-national localism*, something sub-national and anti-transnational seeking to find its own form, its own structures of space, time, feeling, and political realization as sovereign "nation within a nation."

Seizing the narrative apparatus, as it were, is part of any culture's struggle to emerge, exchange, and legitimate its deepest concerns: this is particularly clear in Hawai'i, where Hawaiian was banned as a language of public instruction from 1898, when the nation was annexed into a US territorial possession, until 1986,when Hawaiian served not only in language immersion programs but also as the basis of a large-scale cultural revival of symbols, stories, cultural imagining in the arts and, at the strongest extreme, the push towards recovered political sovereignty in Hawai'i. The invention and normalization of an "American Pacific" was based, to a large extent, on the hegemonic everyday spread of Anglo-American culture in English, and English departments spreading "the literature of the Pacific" as something written primarily by James Michener, Jack London, and the white gaze of exoticizing representation.

The linguistic imperialism of English, domineering and at times eradicating the use of Hawaiian, went hand in hand with the political and economic takeover of Hawai'i: it is no accident that Haunani-Kay Trask, the fiery Hawaiian activist, subtitles her new collection of essays, *From a Native Daughter*, with the stark binary opposition, *Colonialism and Sovereignty in Hawai'i*. Hawai'i is not "postcolonial" to Trask, not just hybrid and global/local: it is simply *colonized* by the US military, commercial and state apparatus. This push towards decolonization is echoed by indigenous Pacific critics in Australia and New Zealand, who argue that the Maori and Aborigines have likewise been colonized into minorities by the settler peoples. As a timely special issue of *Cultural Studies* (1995) on Australian land and language perspectives acknowledges, these "First People" voices need to be heard, circulated, and debated in Asia-Pacific Cultural Studies. Such claims also deserve to be heard and adjudicated, I would argue, not just in courts and state-political forums, but in cultural and literary contexts of Asia/Pacific pedagogy.[10]

Globally and locally, influenced by strong native and foreign currents, Hawai'i (like Taiwan, an island state tied to, yet separated from, a mainland national culture) is tangled and tormented, driven by complex and contradictory claims upon its political-cultural identity as a Pacific island with imposed New England mores colliding with waves of Asian migrant settlement as well. Bamboo Ridge Press, named after a fishing place on Oahu island where generations of Asian-Pacific peoples have fished, eaten, drunk, and sung with locals and Hawaiians, has been since its founding in 1978 a key forum and outlet, its place-based aesthetic supporting the poetry of Eric Chock and Louis-Ann Yamanaka, and the fiction of Darrell Lum, Gary Pak, Mari Hara, and Rodney Morales, just to name some of the more locally — and some, nationally — prominent authors published by the press. Key collections of Hawaiian cultural activism and land struggle, edited by Dana Naone Hall and Rodney Morales, have also been published by Bamboo Ridge Press as well. Bamboo Ridge itself is named after a local fishing ledge on East Oahu where the small statue of a Japanese fishing god watches over the treacherous waters of the deep-blue Pacific. Still called *Halona Point* by Native Hawaiians, Bamboo Ridge is situated between the Blow Hole fetishized by camera-touting tourists and the cove where the famous lovemaking scene in *From Here to Eternity* took place between Burt Lancaster and Deborah Kerr playing displaced *haole* locals at and around Pearl Harbor. The name of the press, founded by two local Chinese writers, Lum and Chock, recalls as well the poetic associations bamboo has in the Chinese literary imagination, evoking the carefree poets of the "Bamboo Grove" in the Jin Dynasty, although some disgruntled writers in Hawai'i see the press operating at times more like the so-called Taiwanese syndicate the "Bamboo Gang." Each local poet, as the myth has it, goes "fishing for his/her god off Bamboo Ridge." The press's journal, *Bamboo Ridge: The Hawai'i Writers' Quarterly*, which comes out sporadically, in group readings when the moon is new, has already published over 80 issues since its founding in 1978 and has virtually forged the making of a counter-canon of predominantly monochromatic, Asian-local ethnic literature in Hawai'i.

This tension-wrought "local literature" movement of Bamboo Ridge culture registers a full expression of this Asia/Pacific culture, especially the experience of Asian workers from China, Japan, Korea, and the Philippines who settled and worked the sugar plantations in the late nineteenth century and worked their way into social and political prominence during and after World War II, expressing the democratic (and Democratic Party) march to American statehood.[11] This Asian-Pacific-based localism emerged in the 1980s as a regional strategy of cultural survival and affirmation in an era of transnationalization and postnational unrest when the US nation-state was coming globally and locally unglued — as Stuart Hall has intuited of the UK — above and below the level of its own long-wrought cultural hegemony.

Albert Wendt said in his keynote address to the "Inside Out: Theorizing Pacific Literature" conference held in Honolulu, September 1994, "For me, the *post* in *postcolonial* does not just mean *after;* it also means *around, through, out of, alongside,* and *against*."[12] What would a postcolonial Asia/Pacific Cultural Studies look like? At the outset, Asia-Pacific Cultural Studies will look like a *threat* to the disciplinary arrangements, professional training and nation-based expertise, cultural capital and vision of vocational purpose in any good-sized and well-entrenched English department like the one in which I taught until recently: the University of Hawai'i at Mānoa, ironically situated right square in the troubled waters of the American Pacific. But it need not be so: the move towards defining and shaping an "Asian-Pacific" concentration in our masters degree program, as well as emphasizing such work in recent hires at the assistant professor and at the Citizen's Chair levels in fact enriched our program and gave it focus and direction as we concentrated on materials we were historically situated best to deal with.

The English Department of the University of Hawai'i at Mānoa, the flagship research campus for a complex array of universities and colleges serving the multilingual and complexly multi-ethnic state of Hawai'i, has offered an MA in English since 1937 and instituted a PhD program in 1987. This program, at both undergraduate and graduate levels, is still grounded in a period-and-genre coverage model of literary training and is heavily weighted toward studying British literature, with a more recent emphasis on American and contemporary literatures as a critical focus. Although the department has been teaching a course called "literature of the Pacific" since the late 1930s — the first and most enduring course of its kind in the United States — it still largely teaches what one disgruntled graduate student, chafing against the MA exam system, called "the canon, Beowulf to Virginia Woolf."

During the past twenty years, however, there has been expanding critical interest in teaching the local Asian-Pacific American literatures as well as a broader base in theorizing the literatures of the Pacific. In Spring 1994 some younger colleagues (Laura Lyons, Ruth Hsu, Paul Lyons, Susan Schultz, David Baker, and Beth Tobin) and I proposed the following Asian-Pacific graduate-level "concentration": "We propose the English Department create a *recognized concentration* that would enable and encourage research in Asian-American/ Pacific-Asian local/postcolonial literatures. As the hyphens and slash marks indicate, these emergent literatures do not fit under a single rubric. In the complexity of their origins and influences, these literatures share characteristics with both non-Western and Western literatures of various periods, from medieval to modern. This historical interplay would be addressed . . . the concentration would explore local/global relations that are now producing such hybrids within 'English' literature," and so on. The rationale for the concentration was based on a pedagogical commitment to exploring the complexities of "local" place and community and redefining cultural identity: "Developing a concentration around issues in Asian-American/Asian-Pacific/local/postcolonial literatures would not only make us more responsive to the community in which we are located," we said, "but might also allow the Department to acquire a special character that would potentially carry with it both more graduate students and national recognition."

Hearing this plan in a department meeting where issues involving race, class, gender, colonialism, and critical theory were also put on the agenda, one colleague began to wonder out loud afterwards: "You mean I can't teach Shakespeare anymore? Has all my training gone to waste?" Others began to worry that they would have to leave Hawai'i for good and relocate on the mainland where, presumably, they could teach an Anglo-American-centered canon to a like-minded audience/class of Anglo-American students. (This assumption of benign and delocated universality is getting harder to make on the continental US, too, as literature departments begin to respond to the ethnic, race, and class needs of local constituencies in communities such as New York City and Los Angeles.)

In its final version, ratified by the University of Hawai'i Mānoa English Department in May of 1996, the concentration is now called "Cultural Studies in the Asia/Pacific" and its organizing rationale reads in part:

> This concentration will focus upon the historical emergence and representations of the Asia/Pacific as a site of cultural struggle, discursive contestation, and literary creativity. By "Asia/Pacific," we intend to open up a discussion of the mixtures, contradictions, and overlapping of histories and trajectories that comprise the term "Asia/Pacific" as site of identity and location. An understanding of "location," in this fully historical and cultural sense, is important because one of the hallmarks of cultural studies is its concern with location and its commitment to scholarship which takes into account the cultural terrain in which the scholar is located. This concentration will contain courses that account for our distinctive history and location in the Asia/Pacific — that is to say, cultural studies that are situated simultaneously among the US and the Americas, the Pacific, and Asia. From this location in Hawai'i, students will be able to study literature and other forms of cultural production in relation to theories of minority discourse, postcolonialism and transnationalism, popular culture, and gender and queer studies as well as film and media studies.

This focus allows for a more fully genealogical understanding and critical excavation of this Asia/Pacific locality as well as a more historicized understanding of "orientalism" as a Euro-American heritage being dismantled.

It also creates an open site for theoretical speculation and cultural production of "Hawai'i," "the Hawaiian," and "the local" as national, anti-national, sub-national and international configurations. This seems as valuable as transmitting the national classics of the continental US and the United Kingdom. I can still vividly recall my days as an assistant professor of English when I was told that I could not teach undergraduates Milton Murayama's novel *All I Asking For Is My Body*, a richly creolized local novella about a Japanese family's struggle on a Maui plantation in the 1930s and the trauma of Pearl Harbor, because it "was not a recognized example of American literature." In fact, I was even told by a person in power that my research on Murayama and publications and poetry in *Bamboo Ridge* journal would do my career no good at all, since it would be considered a kind of "slumming with the natives."

The attitude was to some extent expressive of white colonialism, rephrased of course in the more delicate tones of its liberal-political unconsciousness and American imperialist disavowal: Harvard and California PhDs teaching high Euro-American culture in the Pacific who remained *in*, yet not *of*, the place and culture in which they taught and who, for the most part, maintained a cautious distance from, if not snobbery towards, the local and native languages and ways — at times practicing towards the cultural other in Hawai'i "a kind of sentimental imperialism that the United States is only too famous for" (Rafael 1215).[13] There were always strong-hearted exceptions, like Joseph Baucus and Basil Kirtley, and even the extensive scholarly work of A. Grove Day provides an important groundwork in the terms, canons, and authors he establishes to articulate a certain kind of "Pacific literature" written by and for visiting Euro-Americans and propping up the project of Euro-American modernity.

I could go on citing such locally grounded and globally attuned cultural labors — not just lamenting the past but forging a different, postcolonial future. I would like to talk about my own and other courses offered by Rodney Morales, Candace Fujikane, Vilsoni Hereniko, Paul Lyons, Caroline Sinavaiana, Dennis Kawaharada, and Richard Hamasaki in Pacific local literature in Hawai'i, which provide dialogical perspectives, or courses in "Pacific Rim Discourse" taught by Chris Connery at the University of California, Santa Cruz, which use films like *Black Rain* and *Yakuza* and books like *Megatrends* 2000. The helpful new series of Pacific literature called "Talanoa," initiated and edited by Vilsoni Hereniko at the University of Hawai'i Press, has kept works by Wendt, Grace, Alan Duff, Epeli Hau'ofa, and the poems of Hone Tuwhare in print and usable as paperbacks for college courses. The new series in Asia and the Pacific books started by Duke University Press under the editorship of Masao Miyoshi, Rey Chow and Harry Harootunian puts politics and culture together; another, edited by Bruce Koppel, focuses on issues of social and cultural change in the Asia-Pacific for Stanford University Press. There are the "Critical Workshop in Asia-Pacific" forums and scholarly research projects guided by Arif Dirlik at the Asia-Pacific Studies Center at Duke University and at the University of Oregon; and Masao Miyoshi's refiguring of International Relations and Pacific Studies at the University of California, San Diego, into a more critical and interdisciplinary research agenda where "area studies" of Japan or China are no longer allowed to segregate global political economy from issues of culture and social analysis. There is the work in film and "internationalizing of cultural studies" guided by Geoffrey White and Wimal Dissanayake at the Program in Cultural Studies at the East-West Center in Honolulu. The Program in Asian-Pacific Cultural Studies founded in 1992 at National Tsing Hua University in Taiwan links up with many of these other Asian-Pacific research projects and teaching innovations as well as intervenes locally in contemporary issues of national and local identity and struggle: "to situate ourselves in a present-day and everyday Taiwanese context" as the program says. Multi-sited, translational and transnational journals of the mongrelized Asia-Pacific region, like *positions*, *Inter-Asia Cultural Studies*, and *Cultural Studies Review*, are also reflecting and refracting the re-location and situated struggle of transnational cultural and literary studies in the APEC region.[14]

Although I have touched upon various issues, jumped across disciplinary borders and national frames, and made many rash assertions, I would like to remain critically *affirmative* of the kind of relevant, engaged and fresh work such interrelated research and teaching projects can do in forging a new vision of Asian-Pacific Cultural Studies that will be of some use, even in *English* departments in the region. When Bruce C. Galloway, the vice chairman of the Royal Bank of Canada, was in Taipei, Taiwan, scouting out this global city as a possible Asian-Pacific headquarters for his international bank, which had moved shop from Hong Kong to Tokyo and finally to Singapore in 1993, he assured people on the complicated island polity that "Taiwan had the potential to be an Asian-Pacific financial hub." "Everything is possible!" he affirmed. I would like to be that affirmative and hopeful about the possibility, not of promoting transnational banking, but of doing critical cultural studies inside APEC in these days of "late capitalist weather" in the Asia-Pacific region.

7

(The) Nation-State Matters:
Comparing Multiculturalism(s) in an Age of Globalization

Brook Thomas

Multiculturalism and globalization, two of the most frequently discussed topics at the beginning of the twenty-first century, seem to feed off of one another. Encouraging the flow of people across national boundaries, an increasingly globalized economy generates more and more culturally diverse countries at the same time that individual nations have discovered that a multicultural workforce helps them compete more effectively in that same economy. Despite this mutually reinforcing relation, most discussions of multiculturalism continue to focus on a single nation. Studies of multiculturalism, it seems, need to follow Pheng Cheah and Bruce Robbins' call "to think beyond the nation." Paradoxically, however, to abandon a single-nation approach to multiculturalism is to become aware of the reasons why it persists. Multiculturalism might be an increasingly worldwide phenomenon, but it manifests itself differently in different nations. Thus rather than lead to the posting or transcending of the nation, an approach to multiculturalism that moves its focus beyond one nation actually highlights the continued importance of the nation-state.

In fact, the very concept of multiculturalism as we know it is implicitly linked to the nation-state. People have long recognized that the world is culturally diverse. But they have not generally accepted that individual nation-states are. On the contrary, people believed — and many still believe — that for a nation-state to have a clear sense of identity it must have a unifying culture. Even the United States, which has long been recognized for its diversity, has been sustained by the myth of the melting pot in which newly arrived immigrants undergo a ritual process of Americanization that allows them to share the language, values, and culture of their new land, not the land from which they came. "Multiculturalism" has gained its worldwide currency because it implies not only that the world is a heterogeneous cultural mix — something that everyone already knew — but that the cultures of individual nation-states are too. One debate that crosses national boundaries is, therefore, whether or not multiculturalism can unify a nation.

The pressures that multiculturalism place on the traditional notion of a unified nation-state are immense. Those pressures help to account for many of the heated debates that multiculturalism has provoked. But because multiculturalism is manifested differently in different countries, it also places pressure on accounts of globalization coming from both left and right. On the left, for instance, there is Slavoj Zizek's "Multiculturalism, or the Cultural Logic of Multinational Capitalism," which bristles with interesting speculations but is almost devoid of empirical evidence. Zizek provocatively challenges people who continue to subscribe to the old Marxist model in which a universal logic of capitalism works through individual nation-states turning some into colonizers and others into the colonized. But unlike others who have made a similar challenge, Zizek does not argue that nation-states are in fact one possible site of resistance to the unrestrained flow of capital (Jusdanis). Instead, he claims that we have now reached "the final moment" of global capital's reign: "the paradox of colonization in which there are only colonies, no colonizing countries — the colonizing power is no longer a Nation-State but directly the global company."

A victim of compulsive-polemic disorder, Zizek exaggerates the demise of the nation-state and perpetuates a frequent mistake within Marxism of assuming that there is a universal logic of capitalism that manifests itself globally. Thus when he identifies multiculturalism as "the ideal form of ideology" of this new form of "global capitalism," the problem is not that he links multiculturalism to an increasingly global economy — there are definite links — it is instead that in ignoring the mediating form of the nation-state he cannot describe the complicated process by which multiculturalism challenges the inherited identities of various nation-states at the same time that some — not all — nation-states try to use it — in different ways — to respond to the global economy. As a result, he establishes a far too tidy relation between multiculturalism and global capitalism, one assuming both that multiculturalism is the same in all of its manifestations worldwide and that there is a global logic to capitalism that governs all of those situations.

Zizek may be critical of capitalism's effects, but his assumption that there is a global logic to it is shared by many of its defenders. For instance, celebrants of a global economy claim that an unrestrained worldwide flow of capital will produce a uniformly egalitarian world. That assumption has been challenged persuasively on the left by people like Zygmunt Bauman and on the right by Samuel Huntington who cites compelling evidence to show that economic and political systems manifest themselves differently in groups with different cultural histories. But if Huntington provides a helpful corrective from the right to celebratory narratives about globalization, he errs in assuming the existence of relatively fixed and homogeneous zones of culture. The boundaries between cultures are much more fluid than Huntington allows. Cultures are not set, but are in a process of being continually remade through a process of contact and interchange, contact that forces of globalization have accelerated, although by no means initiated. Indeed, Huntington's notion of a "clash" of civilization is a turn-of-the-century version of Cold War containment policy. The West, according to Huntington, needs to contain the threat of competing cultural systems just as once it had to contain Communism.

By assuming the incompatibility of different cultures and advocating a strategy of contained co-existence, Huntington avoids one of the most important questions facing multiculturalism in a world of globalization: how do people from various cultures interact and influence one another without repeating patterns of domination? Indeed, in Huntington's map of the world there is no space for multicultural nations since by definition a nation must fit into one of the preexisting cultural modes that he identifies. Similarly, Huntington's map of the world renders virtually invisible indigenous cultures located in his Western zone.

Diasporic studies, which trace the migration of people across national and cultural boundaries, is therefore an excellent corrective to Huntington's view. Nonetheless, people in diasporic studies themselves have a tendency to indulge in a different, if more subtle, form of cultural essentialism.[1] If Huntington assumes the persistence of a culture within geographic boundaries, diasporic studies is prone to posit the persistence of cultural identity in a group of people dispersed around the globe. But a diaspora is not united by an unchanging racial or cultural essence. Chinese immigrants in Australia, for instance, develop a different cultural formation from the one in the United States or in Canada because of the national cultures with which they interact. There can even be important differences within nations, such as between Japanese-American cultures in Hawaii and on the mainland.

Those differences should not, however, lead us to assume that the city should replace the nation as the most important unit of analysis for how different diasporas interact ("Cities and Citizenship"). As "cosmopolitan" as some cities have become, the nation to which they belong still matters. For instance, despite important similarities between the communities of Chinese descent in Vancouver and Seattle, their make-up is different because Canada's inclusion in the British Commonwealth means that a much higher percentage of recent Chinese immigrants in Vancouver come from Hong Kong rather than from Taiwan or mainland China. The altered status of Hong Kong may eventually influence that difference, but the altered status itself cannot be understood apart from Hong Kong's relation to different nations.

If neglect of the importance of the nation-state contributes to the tendency in diasporic studies to lapse into essentialism, it also affects one of the most concerted efforts to avoid essentialism: post-colonial studies' theorization of hybridity. Following the lead of Homi Bhabba, many in post-colonial studies celebrate hybridity as a mode of resistance to colonial domination. But the nature of post-colonial hybridity is not uniform. It varies from former colony to former colony, from new nation to new nation. As Chadwick Allen notes, hybridity as a mode of resistance "is untenable as a generalization across diverse histories of colonial encounters" (61).

What many of these examples illustrate is the unconscious tendency to map today's pairing of the global/local onto the traditional pairing of the universal/particular. Although a new generation of thinkers has been trained to be suspicious of an earlier generations' organicism that attempted to make the particular a synechdochal embodiment of the universal, too often the global simply replaces the universal as a perspective that those hoping to transcend the local and particular claim to achieve. But even though new technologies have helped scientists achieve a global perspective on the earth's physical environment, they have no more allowed us to achieve a truly global perspective on cultural, social, and political matters than they have allowed us to achieve a universal perspective on values. To be sure, just because no human is capable of achieving a universal perspective on values does not mean that appeals to universals cannot serve useful functions in concrete situations. As a way of keeping open the possibility of alternative arrangements to existing orders in the world, appeals to the universal — recognized as a counterfactual condition — remain powerful rhetorical weapons potentially — though not inevitably — serving the cause of justice, a concept that itself entails a sense of universality. Appeals to universality become most dangerous when they lose their counterfactual status and claim a particular embodiment within the world, such as when one nation claims synechdochally to embody universal values. The problem with substituting the global for the universal is that the global implies such a concrete embodiment, one that controls the operation of all of its local manifestations. A global perspective is as much a fiction as a universal perspective; yet, unlike appeals to a universal perspective, which become useful when acknowledging their counterfactual nature, appeals to a global perspective retain their force only by claiming to represent a concrete embodiment of the condition of the globe.

Recognizing the need to move beyond the perspective of a single nation while refusing to claim a global perspective, I will conduct my study of multiculturalism in a global economy comparatively. To keep my comparisons manageable I focus on four nations: the United States, Canada, Australia, and New Zealand. There are obvious reasons for choosing these four. Constituted in part by a British diaspora, all share a British legal and cultural heritage. All are countries of immigration and yet have within their borders indigenous populations who were deprived of their lands through a complicated process of colonialism. Similarly, bordering the Pacific, all have closer and closer ties to Asia. Finally, all are attempting to move beyond a history of officially sanctioned racism.

Choosing these four has another advantage. Half a century ago, Erich Auerbach recognized that "The more our earth grows closer together, the more must historicist synthesis balance the contraction by expanding its activity," and argued that "our philological home is the earth; it can no longer be the nation" (16–7). Nonetheless, he also acknowledged that the critic's *Ansatzpunct*, or point of departure, remains the language and culture into which he was born. My point of departure is the United States, the country into which I was born. More has been written about multiculturalism in the United States than in any other country. Yet, except for occasional references to Canada, those writings are almost devoid of comparative analysis.² That lack leads to some serious blindnesses. For instance, although multicultural advocates in this country stress the importance of difference, they almost always ignore the multiculturalisms of other countries, even those with shared historical links to Britain. The result is a provincialism that affects even some advocating a post-national or transnational turn to American Studies. For instance, Gregory S. Jay has written an essay advocating "The End of 'American' Literature: Toward a Multicultural Practice." But at the same time that he would put an end to "American" literature his multiculturalism is based exclusively on the American model. To bring discussions of multiculturalism in the United States into dialogue with discussion of the other three countries is to benefit from comparative work already done among these members of the British Commonwealth (Gunew, Pearson, Fleras).

A comparative approach also combats a blindness where we might least expect to find it. One of the most interesting developments in American Studies in the past generation has been the large-scale importation of "theory." Theory, especially continental theory, has helped to combat the tradition of exceptionalism that has haunted American Studies from its inauguration. But the importance of challenging the still persistent narrative granting the United States a unique moral role in the world should not cause us to neglect the equally important study of how the United States is different from other nations. When continental theory is applied to the study of the United States without taking into account differences between and among nations, the analysis is too often flawed. These flaws are especially telling in attempts to apply general theories of the state — often derived from France — to the United States. To compare multiculturalism in these four countries is to see that — despite the fact that all four owe a major debt to British political traditions — no one theory of the state can cover all four any more than can a universal theory of globalization.

To argue that no theory of the state can cover all situations is not to deny the importance of clarifying terms of analysis. On the contrary, such clarification makes comparisons more fruitful. What, for instance, is the difference between "nation," "state," and "nation-state?" Max Weber called a nation a common bond of sentiment between people whose adequate expression is usually a state of its own. Nonetheless, it is important to remember that not all nations have had their own states. Throughout the period of partitions, for instance, Poland had a sense of national identity even though it had no state. Similarly, a state can exist without a nation, such as might have been the case in the last days of the Communist regime in East Germany and was certainly the case with ancient and medieval city-states, in which a state ruled a city not a nation. A nation-state is, therefore, a nation with its own political institutions that claim to represent it.

These distinctions are important for the Canadian Will Kymlicka, who distinguishes between two types of multiculturalism in relation to the state: multinational states and polyethnic states.

One source of cultural diversity is the coexistence within a given state of more than one nation, where 'nation' means a historical community, more or less institutionally complete, occupying a given territory or homeland, sharing a distinct language and culture. A 'nation' in this sociological sense is closely related to the idea of a 'people' or 'culture' — indeed, these concepts are often defined in terms of each other. A country which contains more than one nation is, therefore, not a nation-state but a multination state, and the smaller cultures form 'national minorities' (11).

A polyethnic state is also made up of people with different cultural heritages, but it is not multinational. Polyethnic states usually result when a country accepts "large numbers of individuals and families from other cultures as immigrants, and allows them to maintain some of their ethnic particularity." A particular nation can be both a multination state and a polyethnic state as in the case of Canada.

Kymlicka's distinction is helpful, but it is worth noting potential problems that are signaled by an inconsistent use of hyphens. The hyphen in nation-state is crucial because it marks a relation between the nation and the state by which the state gains its legitimacy through claims to represent the nation. By leaving out the hyphen in "multination state" Kymlicka unconsciously calls attention to one of the major areas of contention raised by the existence of many nations in one. A multination state still has one state that claims to represent the multinational entity and to have sovereignty over it. To be sure, different nations can exist in a federation, with each having its own governmental structure. But even in a federation each nation is ultimately subordinate to a central, sovereign national state. Disputes often arise over the relation of different nations within the nation to the central state.

Those disputes are especially important if we are to understand the sovereignty movements of indigenous peoples and their implications for multiculturalism and the present configuration of nation-states. Thus, although the phrase would be somewhat awkward, it would be more accurate to use the term "multination nation-state" rather than "multination state." Similarly, a major question that multiculturalism raises within what Kymlicka calls "polyethnic states" is the relation various ethnic groups have to the nation as a whole and to the state. Thus, once again it would be more accurate to use the term "polyethnic nation-state" rather than simply "polyethnic state."

One advantage of drawing attention to these distinctions — even if awkwardness will prohibit consistent use of the phrases — is the reminder that a polyethnic nation-state can decide to relate to its polyethnic population by not recognizing cultural/ethnic/racial distinctions at all. To a certain extent this is true of the United States, which has no official state policy on multiculturalism. In contrast, all of the other three countries have explicit governmental recognition that their national cultures are not singular, although in New Zealand, as we will see, the emphasis is on biculturalism rather than multiculturalism. Canada, for instance, has been officially multicultural since 1971 and in 1988 passed the world's first Multicultural Act. The government includes a bureau for "Multiculturalism and Citizenship" which oversees multicultural policy. Australia, following Canada, has a Multicultural Agenda announced in 1989 and for a while at least had a Ministry of Multicultural Affairs. To be sure, there is an important difference between an act and an agenda. An act carries the force of law, whereas an agenda tends to be more of a signal of governmental support than legislated policy. Nonetheless, both an act and an agenda stem from the state.

As is to be expected, state-sponsored multiculturalism has been attacked by those on the right and left suspicious of state involvement of any kind. For instance, William Gairdner, linking Canada's policy of multiculturalism with the government's attempt to impose socialism on an unsuspecting nation, writes in a chapter entitled "The Silent Destruction of English Canada," "The purpose of ... one-world socialism was and remains the eventual achievement of a world-wide equality of social outcomes; a forced equalization of wealth, regardless of merit; and the neutralization of all value-preferences between different peoples and cultures. The goal of this policy is to replace all *natural* cultures with the idealistic, *artificial*, bureaucratic culture of the State itself" (Trouble 390). In contrast, Linda Carty and Dionne Brand, assuming that the state is inevitably in the service of capitalism, fault Canada's state-sponsored multiculturalism for co-opting grass-roots movements by women of color through the establishment of national organizations supposedly responsive to their needs. "Because the state in capitalist society, by virtue of its goals and interests, does not operate within the interests of the working class — to which most immigrant and visible minority women belong — the limitations of state-formed organizations with a mandate to do so must be recognized and questioned" (170).

If it is tempting to dismiss these responses as paranoid fears about state power, problems associated with state-sponsored multiculturalism cannot be ignored. Whereas those problems vary from nation-state to nation-state, some are similar. For instance, in both Canada and Australia the delivery of welfare services in part according to ethnic groups rather than to class has led to three related problems: (1) control of groups by making them dependent on the government; (2) creation of governmental bureaucracies whose own interests sometimes conflict with those of the groups supposedly served; and (3) reification of various groups (someone has to belong to a particular group to get services).

Of these problems the reification of groups is the one most often cited by critics of both official and unofficial versions of multiculturalism. In addition to seeming to rule out hybrid identities it tends to create groups, not simply describe them. For instance, in the United States a much cited precursor of multiculturalism is a vision of "cultural pluralism" articulated in the early years of the twentieth century by Horace M. Kallen. But whereas there are important similarities between Kallen's cultural pluralism and today's multiculturalism, there are also important differences that affect the groups that each identifies. Kallen's cultural pluralism responded to the massive immigration occurring in the country at the end of the nineteenth century and the beginning of the twentieth and fears that the new, primarily non-English-speaking immigrants, could not assimilate into the American melting pot. Opposing the assimilationist model, Kallen's questioned the need for a core Anglo-Saxon culture. Nonetheless, it is no accident that Kallen's most important book, *Culture and Democracy in the United States*, appeared in 1924, the same year that Congress dramatically curtailed immigration from southern and eastern Europe and halted Asian immigration. In turn, discussions of multiculturalism began shortly after changes in immigration policy in the 1960s. That new state policy helped to produce a multiculturalism that is noticeably different from Kallen's cultural pluralism, since under it only 18 percent of immigrants in the 1970s and only 10 percent in the 1980s came from Europe.

In large measure Kallen was concerned with the cultural difference of ethnic groups; multiculturalism, as articulated in the United States today, usually suggests racial difference. That suggestion is not accidental. Early advocates of multiculturalism in the United States hoped that by using "culture" instead of "race," they could help to combat racism by emphasizing cultural rather than biological difference. For instance, in 1991 the National Council for the Social Studies revised its 1976 "Position Statement: Curricular Guidelines for Multicultural Education." The revised edition, it notes, "focuses more on race than the original does. We rarely used the word race in the first edition, perhaps because of our vain hope that silence would facilitate racism's disappearance."[3] People like Walter Benn Michaels have argued that to substitute culture for race is to produce a cultural determinism to replace an older biological one. From a different perspective, Étienne Balibar has described the persistence of "racism without race." A look at the categories created by United States multiculturalism helps to explain why such criticism has force.

The five categories used to categorize people on many public and private documents are European-American, African-American, Asian-American/Pacific Islander, Hispanic/Latino, and Native-American. If this so-called "racial" pentagon of multiculturalism serves to register awareness that the country is comprised of people from around the globe, it also disguises the very diversity that it is supposed to reflect. Why, for instance, are people from India, Japan, Korea, China, the Philippines, and Polynesia lumped together? That grouping would make no sense at all in New Zealand where Maori distinguish themselves from other Pacific Islanders, not to speak of people from Asia. In fact, a part of the United States itself — Hawaii — is much closer to the situation in New Zealand than it is to the United States mainland.

Another problem with the pentagon is that, like Kallen's cultural pluralism, it seems to have no category for people with mixed backgrounds. In fact, its categories are already composite categories bringing together groups that in other contexts would be differentiated — the various tribes of North American Indians and the various people from many different Asian, African, Hispanic, and European backgrounds. Indeed, the category European-American brings together the very ethnic distinctions that made up Kallen's cultural pluralism.

The fact that this category comprises only one part of the pentagon worries some people that multiculturalism is intent on denying the importance of the country's European inheritance, while for others it disguises the fact that, despite changing demographics, those of European descent continue to occupy a privileged position of power. As recent work in the budding field of "whiteness studies" has shown, "white" is the only racial category that empowers rather than disables its members (Hill, Ignatiev, Lopez, Roediger). What unites both sides of this debate is the tendency to oppose multiculturalism to a somewhat mystified and undifferentiated "Eurocentrism." Neither side is prepared to deal with someone born in Europe of African descent who then immigrated to the United States. The label "Eurocentrism" both ignores historical differences within Europe and fails to keep up to date with changes within Europe today.

Although all most versions of multiculturalism are guilty of creating reified group categories, comparing its different versions highlights the socially and historically constructed nature of categories, like "European-American." For instance, the 1990 edition of the *World Almanac* lists the population of Australia as European 93%, Asian 5%, and aborigines (including mixed) 1.5%, that of Canada as British Isles origin 47%, French 27% and other European 23%, and that of New Zealand as European (mostly British) 87% and Polynesian (mostly Maori) 9%. By 1996 "European" under Australia had been replaced by "Caucasian" and "British Isles origin" under Canada by simply "British." As these statistics reveal, the tendency to create a category of whiteness called "Eurocentrism" may exist in Australia, Canada, and New Zealand as well as in the US; nonetheless, the closer ties these three have with Britain means that they are less likely to ignore the differences between British and other European cultures. The mistake of ignoring them is most obvious in Canada.

In Canada multiculturalism in large part developed in response to the tension arising from conflicting cultural and political heritages from Europe: French and British. The colonial history of Canada has given France and Britain the privileged status of being its two settler countries. That history includes the complication that the British then incorporated French-speaking Canada into its empire in 1763 after winning the battle fought on the Plains of Abraham. Canada remains part of the British Commonwealth as do Australia and New Zealand; nonetheless, in 1963 nationalist stirrings in Quebec caused Prime Minister Lester Pearson to appoint a Royal Commission on Bilingualism and Biculturalism to examine the potential crisis between Canada's "two founding races." The recommendations of this commission led to the Official Languages Act of 1969 passed under the leadership of Prime Minister Pierre Trudeau, and French as well as English became an official language.

The Multicultural Act of 1988 grew out of the Commission's work. In 1971 Trudeau announced a policy of multiculturalism. This policy responded to two pressures. The most important was a potential division between Quebec and the rest of Canada. The second came from those that were neither British nor French Canadians, the most vocal of whom were groups from Eastern and Central Europe who began arriving in the late nineteenth century to help settle the plains states. The policy and later the Act were designed to combat separatist calls from Quebec by proclaiming Canada a nation tolerant of cultural difference. Under state-sponsored multiculturalism

British and French cultural traditions are included as simply part of a Canadian identity of diverse cultures. The metaphor for this diversity is a mosaic, which is quite different from the metaphor of the melting pot long dominant in the United States but now questioned by multiculturalists. Many people in Quebec, however, are reluctant to see French culture as simply one piece of a national mosaic. Claiming a special status because of settlement history, they see themselves not simply as one culture among many but instead as a nation within a nation.

The fact that official Canadian multiculturalism is a state-sponsored policy designed to foster national unity is completely at odds with its image perpetuated by multicultural opponents in the United States, who portray it as a cause of division, implying that a similar state policy south of the border would lead to "the disuniting of America." What opponents fail to acknowledge is that Canadian multiculturalism, resulting from a different history and responding to a different set of problems, is quite different from its nominal counterpart in the United States. For instance, in responding to the threat of French and British conflict it has stressed ethnic more than racial difference. In 1971 addressing the issue of multiculturalism, Trudeau argued that "there is no official culture, nor does any ethnic group take precedence over any other." One result is that, whereas in the United States many people assume that multiculturalism silently stands for multiracial, in Canada the term — "visible minorities" — had to be coined to designate minorities racialized according to skin color. The presence of "visible minorities" has become more apparent because of changes in immigration policy. The Immigration Act of 1910 provided for the prohibition of immigrants "belonging to any race deemed unsuited to the climate or requirements of Canada, or of immigrants of any special class, occupation, or character." In the 1960s this racial clause was eliminated. Then the Immigration Act of 1978 established a point system designed to attract highly skilled professionals from around the globe. Nonetheless, many who came from non-European countries experienced racial discrimination. Even though the Standing Committee on Multiculturalism recommends antiracist awareness, Canadian multiculturalism, aimed at quieting tensions between two communities of European descent, has frequently been attacked as inadequate to deal with racism. A symptom of the lack of attention given to visible minorities is the fact that they remained invisible in the *World Almanac's* population statistics until 1998 when the category "Other (mostly Asian)" was finally created. But even that category leaves African-Canadians virtually invisible, causing George Elliott Clarke to lament: "the general incoherence of color-based identity in Canada permits Canadian whiteness to exist ... as an ethereal force" (100).

The Committee's recommendations raise questions about another issue of great importance to any vision of multiculturalism: what is the relation between language and a culture? Canadian multiculturalism, the Committee notes, should be implemented within a bilingual framework. This loosening of ties between language and culture upset some Anglo- and Francophones, who resented any implication that their cultures had the same status as those of other groups. At the same time, despite the Committee's call to enhance "heritage languages," groups, like Ukrainian-Canadians, protested the favored status given to British and French cultures because of the failure to give multiculturalism a linguistic basis.

In a much cited formulation, Arjun Appadurai has argued that the flows of people, images, technologies, capital, and ideas around the globe are rendering the territorial boundaries of nation-states obsolete. In the midst of the same flows as its neighbor to the south, Canada has developed a different version of multiculturalism because of a complicated and dynamic relation between and among the particular groups that inhabit its territory, a relation that is influenced and influences those groups' relations with the particular form of the state that has developed and continues to develop in part as a response to the same groups.

The Canadian state was formed by the British North America Act in 1867. Passed by the British Parliament, not "authored" by "We, the people," that act declares as its aim "Peace, Order, and good Government," which is subtly different from the United States' Constitution's aim "to form a more perfect Union, establish justice, insure domestic tranquility, provide for the common defense, promote the general welfare, and secure the blessings of liberty to ourselves and our posterity." With the American Civil War fresh in its authors' minds, the British North America Act established a federal system and a relation of individual provinces to the federal government notably different from the relation established between states and the federal government in the United States. Although not explicitly altered, the Canadian federal system was greatly affected by the establishment of the Charter of Rights and Freedoms, a change linked to Trudeau's move toward state-sponsored multiculturalism. Allowing for judicial review, the Charter undercuts the sovereign power of Parliament. For this reason it is frequently compared to the United States' Bill of Rights. But it is also indebted to a

French tradition that includes the Declaration of the Rights of Man and the Citizen and the powerful influence of Rousseau. Gairdner, for instance, blames Trudeau — the son of a Scottish mother and a French-Canadian father — and his fascination with Rousseau for moving Canada from its true English heritage down the road to multiculturalism and socialism. The Charter, Gairdner claims, was Trudeau's attempt to impose his own sense of a Canadian "national will" on the country, a will, that because it is derived from Rousseau's notion of a "general will" is French, not English, in spirit (Crack-Up).[4]

One can strongly disagree with Gairdner's politics and still grant that his sensitivity to differences between French and English traditions keeps him from falling prey to a confusion that plagues the work of a number of critics who have written on multiculturalism in the United States.[5] Anglo-American political thinkers have traditionally been skeptical of Rousseau. Indeed, his theory of a pure and infallible general will is opposed to those fundamental elements of liberal theory, the division of powers, the existence of alternative associations in a relatively independent civil society, and pluralism. As a result, he, along with Hegel, has been blamed for providing the theoretical justification for turning the state from liberalism's "instrument" of freedom into totalitarianism's "embodiment" of freedom. Isiah Berlin, the famous expositor of negative and positive freedom, went so far as to call Rousseau "the most sinister and most formidable enemy of liberty in the whole history of modern thought."[6] Even before twentieth-century totalitarianism, A. Lawrence Lowell, who would become President of Harvard University, in 1887 linked Rousseau to the French Revolution, which "was destined to leave political power as concentrated and despotic as before; only substituting in the place of the king of France some assembly, directory, emperor, or at the very best some chance majority," which "could not fail to govern arbitrarily" because of its disregard for rule of law (758).

Completely ignoring this historical distrust of Rousseau, a number of people who have written on multiculturalism, assume that his notion of the state operates in the United States. Donald Pease, for instance, equates the United State's notion of a "public will" with Rousseau's "general will" (74); Iris Marion Young provides a multicultural "critique of the ideal of universal citizenship" that mistakenly confuses the ideal of a "common good" with that of a "general will" (253); and Lisa Lowe, critical of multiculturalism, claims that the incorporation of US citizens into the state "asks that individual differences (of race, ethnicity, class, gender, and locality) be subordinated to the general will of the collective polity" (144). By drawing on Rousseau, these critics inevitably produce distorted analysis of conditions in the United States. Those distortions multiply when Lowe combines Rousseau's general will with Louis Althusser's theory of the state.

Althusser does not accept the purity and infallibility of Rousseau's general will, but he does grant the state a homogeneous will that "interpellates" its subjects, not only through traditional apparatuses, such as the police and the legal system, but also through "ideological state apparatuses" that control all aspects of civil society through institutions like the family and the education system.[7] Not necessarily authoritative in any context, Althusser's account of the state's power to interpellate its subjects makes more sense in a highly centralized system, like France, than in federal ones like the United States and Canada. In the United States, for instance, education policy varies not only from state to state but also frequently from school district to school district. Those variations directly affect multicultural education. Some states have made no attempt to introduce multicultural education whereas New York's 1991 multicultural plan is markedly different from California's 1987 one that "incorporates a multicultural perspective throughout the history-social science curriculum" (5).

Any thorough study of multiculturalism's relation to globalization in the United States and Canada would have to pay detailed attention to differences in their federal systems and how those differences affect, not only a nation's but also individual provinces' or states' relations to a global economy in terms of patterns of immigration, histories of settlement, and efforts to export different products. Rather than pay careful attention to such empirical evidence, however, critics like Lowe prefer the universal model of the state provided by Althusser since it allows them to construct a simple narrative about state power, especially on issues of race. For instance, in their influential book about race in the United States Omi and Winant simply assert — without proving — "Despite all the forces working at cross-purposes within the state ... the state still preserves an overall unity" (78).

Like the United States and Canada, Australia has a federal system that affects its version of multiculturalism. It is based on its 1901 Constitution, which forged together a federal system borrowed from the United States with a British parliamentary government. That fusion relied on James Bryce's *American Commonwealth*, which attributed the success of the United States Constitution to the genius of the Anglo-American race, not to the ways in which it helped to constitute a country independent from British rule. Bryce therefore reinforced the belief that in 1901 Australia had simply created a local variant of British governance. Indeed, one function of the new federalism was to provide the machinery necessary to implement a uniformly restrictive immigration policy for people of British descent worried about an influx of cheap Asian labor. The historic links between the 1901 Constitution and the notorious "White Australia" policy are important. If the development of multiculturalism in Canada has accompanied changes in the state, like the 1982 Charter, its development in Australia, though often indebted to the Canadian model, has not seen comparable changes in the structure of the state. As a result, Australian multiculturalism is linked both to 1972 immigration legislation ending "White Australia" and, in complicated ways, to the republican movement that would create a new constitution making the people of Australia, not the British monarch, sovereign. The form of government presiding over this new republic is most frequently imagined as neither the British nor the American model, but the Irish or German one. Indeed, when Alistair Davidson imagines a multicultural contribution to changes in the Australian governmental system, he has in mind theories imported from Italy and other European countries.

Australia, then, like Canada, feels a need to develop multiculturalism against a British, not a broadly defined European, dominance, one defining itself more by ethnic than by racial difference. To be sure, as the *World Almanac*'s categories for Australia's and Canada's white populations indicate, because Australian multiculturalism does not respond to tensions between two European groups it is easier in Australia, as in the United States, to lump all Europeans together. Even so, Australia has English as its one official language. This linguistic dominance means that the category of NESB (Non-English Speaking Background) is closely related to Australian multiculturalism, so much so that when the politician Andrew C. Theophanous claims that "multiculturalism is shifting our identity from its British base to a more cosmopolitan one," he does so in the context of arguing for the removal of "barriers to NESB people's access to the halls of power" (287). British dominance in Australia, however, is not called Anglo-Saxon but Anglo-Celtic, a term fraught with historical ambiguity (Dixson).

Anglo-Celtic reminds us that to posit a homogeneous British culture can be as much of a distortion as to posit a homogeneous European one. At almost the same time that people in Australia began to develop a multicultural vision, the New Zealand-born historian J.G.A. Pocock advocated a new approach to British history that would recognize the history of the British Isles, what he calls an Atlantic archipelago, as the "multicultural" (Pocock's term) history that it is. Of course, one of the major components of such a multicultural version of British history is the way in which the English dominated the Celts, especially the Irish. To lump the English and the Celts together, as the phrase Anglo-Celtic does, would seem to ignore the multicultural nature of British history itself. There are, however, good historical reasons for using the term in the Australian context.

The history of the Irish in Australia recalls the history of English colonial domination at "home," since a number of Celts who are now part of the dominant group descend from Irish political prisoners brought over as part of Australia's history of penal settlement. If in fact the penal colony myth gets overblown and most Irish arrived later as free immigrants, their situation still reflected the dynamics of power within the empire since they were generally worse off economically than their English counterparts (Hughes and Keneally). Nonetheless, after the Second World War the formerly repressed began to join in domination in response to new immigration patterns.

Helping to meet the needs for post-war economic expansion, numerous displaced Southern, Central, and Eastern Europeans arrived in Australia. Not former members of the empire and not English speakers, these "New Australians" were defined against the "Old Australians" of Anglo-Celtic heritage. This distinction created the anomaly that an immigrant from the "British" isles — and Ireland — who arrived after one from Greece was, nonetheless, an "Old Australian" while his Greek fellow citizen was a "New Australian." This distinction led to the racialization of many Europeans who were not "British." Thus if in Pocock's multicultural Atlantic archipelago tensions between the Celts, especially the Irish, and the English remain, in Australia a white supremacist group refers to itself as WISE: Welsh, Irish, Scottish, and English. The unifying work of the category British in many ways worked more effectively in former colonies than in the Atlantic archipelago itself.

The already complicated relation in Australia between descendants of former members of the United Kingdom and other Europeans is complicated even further by Australia's close geographic proximity to Asia. That geographic location has important economic consequences that have affected Australian multiculturalism. The 1989 National Agenda for a Multicultural Australia has three principles. The first two are predictable: the importance of cultural identity and the achievement of social justice for all groups. The third is not. It stresses the economic importance of a multicultural policy. As with much of Australian multiculturalism, the model for this economic principle came from Canada, which in 1985 under the Mulroney government concerned about Asian economic growth and investment, proclaimed multiculturalism an economic resource. Nonetheless, it was Australia that first articulated this economic factor as one of the basic principles of its multicultural vision. Indeed, multiculturalism is most noticeably an economic resource in defining Australia's relation with Asian trading parties, since for them it matters whether or not they are dealing with a "white" or a "multicultural" Australia. The new economy may be global, but Australia recognizes that economic forces necessitate paying closer attention to its neighbors and less attention to an island country many time zones away. Thus at the same time that it establishes Australia as a player in a world economy, not simply a member of the British Commonwealth, multiculturalism also affirms the country's location as part of Australasia. Such an Australia, advocates of republican government argue, demands the creation of a new state.

Nonetheless, the course of breaking with the empire runs no more smoothly than did the course of the empire itself. To embrace a multiculturalism that includes Asian immigrants as well as European means that Australia's ethnically defined multiculturalism, like its counterpart in Canada, has to deal with issues of race. It also means that it is a policy that forces Australians themselves to deal with the issue of race. That, despite economic benefits, the country might not be willing to do so was signaled by a change of government in 1995 that abolished the Office of Multicultural Affairs and has threatened implementation of the agenda and perhaps the agenda itself. This backlash against multiculturalism has been accompanied by a rise in racist rhetoric, an indication that not all Australians are willing to break with the image of White Australia.

New Zealand is also closer to Asia than Britain, also has a history of denying entry to Asian immigrants, and also has evoked a multicultural image in response to its changed position in the global economy. Indeed, as the smallest of our four countries, New Zealand is most vulnerable to the dictates of global economic forces. For instance, in the late nineteenth century it was hailed as the most democratic country in the world for granting women the vote and for instituting programs like old age pensions. Since 1984, however, the country's hard won social safety net has been dismantled as a once highly regulated economy adopted radical "free market reforms" in an effort to compete globally. The government's multicultural posturing is connected to that effort. The image of a multicultural New Zealand, the government hopes, will be attractive to rich Asians, especially from Hong Kong or Malaysia, who benefit from a point system like Canada's that makes it easier for the wealthy to immigrate.

But if New Zealand multiculturalism, like its Australian and Canadian counterparts, is part of a self-conscious economic strategy, it is also a poignant example of how particular national concerns alter the formation of different multiculturalisms. Multiculturalism may be linked to the nation's effort to reposition itself in a global economy, but it has been overshadowed by an official bi-cultural policy that addresses the country's need to come to terms with the 1840 Treaty of Waitangi signed by over 500 Maori chiefs and a representative of the British crown. The signing of the Treaty is celebrated every 6 February as the national day, even though the Treaty's exact meaning was — and is — open to dispute. English and Maori versions, it turns out, do not say the same thing. In English Maori got certain rights and guarantees but gave the British absolute sovereignty over the islands. In Maori "kawanatanga" or governorship went to Britain, but "rangatiratanga" or chieftainship was retained by the Maori (Kawaharu, McHugh, Orange).

Any question about which interpretation would reign was decided in the course of the nineteenth century as British settlers gained more and more power. Nonetheless, the Treaty was at least indirectly responsible for Maori getting generally better treatment than indigenous peoples in the other three countries. For instance, as New Zealand developed its own representative government, four seats in 1867 were reserved for Maori. As claims for Maori rights gained force in the second half of the twentieth century, the Waitangi Tribunal was established in 1975 to give effect to the Treaty. In 1984 the scope of the Treaty was widened to hear Maori land claims dating back to 1840. The existence of the Tribunal signals a move toward recognition of New Zealand as a bi-cultural society, a recognition that tries to reconcile the interests of Maori and Pakeha citizens. That effort leaves little room for multiculturalism, since Maori are as reluctant as Quebec nationalists to see themselves as simply one culture among others. But if Quebec claims special status because the French were one of two colonial powers occupying Canadian territory, the Maori see themselves as victims of European colonial expansion.

The Maoris' insistence on biculturalism shows how much tension there is between indigenous groups and visions of multiculturalism despite governmental efforts to reconcile the two. As recently as 1996 in his annual report the country's Race Relations Coordinator, Dr. Rajan Prasad, insisted that "From a race relations perspective in the New Zealand context, it is inappropriate to see biculturalism and multiculturalism as polar opposites. The term biculturalism is appropriately used to describe the Treaty relations between Maori and the Crown, and from this relationship emerge a number of rights and responsibilities. Multiculturalism is therefore not a counter to biculturalism because it refers to quite a different image of a society and one that rests comfortably with the concept of biculturalism described above" (215). But despite Dr. Prasad's optimism, the New Zealand experience does not give a lot of hope that the two will indeed rest comfortably with one another. Describing Maori reaction to the rise of multicultural rhetoric in the 1980s, Andrew Sharp writes, "The multiculturalist mode of thought made each culture equally important, and so te iwi Maori took its place as only one people among many, with no special claims against other iwi, and no special place in Aotearoa. They for their part wished to restate their special claims against others and to assert their unique place in the land" (Sharp 229).

New Zealand's biculturalism and its complicated relation to efforts to assert a multicultural vision have developed, as in Canada, during a period of dramatic changes in the country's governmental structure. New Zealand may be officially bi-cultural, but sovereignty still rests with the Crown. Indeed, New Zealand is the only of these four countries that can trace its history directly to its founding as a British colony. The other three are all federations of different colonies and other entities. Even so, there is more talk in New Zealand than in any of the others, with the possible exception of Canada, of the possibility of a confederation. But speculation about some future confederation in response to its national history occurs at the same time that concerns about national survival in the new global economy place other pressures on governmental reform. The result of these and other pressures has often been contradictory.

In 1996 a system of proportional representation on the German model was set into place. It lessens the power of the two traditional parties and makes coalition governments more likely. At the same time, as we have already seen, New Zealand's welfare state was dismantled in an effort to compete globally. Neoliberal concerns have also had an impact on settlement treaties with the Maori, since large settlements affect the national debt. Thus, the same Labor government that tried to bring about increased reconciliation with Maori by moving forward on treaty settlements, undermined the potential effect of its efforts through its economic policies. A further contradiction arises from the same government's attempt to introduce a Bill of Rights modeled on the Canadian Charter, which would have introduced judicial review as a way of limiting the sovereign power of Parliament. That attempt failed, but The New Zealand Bill of Rights was passed in 1990 as an ordinary act without authority to invalidate any act of Parliament.

Largely a symbolic acknowledgement of New Zealand's commitment to international accords on human rights, the Act has a number of interesting provisions. For instance, in a section on "Non-Discrimination and Minority Rights" it establishes a right to be free from discrimination as well as a right of members of "ethnic, religious or linguistic minorities" "to enjoy the culture, to profess and practice the religion, or to use the language of that minority." It also adds a provision that "Measures taken in good faith for the purpose of assisting or advancing persons or groups of persons disadvantaged because of colour, race, ethnic or national origins, sex, marital status, or religious belief do not constitute discrimination." If such a provision existed in the United States, it would conflict with efforts, like Proposition 209 in California, to undermine affirmative action.

New Zealand's biculturalism calls attention to the condition of indigenous peoples as yet one more "global" issue. Indeed, all four of our countries confront complicated indigenous issues, ones that challenge their versions of multiculturalism, challenges that advocates of multiculturalism have never fully answered (Michaelsen). To be sure, insofar as multiculturalism emphasizes the heterogeneity of cultural formation, it would seem to have an important place for indigenous cultures. For instance, the California "History-Social Science Framework" uses the presence of indigenous peoples at the time of European exploration to claim that "American society is now and always has been pluralistic and multicultural" (20). In Australia and New Zealand the Aboriginal and Maori heritages play a crucial role in the countries' efforts to distinguish their versions of multiculturalism from one another. That role is especially apparent in current productions of visual art in which unique styles have developed that incorporate Aboriginal and European or Maori and European traditions. It is also apparent in advertising as both countries broadcast images of their indigenous peoples to lure tourists from all over the world. Nonetheless, insofar as multiculturalism grows out of these countries' traditions of immigrant openness, it often conflicts with the interests of indigenous people. The question of whether the cultures of indigenous peoples should be seen as just one of many cultures co-inhabiting the land or as having a special status that distinguishes them from the various groups of settlers is not confined to New Zealand alone. A symbolic embodiment of this dilemma is the design of a bill of Australian currency issued in 1988 to mark the country's bi-centennial. It included both a depiction of the history of various settlers and an image of Aboriginal art, but the two were on different sides of the bill, joined, yet opposed. A practical embodiment occurs in Canada where some indigenous peoples' cultural productions have not been funded by the Ministry of Multicultural Affairs because there is a separate Department of Indian Affairs.

Tensions between indigenous peoples and multiculturalism exist in all four countries, but the tensions manifest themselves differently because those peoples have different relations to the state. If in New Zealand the country was founded by a treaty between Maori and British settlers, in Australia Aborigines received little or no official recognition. In Canada and in the United States the situation was somewhere in between. For instance, in *Cherokee Nation v. Georgia* (1831) the Supreme Court ruled that a Native American tribe existed in a "state of pupilage" with respect to the United States resembling the relation of a "ward to his guardian." Nonetheless, the tribe was acknowledged as a separate nation, even if a "domestic, dependent nation" (17). As limited as that acknowledgement is, it was cited in Australia when the high court in the landmark *Mabo* and *Wik* cases overturned two hundred years of history in which the continent of Australia was legally classified by Europeans as *terra nullius*, that is uninhabited land. The result is circumscribed recognition of some Aboriginal land claims (Attwood, Reynolds, Neumann, Thomas and Ericksen). The fact that the common law precedents cited in both of these cases recognized the national status of indigenous peoples should temper the enthusiasm of anyone who sees the demise of the nation as a necessarily progressive move. Certainly, many members of Canada's First Nations would take issue with that premise.

Augie Fleras stresses the need to distinguish between multiculturalism as "(1) fact, (2) ideal, (3) policy and (4) reality" (54). Multiculturalism as fact is an empirical statement about the diversity of cultures; as ideal it is a normative statement about how those cultures should relate to one another; as policy it is an attempt by organizations, often educational or governmental, to implement an ideal. The reality is, as Fleras notes, a gap between ideal/policy and actuality. Intricately linked to forces of globalization, multiculturalism varies, nonetheless, as fact, ideal, policy, and reality in the four countries we have looked. Those variations are due in part to different state formations in each country. At the same time, a state is not a fixed or transcendental entity. Instead it is "a contingently linked assemblage of institutions which have emerged over time in *ad hoc* responses to political and social pressures."[8] As the United States, Canada, Australia, and New Zealand respond in their own ways to a global economy, they have also developed their own responses to the people from different cultures who make up the body or matter of their nations, nations whose particular state formations continue to matter in terms of how multiculturalism is embodied within each one of them.

Part II

Virtual Worlds and Emergent Sensibilities

8 The Growth of Internet Communities in Taiwan and the Marginalization of the Public Sphere

Allen Chun and Jia-lu Cheng

CYBERSPACE, VIRTUAL COMMUNITIES AND THE LIMINAL SOCIAL

To say the least, the Internet has experienced exponential growth over recent years both in user activity and academic attention. The technological developments that have contributed to its media as we know it today and the changing sociological landscapes of the media themselves are, however, analytically distinct aspects that must be seen in their own light. Contrary to common misconception, the Internet is not, strictly speaking, a network but rather a common protocol (TCP/IP) that formed the gateway for linking separate networks.[1] The protocol was initially designed in 1969 by the Department of Defense and established in 1982 to link its ARPANET (Advanced Research Project Agency) computers. The success of this protocol enabled TCP/IP to link competing networks such as CSNET, USENET and BITNET, later NSFNET, which in 1986 became the backbone of major university computing centers.[2] Thus by the time ARPANET ceased to exist in 1990, its protocol lived on to become the standard for a true Internet that linked different networks of computers, as though they operated seemlessly as part of the same system.[3]

The cumulative history that characterizes the infrastructural development of what one popularly refers to now as Internet contrasts ironically with the notions of cyberspace and virtual reality that one usually uses to designate the nature of the media, as though removed from actual, physical communication. In the latter, it is as if one is linked across incongruent space by acts of transcendence or simulation. This discrepancy between technology and the imagination invoked by that technology on the other hand raises then crucial questions not just about the nature and meaning of "globalization" but also the kinds of social spaces created by that globalized media.[4]

The concept of cyberspace was first mentioned in William Gibson's novel *Neuromancer* (1984). The kind of community utopianized in this book was in essence a computer culture that, through technology, extended as well as transcended physical limitations. Cyberspace has faint associations with Norbert Weiner's (1948) notion of cybernetics as the re-imaging of the human body into digital information, creating hybrid notions of humans-qua-machines, namely cyborgs. Nonetheless, the overlap between corporeal and electronic reality (or the erosion of the former by the latter) is an implicit nuance invoked by the phenomenon of cyberspace communities.[5] Recent theoretical writings on cyberspace and its related social manifestations have epitomized the decentered, free-floating exchanges between culture, society and technology. Thus, Featherstone and Burrow's (1995) call cyberspace and related phenomena "cultures of technological embodiment", as though hailing a new stage of integration between lived experience and information, or a blurring of its existing boundaries. Virilio and Riemens (1995) cite Harvey's concept of time-space compression to argue that loss of orientation will rise with the chaotic advent of cyberspace and its unregulated globalization. Gunkel and Gunkel (1997) adopt a similar culturalist perspective to map out the "virtual geography" of cyberspace that mirrors, to a degree, the colonial logic of discovery in an earlier era of European expansionism. The logic of extension overlaps with repeated references made by other writers to mediation or the construction of social bonds in incorporeal form.[6] The constant flow between global and local, public and private, corporeal and incorporeal, etc., is then precisely what leads Shields (1996) in the final analysis to connect the cyberculture of Internet to real technological histories, abstract processes of embodiment and flexible, virtual spaces.

The interchangeability of cyberspace and virtual reality in some instances and the overlap between the socially real and digitally symbolic invoked by these concepts in effect confound our attempts to determine whether the medium itself is an appropriation of the real by the imaginative or vice versa. This ambiguity is best exemplified perhaps by Kroker and Weinstein's (1994) term "virtual capitalism." Instead of speculating on the nature of communication in such a medium, it is more constructive, in our opinion, to investigate the kinds of concrete communicative activities that have emerged in this medium, then determine the nature of technological input and cultural values that have contributed to this community. More than just extensions of a globalized medium and transformations of the real into the surreal, the technological capacities of the Internet have more precisely created niches for the emergence of communities and social relations that should be viewed in their own terms and in their ramifications for a wider public.

In retrospect, the emergence of Internet cultures in the context of globalization has raised the possibility of radically new forms of *community* as well as *communicability* that differ from the boundedness and sociability intrinsic to public cultures in the modern era. Virtual technology has in certain contexts, of course, made face-to-face interaction and work practices replaceable by other kinds of media by accelerating the break-up of physical distance and time, in effect making communities based on more traditional kinds of social relationships obsolete. Such new forms of interaction in turn deserve attention for the simple reason that they have important ramifications for the exercise of power, practice of everyday life routines and operation of institutions. Toward this end, it is necessary to carefully delineate the ways in which technological developments create the basis for new cultural spaces while at the same time providing a ground upon which cultures meaningfully and actively appropriate. Globalization (incorporation of the local within a global), transnationalism (blurring of boundaries between traditionally discrete entities), decentering (shifts in power between core and periphery) and time-space compression (dissolution of physical time and distance by technological progress) have variously contributed to functional disjunctures in the system. However, it is important to also emphasize the *perceptual* mechanisms in a *local* context of culture that serve to interpret, synthesize and negotiate these external material processes.

Cyberspace communication lumps together phenomena that should be technically termed Computer Mediated Communications (CMC). The latter includes email, Multiple User Dialogues (MUD), Internet Relay Chats (IRC), object-oriented games, Usenet newsgroups, bulletin boards (BBS), interactive virtual reality and teleconferencing, not to mention interfaces to information networks such as gophers and World Wide Web (WWW). Advances in and links between these various telecommunications techniques will no doubt expand this list.[7] Escobar (1994: 214) notes that while computer mediated technologies have brought about a regime of technosociality within a broad process of sociocultural construction, biotechnologies have brought about a regime of biosociality by intervening into the production of life, nature and the body to create a new order. Distinctive domains of human activity are generated by discourses and practices within this medium, which can vary in different socio-cultural settings and can affect labor processes, stratification and culture. By far, the most ambitious articulation of the extent to which computer mediated communications have transformed modern disciplinary regimes is Hardt and Negri's *Empire* (2000) and their Deleuzeian conception of "smooth world." As the title of their book indicates, such a regime of bio-techno-sociality represents above all a new form of sociopolitical domination. The extent to which this Foucaultian notion of a disciplinary society has been refined by the kind of global neo-imperialism that Hardt and Negri ultimately allude to is debatable, but one cannot deny that technosociality of a new kind has impinged directly on the constitution of cyberspace communities. The way these communities function in turn has produced wider ramifications for the practice of a public sphere.

Castells' *Rise of the Network Society* (2000) offers a lucid interpretation of how the revolution in information technology has in effect provided a political economic platform on which networking has become a new mode of sociality. Unlike previous perspectives on cyberculture that have dualized technocratic and culturalist approaches to the understanding of this new medium, Castells sees informational economy and network communication as integrated. To him, the informational economy is a distinctive socioeconomic system vis-à-vis early industrial capitalism, in that it has realized the productivity potential contained in the mature industrialized economy because of the shift toward a technological paradigm. As a system, its organizing trajectories are reflected in the restructuring of capitalistic modes of production that has taken place in all other sectors of the economy, not just informational. Whether we call this transformation post-Fordist or phenomena based on principles of flexible production and horizontal incorporation is insignificant. Perhaps more importantly, Castells views "the culture of real virtuality" which emerges from this network society as a mode of communicative interaction that is built largely on the basis or in the confines of the structure of this informational economy. Its openness is isomorphic with the flexible spaces of production created by that economy. In this case, the imaginative aspect of cyberculture that forms the substance of culturalist (essentially escapist) approaches to (the technological reality of) the Internet is for Castells hardly autonomous. It is largely grounded in an evolving socio-economy.

Institutional spaces are important, but they need not be narrowly political-economic in the way Castells casts them (especially in his adherence to a Marxist framework of social production). The Internet is largely a technological revolution but not necessarily in a socially systemic or politically conscious sense. Political contestation in a Cold War era prompted the heavy-handed role of the state in defining a TCP/IP protocol, but the openness of its system eventually combined with other hardware developments based on similar compatible principles of decenteredness, such as WWW. This then contributed to its own development, but in a context necessarily influenced by other institutional factors, such as government intervention, legal regulation, market forces, etc., which are in large part locally defined. In this regard, the emergence of Internet communities as well as the nature of their social communicability must necessarily be local phenomena, but their cultural "authority" must be seen in the context of their interaction with other local institutional forces. Identity and sociality operate within the interactive spaces marked by persons and institutions.

INTERNET DEVELOPMENT IN TAIWAN AS EXTENSION OF THE GLOBAL

Prior to the worldwide adoption of the Internet, strictly speaking, initial attempts to develop a computer network in Taiwan were funded by the central government. In April 1985, the Ministry of Education Computation Center established an "Education and Research Information Support Service Center" (*jiaoxue yanjiu zixun zhihuan fuwu zhan*) that served as the hub for network development. In 1986, under the auspices of the National Science Council, National Chiao-tung University established a similar IFNET, which served primarily to link the computer centers and departments at major national universities. It was later expanded to include various polytechnic universities and Academia Sinica and encompassed over forty nodes. However, lacking additional government funding to maintain it, IFNET eventually died out. In July 1987, with assistance from IBM, the Ministry of Education used a BITNET system that linked universities worldwide and provided services for email, file transfer, interactive dialogue, listserv discussions and fileserver access. However the closed nature of the system, which lacked remote login, among other things, led to the eventual adoption of the TCP/IP standard and gradual phasing out of BITNET.

The Taiwan Academic Network (TANet) was established in 1989 under the auspices of the Ministry of Education in conjunction with major universities to provide the backbone for a nation-wide information infrastructure. Built on the Internet TCP/IP, it provided the major hardware conduit for email, ftp, telnet, bbs and netnews, which later expanded to include IRC, gopher and WWW services.[8] In addition to ftp, hytelnet, archie, WAIS and on-line library catalog servers that linked major universities and commercial-polytechnic colleges, government research and information centers and municipal libraries, by far the most widely used and rapidly expanding domains on the TANet were gopher, netnews, BBS and WWW sites. Not until April 1991, when the Ministry of Education network was linked to a server at Princeton University, was TANet directly connected to NSFNET, then in turn a global network. Through the global network, other local servers, such as gopher, became linked to the outside via TANet.[9] At the same time, newsgroup and BBS Usenet sites became established on university sites through TANet as well. WWW sites developed later but grew exponentially with the evolution of graphic interfaces to a point now where there is probably no way to get an accurate count of the sites. The academic network later saw the rise of other networks, such as SEEDNet, established with the assistance of the Ministry of Economics Technical Guidance Office, largely for commercial use, and HiNet, which was established by China Telecoms for general and commercial use.[10]

Of the commercial servers, SEEDNet (Software Engineering Environment Development Network) was developed from July 1988 to June 1992 to provide a Chinese UNIX system for software production. However from 1990, it shifted its emphasis to the Internet, and from 1992 it began to provide services to the commercial sector. In July 1995, after a two-year experimental period of free access, it began to operate on an official fee-paying basis. HiNet, on the other hand, was developed under the auspices of the government's National Information Infrastructure (NII) Policy. It was first installed in March 1994 on an experimental basis before being made open to commercial and private use in March 1995. In a brief period of time, it became the nation's largest and most active commercial network, with fast links to Internet backbone servers abroad.

Taken together, TANet, SEEDNet and HiNet form the three major nodes that connect Taiwan's networks to the rest of the world. Each of them has links with smaller local networks. It is difficult to accurately document the statistical range and distribution of Internet activity in all its domains. While the number of user accounts doubled each year in the early years, the total number of servers has more than tripled in recent years. By far, the biggest increase has been in the number of WWW servers, which has nearly quadrupled, followed next by FTP, then news and BBS discussion servers. During the early stage of development (March 1993 to December 1996), the total volume of user activity in TANet overall had experienced exponential growth. In the long run, FTP activity had gradually declined proportionately, while WWW activity had increased most visibly (1%–23%), followed by newsgroup activity (3.5%–30%).

Another survey of servers shows that computer networks began earliest in the national universities, especially those with information science departments, and tended to develop more rapidly than private universities, polytechnics and government institutions. The initial association of networks with special computer-related services explains, without doubt, the high number of FTP and gopher sites, but the popularity of these sites has gradually given way to increased BBS and newsgroup activity along with construction of WWW sites. It is difficult to assess the extent or nature of such activity without looking at each in detail, but it is clear that, at least on the BBS and newsgroup sites, it is dominated by "discourse" of all kinds, not just specialist or academic. A cursory scan of discussion topics on these sites shows a diverse distribution that covers not just technical issues but also concerns ranging from everyday life to high politics (see Table 8.1). A random survey of the most popular weekly topics over a six-month span in the first half of 1996 demonstrates the equal proliferation of topics pertaining to computers (10), leisure culture (3), media and society (3), current politics (5), and relations between the sexes (4) (see Table 8.2). This diversity should be a function of democratic access in the media (institutional decentralization) as well as the diverse interests (communicative freedom) for which such medium is used. Institutional decentralization and communicative freedom are two socializing aspects of the medium, but more importantly they invoke two distinct notions of power thus have different impacts on the "public."

Thus, the development of Taiwan's Internet is in technological terms clearly an extension of a global medium or more precisely a natural outgrowth of initiatives in the information sciences to link globally, which was made possible by the adoption of a TCP/IP network standard. The adoption of a common interface enabled computers actually running on different networks to act seamlessly as though they were part of the same system. The specialist priorities that enabled the establishment of a global informational system were distinct from but nonetheless contributed to its eventual popularization.

In other words, time-space compression maximized the efficiency of specialist communication (to diverse sources of data) and facilitated its popularization as well (by making traditional forms of communication routine and providing access to the "public" domain in a way that was not possible previously). But it is perhaps equally important to note that specialist and popular participation in the same medium tended to be driven by different needs and goals.[11]

The kind of globalization taking place here is perhaps consistent with what Lash and Urry (1987) calls "disorganized capitalism", following Claus Offe, in the sense of being decentered. Lacking a regulative core, the kind of network space so engendered does not appear to be culturally hegemonic, thus does not seem prone to the homogenizing tendencies of an earlier modern world system. Discursive communities emerging in such a space would also appear to be spontaneous in a way that maximizes local autonomy. By being part of a seamless informational economy that mirrors the global cultural economy, marked by what Appadurai (1990) terms functional disjunctures between ethnoscapes, mediascapes, technoscapes, finanscapes and ideoscapes, such disorganized flows of people, images, technology, capital and ideologies inevitably bring about incipient crises of identity. But in what sense do these crises directly engender changing public spaces, if at all?

Seen from the perspective of its material infrastructure, there is perhaps little to justify the thesis that cyberspace communication is a "virtual" reality in the sense of being transcendent, simulative or even radically different from the processes of modern time-space compression. The appearance on the Internet of the same kinds of discursive activity that one would find in other public domains implies that the network is largely an extension of ongoing social communication. However, the function of the medium in facilitating ongoing social communication is distinct, on the other hand, from the nature of communicability that defines the form and content of this discourse. The fact that specialist and popular appropriation of the same medium differs suggests then that there must be different processes of meaningful localization or different structures of perception, accommodation and negotiation. The nature of such discursive communities should, moreover, ultimately reflect upon the perceptual mechanisms that serve as a vehicle for invoking radically new cultural values, while outlining the possibility of resistance to and co-optation with accepted norms. One may ask, to what extent does "countertalk" represent an alternative mode of rational communication, and in what sense do or can such communities engender "counterpublics"?

From a technical perspective, it is clear that the advent of networking represents the ultimate extension of personal computing. Its revolution is not one of providing more computing per byte, as might have been the case in the age of supercomputing, but one of maximizing user-friendliness, to reiterate a term of the times. Yet the motto of user-friendliness simply underscores the importance of articulating the perceptual process that drives the construction of user interests. As can be seen from the evolution of Internet communities, far from being a cut and dry matter, user interests are largely a function of who the user is and how the rules of the medium invoke and engage his or her participation. Although specialist dialogue on the Internet still figures prominently in the overall field of activity, the popularization of the medium (its increased access to the general public as well as its increased facility of use) is really what has attracted recent scholarly attention to Internet cultures and cyberspace. In any case, such communities as things in themselves deserve further scrutiny. Quite apart from the technological advances that have given rise to networking and the functional disjunctures of the globalization process, the rules of communicability that have shaped the formation of Internet communities have important ramifications for a newly emerging public. They have defined new rules of discursive acceptability and boundaries of sociability. Its facility of use has in effect made the medium an extension of private, individual interests. Thus, for example, email has maximized personal freedom by freeing correspondence from the institutional and economic limitations of regular mail and other telecommunications. But this extension of the private into the realm of traditional communication has also created new rules of etiquette (hence sociability) or just the breakdown of old ones. Moreover, the increased access to the public realm provided to social groups and dissonant voices normally excluded from a traditional public sphere has subsequently contributed to greater multivocality and indigenization of that public. Typically marginalized groups or outcasts, such as ethnic minorities, homosexuals and political or artistic dissidents, thus now have a venue for public expression that has been traditionally closed to them.

In short, the advent of Internet communities and communicability in sociological terms reflects less the transcendence of the traditional real by an imaginary postmodern or global than the conflated and often incongruent overlap between an extended private and extended public. This disorderly overlap of private and public domains is what is most characteristic, we argue, of the new spaces emerging from this Internet public. Its liminality should not be confused with the constant flow between global and local or the disorganized spaces of the informational economy. At the same time, one may ask what kind of public sphere is engendered by this disorderly overlap between an extended private and extended public? In what senses do the latter really conflict?

THE EXPLOSION OF MULTIVOCALITY AS EMANCIPATION OF THE INDIGENOUS

The explosion of "talk" on the Internet deserves serious attention, and it is easy enough to note how advances in technology have made access to information faster and more convenient, which has in turn facilitated the management and production of knowledge in all other regards. Time-space compression has made the whole world accessible and in turn collapsed the traditional barriers that have in the past maintained the boundedness of communities, such as class, society and polity. Without the ethnic and nationalist stigmas attached to objects, ideas and information, it would appear that all things have become cosmopolitan in nature, while in the long run one may question whether the question of origin is relevant at all.

As communicative technologies, there are differences between the "cultures" that emerge in non-interactive media, such as WWW, in contrast to the discussion groups located on various listserv boards, newsgroups and BBS forums. Listservs and other interactive groups, such as TWICS, CIX and the WELL, documented extensively by Rheingold (1993), are all examples of virtual communities based on mutual interest and specific membership criteria, where social relationships are formed between named and known individuals. Yet despite its virtual character as a non-residential community tied together by the seamless nature of the media, the bonds of sociability that characterize this community are really no different from traditional social groups. In lieu of face-to-face relationships based on propinquity, one might say that sociability is dependent more on network capital, knowledge capital and spiritual communion. Similarly, Reid (1991) notes that IRC does not fit well with conventional theories of human communication insofar as it reverses the role of social context in shaping conversation and community. Because one is always free to experiment with different forms of communication and self-representation, IRC participants have developed rules, rituals and communication styles. Social conventions based on physical markers, such as dress codes, and verbal etiquette are replaced by various linguistic conventions. On the other hand, newsgroups and BBS forums, due to the anonymous nature of the contributors, shed a different light on the notion of sociability that has not been clearly addressed in the past.

The concern with communities, virtual as well as real, was one of the issues raised in a workshop on "Culture, Society and Advanced Information Technology" that was cosponsored by the American Anthropological Association and Computing Research Association.[12] From their discussion, it was clear that the advent of technology could cut both ways: it could have a positive effect by bridging social relationships over insurmountable geographic distances, but it could also alienate and undermine local communities. Utopian and dystopian views divide the literature on cyberspace communities. For instance, Rheingold (1993) and Mitchell (1995) both argue that technical enhancement of communication is the basis of community, which transcends the need to maintain concrete face-to-face relations. In contrast, Slouka (1995) and Stoll (1995) accent the potential of the Internet to blur distinctions between reality and fantasy, while Stone (1995) and Turkle (1995) take a conciliatory approach by arguing that, instead of being a substitute for real life, this new technology can also represent possibilities for refiguring identities and redefining self-perception. These differences of opinion are, as was mentioned at the outset, largely a function of whether one sees these communities as an extension of existing technologies of communication or the result of differently imagined social worlds. To this, however, one must add the important role of rules in defining the conditions of access to and use of the Internet. In reaction to Volokh's (1996) argument that the "cheap speech" brought about by technological advances will ultimately make communication more democratic, Kling (1996) points on the contrary to the deleterious influence that the telecommunication revolution might have on institutions based on traditional print or mass media. This then prompts Winston (1996) to add that the radical advantages bringing about easy, unregulated access will inevitably be countered by legislation regarding (unlimited) access or (unrestricted) use and the charging of fees.

First of all, there are on the Internet different communicative communities characterized by different modes of symbolic representation and social interaction. Secondly, one must note that the nature of ground rules defining access to the media, their conditions of use and limitations on discourse can also have serious impact on the nature of community so engendered. Without making generalizations on the effects of "cyberreality", it is necessary to view these communities as concrete entities in themselves and with reference to the larger social context that forms them.

We have focused particular attention to the proliferation of "countertalk" in Taiwan's BBS discussion groups and, to a lesser extent, newsgroups, which are in some ways similar. Contrary to listservs and virtual communes, like the WELL, BBS bulletin boards form no community in the sense of interpersonal attachment between its members, despite the existence of common interest. Nonetheless, their popularity of use obviously indicates that they serve certain needs, if not certain sociological functions. Each institutional site usually has its own BBS or news node, which may include internal discussion groups as well as links to other newsgroups at related campuses. No one, to our knowledge, has done a study of these groups; that is to say, their emergence over time, popularity in terms of volume of dialogue, discursive content and the nature of communication between users. Talk groups at Academia Sinica can be broken down as follows (see Table 8.3).

The structure of discussion groups is not unusual, and in descending order of popularity, talk is centered on computers/software, news and queries, recreational hobbies, intellectual talk, socializing and sexes, campus activities, announcements, culture and fine arts, society and politics, career and health, then sports.[13] The high proportion of "for sale" announcements, employment ads, newsgroup question and answers, and local activity notices within their respective categories shows that such newsgroups can have a practical function, where people post and seek matters of routine need within a medium of convenience. While the prevalence of computer tech talk is expectedly the highest of all categories, the volume of non-serious discussion is also quite high. Intellectual talk occupies a high percentage of overall discourse, but exactly half of such talk is devoted to astrological queries. Pop music gossip, basketball trivia and gastronomic chat appear to be prominent topics under the general categories dealing with recreation, while the headings of society/politics and socializing/sexes appear to be the most internally diverse. Broad discussions on Chinese society and love talk in general are the next most heated subtopics in their respective categories, occupying about 25% of total messages. While the figures do not necessarily mimic those found elsewhere, the same categories of talk groups exist everywhere. On a campus BBS, one would expect a higher proportion of talk on youth-related topics, which reflects the higher percentage of students who actively participate on the network, in addition to official circulars.

A statistical survey of BBS discussion groups in Taiwan shows that the total number of sites has from August 1994 doubled in just less than four years. The gradual increase in and diversity of sites over time reflects for most part the growing and maturing interests of the users. As might be expected from general headings such as alumni, recreation, computer and society, each year witnesses the addition of new schools, hobbies, specializations and localities that are the natural result of new and changing interests. On the whole, many of the topics appear to be subjects for discussion groups that could be formed anywhere else. This thus raises the question, what is the utility provided by the electronic media in particular? In contrast to the mainstream mass media, one definitely finds a higher diversity of representation by minority and niche groups made possible by "cheap speech" or the facility of gaining "public" presence. This would include those representing localities, ethnic minorities, political parties, religious sects, environmentalists, homosexuals and special interest groups, such as consumer activists and the handicapped. The fact that these niche groups represent minority interests not necessarily given an explicit or strong voice in the mass media suggests that such online discussion is an effective conduit for democratic expression. Multivocality at some point also eventually overlaps with counterdiscourse in terms of alternative and dissonant voices. In other words, it is imminently a fertile ground more for the spawning of non-mainstream causes, such as opposition politics and disadvantaged minorities, than for other specialized interests, such as rich capitalists and political elites, who thrive more on exclusivity and hegemony instead of anonymity and openness by limiting access.

The appearance of BBS discussion groups devoted to ethnic minorities and indigenous cultures has been in line generally with the government's promotion and preservation of local histories and cultures since 1988. It is interesting to note first of all that those contributing to newsgroups on particular localities do so to exchange common interests in local history or folk culture. Although most seem to come from these places, the discussion sites function less as a hometown association (*tongxiang hui*), where people from the same localities keep up social ties through exchange of information and discussion, than as forums for mutually disinterested people. In this regard, virtual communities, even when they may overlap in discursive content and social makeup with traditional associations, nonetheless function differently from the latter.

Similarly, a large aboriginal discussion newgroup named after the Atayal, one of the nine major Austronesian cultural groups in Taiwan, has served less as a social network for indigenous comrades than as an information center for activities and opinions pertaining to aboriginal culture and welfare. In general, topics of inquiry have tended to center around the nature of aboriginal languages, cultures, myths, legends and artifacts, and less frequently about current local activities, information about aboriginal service teams, museums and social problems, including alcoholism and unemployment above all. Occasionally, there is discussion concerning relationships between natives and anthropologists or urgent political concerns, such as anti-nuclear and environmental issues. Thus, while the discourse that characterizes these newsgroups does not appear to differ radically from the social communication found in traditional communities, it is clear nonetheless that the social functions of these groups do differ. They resemble less social clubs, by virtue of their open nature, and their continuity tends to be sustained more by common discursive interests than by the ongoing social commitment of their member-participants, who may come and go.

In this regard, the sense of community invoked by such newsgroups is quite analogous to similar newsgroups elsewhere. On discussion groups where utilitarian interest is at stake, for example, stock market investor groups, the lack of *a priori* social relationships does little to deter the efficacy of communication on the whole. In essence, anonymity of participants without doubt makes the nature of communicative interaction democratic, but the lack of moral obligation, other than dictated by communicative necessity and interests, means also that its ability to construct a socially cohesive community, not to mention a rationally communicative "public", is somewhat dubious. Thus in comparison to the kind of utopian WELL community that Rheingold (op. cit.) describes, it would be more accurate to say that there are different kinds of communities, which invoke different kinds of sociability through the regulation of different kinds of discursive rules. From an egocentric perspective, it would be more accurate to say that any such community can serve as extensions of a routine lifestyle, instead of clashing with it (as a kind of virtual, counter-, or simulacrum of "reality"), by serving various niches. Such communities do more than realizing a "democratic" public; by ramifying the meanings of "social", they in effect redefine "the public."

In addition to empowering the emancipation of subaltern voices in society, another new development in this medium has been the explosion of open discourse by other repressed voices on matters traditionally relegated to private or even socially taboo domains. In particular, the keen proliferation of sex talk differs significantly from political discussion groups in that most people use pseudonyms or at least are more unwilling to divulge their real identities. In addition to explicit pornographic talk, it is interesting to note that much talk is devoted to inquiries about sex, presumably by inquisitive, inexperienced youth. Discourse ranges from obscene interventions by macho males to explicit descriptions of sexual positions to Dr Ruth-type dialogues about menstruation, AIDS, virginity and circumcision. Not only do conversations in each case tend to be explicit and uninhibited, but more importantly the very openness and anonymity of the medium makes possible a realm of discourse which is not normally acceptable in other "social" contexts, public or private. Like the political minorities newsgroups, this medium is clearly an extension of the public in a way that is insured by its open but anonymous nature of communication. Especially in the case of sex talk, which would be particularly sensitive in traditional familial or personal circles, this medium would thus appear to offer a conduit of expression not prone to adverse shame. The degree of uninhibited talk is also a function of regulation or censorship exercised by bulletin board controllers, but the medium itself can be exploited equally by those attempting to transcend the traditional public as well as the individually private domains.

The social ramifications of BBS newsgroups in the public sphere differ on the other hand from the explosion of democratic access seen on the WWW sites that has witnessed the growth of e-commerce and seemingly limitless conduits for individualistic expression through the creation of personal websites. The decentralized nature of Internet networking has subverted any basis of hegemony. At the same time, accessibility of service on the Web, in the form of virtual commerce and electronic brokers, with their ability to expand economies of scale (in ways that supermarkets have transformed the modern landscape) have expanded capacities of the public media largely to the detriment of traditional services. However, the blurring of public and private here on what obviously is an open medium is really the consequence of the inability of legal institutions to define and regulate the rules of dissemination and consumption. This is the dilemma experienced by the inability to control pornography on the Web, for example, which is driven by an assumption that the Web differs fundamentally from other forms of mass media.[14] E-commerce has been popular in Taiwan too, but its current acceptance as a public institution is a function of its legal ambiguity.

"COUNTERTALK" IN AN ERA OF DEMOCRATIZATION, OR THE END OF "THE" PUBLIC

In short, the explosion of "talk" and representation on the Internet is in the first instance the consequence of certain hardware developments that may be viewed as an extension of the communications media in ways that do not differ from the processes of time-space compression of a previous era. The decentered nature of the network results in the democratic dissemination of information by virtue of its lack of redistributive control, which complements democratic assess to the media made possible by its open and anonymous nature of communication. Democratization in both these senses can explain the proliferation of voices that have routinely been denied access or expression in a traditional or mass media. But the extent to which multivocality in the public media produces the social articulation of difference that leads to a critical public sphere impinges more importantly on the kind of sociability invoked in such discursive communities. One must ask in what sense the sociability and communicability associated with such groups can be called "cultures", insofar as they follow accepted social values, rules of etiquette or linguistic codes? To what extent do they not only spawn rational communication by Habermasian definition but also engender the constitution of a polity and the participation of free individuals in civil society? The semantics and pragmatics of talk ultimately reveal in this regard significant features of these social communities, the continuing influences of cultural values and the limits of political impact that such communities have in the structuration of public spheres, despite the possibilities of resistance and counterculture in rationally communicative terms.[15] If anything, multivocality and democratic discourse alone are insufficient conditions for making critical discourse socially effective insofar as they are constrained by the liminal nature of the medium. They must also be seen in social context.

The most obvious sites for "countertalk" concern politics, sex and bureaucracy. These subjects are not insignificant, given the decades of martial law exercised in the postwar era and the subsequent liberalization of the economy that reverberated into areas of politics and culture. In Taiwan, democratization was anything but a natural consequence of market deregulation but a deliberate policy of state to localize the nation to suit changing political realities.[16] In this regard, the liberalization of the economy was coupled with a diversion away from cold war politics as well as the indigenization of ethnic relations. Political liberalization was orchestrated in a manner that enabled economic progress to undercut support for an opposition party based on a policy of ethnic nationalism. Similarly, the loosening of media control and the rise of youth countercultures were promoted as direct consequences of the government's policy of "democratization" despite decades of stark repression. The emergence of a public sphere must thus be viewed as a function certainly of the autonomous actions of free individuals in civil society but within social spaces controlled carefully by discourses and practices of the state. The transnational and free-floating space of Internet communities represents perhaps an ideal venue for observing the autonomous and deregulated communication of a wholly civil public sphere. But one must ask to what extent is countertalk just discursive and under what conditions does or can discursive democracy become socially transformed into a politically oppositional public sphere?

Countertalk on political bulletin boards has no doubt become an important conduit for disseminating discourse in virtual space, minimizing the necessity for face-to-face interaction in the form of social movements, for instance. However, the existence of such groups during the run-up to the recent presidential elections had not lessened the frequency or weight of social activity but just supplemented it. Moreover, the virtual medium had been exploited with equal vengeance by both mainstream and opposition parties, thus it is difficult to assess the impact of such media alone. While public media such as newspapers and radio have increasingly become permissive, given their traditional conservativism, it is clear that public expression has a certain range of tolerance so long as identities of individuals are named. However, in the case of such BBS groups, anonymity in itself has guaranteed the possibility of total nihilism by producing a peculiar kind of public (or liminal) niche for the expression of thoughts and sentiments that would be repressed in a social or personally intimate context. Bogard (2000) phrased it most accurately, when he observed that "distance" and "strangeness" in Simmel's terms seems to characterize most aptly the postmodern condition of cyberspace, which claims in theory to efface distance and create intimacy between otherwise nameless and unknowable people. In other words, one can very easily disappear into the niches of the medium instead of opting to maximize its public effects.

The advent of BBS as a means of making the bureaucracy more accessible, at least in communication terms, to the masses has similarly provided a conduit for unintended countertalk. The departmental BBS at National Tsinghua University, for example, was during its inception used less effectively for electronically posting information that would normally circulate by paper than by students to vent their frustrations regarding official policies and complaints about things in general. At National Sun Yat-sen University, the busiest BBS node, judging by the sheer volume of messages, tends to involve campus police, with the most frequent complaints having to do with parking scarcity and various "attitude" problems. In such cases, rather than making resistance more public, as one might expect from increasing democratization of the institutional apparatus, the openness of the medium has made resistance somewhat more subversive by giving credence to liminal channels of communication. In many instances, media events have also become a popular focus for dialogue on newsgroups. The sex scandal surrounding official government spokesman Huang I-chiao and the brutal murder of a university student by her classmate in an apparent love triangle are recent examples that have incited considerable BBS discussion. In both cases, the mass media coverage still lacks the uninhibited quality of opinions on the BBS, and in the latter case one may question whether participants had as their goal politically effective communication.

The World Wide Web has provided another conduit for the proliferation of alternative voices whose existence would not have been possible in a once heavily regulated media. Despite the lack of interaction characteristic of newsgroups and listserv discussion groups, the flourishing of electronic magazines and promotional literature created by groups as diverse as religious cults to student radicals merits consideration. For example, a website at National Tsinghua University entitled "Sinland", compiled by students and faculty, includes two intellectual feminist magazines, a gay magazine, two cultural magazines featuring essays by radical academics, an architectural forum weekly, two softcore magazines entitled "Menstruation" and "Freegirl", a politically offbeat magazine called "Anarchy", a satirical magazine entitled "Slobber", a magazine of nihilist poetry entitled "Hypertext Wonderland" and one totally indescribable magazine named "Shit."

Commercial interest aside, the proliferation of electronic journals seemingly catering to all possible tastes, yet without any intended market except for the purposes of self-gratification and exhibition, raises questions about the kind of communication engendered between suppliers and consumers of the text. From a broader perspective, unlimited access to the media of the kind made possible by virtual technology raises questions ultimately about the fate of cultural cores and hegemonies characteristic of the modern nation-state. As long as access to the media remains unrestricted and the possibilities for alternative discourse remain open, resistance to dominant discourses and ideology always exists. But rather than presenting itself as an expanded political public, as envisaged by critical theory (characterized by increased participation of free individuals in the social realm and committed to purposive and rational communication), the self-regulating and ever expanding medium of cyberspace seems instead to have opened a back door to the public sphere, characterized by relations of distance and strangeness.

In actual fact, the uninhibited nature of both BBS discussion groups and websites have changed considerably since their formative years, to say the least. For one thing, the increasing popularity of graphic interfaces have shifted much activity away from Usenet communities and Unix text-based newsgroups to website chat rooms and other interactive media. Secondly, the ubiquity of email as a mode of routine communication within an office environment has moved the site of student online dialogue to other non-official venues. Thirdly, greater awareness of Internet communication within institutions as a whole has led to increasing regulation of or control over institutional website content and form. All of these developments have made it harder for people to get unrestricted access to the dissemination of public material and inhibited expression in web content. At the same time, the growth of commercial servers and websites has provided space for the expansion of these private interests away from institutional sites *per se*. Internet governance has thus become an increasingly important factor in guiding maturation of the medium by defining the acceptable parameters of both content and form. By restricting pornography and violence, for example, it has imposed guidelines that make it comparable to any public media. However, the limits to such conformity will, on the other hand, be conditioned by its ability or willingness to give leeway to individual access and expression. This will continue to be a topic of ongoing definition and debate, but it clearly will have ramifications for the way the private and public liminal overlap.

The early formative history of the Internet has perhaps in the initial stage facilitated the emergence of multivocality and democratic access that in turn transformed the use of the medium from a preserve once dominated by computer specialists and hackers to one catering to diverse and unregulated interests. This has led many, including Castells, to view the Internet as a venue for chaotic counterdiscourse, oppositional movements and millennial projects of all kinds. Yet in the process of popularization, it has become a locus of institutional appropriation and routinization in a later stage of maturation. Email has replaced other traditional forms of communication to a point where it has become in most places a ubiquitous routine. Electronic control of normative routines has necessarily marginalized use of the medium by other unofficial persons and interests. The restructuring of institutional and commercial space should invariably lead to new polarization between public and private interests, which will in turn increasingly dualize persons and identities. In other words, we have already gone beyond the simple millennial visions presented by utopian network society, yet at the same time we must grasp the contested terrain invoked by governance.

Without any notion of governance, these liminal spheres risk becoming cosmologies unto themselves. Rather than conflicting with the public sphere, they occupy parallel spaces. Because they do not aim at constituting social communities in the traditional sense of the term, their communicative function should not be understood in terms of notions of rationality that have direct implications for the nature of the polity. Nonetheless, they serve a function that can be contextualized in a cultural context of meaning; this may be a reason for their continued proliferation. These developments also mirror the cultures of youth resistance portrayed in Paul Willis' classic ethnography *Learning to Labor*. By flaunting their conscious differences with and opposition to mainstream society and values, the groups of counterculture "lads" are nonetheless content to remain socially submerged. The reasons for their inability or unwillingness to socially articulate their differences in politically significant terms appear to have much less to do with their inherent communicative rationality than their positionality in the nexus of institutional or class power. For essentially the same reasons, one must distinguish between the discursive possibilities created by public access to and informational dissemination within the medium from the institutional changes in the structure of power that give rise to a democratic public sphere, only part of which is dependent on its discursive freedom. We suspect that the role of Internet culture and virtual communities in the emergence of a critical public sphere will depend instead on the maturation of the medium to be able to socially articulate or otherwise make manifest the multivocality that it has already spawned, but at the same time peripheralizes by virtue of its inherent decenteredness. In comparative perspective, it is difficult to generalize about other places on the basis of Taiwan's unique developments. In one respect, its early link to a global network combined with the rapid subsidized development of an informational infrastructure has facilitated popularization of this medium in many senses of the term. Secondly, the lack of strong state intervention in controlling the content and form of the medium initially then spawned an unusual multivocality unparalleled in many other places, which was combined with the government's official tolerance for democratic expression. All of this cultivated peculiar uses of the medium as an extension of both private and public expression. This curious overlap between the private and public liminal has in recent years, however, been subtly altered by a restructuring of (official) institutional and commercial spaces in this medium, which has increasingly marginalized a popular public that had initially been a primary beneficiary of the network revolution. Ultimately, this has created a peculiar public sphere. In the final analysis, the distinctiveness of Taiwan's experience is thus less paradigmatic of certain local cultural developments *per se* than its peculiar, selective negotiation of certain general conditions.

APPENDICES

Table 8.1: Most Popular Newsgroup Discussion Groups from 1994 to 1998 (In Order of Weeks of Popularity)

1994	Politics (10), Campus life (1), Comics (1)
1995	TV trivia (10), Campus life (8), Macintosh (4), Windows (3), OS2 (2), Jokes (2), Tests (2), Comics (1), Movies (1), Alumni (1), Politics (1), Baseball (1), Chat (1), Boy-Girl Relations (1)
1996	Politics (8), TV trivia (4), Baseball (4), Tw.bbs administration or installation (3), Campus (3), Hackers (2), PC Hardware (2), Win95 (2), Video Games (2), Friends (2), International Students Association in Economics and Business (1), Alumni (1), DOS (1), Computer Networking (1), OS2 (1), Motorcycles (1), Movies (1), MUD (1), Astrology (1), Religion (1), Jokes (1)
1997	TV trivia (10), Hardware (8), Politics (6), Astrology (4), Campus (4), Motorcycles (4), Jokes (3), Win95 (2), OS2 (2), Video Game (2), Baseball (2), Comics (1), Marvel (1), Weapons (1), Taipei (1), Men-talk (1)
1998	Politics (15), TV trivia (13), Astrology (4), Movies (3), Campus (2), Novels (2), Boy-Girl Relations (2), PC Hardware (1), Motorcycles (1), PC games (1), Weapons (1), Basketball (1), Chat (1)

Table 8.2: Most Popular Newsgroup Discussion Topics in Each Week for the Period of 11/13/95–5/12/96

		Number of Messages:
11/13:	Sign up to protest Apple Taiwan's high price policy (comp.mac)	127
11/20:	The most hilarious names that you have heard (talk.joke)	241
11/27:	Sign up to protest Apple Taiwan's high price policy (comp.mac)	169
12/04:	Have seen these comic super old characters ... (rec.comic)	246
12/11:	Yes, I use OS/2 (comp.os2)	155
12/18:	Question: Power PC superior to Intel? (comp.mac)	303
12/25:	Question: Power PC superior to Intel? (comp.mac)	131
01/01:	Protesting TTV's discontinuation of Star Trek! (rec.startrek)	203
01/08:	A Comparison of Operating Systems (comp.dos)	117
01/15:	Do not overestimate the determination of the Chinese Communists (soc.politics)	124
01/22:	The first Internet Cafe House [27/1/96] (aiesec)	94
01/29:	Men are all really horny? (talk.friends)	103
02/05:	Taiwan independence must win; (new) nation must be established (soc.politics)	676
02/12:	Taiwan independence must win; (new) nation must be established (soc.politics)	442
02/19:	Men are all really horny? (talk.friends)	70
03/04:	Cute girls looking for prospective partners! Please call (campus.nctu)	261
03/11:	Cute girls looking for prospective partners! Please call (admin)	251
03/18:	Election of "worst singing artist" (rec.tv)	167
03/25:	Do not apply for hinet, because one day it may waste you $20 or more (comp.network)	140
04/01:	Vehemently protest the construction of nuclear electric plant (admin.install.bbs)	136
04/08:	Typical mainlander political party (soc.politics)	164
04/15:	A super powerful news/email offline reader-distribution system (comp.hacker)	266
04/22:	A group of Polytechnic students announce — -don't know why (soc.politics)	165
04/29:	Good news! agent 99e has a way to correctly input Chinese (comp.hacker)	283
05/06:	Market survey of Vancouver, B.C. cram schools (alumni)	214

Table 8.3: Sample Distribution of Various Discussion Groups on Academia Sinica News Server (May 1996)

	Talk Groups	Messages (% Total)	Busiest Subgroup	Messages (% Total)
Announcements	17	49,609 (7%)	for sale announcements	48,196 (97%)
News and Queries	3	122,307 (17%)	newsgroup Q&A	102,341 (84%)
Arts and Literary	15	48,316 (7%)	pop music gossip	23,626 (49%)
Intellectual Talk	14	61,177 (9%)	astrological queries	30,352 (50%)
Society and Politics	18	41,151 (6%)	Chinese society queries	11,083 (27%)
Career and Health	3	12,971 (2%)	employment notices	12,199 (94%)
Athletic Sports	7	7,453 (1%)	basketball trivia	5,727 (77%)
Recreation Hobbies	25	91,099 (13%)	gastronomic tips/info	14,021 (15%)
Campus Activities	11	52,282 (7%)	campus activities news	32,615 (62%)
Computers/Software	45	160,428 (23%)	computer hardware chat	29,808 (19%)
Socializing and the Sexes	8	55,595 (8%)	love talk in general	14,419 (26%)
Total	166	702,388 (100%)		

Table 8.4: Major Events in the Early Development of Taiwan's Internet

1985.04	Executive Yuan approves creation by Ministry of Education's Computation Center of a Teaching and Research Information Support Service Center.
1986.01	The computer departments of National Taiwan University, Taipei Industrial Technical College, National Central University, National Tsinghua University, National Cheng-kung University and National Chiao-tung University collaborate to establish IFNET.
1987.07	The Ministry of Education's Computation Center connects to BITNET system.
1987.12	Executive Yuan approves National Computer Network Project for All Information Centers and Universities.
1989.01	Ministry of Education's Advisory Committee promotes Three-Year Project for the Development of Campus Networks.
1989.09	Ministry of Education's Computation Center proposes TANet Project.
1990.01	Information Policy Committee begins development of SEEDNet.
1991.07	TANet construction is complete and becomes officially operational.
1991.12	The Computer Science Department of National Sun Yat-sen University and Lung-Chie Computer Co. begin development of a Chinese BBS (Bulletin Board) System.
1991.12	Ministry of Education's Computation Center connects to NSFNET via JvCNet.
1991.12	Ministry of Education establishes TANet Management Committee to draw up Rules and Regulations for TANet Operation.
1992.06	TANet connects to International Internet and is officially inaugurated.
1992.10	National Sun Yat-sen University inaugurates first-generation BBS system.
1993.01	SEEDNet becomes officially open for commercial use (free promotion until 16 July).
1994.03	Chunghua Telecoms officially inaugurates HiNet for promotional use.
1994.08	Executive Yuan establishes National Information Infrastructure (NII) Subcommittee.
1994.10	National Central Library officially inaugurates online network.
1995.03	HiNet becomes officially open for commercial use.
1995.03	TANet Management Committee draws up Rules and Regulations for BBS operation.
1996.01	Ministry of Education drafts guidelines for the supervision of BBS and network sites.
1996.02	*Fanshuteng*, the first Chinese-language Web search engine is officially inaugurated.
1996.02	TANet Managing Committee establishes Guidelines for TANet Operation.
1996.07	The Taiwan Branch of the International Internet Society is established.

1996.10	The Taiwan Network Information Center (TWNIC) is established.
1997.01	HiNet issues a notice on the TANet BBS prohibiting users from disseminating (spam) commercial messages.
1997.04	TANet Managing Committee establishes sets of Operational Responsibilities for Local Area Network Centers and Provincial Educational Network Centers.
1997.05	Executive Yuan officially opens an electronic mailbox for general opinions/queries.

9

The Internet in China:
Emergent Cultural Formations and Contradictions

Liu Kang

Since the mid-1990s, hundreds and thousands of Chinese-language Internet websites emerged in China, and the number of Internet users has increased dramatically. The Internet has become a dynamic force in China's cultural landscape. It is an important aspect of globalization, and plays an increasingly active role in China's transformation from its Maoist past to a post-revolutionary, post-socialist society. Globalization not only brings China closer than ever to the capitalist world economic system and market, but also generates new forms of culture and social interaction. The Internet has provided a new impetus to this process of transformation. Internet communication and global media have become central components of globalization processes. Given that the United States and Western Europe now dominate both technological developments and contents in global communications, the flow of information on the Internet promotes triumphant ideologies and values of capitalism across the world. China confronts these ideologies daily as it irreversibly moves toward globalization. It has sought to find new values and beliefs that can provide social cohesion and identities to its diversifying population. The state, of course, desperately needs an ideology, whether explicit or implicit, to ensure its legitimacy.

The Internet emerges in the midst of serious political and ideological changes. Can the Internet open up a new public sphere that will foster democracy for the Chinese people? To what extent will Internet communication erode the social and cultural fabrics and affect Chinese society negatively? Along with the technological and economic potential and promise it brings, the Internet will surely subject China to the ideologies of global capitalism under the various guises of "cultural imperialism," post-colonialism, and consumerism. What are the ideological impacts of global capitalism on Chinese culture and society? These questions cannot be answered with certainty; around the world people have been scrambling to find explanations for the sea changes in social life under globalization. But what the Internet can do in China is of critical importance to those aspiring to build a more democratic public life across the world, as well as those determined to amass unimaginable profit and power.

Communication technologies in the world at large provoke high hopes and anxieties primarily in technological and economic sectors. In China, the self-styled "largest developing country," technological and economic developments are set as its utmost priority. Ironically, however, rather than in the economic sector, the Internet has ignited a social engine mainly in the political, ideological, and cultural arenas. This chapter examines three distinct aspects of Internet development in China. First, the Internet creates a new press, which links to the global communication network. It trespasses the boundaries between the state-owned, centralized press and commercially-oriented local press, and between international press and national press. This new press inevitably affects Chinese media structures and practices, and will have profound implications not only on the Chinese media but also on the future of China's state ideological apparatuses. Second, the Internet provides an alternative public forum for political and intellectual debates that are rarely allowed in state-owned media. It appears as a virtual public sphere where the most politically sensitive issues — such as reforming the one-party system, fallacies of the past and present state and the communist bureaucracies — are being heatedly debated. As the Internet has become a site of fierce ideological and political contention, what will eventually transpire remains unknown. But the Internet political forum will undoubtedly alter the structure of public discourse in the political and ideological arenas, and will significantly affect China's political future. Third, an Internet literature has emerged, serving as the aesthetic representation of the urban youth generation, largely born in the 1970s and 1980s. As today's urban youth culture has largely been shaped by television and other digitally-based communication systems, Chinese young urbanites find the Internet a favorite channel for voicing their concerns and yearnings. Thriving literary activities in cyberspace have become a noticeable trend, while public interest in "serious" literature is eroded by the entertainment industry and consumer popular culture. Internet literary expressions of the urban youth are sharply divided. While commercialism nurtures sensuous indulgence and pleasure-seeking, some new experimental theaters are using the Internet to revive idealism and heroism reminiscent of the revolutionary past.

GLOBALIZATION, THE INTERNET, AND NEW MEDIA

Globalization coincides with China's economic reform and opening-up, which constitutes the historical condition for the appearance of a new media. The Internet not only provides technological means to the new media but also brings to China ideologies and values from the newly developing global media system. The Internet stems largely from the US-based media conglomerates and transnational corporations, and, according to Edward Herman and Robert McChesney, serves as a "new missionary of global capitalism" to spread the gospel of market and profit (1). Such an ideological mission and "thoroughgoing commercialism" of the global media, Herman and McChesnye continue, threatens to undermine democratic participation of citizens and endanger the public sphere in the West. Meanwhile, Herman and McChesney concede that "media globalization" has its positive effects, by "carrying across borders some of the fundamental values of the West, such as individualism, skepticism of authority, and, to a degree, the rights of women and minorities," which can "help serve humane causes and disturb authoritarian governments and repressive traditional rules." (8) This self-contradictory view reflects, however, a deep-rooted conceptual dichotomy of the democratic West and undemocratic non-West, as though that "evils" are different — commercialism in the West, and authoritarianism in the non-West.

By abandoning its revolutionary tradition that was adamantly opposed to capitalist ideologies, and embracing a developmentalism to build a free market and a capitalist economy, China's case defies those simple West/East dichotomies. Deng Xiaoping's developmentalism is premised on economic marketization and corporatization, whereas the political order still rests on the ideological legitimation of socialism. The ideology of socialism still promises socio-economic equality to all citizens, and as such, is fundamentally at odds with the objectives of global capitalism to maximize profit at all costs. The paramount problem that China faces is the incommensurability between socialist ideologies and economic capitalism, which inevitably results in a legitimation crisis.

The media and the press are at the forefront of political and ideological change. The media in Mao's era served as a mouthpiece for the Chinese Communist Party (CCP), which was instrumental in the formation and dissemination of revolutionary ideologies and values. Since the reform, media not only have followed the directives of the Party, but have increasingly been compelled to adapt to the marketization trend that demands a service-oriented, more pragmatic and less politically preaching press. Jaime A. FlorCruz, *Time* magazine's Beijing bureau chief, observes, "The vibrancy, diversity, and enterprise of newspapers, magazines and television shows reflect growing pluralism ... and Beijing's inability to control it." (43)

The Internet has dramatically accelerated the pluralization of media in China. Since the mid-1990s, the Internet has created new media in cyberspace. China began developing the Internet in 1994, as the US federal government announced its agenda of constructing information superhighway. On 20 December 1995, *China Trade Daily* became the first Chinese news medium to have an online version on the Internet. By the end of 1995, only seven Chinese news media had an online service. Beginning in 1996, however, China's Internet development soared. By the end of that year, there were 100,000 Internet users, but by the end of 1998, the number of Internet users reached 2.1 million. One year later, that figure doubled, reaching more than 4 million in December 1999 (Xu). According to the statistics issued by the China Internet Information Center (CNNIC) in December 2000, the number of Internet users in China had leap-frogged to more than 20 million, a phenomenal growth of the cyberspace by any standard (*Beijing Youth Daily*). In a survey released in April 2002, Nielson Net Ratings, a US media research firm, states that "China has taken second place in the race for the world's largest at-home Internet population," as China becomes "the largest Internet in the Asia Pacific region, and the second largest worldwide after the US." According to the survey, in March 2002 there were "56.6 million people living in households with Internet connections" (Chan, Steyn). CNNIC's report on 21 July 2003 indicates that by 30 June 2003, Chinese Internet users reached 68 million.

The news media were among the first in China to develop Internet websites. By mid-1999, of 2,053 newspapers about 300 newspapers and presses had online publications, or about 14.6%. Major national newspapers began to set up online news centers. The Chinese government allocated substantial funds to the five major websites of the state presses: *People's Daily*, Xinhua News Agency, the English-language *China Daily*, China International

Broadcasting Service, and China International News Center of the Internet (*Qiaobao*). China Central Television (CCTV), the national television network with eleven channels, also has a website compatible to these five presses in terms of its resources and audience. These websites have apparently learned formal and technical aspects from the major global media's websites, such as CNN, *New York Times*, and the Reuters, and have integrated the latest multimedia technology in online news reporting.

Although the contents of these websites remain largely identical to their print or electronic counterparts, changes have gradually taken place. First, the online international news coverage is quicker and more open to global media system than the print and electronic media. Online news is an around-the-clock, fast-tracking operation, which makes censorship by higher authorities much more cumbersome and often impossible, particularly when live reporting is called for. Chinese media today still must submit any news report on significant and politically sensitive events (such as the US Congress votes on China-related issues, US air-strikes against Iraq, etc.) to censorship agencies before it can be aired.[1] This normally causes a considerable delay in hours, even days. Live television news coverage is still a rarity in China. However, on the CCTV and *People's Daily* websites international news now appears almost simultaneously with those from CNN, the Reuters, etc. The CCTV online news is often broadcast faster than its TV news programs. The censorship mechanism apparently cannot catch up with the online news program's striving for ever faster headlines.

A significant change is the online interactive journalism and commentaries that major presses have experimented with in a variety of forms such as bulletin boards, chat rooms, online polls, and online opinion columns. The most important is the *People's Daily* online chat room *Qiangguo luntan* ("Strong Power Forum," literally, "strengthening the nation forum.") The chat room was set up in the wake of NATO's 1999 bombing of the Chinese embassy in Belgrade. It has since grown into one of the hottest public political forums, allowing a blend of public debates, news stories, and letters of opinion that cover a wide range of issues. Some are politically highly contentious and sensitive, which can hardly be published by the print and electronic media. The creation of a chat room for public political debate in the most important mouthpiece of the ruling Communist Party indicates the significance of the Internet. The US media, of course, rushed to describe it as an avenue for political dissent in the cracks of the Communist authoritarian rule. The American media's politicizing and sensationalizing penchant aside, the Strong Power Forum of the *People's Daily* website shows that the press is caught between its traditional role as the bastion of the communist ideology and its current role to serve the CCP, which now promotes economic and technological development.

In the meantime, the major Internet portal companies such as Sina.com, Netease.com, and Sohu.com, all established online news websites, with news reported by their own news crews rather than by the official Xinhua News Agency or by other state-owned media. This caused considerable alarm to the government. Since 1949, the Chinese media have always been controlled by the state, and all editorial members and journalists have been selected and trained through an established process that ensured conformity to a standard of journalism. The new commercial website news crews, however, have no institutional bond to the state-owned press and thus are under no obligation to conform to the state criteria. They choose to emulate either Western (mainly) American-style journalism or Taiwan-Hong Kong journalistic practices (the latter largely adopt Western journalism in Chinese language). Lacking Western-style professional training, and free from Chinese-style media control, the online novices, mostly in their twenties, face daunting difficulties in news reporting: they have yet to learn how to tell rumors and libels from real news, and how to verify the news sources and report first-hand news rather than relying on indirect news reports.

Although the government remains ambivalent about the online public debates and loose censorship on the websites of state-owned and semi-state-owned presses, the emergence of new media outside the existing media institutions and organizations was viewed as reaching over the limit. The National People's Congress (China's legislative body) issued in November, 2000, a regulation concerning the Internet and information security. The regulation is comprehensive, covering the potential Internet infringement of national security, as well as Internet violations and crimes in commercial and technological sectors and the news media. It prohibits Internet portal companies from using news reports written by unauthorized press sources, and requires general portal sites to obtain permission to use news from foreign media and to meet strict editorial conditions when using their own crew's news reports (AP).

The US media reacted with scorn for the "Chinese communist regime's dilemma," asserting: "Chinese leaders have been ambivalent about the Internet since its first explosive growth in China in the mid-1990s. They want to harness it for business and education while preventing it from becoming a tool of political discontent. The difficulty over managing bulletin boards is one of many dilemmas China faces in its effort to police the Internet, which the communist leadership has accepted as a necessary but awkward tool for modernizing the economy." (AP) It is true that the Chinese government is wary of the "the political discontent" that the Internet might bring, a worry that US media often reinforce by celebrating the political and ideological empowerment that the global media system can effect in China. Thomas Friedman, a *New York Times* neo-liberal media pundit, prescribes an emancipatory mission for the Internet in China: "Deep down, the leadership here [in China] knows that you can't have the knowledge that China needs from the Internet without letting all sorts of other information into the country, and without empowering more and more Chinese to communicate horizontally and create political communities. In the long run this will only give more tools to the forces here pushing for political pluralism" (A2).

Friedman and his cohorts are hopeful that the Internet will push for the kind of "political communities" that they preach every day to the "authoritarian" countries via the *New York Times*, CNN, *USA Today*, and so on. Their discourse reflects the dilemma that China faces, but not in the way they describe. The political communities and pluralism that the global media try to help create in China may serve a variety of purposes, which are not necessarily democratic or inherently good. Recent critical reassessments of "civil society" caution us not to automatically associate "civil society" and "pluralism" with democracy and equality in political and economic life. A civil society for democratic participation depends much on the state, which provides legal protection and resources and which implements an economic policy that aims at equality and justice for the majority (Ehrenberg, Cohen and Arato). China, in its transition from a highly centralized political system and a planned economic system to a market-oriented society, faces a dilemma: on the one hand, there is an imperative to further the process of decentralization; on the other, there is the danger of total social disintegration and fragmentation. Hence, some critics argue that what China needs now, first and foremost, is a state-rebuilding to re-establish an effective government system, in order to implement and reinforce law and to oversee democratic political participation (Ding). Ideological legitimation is a crucial aspect of state-rebuilding and social reconstruction. By issuing a series of laws of Internet media in order to establish normative regulation over the arena of ideology and values, the Chinese government faces ever increasing challenge from the pluralization and diversification of information channels brought about by the Internet and global media system, with uncertain, yet significant consequences to the society.

The Internet news media have attracted a growing audience, especially among the young and educated population. A June 2000 study shows that in the US, daily Internet news consumers consist largely of males (61%), less than fifty years old (75%), and college-educated (47%) (Pew). In comparison, a April 1999 survey of Beijing residents indicates that 25% of the residents, who are among the most educated in all Chinese cities, get international news from the Internet, whereas 48.6 % relied on CCTV's National Evening News (*Beijing Youth Daily*). To be sure, China's modernization will depend largely on the generations younger than age 50 to achieve its preliminary goals in the first quarter of the twenty-first century. The younger Chinese are undoubtedly attuned to the Internet and global media for information and news. Although media pluralism and diversity may spawn more and more fragmentation and specialization of audience, the sheer number of the Chinese population to be affected by the Internet poses formidable problems for building social cohesion and consensus. Diversity without basic societal consensus and cohesion means no democracy but chaos, especially when each of the fragmented, segregated groups amounts to tens of millions of disenfranchised individuals. However, with the collapse of the revolutionary hegemony that once held together — by both ruthless coercion and massive consent — 800 million people in Mao's era, the compelling need to rebuild a social consensus clashes with the imperative of pluralization. This contradiction is especially visible on websites dedicated to political debates.

INTERNET POLITICAL FORUMS: A VIRTUAL PUBLIC SPHERE OR A HOTBED FOR ANTAGONISM?

It can be said that the Internet has served as a political forum for the Chinese since its inception. The development of the Internet in its earlier forms (the ARPAnet, NSFnet, usenet, bitnet, etc.) and email, in the late 1980s, coincided with a period of political and social unrest across the world, especially in the so-called "really existing socialist countries," including China. Apart from the fall of the Berlin Wall that signaled the demise of communism in the Soviet bloc, the events at Tiananmen Square in 1989 are generally perceived by the Western media as a turning point in China's political life (a perception which is nonetheless sharply disputed among the Chinese).

By 1989, there was a large contingent of Chinese students (more than 100,000) studying primarily natural sciences and engineering in the US. These students were, on the whole, sympathetic with the demonstrators in Beijing and outraged by the government's bloody crackdown. As the prominent activists in the demonstrations fled to the West and converged with the existing students there, a new alliance of political dissent was forged, thanks to the fast and convenient links of email.

The first Internet magazine in both English and Chinese, *China News Digest (CND)* <http://www.cnd.org> and *Hua Xia Wen Zhai (China Digest)* <http://www. cnd.org/HXWZ>, appeared at this juncture. *China News Digest*, an English web magazine, was created in March 1989 in Canada, by two Chinese students. They claimed that their purpose was to serve the "need for information exchange on the network among Chinese students and scholars" and "to evade the pressure from the Chinese consulate in Canada, which had a higher degree of control on Chinese students than their US counterparts" (Bo). At first, according to its creators, the CND had about 400 readers in Canada. The Tiananmen events gave the magazine a huge boost. By September 1989 it set up listserver accounts at Arizona State University and Kent State University, serving about 4,000 subscribers in the US and Canada. Then the CND became a full-fledged daily electronic newspaper, having several columns and services, such as Book Reviews, Market Watch, and special packages concerning the Olympic Games, the Most Favored Nation trade status, and Chinese students' permanent residency status. In 1991 the first electronic Chinese-language weekly magazine, *Hua Xia Wen Zhai*, was published by the CND. The CND's initial publication in March 1989 was only less than two years from the first ever web newspaper, *San Jose Mercury News* in California, which was launched in 1987. With the introduction of the World Wide Web in the mid-1990s, the CND rapidly expanded its service and audience. By March 1998, CND claimed that its homepage "receives about 17,000 visits a day, while the *Hua Xia Wen Zhai* sub-homepage is visited by an average of 18,000 times a day." By 1995 CND moved to Maryland and was "officially registered as a non-profit organization, as China News Digest International, Inc." And "on May 9, 1996, CND obtained its tax exemption status as approved by the IRS," according to the same account (Bo).

One may wonder, however, what kind of status (taxational, legal, and financial) the CND had actually had between the years, and one may question the purported nature of it as "a community-based, free news and information service provided by volunteers."[2] But its enormous popularity among the Chinese student communities in North America and in Western European countries was beyond any doubt, especially before the World Wide Web was launched in the mid-1990s.

CND was attractive to the students not only because it was cost-free and convenient, but also because it was available to most Chinese students who spent days and nights working on their computers in engineering laboratories, toiling over projects assigned by their American academic advisors and lab supervisors. It struck an emotional chord, and offered practical assistance to tens of thousands of Chinese students deeply estranged from the Chinese government, and determined to seek long-term career and personal development in the West. Students were particularly enamored of *Hua Xia Wen Zhai* because it publishes anecdotes, memoirs, stories, prose essays and investigative reports that are free from political cliches. *Hua Xia Wen Zhai* was, for a considerable period of time, an indispensable resource for tens and thousands of Chinese students in the US, providing news and useful information concerning immigration status, job opportunities, leisure, and entertainment.

But make it no mistake that the foremost objective of the CND and *Hua Xia Wen Zhai* is political and ideological, despite its editorial disclaimer to the contrary. Its editorial policy echoes most of the mainstream Western media in terms of "independent," "impartial," "balanced," and "unbiased" news and analysis. Its contents also resemble much of the Western mainstream news media in covering China-related news and in commenting on China's affairs. CND's editorial policies and orientation largely represent the overseas Chinese political dissident groups, aggregated mostly in the US.

Take one issue of *Hua Xia Wen Zhai*, No. 507 (15 December 2000), for example. There was no particular "newsworthy" event during the week in which the issue was published, and there was no special occasion marked during the week either. The issue consists of nine sections, which begins with the weekly news summary, and ends with a table of contents for its special issues on the Cultural Revolution. The other seven sections are journalistic and literary essays. The news section is divided into Chinese news and international news. The Chinese news section contains sixteen brief news items, of which five items concern "human rights abuses" (the alleged "government persecution of the Falun Gong members," US Congressman's accusation of China's "worsening human rights conditions," etc.); four about disasters and crimes, two about Hong Kong's legal battle with mainland illegal residents, two about Taiwan independence, the rest of the section about China's negotiation with the WTO (1); China's president Jiang Zemin's congratulations to George W. Bush for his US presidency (1); China's corruption trials (1), and so on. These news briefs are apparently either translations of the mainstream US media or headlines taken from Taiwan media. Its ratio of news categories corresponds to US media coverage of China, too: "human rights" news about 25–35%, crimes and disasters about 25%, and Sino-US relationship 10–15%, Taiwan and Hong Kong about 20%, and the rest (China's politics, economics, science and technology, social and cultural events, etc.) about 10–15%.

News categories thematize and frame worldly events according to certain agenda setting. In the early 1990s, as most overseas Chinese students were still caught in the anger and frustration of the "post-Tiananmen syndrome", *Hua Xia Wen Zhai's* agenda setting was in tune with this general mode. However, as China's reality has evolved in the mid-1990s beyond the politics of Tiananmen, and, in the meantime, the tension between China and the US has steadily risen, the mood of the overseas Chinese communities altered significantly. By the end of the 1990s, CND and *Hua Xiao Wen Zhai* no longer enjoyed the almost monopolizing power it once had among overseas Chinese students. Part of the reason is that booming Chinese-language websites offered more options. The fact that CND refuses to move beyond the "post-Tiananmen syndrome" is the primary cause of its loss of popularity among overseas Chinese readers.

By the late 1990s, new online Chinese-language forums and chat rooms began to boom. The most dramatic of these is unquestionably the Strong Power Forum, or *Qiangguo luntan*, *People's Daily* online chat room <http://www.peopledaily.com.cn>. *The New York Times* report asserts that "For the government, the Internet has been, at times, a useful tool: after the embassy bombing in Belgrade, for example, chat rooms gave Chinese an outlet for their anger. But it is clearly a double-edged sword" (*New York Times*). The report continues that "In early May, for example, most of the entries were attacks on the United States, NATO and President Clinton, reflecting the widespread view that the Chinese Embassy had been deliberately chosen as a target. But by the end of the month, the anniversary of the June 4, 1989, crackdown in Tiananmen Square was fast approaching. Along with thousands of patriotic entries, a few more controversial thoughts occasionally made their way online — if only for a few minutes. On the chat room Netease, which was devoted to the embassy bombing, one person ventured: 'June 4 is coming. What do you think?' The events of June 1989, during which tanks moved into central Beijing, killing hundreds of civilians, are among China's ultimate political taboos."

The New York Times report catches the obvious timing of the tenth anniversary of the June 4, 1989 Tiananmen events, which by coincidence was only one month away from the May 7, 1999 embassy bombing that led to the launch of Strong Power Forum. But it misses the irony there. In ten years, icons about China have changed from a universalist symbol — the Goddess of Democracy at Tiananmen Square in 1989 — to a set of particularistic images in the spring of 1999 in Beijing. There were crying mothers of the victims of the NATO's embassy bombing, which only appeared in the Chinese media. By contrast, the predominant image in the US media was the sullen face of James Sasser, the US ambassador to China, looking out from the broken window of the American embassy in Beijing, damaged by angry student demonstrators. Deliberately or unwittingly, the US media created (or excluded) these images to reaffirm certain ideological messages, but the irony is that the discourses used to narrativize the Beijing student demonstrations that took place in both 1989 and 1999 had to effect a thorough about-face. In 1989, at the triumphant moment of globalizing and universalizing ideologies of freedom and democracy, the US media touted the Chinese students as young heroes and heroines embracing the pro-American symbol of white-woman-as liberty. Only a decade later, the same kind of Chinese students from the same universities was portrayed by the same US media as mobsters, mobilized by the Communist regime for an anti-American, ultra-nationalistic, and xenophobic cause. What is absent in the 1999 discourse of the US media, though, is the universal and idealist claims of freedom and democracy, the individual plights of the bombing victims and the emotional reactions of the Chinese public. Much accentuated, instead, is equally particularistic, and nationalistic assertions by the US media of the "threat to American interests by Chinese mobsters" and the "rising tide of Chinese nationalism." In hindsight, one can now discern in the 1989 universalizing discourse of freedom and democracy the particularistic, Cold War ideological agenda to end communism, and to bring China under the geopolitical order set forth by the United States as the only remaining superpower.

Just as the particular American geopolitical motive to overthrow communism was largely concealed under the universalizing symbolism of freedom and democracy in the Tiananmen events, the truly universalist concerns of the Chinese people for progressive and democratic life in modernization and globalization become submerged in clamorous particularistic and nationalist rhetoric, derived from both Western censures against the alleged "upsurges of Chinese nationalism" and radical anti-Western forces, and the official versions of "patriotism" within China at the turn of the century.

These dialectic twists and turns constitute the context in which Strong Power Forum emerged, and the debates in the forum encompass the full complexity and contradictions of China's historical conjuncture. The universalizing, globalizing, and local, particularistic discourses of China's modernity and globalization, China's domestic politics and Sino-US relations, China's economic marketization and capitalist world system, China's state rebuilding, social and cultural reconstruction and global geopolitics, are all deeply entangled. Complex as they are, the discussions attract a great deal of participants. On its first day, 9 May 2000, one day after NATO warplanes bombed the Chinese embassy in Belgrade, Strong Power Forum had 50,000 visitors within 24 hours. It now averages 70,000 page views a day, primarily among people ages 19 to 35.

Apart from its regular chat room BBS which posts hundreds and thousands of messages daily, the forum has several special sections. One is the interactive live forum, which invites scholars, specialists, government officials and celebrities to "chat" online with the audience on certain topics. The other is a section of "In-depth Discussion," where contents of the messages are screened by editors with more rigor, and tend to be more focused. The third section is the "Forum Digest," which is broken down into 80 to 90 subcategories, ranging from "Taiwan Strait issues," "Political Democracy and Political Reform," "China's Military Buildup," to "Anti-Corruption," "Sovereignty and Human Rights," "China and Olympic Games," "Humors and Jokes," "Stock Market," and "Marriage and Law." Selected messages are posted and reposted in the "Digest" section, which resembles the size of a US Sunday newspaper, only without advertisement.

A random browse at one day's contents will illustrate the diversity of messages. The selective section of "In-depth Discussion" on 21 December 2000 (an uneventful, "normal" day) contains 114 messages. The first ten messages are as follows: (1) "Jiang Zemin spoke out!!!!!"; (2) "In 15 years Japan's second economic power status will be replaced by China and India — if we believe this we'll be utterly deceived"; (3) "This morning China launched its last satellite in this century"; (4) "National college entry examination frauds reflect China's social reality — what kind of 'stability' do we need?"; (5) "Attention to our peasant brothers (I) — who treats peasants as human beings?"; (6) "Attention to our peasant brothers (II) — how are the 'rogues' singled out among peasants?"; (7) "Attention to our peasant brothers (III) — the peasant problem is China's central problem"; (8) "China's old friends are vampires sucking Chinese blood!"; (9) "the key to China's economic problems is political reform"; and (10) "On advantages of public ownership of property."

Not only the issues vary a great deal, so do the forms and contents. Some messages are news stories taken from news media. Message 3 on satellite launch is a report from China News Agency (a state-owned media service catering to the international community). News from US, Western, Taiwan and Hong Kong media often sneak in as messages attached with comments. This kind of news reports or analyses do not appear even in *Reference News* (*Cankao xiaoxi*), China's largest newspaper carrying translated news from foreign presses, edited by Xinhua News Agency. Although Chinese readers can usually see websites of *New York Times* and other Western presses by dodging the official Internet blockade, the news stories that appear in Strong Power Forum in Chinese translations give readers a more direct access. Apart from news, there are long essays in several segments, such as Messages 5 to 7 on "peasant problems," which are written in serious academic style, backed by considerable research. Some are very brief, perfunctory remarks, such as Messages 2 and 8.

A long essay (about 7,000 words), posted on 2 December 2000 by Zhou Xincheng and Chen Xiankui, warns the ideological and cultural infiltration of the "Western antagonistic forces." To emphasize their seriousness, the authors use their real names rather than nicknames used by most chat room participants. The essay lists seven major ways by which "the Western forces" infiltrate Chinese cultural and ideological domains, which include forcing China to accept "international and global standards" set up primarily by the US, "dismembering socialist China through globalization," and "spreading Western ideologies and values through high tech means, such as the Internet and information superhighway." The essay calls forth "opposing both 'leftist' and rightist trends," asserting that "under the current condition of globalization, we should remain vigilant primarily against rightist trends as we must fight peaceful evolution and ideological infiltration in dealing with Western countries" (Zhou and Chen). The essay apparently reflects the views of old communist ideologues, who have lost most of their political power but nonetheless still have considerable influence in the ideological domain, simply because institutionally and structurally that domain has been, and still is, the least touched estate during Deng Xiaoping's reform.

Not only has the *People's Daily* to pay some tribute to the old guards of communism in the Strong Power Forum, important media such as the People's Liberation Army (PLA)'s newspaper, *PLA Daily*, echo their concerns in their editorials. *PLA Daily* warns that the "information colonialism" is a real threat to national security and the cultural, ideological values of many developing countries, as most information in the global information network, the Internet in particular, comes from English-speaking nations, primarily the United States. The editorial demands that China establish its own information network by making use of technological innovations, and by "studying rigorously the strategies of the people's war in the information era" (*PLA Daily*). On the one hand, the concerns for national security and "information colonialism" is not unwarranted, given the US domination of the global information network and geopolitical assertions of the United States in the cultural and ideological domains. Joseph Nye, former assistant secretary of defense and Dean of Harvard Kennedy School of Government, argues in the major US media that exercising "soft power" in the ideological and cultural arena is critical in consolidating US interests globally (Nye). On the other hand, vigilance for security can readily become an excuse for suppressing free exchange of ideas on the Internet. Moreover, any slightest sign of the Chinese government's interference in ideological and cultural domains will inevitably invoke criticism and protests. This in turn will give the leftist old guards more ammunition to fire at "bourgeois liberalization" and "peaceful evolution." The vicious circle spins from there, and the authorities cannot effectively stop it. The government seems to have adopted a low-key, ambiguous tactic when tensions between the left and the right are on the rise, at least in the Internet forums, allowing both camps to air their grudges against each other without tipping the balance.

The contents of Strong Power Forum indicate the extent to which the Chinese Communist leaders are willing to tolerate, if not to endorse, this free flow of ideas in cyberspace. Yet the existence of the forum itself cannot testify whether it is a true public sphere for democratic participation, or simply a hotbed for antagonistic ideas spawning more cleavages. Under the present circumstances when laws of news press are non-existent, and the traditional censorship mechanism is increasingly ineffective and outdated, no one knows where the Internet forums in the state-owned media are heading.

The state-owned media, of course, no longer have the monopoly in China today. Many independent websites have mushroomed in recent years, and are dedicated to social and political debates. Some websites gain popularity in intellectual circles by their controversial standpoints, and some by extensive coverage of debates. Visions and Thoughts (Sixiang de jingjie, <http://www.sixiang.com>) was a website produced by Li Yonggang, a lecturer at Nanjing University's Department of Political Science and Administration. It includes essays authored by some 50 scholars, covering the major issues of intellectual debates. The scholars represent a broad spectrum of views, from neo-liberalist, the New Left, to neo-conservative, and debate among themselves on a wide range of issues, such as China's modernity, political reform, economic developments, and social problems. Authors also include some exiled intellectuals known for their dissident politics, such as the journalist Dai Qing. The website was created in September 1999, and closed down in October 2000. This caused considerable stir in the media outside China. Some overseas Chinese media were quick to accuse the government of forcing the website to shut down, saying that "it again showed that there is no legitimate space in China for moderate, rational, gradualist, and open debates about reform as long as political issues are touched" (Chinese News Network). Inundated by hundreds of inquires immediately after the closing of the website was announced, the owner of the website had to send a long public statement to clarify that his decision to close it down "has nothing to do with the government and politics, and it's entirely my personal decision, for private reasons" (Li Yonggang). The essays of this website, however, reappear in many other websites as Internet forums and journals continue to grow.

These semi-independent or independent Internet forums are quite explicit in their political and ideological orientations and are sharply divided. Culture China (*Wenhua zhongguo*, <http://www.202.106.168.89/~culturechina>) is owned by Yu Shicun, editor-in-chief of *Strategy and Management* (*Zhanlue yu guangli*), a well-known journal with some military backgrounds, which often publishes controversial articles in social sciences and humanities. The website is not, however, an online version of the journal. It carries articles with poignant views critiquing social ills, moral and ethical problems that China faces from "secular and humanistic viewpoints." Recently, a few websites with strong New Left inclinations have attracted a lot of attention. Shibo Forum (Shibo luntan, <http://www.pen123.net.cn>) carries mostly articles authored by scholars affiliated with the New Left or nationalist camps, and it also opens a section publishing articles by neo-liberalists, debating intensely over the issues of free market, liberalism, socialism, economic inequality and injustice, and authoritarianism. Most authors that publish in Internet forums and journals are well-known activists in China's intellectual debates now, and some are Chinese scholars residing in the US and Western Europe. They invariably take an active part in the Internet forums and journals, and are eager to disseminate their views first on the Internet. Apart from the China-based websites, there are many Chinese-language websites in North America and elsewhere, which participate in the heated online debates. Huayue Forum (Huayue luntan, <http://www.huayue.org>) is a popular US-based forum and chat room, which resembles Strong Power Forum in its format and content, with much less editorial constraints. China and the World (Zhongguo yu shijie, <http://www.chinabulletin.com>) is a well-known US-based website that is divided into an online journal, a historical archive and a chat room. The website has an ostensible leftist orientation, criticizing the neo-liberalist free market ideologies and Deng Xiaoping's developmentalism.

The Internet offers a major venue for China's political, ideological, and intellectual debates, with little and largely ineffective censorship or official interference. Hence, it can be viewed as a rare space for almost unrestrained free speech that hardly exists in China's mainland. Despite the sporadic tightening-up and crack-downs, and contrary to the reports of the Western media, the Chinese government in general has kept a low-profile and ambiguous gesture towards the Internet forums, tolerating their growth as long as no one publicly advocates the overthrow of the current regime. It is safe to predict that the Internet political forums in China will continue to grow and play more significant roles in China's social life. But what remains to be seen is whether the Internet political forums will lead to a democratic public sphere or a nursery for social antagonism.

LITERATURE IN CYBERSPACE: URBAN YOUTH'S SEARCH FOR AESTHETIC EXPRESSIONS

Apart from having access to news and participating in political debates, interests in literature, or rather, in literary self-expressions have become another major attractive facet of the Internet among the Chinese net users. According to the estimates by the Internet Information Center of China,

80% of China's net users live in urban areas, and have a high school education or above. A significant portion (about 45%) of these urban net users are between 20 to 30 years old, or were born in the 1970s or later (Li Xiguang). This generation in a way is the main beneficiary of the reform in terms of material and economic prosperity, but it also bears the brunt of the transitional time in terms of the confusion and loss of values and ethical norms, as revolutionary idealism clashes head on with consumerism and egotism. As the turn of the century marks the coming of age of this new generation, a distinct urban youth culture is taking shape. Nurtured largely by an electronically-based consumer culture, this youth culture is the embodiment of globalization: it draws its icons, styles, images, and values mainly from the "global" (read: Western) consumer cultural production and entertainment industry. In the meantime, they have a much stronger desire than the "Mao's children" born in the 1950s, who have now become parents of the 1970s and 1980s generation, for a distinct cultural identity that marks their local, regional, ethnic and national differences.

Compared with their parents or their older siblings, this urban youth generation by and large seems much less interested in political debates. Rather, they are more drawn to pleasure-seeking, sensuous, or aesthetically-pleasing life-styles and expressions. The Internet hence provides the techno-savvy youth with a much freer and trendier (or "cooler") venue for self-expression in artistic and literary forms. The recent proliferation of e-fiction sites and the rise of several "e-fiction star writers," whose writings were published first as Internet literature, and later turned into bestsellers in print, have constituted a thriving cyberspace literary field. Not surprisingly, the Internet literature arouses both suspicion and enthusiasm from established writers and literary critics, but it will be too simplistic to brush it aside as merely a high-tech offspring of consumer culture. While the predominant mode of the Internet literature is that of pleasure-seeking and romanticizing, one also witnesses a recent surge of interests in revolutionary idealism in new experimental theaters and their websites, particularly the play of *Che Guevara* (2000) that has toured the country in recent months with remarkable success. The Internet has been most active in disseminating the information and debates about the play, creating an interface between theatrical performances and online discussions.

In a more general sense, the Internet also serves as an interface for the self-identities of the urban youth, consumer culture, global fashions and cultural trends. The urban youth often identify themselves as the New

Humanity (*Xin renlei*), or the "Newer, New Humanity" (*Xin xin renlei*). The term was coined first in Taiwan in the mid-1990s, and reached the mainland China quickly. The Newer, New Humanity is said to have the inclination to "chase anything new, fashionable, vanguard, love cartoons, tattoos, disco, etc., and they are crazy about new life-styles, new technology and freedom. ... They are the generation of information technology and the Internet. Their shared language is a cryptic 'digital slang' and 'Internet slang' " (*China Youth Daily*). A self-styled manifesto claims that "the Newer, New Humanity is born at the age of globalization and technological innovation," and "they consist of middle-class Internet and e-commerce specialists, cartoon- and disco-loving generation, McDonalds, CocaCola, tele-marketing, independent workers, avant-garde artists. They are transforming the old values of life and relationships with their own life-styles, in order to fulfill the goal of more humane and self-pleasing existence" (Ye Niu). While the goal of this generation is both vague ("more humane") and pleasure-oriented ("self-pleasing existence"), it is clearly linked with the global (Western) trend.

The Chinese Newer, New Humanity embraces the Internet as the new literary starlet. A click on search engines of Sohu.com and Chinese Yahoo.com, two major Chinese-language website search engines, produces more than 200 websites dedicated to literature. Taking advantage of the virtual non-existence of online copyright laws, a majority of these websites simply put online published literary works from canonical classics to latest best-selling martial arts fiction (a popular genre analogous in its status to science fiction in the US) for free download or browsing. Still, a significant number of websites are devoted to original online literary writings, providing a venue for literary aspirants to freely publish their writings without the editorial screening and sifting of print presses and magazines. The Newer, New Humanity can practically experiment all sorts of writing styles and techniques, using interactive chat room to "collectively" produce literary works and creating "Internet slang" as a "cool," special kind of self-expression among the group.

Although the bulk of Internet literature looks largely like sophomoric composition, outstanding works have emerged, and several Internet writers have become consumer culture stars ever since. In the fall of 1999, Netease.com, a leading portal company, and Under the Banyan (Rongshuxia) <http://www.rongshu.com>, a website dedicated to Internet literature, organized separately two Internet Literature Contests. Rongshuxia received 7,000 e-fiction and e-prose essay submissions, and 50,000 readers participated in the two-month contest. The Contest Committee, composed of a host of China's most famous writers such as Wang Anyi, Jia Pingwa, Yu Hua, and Wang Shuo, selected 18 pieces for awards. Netease.com also asked such literary luminaries as Wang Meng and Liu Xinwu to select 30 winners among 3,000 submissions (Rongshuxia). And apart from the fanfare and pomp of these contests which smack of strong commercial calculation, a number of e-fiction writers have indeed gained widespread popularity.

In 1999, an e-fiction writer with a pen-name Long Yin (Dragon Singing) produces a new genre of "literary knight fiction" (*wenxia xiaoshuo*), as a parody-travesty of the popular, traditional genre of martial arts fiction or "knight-errant" fiction. He published in the literary website, Great Tang Dynasty Chinese (*Da Tang Zhongwen*) <//dtnets.com" http://www.dtnets.com>, a trilogy, *Wise Sage Donfang Shuo* (*Zhisheng Dong Fangshuo*). The trilogy is based on the legends of Dongfang Shuo (154 BC–93 BC), an off-beat humorist and court-entertainer during Western Han Dynasty. The hero's satirical discourse and quick wit are often described as a counter-weight to the stern, heavily didactic, moralistic Confucian literary canons in Chinese literary history.

Wise Sage Dongfang Shuo is filled with satire and humor, parodying the literary convention of martial art fiction and its hackneyed character types and stereotypes. The author is apparently well-versed in martial arts fictional styles and narrative techniques, and adaptable to the fad of "rewriting/dramatizing history" in the 1990s. A deluge of popular fiction, TV soap operas about emperors and their concubines, mistresses and romantic affairs of politicians, warriors, and writers in China's imperial past prevailed China's consumer culture scene. The e-fiction *Wise Sage Dongfang Shuo* adroitly gets on the bandwagon of romanticizers of the imperial glory, and wins the sentiment of the reading public instantaneously. The traditional print press immediately took note. In the spring of 2000, Writers Press (Zuojia chubanshe), one of the most prestigious literary presses in China, decided to publish the trilogy, and in less than a month about 10,000 copies were sold out, making the trilogy a first e-fiction-turned-into-bestseller. CCTV's TV Series Studio, China's largest TV soap-opera syndicate, bought the TV adaptation rights before the print books were on the market (Da Tang).

The commercial success of *Wise Sage Dongfang Shuo* in both cyberspace and traditional print book forms creates a new literary market in China. Many traditional presses follow suit, publishing popular e-novels and stories as bestsellers. Under the Banyan claims that it has signed contracts with 23 presses since the spring of 2000, and published 56 books of fiction, poetry or prose essay, which were all first published online, and the print books of e-literature by March 2001 already sold over 1,240,000 copies (*Da Tang*, 22 March 2001). The "e-fiction" label adds much to the appeal of this newly-cooked popular genre. It becomes a popular genre in commercial culture, along with other popular genres, such as the fiction of "beauty-baby authors." The "beauty-baby authors" are a group of young female writers, represented by Wei Hui, a Shanghai-based, Newer, New Humanity freelance writer. Wei Hui's novel, *Shanghai Baby* (*Shanghai baobei*, 2000), gained her popularity or notoriety for its graphic and allegedly "pornographic" depiction of sex, lust and drugs of Shanghai young women with leisure and money, made possible by high-pay jobs at transnational corporations and contacts with their Western executives and businessmen.[3] Not surprisingly, the Internet literary websites play a very active role in promoting the "beauty-baby authors" by publishing online all their works, some of which, including *Shanghai Baby*, are banned publicly because of their alleged obscenity.

Despite the alarms and warnings of parents and moralists, the Newer, New Humanity are determined to pursue their happiness in romantic adventures and sensuous experiences. E-fiction writers, who are most audacious and trendy, capture the emotions of the pleasure-seeking, desire-driven youth in their works, and are thereby made into stars by both the Internet and publishing industry. Of a dozen or so e-literary stars Bum Cai (Pizi Cai) is arguably the best known. Bum Cai is the pen-name of Cai Zhiheng, a 30-year-old Taiwanese who was working on his doctoral degree in hydraulic engineering in Taiwan in the spring of 2001 (no further information available concerning Cai's academic study). As a graduate student, Bum Cai was said to have played on the keyboard of his computer hours after hours, surfing the net and chatting, while working in the engineering lab, like most other "net worms" (*wangchong* — a nickname coined by net users) of his age. Then he was said to begin writing down his fantasies about romantic adventures through the Internet, thus the making of his first novel about Internet love, *The First Intimate Touch* (*Di yici qinmin jiechu*).

The impact *The First Intimate Touch* has on mainland readers is phenomenal. Sina.com, which publishes the e-novel on the mainland, asserts that the novel is the first landmark Internet novel in Chinese and that it "makes the underground Internet literature emerge above the ground" (Sina.com). Lest that any political connotations with "underground" be invoked, the novel actually has nothing whatsoever to do with politics, literally or metaphorically. It is a cyberspace romance populated by the Newer, New

Humanity, embodied by the first-person narrator-protagonist Bum Cai —
identical to the pen-name of the author. And the protagonist Bum Cai himself
resembles the actual Bum Cai the author in the real world. The hero Bum
Cai is an engineering graduate student in Taiwan, who buries himself in
endless lab works and mathematical calculations in front of his computer.
Often bored by the mechanical and repetitive work, he fantasizes about
romantic encounters with beautiful girls, and finds the Internet chat room
the best venue to share his fantasies with other net users who use pseudo-
names and make up their gender and age at will. It is a unique way of
fantasizing sexual encounters by remaining anonymous and sharing the
private, intimate thoughts and desires with an equally anonymous other.

What makes the novel so attractive to the Newer, New Humanity is
obviously not psychological (or psychoanalytical) intricacies about the Self/
Other, absence/presence binary oppositions. Quite on the contrary, there is
hardly any sign of such intellectual and linguistic plays that inhabit many
post-modern or neo-avant-garde fiction. The novel's primary appeal lies in
its language. The narrative discourse is mostly simple and straightforward,
casual and conversational, akin to that of most popular fiction on the market.
However, it creates freely Internet slang and neologism out of the Mandarin
Chinese urban dialects, mixing English acronyms with Chinese short-hands,
swear-words and even obscenity with high-tech jargon. The profuse usage
and coinage of new slang in depicting cyberspace romance — anonymous
"Internet lovers" who use very graphic and intimate languages to each other
in reference to their bodies, innermost desires, sexual fantasies and habits —
tend to have a liberating effect not only on the subject of the novel, i.e.
romantic love and sexual anxiety, but also on the discourse about sex and
desire. In other words, the Newer, New Humanity find Bum Cai's Internet
slang a new, exciting discourse to articulate their "liberated" experience. Bum
Cai's slang and stock phrases such as "beautiful brow" for "girls" (a homonym
for "sister" or *meimei*), "dinosaur" (*konglong*) for "men in cyberspace," and "I
love you ten thousand years," have created a mesmerizing appeal to the
Newer, New Humanity who are nurtured by TV commercials and the MTV
culture, and are long accustomed to the short-hand, yet "cute" and "cool"
phrases articulated by the starlets.

The liberating effect of Bum Cai's Internet slang can be highlighted by
contrasting it with the language of two bestselling novelists in China today:
first, that of Hong Kong-based Jin Yong, China's foremost martial art author,
and second, Wang Shuo, whose Beijing-dialect novels have won him the

title of "the master of hooligan literature." Unlike Jin Yong who insists on an elegant literary style and Wang Shuo who relies much of his appeal on his superb reproduction of contemporary Beijing dialect and slang, Bum Cai's discourse neutralizes the vernacular, dialectal aspects of Chinese language, while globalizes the Chinese by mixing the "coolest" American English slang of the US "yetties" directly with the idioms of Chinese techno-savvy urbanites. It is an online linguistic hybridity, an incipient "globalized" Chinese favored by the Newer, New Humanity.

The literary devices and techniques that Bum Cai uses in his e-novels, however, are nothing innovative. The novel largely adopts rather worn-out formulae of melodramatic plots and "comedy of errors." Furthermore, its carefree depiction of love, sex, and human relationship is couched in technological and scientific jargon, in order to give its naked pursuit of sensual gratification an educated and high-tech facade. It can, however, hardly conceal its uncritical endorsement of pleasure-oriented, individualistic values and beliefs. It is hence disturbing to see that the Chinese urban youth culture is grounded on such an ideology of global consumerism and egotism. The consumer culture's tireless promotion of the ideology of unbridled individualism and consumerism severely obfuscates the social conditions of China today, and is detrimental to its social reconstruction, which calls forth social commitment and dedication of its citizenry.

The Internet has yet to become totally penetrated and dominated by consumer culture, and it offers opportunities to other alternative and radical aesthetic and literary expressions. A number of websites have appeared recently. They are dedicated to literary and artistic experiments that try to revive radical revolutionary idealism. These websites often collaborate with other groups, such as artists, musicians, dramatists, historians and literary critics who contribute frequently to the websites, or are website makers themselves. Together with the political and intellectual online forums and chat rooms, these literary and artistic websites have constituted a New Left presence with considerable constituents among the net users. A noticeable case is the interactive website discussion, dissemination and theatrical experimentation of *Che Guevara*.

Che Guevara is collectively written and directed by Beijing-based musician Zhang Guantian. It debuted as a small-theater, experimental play in Beijing in the spring of 2000. The crew members are not affiliated with any state-owned dramatic troupes or institutes and are financially self-supporting and artistically independent. They are professionals who work for the play part-time. Except Zhang Guangtian who was born in 1966, other members of the *Che Guevara* team were mostly born in the 1970s, that is, the generation of the Newer, New Humanity. The *Che Guevara* team runs in a similar way to China's rock star Cui Jian and his team, who are largely independent of the state institutions. Yet, the ideologies of *Che Guevara* team and Cui Jian's rockers are visibly different. While Cui Jian draws on the protest songs of the 1960s and the American rock 'n' roll tradition as a way to renounce and satirize China's revolutionary legacy, the *Che Guevara* team wants to reinvigorate the revolutionary spirit, incarnated by the legendary Argentinian guerrilla leader, in order to wage new campaigns against social injustice and corruption in contemporary China and the world. The play is a medley of music, dance, mime and drama, poetry recitation and chorus singing. It is an experimental, non-realistic play with few state settings and props, drawing apparently on Chinese experimental theater of the 1980s and Western experimental theaters of Brecht and Beckett. The protagonist Che Guevara never appears on stage, only his voice is heard off-stage. The plot has two parallel lines, one tracing Che's revolutionary journey from the Cuban revolution to his final destiny in Bolivian guerrilla warfare in 1967, the other presenting contemporary, post-Cold War, post-revolutionary reflections on the revolution and its meaning in the face of rampant corruption and social injustice in China and the world. The two story lines are juxtaposed and intertwined, punctuated by sometimes solemn, and sometimes rueful, songs and dances. The message of the play is fairly explicit: calling for a revival of revolutionary idealism to right the wrongs in this materialistic, consumer-oriented, yet unjust and undemocratic world. The play is also a strong critique, cast in poignant satirical tone, of the current social ills in China and the lopsided official ideology of economic determinism and developmentalism.

The Internet websites Blackboard Literature and Arts (Heibanbao wenyi, a reference to Maoist practice of "culture of the masses") <http://www.heibanbao.com>, Music Big Character Posters (Yinyue dazibao, a reference to the Cultural Revolution's "big character posters") <http://www.person.zj.cninfo.net/~dazibao>, and Sina.com covered the tours and staging of the play extensively. They also launched a continuous publicity campaign for the play. The director Zhang Guantian and a major playwright Huan Jisu published a number of theoretical and critical essays expounding their aesthetic views, and a number of online discussion panels were organized by these websites. The play's success owed significantly to the dissemination and publicity of the Internet websites as a much faster and alternative medium (the state-owned media remained somewhat ambiguous and largely silent on the play because of its critical stance on the official ideologies and policies). By the same token, the Internet websites involved in the play received a big boost, thanks to the success of the play.

Yet, does *Che Guevara*'s radical revolutionary rhetoric reawaken a sense of social commitment among the young generation? Or does it reproduce a nostalgic feeling that merely valorizes the aesthetic dimension of the revolution? Che's decision to sacrifice himself in guerrilla battlefields may elicit a quasi-religious sense of the sublime among the post-revolutionary urban youth, but it hardly constitutes a viable alternative to the hegemony of global capitalism and its ideologies.

The Internet in the global information and media system embodies the dialectic tension and contradiction of globalization in terms of its democratic potentials for the disempowered majority, and its instrumental capacity in the service of global capitalism. And its double-edged capability is shown clearly in China today. The more specific or local issue in China can be seen as tensions between needs for normative regulation, state-rebuilding and social reconstruction on the one hand, and democratic participation of its vast population in a public sphere sustained by strong societal commitment on the other. In the three critical areas of ideology and values, namely the news media, the public political forum, and literature and the arts, the Internet has become one of the most dynamic driving forces. The Internet has been active in dismantling the discursive, institutional infrastructures of the revolutionary hegemony, and in disseminating global consumer culture to the Chinese urban youth. However, it has yet to vindicate itself in terms of its constructive potential in reinventing an ideological consensus conducive to China's social reconstruction. For the majority of the public this entails not only local (Chinese) restructure and reinvention, but resistance to global consumer culture and the political and economic hegemony of global capitalism.

The Internet holds out the promise of a new democracy and equality by nurturing a creative and constructive literacy and egalitarian social consciousness. Yet the promise can only be delivered by ceaseless and concerted efforts of the state and individual citizens. The Internet's constructive role in China depends on the social and cultural reconstruction, and as such, it is also an integral and constitutive part of the reconstruction. Under the condition of globalization, there are equally concerted but much more powerful efforts of global capitalism and its political agencies (IBM,

Microsoft, Hollywood, etc.), and the governments and state institutions, to consolidate its global domination. And the Internet is a critical arena in which new forms of domination, inequality, and exclusion fight with forces for democracy and justice. Such a battle is thoroughly deterritorialized, and China is no exception.

10

Home Pages:
Immigrant Subjectivity in Cyberspace

Sangita Gopal

In Arjun Appadurai's now classic formulation media and migration are the two major and interconnected diacritics that constitute subjectivity in the present time (*Modernity* 3). Global subjects emerge in the simultaneous circulation of bodies and images, through motion and mediation. Yet motion and mediation function contrapunctally. The former works through expansion — as agents are displaced, their experience of space is dispersed. The place left behind, the spaces traveled through survive as memory and nostalgia. A diaspora is defined by the multiplicity of location. The plural experience of space accounts, in part, for the so-called "double" consciousness of diasporic populations. The latter — mediation — works through contraction. Space condenses into images that serve as metonymies for motion. This is most clearly literalized by new media technologies like the World Wide Web. The world shrinks to a network. In this alternate spatiality, as virtual links proliferate, the need for real motion diminishes since motion is a way of establishing connections. In the network, all sites are always already available. Thus diaspora and cyberspace serve the ends of globalization through real and virtual means. To be global today is to be scattered and wired, for these two elements in tandem express the simultaneous expansion-contraction that is the ideal form of globalism.[1]

Globalization is everywhere manifested via this double form. This is best illustrated when we contrast the global form to that older form it is said to have supplanted: the form of the nation-state. The global is not only instantiated through prefixes like *trans-* and *multi-* in relation to the nation but also *sub-* and *contra-*. Thus if the movement of peoples accelerated by the needs of global capital has resulted in an unprecedented increase in immigrant/migrant communities within North America, the movement of capital, conversely, facilitated by a multinational division of labor has created a growing number of internal migrants[2] who occupy what Saskia Sassen calls the "frontier zones borne of the interactive overlapping of global and national orders" (219). These frontier zones function "below" the nation-state, using the logic of the "beyond." Stated otherwise, the global is not in opposition to the local but rather subtends a "local" that expresses the "global."[3] This particular form of the global, a form that both displaces and substitutes the nation form, critically depends on and is produced by electronic mediation, particularly Internet technologies.

The fused nature of these two processes — motion and mediation — that accounts for the ideal form of globalism is *literally* instantiated by the Indian diasporic community and its relationship to the Internet. We will examine the participation of Indians in the technology industry to see how this new mode of production constructs a certain type of diasporic subject (both inside and outside the nation, neither "native" nor "immigrant") the trajectory of whose being is mediated largely by global technology flows and its distinctive consumption interfaces. We will look at how this diasporic "Indian" subject globalizes the nation space by localizing it, such that these different locales end up as versions of the same ideal that is Silicon Valley. This "equalizing" logic replicates the so-called democratic underpinnings of cyberspace where space is virtualized as a network of "sites" — decentered, accessible, traversible. I will analyze certain websites and portals that cater to Indian (in one case putatively "South Asian") Internet users to show how they destabilize traditional categories like "immigrant" and "native" by reconfiguring the terms of psychic, affective and material exchanges between the "migrant" and her "homeland." It is my contention that by making "new" modes of communication possible, cyberspace undermines some of the enabling conditions for immigrant subjectivity. I will focus, in particular, on the vicissitudes of immigrant nostalgia and ask to what extent the re-coding of nostalgia causes things to fall apart.

PART 1: THE DIASPORIC "INDIAN"

In recent years, Indian immigration to the US has been almost entirely dictated by the needs of new media and communication technologies. The recent diaspora is almost exclusively comprised of high-tech workers, a significant percentage of whom were brought here on temporary work visas (H1B's) to prepare for Y2K — a non-event that announced, if anything, the coming of age of electronic globalism. By all accounts, information technology in the United States depends strongly on immigrant Indian expertise: Over 50,000 Indian engineers work in the Valley, there are more than 100 Indian-owned or Indian-backed companies in the area and these have combined market cap of over $40 billion. Ten percent of all Microsoft employees are Indian ("Oh Brave New World"). An Indian, Sabeer Bhatia started Hotmail. Vinod Dham was one of the fathers of the Pentium chip, K.B. Chandrasekhar's company Exodus is responsible for carrying 30% of all traffic on the Internet, Lata Krishnan is the highest paid woman in Silicon Valley and in a recent article in the *New Yorker*, David Denby describes financier Vinod Khosla as being "by common consent ... the most important money guy in the entire fibre-optic world" (139). People of Indian origin (POI) make up a whopping 30% of software workers worldwide and this "high tech army performed one third of the pre Y2K fixes in the world's corporations and governments" (Denby, 140).[4] The drive for digital excellence begins at "home." In his recent bestseller, *The New New Thing*, a book on entrepreneurship in the Valley, Michael Lewis devotes an entire chapter showing how the Indian Institutes of Technology are instrumental in producing some of the best IT minds in the world today.

Interestingly, this digital diaspora includes not only those Indians who have migrated to other countries, particularly the United States, but also an emerging class of internal migrants — invariably high-tech workers and entrepreneurs who serve the corporations of the world via the Internet. This class, I suggest, is distinct from the national elite that emerged in the wake of postcoloniality insofar as it is defined neither in relation to the nation, nor is it inscribed in the classic dialectic between the new nation and its former colonizer (in this case, the United Kingdom). Rather, this "new" elite locates itself in global digital culture, producing lifeways that are simultaneously mobile and electronically mediated. Often self-consciously distanced from the nationalist project, the "new" elite inhabits national space at once remove, cultivating the sensibility of displacement often associated with diasporic populations. It is constituted, in other words, by the localizing logic of the "global."

This logic accounts for the fact that much of the country's recent economic activity, driven by global IT needs, is marked by the emergence of the digital cities — Bangalore and Hyderabad — touted as India's response to the Silicon Valley in California and the Silicon Alley in New York.[5] Not among India's major metropolises, Bangalore's pre-digital identity was regional rather than national. Located in the heart of the Deccan peninsula, blessed with a temperate climate and a certain small city grace, Bangalore was relatively unfettered by the burden of colonialist or nationalist historical memories. This made it ripe for reinvention on global terms. A recent article in *Wired*, titled "Boomgalore," illustrates this well. This article is an ethnography-cum-travelogue of Bangalore. Author Brad Wetzler effectively tracks what is becoming a ubiquitous feature of so-called global cities — the emergence of global zones within national spaces that split the national space, as it were, introducing into its midst an alternate logic of living and belonging. Wetzler characterizes this as a phenomenon where "boomtown riches [are] dropped into the middle of a third world city." These zones and the people who inhabit them have created a parallel universe, thus mimiking, as it were, the relationship of cyberspace to real space. Koramangala, the southside neighborhood that is home to most of Bangalore's 300 software companies, is most appropriately represented not in terms of the greater city of Bangalore (of which it is a part) but on the pages of its resident website "kormangalam.com."[6]

Wipro, arguably the most successful software company in Bangalore, started out on a simple premise: the Net can serve as a prosthetic that turns an office in Koramangala into a development and maintenance center for global software needs. Called "offshore development centers," these offices conjure away spatial distance and accelerate time. Thus while India's geographic remove from the United States (home to Wipro's major clients) is moot, the fact that Bangalore is 10.5 hours ahead of New York presents *the* competitive advantage: it means that Wipro engineers can work while the US sleeps thus extending the workday 24/7 ("About the Company"). Wipro keeps global rather than local time. The emergence of these "offshore development centers" is a perfect illustration of what Sassen describes as a "partial unbundling of nation space" (217). One such site, the International Tech Park with its private sewage system, power plant and satellite dish is quite literally a "global village" — indistinguishable from any Tech Park anywhere else in the world and quite abstracted from the nation-space of which it is nominally a part ("Boomgalore"). What we witness in Bangalore, Koramangala and the proposed Tech Park is a progressive contraction of global space into the "local" and yet this locality is not moored in the context of which it is a part.

Yet, the very fact that people of Indian nationality comprise a large proportion of the digital diaspora is an outcome of colonialist and nationalist history, a history that this diaspora is willed into forgetting. For one, India's initial "failure" to keep pace with global infotech can be attributed to a postcolonial socialist government dedicated to developing "native" industry. The protectionist policies of the 1970s established high tariffs and placed restrictions on foreign investments (Das, 213–67). Indian programmers had no access to newer computing equipment and compensated for their clunky machines by developing precise and elegant code ("Boomgalore"). When American companies arrived in the more hospitable climate of the 1980s, they found a treasure trove of highly exportable English-speaking professionals. This marked the beginnings of the "body-shop" wave that peaked in the early 1990s. With the development of Internet technologies, the logic of body-shopping was recast in the form of the "offshore development center." But it is this historical trajectory that Azim Premji, CEO of Wipro, both evokes and subverts when he says to Wexler, "We are gifted scientists and mathematicians by *nature* ... we invented the zero and integers and other crucial elements of modern mathematics — and we have never been compensated for that" ("Boomgalore"). By tracing a straight line of descent from India's distant pre-colonial past, Premji invokes a debt that goes back to the time when India was an empire rather than a nation and by locating technology in "nature" (rather than in the messy muddle of postcolonial culture), he rhetorically paves the way for a new kind of digital (and global) subjectivity. As Wexler slides down the tech chain and interviews programmers, another facet of this new subject self-making emerges. The digital workers see themselves as possessing a new relationship to consumption. As Meena Nagarajan puts it, "the biggest change is that we don't think twice about buying something if we want it. With them (her parents), providing for your family took every rupee you had. Personally, I'm working on building a large CD collection and a library full of good books" ("Boomgalore").

One must emphasize two aspects of this new consumption pattern: that buying power is restricted almost exclusively to this "new caste" and the cordoned-off world in which they move and, more interestingly, that the structure of desire exactly resembles that of such digital communities elsewhere, most notably Silicon Valley, adjusted to cost-of-living and exchange rate indices. The fact that an impoverished postcolonial nation should aspire to US commodity culture is entirely understandable — that, after all, is the reason why Indians emigrated to the US in the first place. What is new is a pervasive sense that information technology can level the playing-field, thus making the question of immigration moot. As portions of the national space transform into global space, the internal diaspora increasingly takes the place of the diaspora proper. The fact of reterritorialization implicated in immigration is superseded by the deterritorialization enabled by cyberspace.

Given this mutual imbrication of networking and the Indian diaspora(s), we must now investigate how the operations of the Internet and the World Wide Web reconfigure the very nature of immigration, thus bringing into being new kinds of immigrant subjects. Our questions can be formulated thus: does cyberspace disable the very conditions of possibility for immigration, conditions that have hitherto determined the vectors of immigrant desire and produced the immigrant as a nostalgic subject who lives in one place and pines for another? As Stuart Hall puts it, "identities are the names which we give to the different ways we are positioned by, and position ourselves in, the narratives of the past" (quoted in epigraph to "Twilight Memories"). Rather, does cyberspace bridge and ultimately cancel out the lag in space and time through which the immigrant constitutes "such narratives of the past"? Widely referred to as an alternate diasporic public sphere, what "new" kind of subject does cyberspace bring into being? But first, we must take a detour via nostalgia.

PART 2: THE PAST IS ANOTHER COUNTRY

What distinguishes cyberspace is less its putative global reach and more its emergence in Timothy Luke's words as a "third nature" that "fuses the local and the global in new everyday life worlds" (91). It is a "nature" moreover that reverses the spatio-temporal configurations of both the first nature of the biosphere and the second nature of the industrial technosphere. As Luke convincingly demonstrates "cyberspace" operates both above (in the form of the multi- and trans-national) and below (in the sense of micro- and contra-national) the nation-state and provides an alternative to the nation-states' location in perspectival space and neutral time (93). In being the instance, par excellence, of Baudrillard's hyperreal, it simulates, rather than represents, reality. As such, it emerges as an "other" space operationalized by different technologies of time and space.[7] Thus the utopian vocabulary associated with cyberspace is not merely the hype that greets new technologies but rather that cyberspace in being virtual is quite literally the stuff that dreams are made of. It takes us out of the strictly enforced borders of the nation-state into a perfectly elastic domain that can be as intimate or expansive as the number of links we choose to explore or embed. We can travel as near or far as we wish since all our itineraries are equally fantastic. For the privilege of free travel we must submit to the lures and temptations of commerce on the information superhighway. The fantasy that underpinned cyberspace was, after all, that of a sovereign zone created for the workings of friction-free capitalism, unburdened by history, memory and national ideologies.

It is this fantasy of collapsing space into time that pulls the immigrant into cyberspace.[8] The relationship of immigration to the nation-state, as theorists of nationalism have long noted, is a complex one. The immigrant, at once affirms and subverts the finitude of the nation-state. As that agent who leaves one nation-state to make her "home" in another, the immigrant performatively reiterates the rituals of national belonging. In being subject to naturalization, the immigrant throws into sharper relief the homogenizing "nature" of the nation-state. Immigration in its modern form is ineluctably linked to and shaped by nation-states as finite entities that place certain limits on the nature and duration of movements of social actors across space.

Spatial displacement is but one aspect of the experience of immigration. For immigration in its classic mode is not only a movement in space but also a voyage away from time. To immigrate is to begin anew and therefore to depart from one mode of historicity and arrive at another. As the immigrant moves from the Third to the First World, the south to the north, the postcolonial periphery to the metropolitan center, she is inserted into a different temporality. What appeared from the periphery to be the "future" (the inevitable temporality of the developed West) becomes henceforth her present. The immigrant is frozen, sealed within a previous time even while constructing another story in the present time. This splitting of time by immigration is analogous, though not equivalent, to the splitting of the national subject in the narration of nation. As Homi Bhabha has pointed out that while nationalist discourse requires the unitary category of the "people," the enunciation of nation demands "that the people must be thought in a double-time." The people are both objects based on the pre-given or constituted historical origin or event; they are also the subjects of a process of signification which erases the past to enable the process of repeating and renewing the nation. "In the production of the nation as narration" Bhabha observes, "there is a split between the continuist, accumulative temporality of the pedagogical, and the repetitious, recursive strategy of the performative" (297). This is what makes the immigrant, in some senses, the nationalist subject par excellence.

The double-time of immigration has a sharper divide than the double-time of the nation; what intervenes between the performative and the pedagogic is the element of space. Space in its alienating function introduces a bar on repetition and performance and encases origin in an ever-receding frame, like the coastline in an actual journey. Immigrant subjectivity therefore tends to a single, vanishing, archaic time, the only conduits to which are memory and nostalgia, and whose recovery is only made possible by the excavation of part-objects. As the immigrant makes her home in the new land, memory — constituted by specific remembrances — morphs into nostalgia — characterized by longing for a past that no longer exists or has never existed. Paradoxically, though the initial act of immigration involves a movement through space, the immigrant comes to experience the place left behind as a time past.[9] In this transformation effected from the vantage of distance what was (the actual past) shades into what might have been (the perfect past); memory mingles with fantasy to create a past shot through with imagined desires and affects. It is for this reason that the object of nostalgia — what the nostalgic pines for — is always elusive.

Nostalgia, as Svetlana Boym in her remarkable book, *The Future of Nostalgia*, notes, is dependent on the modern conception of unrepeatable and irreversible time. A product of linear time, modern nostalgia is necessarily the other face of progress. In the rush forward, nostalgia emerges as the look backward; it is, what Boym calls a "side effect of the teleology of progress" (10). While Boym identifies the rise of nostalgia as central to the coming of European modernity and its radical rearranging of space and time, the immigrant who leaves her homeland to make a better life elsewhere must necessarily invest in this temporal narrative of progress. As such, she serves as the perfect vehicle for the making of the nostalgic subject.[10] Immigrant subjectivity is sutured by nostalgia.

Since nostalgia is operationalized by time rather than space — the objects of nostalgia dwell in the past rather than in the contemporary elsewhere — a return to the site of nostalgia is necessarily impossible. The "home" to which the immigrant returns for occasional visits is always other than she remembers it. It provides, at best, the disorienting experience of the uncanny. Immigrants realize quickly, if painfully, that nostalgia can only be nursed from a distance. Nostalgia introduces into the new home poignant vestiges of a past (and more perfect) time. The statues and figurines, the carpets and rugs that adorn the immigrant home serve as so many evocations of the past, evocations that defamilarize the present. Putatively meant to make the home more heimlich, immigrant souvenirs introduce an otherness into the heart of the home. They interrupt the process of assimilation by introducing another order of cultural specificity, an order, at once, intimate and inaccessible. Far from being a catacomb of dead objects that museumize memory, immigrant souvenirs signify the constitutive lack of diasporic subjectivity.

The objects themselves are often mass-produced kitsch. As inauthentic objects (the kind, for instance, that tourists would bring back from a trip to abroad as a record of the trip) they underscore that "nostalgia is the repetition that mourns the inauthenticity of all repetitions and denies the repetition's capacity to define identity" (Stewart, xviii). They are versions of the "exotica" that adorn the walls of innumerable Indian restaurants — a marble miniature of the Taj Mahal, a generic Rajasthani mirrorworked wall hanging, painted wooden tables from Gujarat — in brief, the cultural clichés that represent India to the world. These clichés, rather than the unique objects of a more individualized history, by their very reproducibility (the same objects with minor variations show up in countless immigrant homes) turn immigrant nostalgia into a collective act. These objects never quite attain to the status of commodities but function rather as prompts to nostalgic affect. These souvenirs, in their very banality, can stand in for the elusive and fundamentally unrepresentable past. Never a part of the décor, these objects give poignant witness to the asymptotic nature of immigrant desire, the impossibility of the return home. It is, as if, in collecting the souvenirs of tourists, the immigrant acknowledges that the immaterial stuff of nostalgia can only be materialized through catachrestic objects. Finally, as fragmentary symbols of the "old" nation, these objects testify to the precarious fantasy of national belonging. As Boym reminds us, the rise of nostalgia corresponds exactly with the rise of nationalism in Europe. The production of a country's past as sacred and unrepeatable helps secure the fragile contours of national identity by providing a unique history of that identity. Representations that congeal this historical narrative attain to the status of nostalgic objects. The rise of the national museum is paralleled by the entry of nostalgic objects into bourgeois living-rooms. The immigrant's mimicry of this act in reference to the nation *left behind* subverts the workings of nationalist nostalgia.

Nostalgia thus serves as a condition of possibility for immigrant subjectivity. It emerges in the splitting of space by time involved in every act of immigration. As modernity's other, it interrupts the teleology of progress that motivates immigration and produces the immigrant as a creature alienated by longing. It crucially defines the diasporic sensibility, never quite at home here or elsewhere, as *the* uniquely modern sensibility, thus making the immigrant the "modern" subject par excellence.[11] As such, the nostalgic immigrant prefigures the so-called nomadic subject of globalism. Except that the technologies of globalism, particularly and most recently cyberspace, derail the classic workings of nostalgia.

PART 3: THE WANING OF NOSTALGIA

Mingling fact and fiction into a dream of the past, nostalgia had served as a sustaining fantasy rather than as a reliable route to the past. Nostalgia is always contaminated with imaginings and therefore the objects of nostalgia, as we saw, are unrepresentable. The inherent unreliability of nostalgia, its limited truth value, makes it susceptible to bad reproductions. Of late, as both Jameson and Appadurai have observed, there has been an explosion of ersatz nostalgia: nostalgia for a past that never was, nostalgia without memory. Jameson and Appadurai link this phenomenon to a revolution in consumption brought about through what Michael Hardt and Antonio Negri have called "informatization" (298–300). As Appadurai, developing Jameson's concept of the "vanishing present," argues mass merchandising and advertising (rendered all the more efficient through new media) coax customers into "missing things that they have never lost" (*Modernity*, 77). In a variation on the classical theme of "carpe diem", postmodern consumption cultivates, what Appadurai calls, an "aesthetic of ephemerality" (*Modernity*, 83) whereby the rapidly dissolving present (and therefore the future) can only be secured through innumerable objects that embody the "period" style. The aesthetic of ephemerality gains particular momentum in the digital age where speed is everything and time is, quite literally, money. In late capitalism, via a subtle reversal of earlier capitalist logic where consumption signified leisure, time is created by the very act of consumption. The objects purchased simultaneously represent and commodify time so that any time spent not consuming becomes a waste of time. To this can be traced the beginnings of e-commerce where entrepreneurs wanted to cash in on the time we spent surfing the web. One of the primary factors used by venture capitalists to evaluate web-based business proposals was "stickiness" — how often a surfer came to a site and how long she spent there.

This aesthetic of ephemerality works not only in the present but spills into the past. Thus, as any reader of Baudrillard and Lyotard knows, the past turns into a clearing house for different styles displayed for effortless appropriation. The postmodern nostalgic's longing can be adequately mapped onto objects that materialize the past. The concept of irreversible time which enables the bittersweet yearnings of nostalgia makes for a notion of time as repeatable. Time, in other words, enters the domain of exchange to circulate as images and objects. The breakdown of linear time is attributed by postmodern theory to the dizzying circulation of signs unhinged from social and historical signifiers. But this explanation needs to be supplemented by an analysis of the almost instantaneous and global exchange of images made possible by electronic mediation. Such exchanges between "worlds" (first, second, third) makes the disparate chronicities of the globe simultaneously present. Thus the metropolitan subject sees her "past" appear in the periphery as their "present", her "present" their dreamed-off "future" — such spatialization evacuates temporality, turning time into, what Appaduria calls, a feature of the image. Such an understanding of time is properly post-nostalgic (*Modernity*, 37). This phenomenon is most accurately realized in the World Wide Web, a network that enables the continuous circulation of images by replacing linear time with simultaneity.

What further distinguishes authentic nostalgia from its postmodern copies seems to be the nature of the nostalgic object itself: in the first case the object is never quite a commodity, it is an imperfect (kitschy, fake) representation of "the obscure object of nostalgia" and as such marks the beginnings of longing; in the second case of ersatz nostalgia, the object is fully commodified and appears as the very thing that satisfies longing. Such longing approximates to the condition of consumer desire. In this scheme the nostalgic is none other than the desiring consumer whose yearnings for the past, whose fears about the vanishing present can be fulfilled by the proliferation of objects. Postmodern nostalgia is "inauthentic" not on the basis of the thing being remembered (since all nostalgia has an element of fantasy) but rather in that it can be induced, cultivated as affect even in the absence of loss and dislocation. We can all refashion ourselves as nostalgics. What happens, then, to the "real" nostalgic, the one whose being is constituted by an experience of loss? The immigrant, for instance, whose subjectivity is traversed by nostalgia, whose past is another country?

PART 4: HOME PAGES

Yet, there appears to be a formal equivalence between e-subjectivity and diasporic identity. Recent work has stressed the fragmented and fluid nature of self and identity in cyberspace. In her book, *Life On The Screen*, Sherry Turkle notes that virtual reality verifies poststructuralist theories of subjectivity for "more than twenty years after meeting the ideas of Lacan, Foucault, Deleuze and Guattari, I am meeting them again in my new life on the screen. But this time the Gallic abstractions are more concrete. In my computer-mediated worlds, the self is multiple, fluid" (114). Such a development is welcome for "the culture of simulation may help us achieve a vision of multiple but integrated identity whose flexibility, resilience, and capacity for joy comes from having access to our many selves" (117). The special environments of cyberspace — chat rooms, MUDs, MOOs — enable users to create and articulate multifaceted and multifaced identities. Cyberspace, it would appear, is the natural medium for the expression of split immigrant subjectivity. And yet, paradoxically this formal equivalence conceals a radical difference between immigrant and cybersubjectivity for whereas the former is structured by lack, the latter promises prosthetic plenitude.

In an article entitled "Cyberspace, Or the Unbearable Closure of Being," Slavoj Zizek draws attention to one constitutive feature in the discourse of cyberspace: that it is a space without lack. This corresponds exactly with Bill Gates' prediction that the information superhighway would promote friction-free capitalism, a prediction that led to the dot.com boom and bust. The problem as Zisek sees it with this formulation is simply that "desire" cannot survive such plenitude, since "desire" in psychic terms is crucially dependent on lack. If the field of free choice is not confined by a forced choice, the very freedom of choice disappears. More is not better. As he puts it: "the vision of cyberspace opening up a future of unending possibilities of limitless change ... conceals its exact opposite, an unheard of imposition of radical closure" (154). It is for this reason that the discourse on cyberspace careens between the wildly utopic and the bleakly dystopic; what such "extreme" responses express is an inability to come to grips with the virtuality of cyberspace which either threatens or promises (depending on your viewpoint) to collapse the rules and limits of real space.[12] Virtualization in canceling out the necessary distance between a neighbor and a foreigner such that both appear *equal* in their "spectral screen presence" undermines the reality of the other. It throws into particular confusion immigrant ontology for the immigrant *is* the neighbor who is *also* a foreigner. This has very important implications for immigrant subjectivity and nostalgia. As Homi Bhabha puts it: "However wondrous the protean possibilities of online ontologies ... there is danger that the instant simultaneity so often celebrated on the Net in the name of instant 'connectivity' may drain everyday life of its historical memory and its capacity to register the contentions of cultural difference" ("Minority"). Like Zizek, Bhabha wants the solid proximity of the "neighbor" rather than the faceless subjectivity promised by cyberspace as the grounds for cultural memory and community building in the diaspora. Pushing Bhabha's logic one could argue that as new technologies make the nation-state progressively redundant as a unit of substantive identity, the *critical* relationship that the migrant has to the nation-state (an unease that reveals, as we have seen, the illusions and exclusions of nation-building) also falls out of the picture. Difference ceases to matter in the same way.

Immigrant subjectivity, then, is crucially defined by a double alienation: from the home left behind and from the adoptive country. This double alienation is signaled by nostalgia, that metaphorical look backward that forever prevents the immigrant from settling in and that creates the longing for that space of her past. Nostalgia stands in for the lack that defines the immigrant condition itself, the blindness at the edge of interpretation. Spatial and temporal distance and catachrestic souvenirs are the enabling conditions of nostalgia. Cyber-connectivity abolishes the effects of space allowing immigrant subjectivity to reiterate and recreate itself through performance, to march properly in double-time as it were. The altar of distant origin, that stuff that the immigrants' dreams are made of, can now be supplemented and supplicated to by the rituals of contemporary practice. Globalism, as effected by e-communication is, as we have seen, a two-way process. It enables countries in the periphery to catch up with the first world creating both internal and external diasporas that tend to each other. Further, it also enables subjects, immigrant or otherwise, in the center to catch up with their peripheral "homes." In brief, it bridges gaps, virtually undoing dislocation, suturing global asymmetries, bringing plenitude where there was lack.

Our analysis of cyberspace will now focus on specific portals and websites targeted to Indians worldwide. We look, in particular, at two of the portals with the highest number of daily page views — rediff.com and netGuruindia.com. We will also turn to a few e-commerce sites hosted by these portals — phooltime.com and blessingsonthenet.com and giftsindia.com — to see how commodities mediate this reconfiguration of immigrant subjectivity in cyberspace. In theory, of course, these sites can be accessed by any Indian with a computer and an IP address but, in fact, the core group of users have overwhelmingly been Indians connected to the technology industry, the global diaspora we have referred to above.[13] This is definitely the case in India, a country where Internet access though growing exponentially is still limited to a very small slice of the upper middle classes, particularly those in the tech-industry.[14] Given the extent to which such portals depend on "integrated sponsorships" from e-vendors, the relative lack of purchasing power in India and the limited nature of consumer credit means that the primary market from the sponsors' point of view remains the global diaspora of external and internal immigrants.[15] In fact, rediff.com, one of the first entrants into the portal segment, started out as an information site based out of Mumbai driven by "the Non-Resident Indian's hunger for news from home." Rediff had defined itself as an "India-centric megaportal" that catered to a worldwide audience. For CEO Balakrishnan, immigrant nostalgia was quite precisely a business opportunity and while there has always been a market in India to cater to the special needs of the NRI (the acronym NRI, Non-Resident Indian, is an official demographic category), the time-space configurations of the Internet made possible hitherto unimaginable synergies. Rediff's corporate goal is thus expressed by Balakrishnan, "What we eventually want the company to become is a kind of all things to all people Website" ("Master"). This bountiful vision of seamless exchange, where community and identity are repackaged as products and where products in turn constitute community and identity, admits none of the asymptotes of nostalgia.

The products of communicative exchange, literally and metaphorically, frame these sites. For instance, the welcoming pages for both netGuruindia.com and rediff.com are embedded within banners that advertise phone cards, cellular service, v-mail video messages from "near and dear ones", airline tickets and online gift services. The gift link brings us to a page which announces "Are you looking for ethnic, cultural nostalgic gift items — look no further." The home page for the "Gift Store" is hyperlinked to cross-referenced menus that provide a precise catalog of objects, sorted by region (crucial in a multi-ethnic society like India and evidence of extensive customization) and category. The categories traverse the gamut from the occasional to the practical: so the buyer can take her pick from TVs and kitchen appliances to regional attires and sweets freshly made in the city of his choice. These gifts, usually local goods delivered by local vendors, mark a radical break in the practice of immigrant gifting.

As Marcel Mauss argued in his classic work on the topic, there is no pure, unmotivated gift. Mauss' analysis of archaic societies shows that there is a logic to the gift for gifts are regulated by rules and the practice of gifting builds social solidarity. As anthropologist Mary Douglas writes in her foreword to the work, "The cycling gift system is the society" (ix). Part of the *price* of immigration was that the immigrant subject was excluded from the gift-giving cycle, and hence from the society she had left behind. However prized the return of the prodigal son, the relation of immigrant to home was not primarily an economic one.[16] The immigrant came home bearing gifts, but these were not true gifts, they assumed no reciprocity, they were loot being given away in charity, as was the practice of remittance. If economy is fundamentally about reciprocity and exchange, then immigrant and home were connected solely in an affective economy — of mutual longing and remembrances, of lockets and fading photographs, of letters to and fro, of visits and departures.

E-commerce introduces the gift into the domain of diaspora, thus providing an entirely new locus for immigrant subjectivity. The practice is banal, with few clicks of a mouse (Balakrishnan guarantees "No more than two clicks will let you make a purchase on our website" ['Marketplace']), one initiates the delivery of some gift to a friend or relative, but its consequences have great import. What is delivered is not merely an object but oneself. Through the prosthetic that is e-commerce, the immigrant self is inserted into the circuit of ordinary life, her gift is one amongst many for the occasion, it becomes a routinized act of the habitus, thoroughly domesticated. Through repetitive gift-giving the immigrant subject becomes reinserted into the circuit of sociality. The fact that these gifts are globally purchased but locally produced is itself significant for cyberspace instantiates the global through the concretely local. The local is thereby produced by the flow of global desires, as we saw above with Bangalore. In place of the approximate part-objects of immigrant nostalgia, the gift store introduces an embarrassment of riches. The immigrant can now order a hot meal from a favorite restaurant to a dear one who is now miraculously near or the latest CD before it is in the stores or movie tickets to the new blockbuster at the neighborhood theatre (www.thegiftstore.com). Even the items listed under the category "souvenirs and handicrafts" are hardly the kitschy wallhangings and statues that adorn immigrant homes in the new land: they are trendy, varied, individualized expressions of the purchasing power of the dollar crosshatched with newly indigenized taste.

This process of "deimmigration," as it were, is played out even at a metaphysical level. Just as one gives gifts to one's friends and kinfolk to remain social, one gives votive offerings to the gods to remain properly Hindu. To be fully efficacious this *puja* or act of worship has to be performed at the right time and directed to the right deity. And the hindu religion (the majority faith in India) has hundreds of thousands of deities, each with its own particular *puja* routine. Enterprises like saranam.com offer the immigrant subject the option of a customized, personalized *puja* performed on her behalf in the temple of her choice. Not only is the devotee's prayer transported across the seas, the gods too answer back through the miracles of e-communication and modern transportation: once the *puja* is performed the *prasad* — food which has been sanctified by the blessing of the god — is packed and sent to the customer by UPS. The immigrant subject then is continually returned home, voyaging back by means of small acts of social and metaphysical manners. Saranam.com's special features include "pujas performed at over 250 top temples, 27 packages and electronic consultations with priests." The home page highlights some of the more obscure deities, providing snappily edited contextual material and offering "specials and promotions" for trying out *pujas* on new dieties. Another site, blessingsonthenet.com, goes a step further and provides realvideo and realplayer broadcasts of *pujas* and festivals. While the philosophically-minded among us might cringe at such crass commodification, there is no gainsaying, that at one level, sites like these both feed and put an end to certain kinds of nostalgic longing for the pujas and festivals of the past.[17]

What are the consequences of this "transportation of presence"? Loss, rootlessness and nostalgia are being replaced by a circuit of commodities which interpellate and reinscribe immigrant desire into the discrete transactions of e-commerce. In other words, the possibility of reinsertion negates those affective and psychic structures that constituted immigrant subjectivity as a tragic one. The constant "being there" made possible by cyberspace leads to a death of tragedy. In fact "being there" proves to be generative of new modes of subjectivity in the homeland. Immigrant subject desire inserts new signifiers into the discursive space of the homeland. Phooltime.com enables its customers to have flowers delivered in any city in India. What is remarkable here is not the convenience, nor the Hallmarkstyle tackiness — arrangements like "Just Because" or "Across the Miles" — but the very existence of the practice. Flowers in India have four main functions, as social decoration, public appreciation (garlanding a musician or leader), religious practice (flowers are thrown at the deity's feet) and for personal adornment (worn on the hair by women). They do not, however, act as signifiers for affective transactions between two people. Phooltime.com then not only inserts immigrant subjectivity into the field of Indian sociality, it also helps to introduce Western subjectivizing devices. The subject who uses flowers as a carrier of emotions is the Western subject of romantic love. Gift-giving through e-commerce then has two aspects: it returns the immigrant subject by locating her desire in day-to-day practice; it displaces the Indian socius by introducing into it new modes of subject-making. The "difference" between subjects and subject-positions — differences that come from the asymmetries of desire and location — are increasingly being eroded in the unvarying spatial environment of cyberspace.

Such a change points to the beginnings of a new formation: a global Indian subject who can be reduced neither to "native" nor to "immigrant." The manifestations of this global subject are often deeply local. The websites and portals pride themselves on the variety and diversity of their localization. NetGuruindia.com is available in several Indian languages and has, at least, five metropolitan editions. Each edition, though created on the same template and advertising the same products, is modified. This is a notion of the local that is driven by the customizing capabilities of a new technology rather than the thick descriptions of context. It is a local produced by the inscriptions of global desire and modeled on a universal template that sets the frames and limits of the particular. At one level, surfing the pages of some of the prominent India-centered sites on the web, we are struck by the extent of customization. As a peculiarly transnational form, these web pages unpack into its many constituting localities and ethnicities the postcolonial abstraction that is India. At the same time, this pluralization occurs through a mode of re-packaging that actually evens out the textures of difference. The new formula seems to read: global frame, local color. The topography of Internet technology — the frontend-backend dualism mediated by middleware — perfectly realizes this formulation. As Appadurai puts it:

> The central feature of global culture today is the politics of mutual effort of sameness and difference to cannibalize one another and thus to proclaim their successful hijacking of the twin Enlightenment ideal of the triumphantly universal and the resiliently particular ... ("Disjuncture", 298)

I want to conclude by examining two sites that illustrate this new formation not only in terms of textual features but also in terms of the subject these texts produce. They are the recently deceased chaitime.com headquartered in Philadelphia[18] and rediff.com based in Bombay. These texts display a complex set of connections, resemblances and linkages. Though emerging from totally different economic contexts, it is hard to tell the difference these contexts make; it could easily be the case that chaitime (with its Indian sounding name, the word for tea in many Indian languages is "chai") was based in India and rediff (with an Anglicized name) in Philadelphia. Both sites seem to be incarnations of the same pan-Indian subject. Chaitime.com itself splits into three "local" selves: chaitime US, chaitime UK, and chaitime India. Locale, however, is continuously framed and transgressed by global hypertextuality. At the top of each page, on 11 December 2000 was a banner for half.com, a company that sells books, CDs, movies and games. Is half.com British, American or even Indian? We don't know. On the same day, chaitime India contains a feature on actor Sunil Shetty in the Bollywood (a name for the Hindi film industry, itself a play on Hollywood) channel, chaitime US has Bollywood dreams, the UK version has its Bollywood channel. Again, while websurfing on 11 December 2000, we see that rediff USA is Indianized by advertising Hanuman Jayanti celebrations and Bhajans, rediff India is Westernized by featuring Christmas offerings. Each approximates to the condition of the other — all things to all people. Everything is linked to something else which is linked in turn to a shopping cart. If there is a dizzying sense of travel between pages, between sites, between locales and between cultures, what stays this motion is indeed a commercial transaction. The time it takes for us to accurately enter in our credit card number and have it approved is a resting place. Indeed, hypertextuality may be the perfect metaphor or trope for describing the emerging global subjectivities. It is not so much that such subjects are split, rather that every subject becomes a node which is linked to a multiplicity of networks. This hypertextual subject exceeds locality, culture and nation; it is situated in the pathways, the vectors of cross-cultural, transnational desire and flow.

The hypertextual subject is spoken in a frenetic and fragmented manner. Chaitime.com describes itself as providing "interactive games, breaking news, downloadable music clips, timely articles, lively chat rooms, free email and a constant revamping of all these features" ("homepage", 4 November 2000). Global subjectivity speaks in a series of blips scattered across many domains.

It thus constitutes a totally new voice and register. The immigrant subject had in the past been compelled to record and discover itself through the totalizing and essentializing forms of lyric poetry and the autobiographical novel. These resulted in objectifications which were meant to preserve the disappearing self, much like the artifacts did for the disappearing culture of one's homeland. Cyberspace endows immigration with an alternate subjectivity. The immigrant subject no longer needs to either collect objects or turn itself into an object, it can now plug into a website and instantly realize desire and memory, no more than two clicks away from the end of nostalgia.

11

Very Busy Just Now:
Globalization and Harriedness in Ishiguro's
The Unconsoled

Bruce Robbins

Readers of Kazuo Ishiguro's novel *The Remains of the Day* (1989) will have no trouble remembering the novel's case against professionalism. "Our professional duty is not to our own foibles and sentiments," the butler-protagonist tells Miss Kenton, "but to the wishes of our employer" (149). Professionalism, the explicit center of the butler's belief-system, seems responsible both for his personal sacrifice of love with Miss Kenton and for his moral failure in backing his employer's pro-Nazi diplomacy. Lord Darlington convenes a conference of European diplomats at Darlington Hall in March 1923 in order to make "a strong moral case for a relaxing of various aspects of the Versailles treaty, emphasizing the great suffering he had himself witnessed in Germany" (92). In the years and pages that follow, we see Lord Darlington as an open anti-Semite whose efforts to stop the approaching war with Germany align him with the fascists. In case we miss the point, the 1923 conference is also the moment when the butler's father, lying upstairs gravely ill, has a stroke and dies while Stevens himself, who has been warned that the end is near, refuses to interrupt his professional attentions to the diplomats downstairs. Told that his father has passed away, he remarks that he is "very busy just now."[1]

It does not seem accidental that Ishiguro's case against professionalism, which leads the butler to serve Lord Darlington's ends so blindly, is simultaneously a case against cosmopolitanism. Each is presented as an unnatural detachment from ordinary emotions: erotic love, love of country. Each also offers substitute emotions, *re*-attachments, and these substitute emotions are reciprocally reinforcing. Lord Darlington's cosmopolitanism, the novel suggests, stems from his aristocratic status; rather than indifference, it expresses a positive solidarity with his German fellow aristocrats that's more compelling to him than the interest she shares with fellow Englishmen of the lower orders. "'He was my enemy,'" Darlington observes of a German diplomat, "'but he always behaved like a gentleman. We treated each other decently over six months of shelling each other. He was a gentleman doing his job and I bore him no malice'" (73). A gentleman doing his job: skipping forward in time, one is tempted to say that doing your job competently has become the modern equivalent of feudalism's pre-national gentility. For it too overrides the moral obligations of national membership by conferring the moral privilege of *trans*-national membership: the privilege of being treated decently despite shelling or other forms of long-range aggression. One can speculate, in other words, that professionalism has replaced aristocracy in providing a social glue and ethical grounding for cosmopolitanism. This would explain why, for example, Alvin Gouldner sees his "New Class," a forerunner of the Ehrenreichs' "professional-managerial class" and Robert Reich's "symbolic analysts," as encouraging "a cosmopolitan identity, transcending national limits and enhancing their autonomy from local elites" (2).[2] With its peculiar ability to produce bonds among detached, institutionally scattered subjects, bonds that are suffused with affect though not always created or sustained by the frequent face-to-face engagements of the same-site work group, professionalism would seem well suited to new trans-national demands for loyalty and solidarity at a distance, whether corporate or quasi-governmental. The question is whether this is any cause for celebration.

Common sense would suggest, with Ishiguro's apparent blessing, that it is anything but. In his book *Famine Crimes: Politics and the Disaster Relief Industry in Africa*, Alex de Waal strikes a representative note of cynicism when he suggests that "the struggle against famine has become professionalized and institutionalized" (5). It has been taken over, that is, by a "cosmopolitan elite of relief workers, officials of donor agencies, consultant academics and the like" (3–4), and these people are mainly concerned with establishing "moral ownership of famine" (xvi), "widening the scope for humanitarian and human rights organizations to intrude (in certain ways) into the affairs of African nations" (xv). Quoting Ivan Illich, who advocates the abolition of schools and hospitals in the name of peasant self-sufficiency, de Waal proposes that "'to help [is] to interfere'" (5). He suggests that "the intrusion of humanitarian institutions represents, in an insidious but profound way, a disempowerment of the people directly engaged in the crisis, which drains their capacity to find a solution ... external involvement, however well-intentioned, almost invariably damages the search for local political solutions" (xvi).

People like ourselves tend to be ambivalent about professional activities, including our own, and about *any* activities that cross national borders, especially when they claim to serve purely humanitarian interests. Given the inequality of access to trans-national mobility and to credentials, as well as the many reasons to distrust those humanitarian, altruistic rationales that cosmopolitanism and professionalism share, and given that warm affective ties within the profession are no guarantee of its ethical value from the perspective of those outside it, such ambivalence is probably on the whole a good and necessary thing. Still, people like ourselves should also suspect the general eagerness to view all professional claims to the "common good" as solely and inevitably a devious form of self-interest. Consider what the model of professionalism-as-disempowerment would suggest about such features of the social welfare state as — to take a pertinent example — taxpayer-supported public education. According to this model, public education would have to be seen as a conspiracy of the Powers That Be to create teaching jobs for the professional-managerial elite while also de-educating and mis-educating the masses. It could not be seen, alternatively, as a political compromise arrived at in large part because working class people demanded free public education for their children and actively fought for it. It's as if providing jobs for middle-class teachers could only be a zero-sum game whereby working class families lost out for each teacher hired.

This zero-sum logic does not seem any more persuasive when it is aimed at humanitarian NGOs (non-governmental organizations) working transnationally, whatever other critiques may apply. Thus the interesting doubling up of anti-professionalism and anti-cosmopolitanism, whether in famine relief or in Ishiguro, provides an occasion when common sense seems to stand in double need of adjustment. That is the first hypothesis here. The second is that, thanks to this same doubling or mutual reinforcement, ambivalence about *work* also expresses ambivalence about *globalization*. In other words, the doubling is a perceptual convenience making it possible to work through the meaning of the latter in terms of the former.

For most of us in the metropolis it is extraordinarily difficult most of the time to register the existence of the global or transnational domain as a matter of personal significance. If we can see it, we can't hold it in focus for very long or assimilate it to the other things we spend our days doing and caring about. And if it is not part of our everyday actions and anxieties, then it will not become part of our fiction. This is the gist of Salman Rushdie's bon mot about the English not understanding their history because so much of it has happened elsewhere. And it is the point Raymond Williams's interviewers make, in the volume *Politics and Letters*, when they remind Williams that even the English social novel of the 1840s had virtually nothing to say about the Irish famine, which was a direct consequence of how English society was organized, and a consequence happening only a stone's throw from England's shores. The empire was not part of the "structure of feeling," hence not easy or convenient material for the novel (164–65). We cannot assume in advance that the international division of labor will somehow inevitably show up in the cultural expressions of the metropolis, even when much of what goes on in the metropolis is arguably determined by its place in that division of labor. So if a window on such determinations does unexpectedly open up, if even a narrow slice of the logic connecting metropolis and periphery suddenly becomes visible, it's in our interest to have a look.

The "very busy just now" moment in *Remains of the Day* offers us such a window not only because it represents the close historical link between professionalism and cosmopolitanism, but also because it stages the intrusion of work into the intimate sphere of the family, and because this somewhat anachronistic intrusion has an obvious basis in the late twentieth-century integration of capitalism on a global scale. What we now perceive as everyday harriedness, the perpetual time deficit and time anxiety associated with what National Public Radio has been calling "the juggling act," results in large part from the so-called "restructuring" of companies, the preference for part-time or "flexible" labor and "just-in-time" production, the systemic acceleration of innovation and cultivation of insecurity in the pursuit of short-term profit that has been called "flexible accumulation" or "post-Fordism." None of this will be news to anyone. Post-Fordism's harried style, speeded-up pace, and sense of being beset by too many tasks and too little time is not limited to the denizens of the new 24/7 digital sweatshops or to stockbrokers pressured to follow the markets in a dizzying multitude of time zones. Control of time has become a scarce and highly valuable commodity for almost everybody, and lacking that control has all sorts of repercussions for gender relations and the quality of family life. Basic acts of citizenship like voting come to seem heroic, and activism almost superhuman. Insecurity about the future, both immediate and distant, becomes a political issue of almost the same order of importance as wages. Especially in families with children where both adults work, as is now the rule, all this harriedness means a new level of generalized stress. On the model of post-Fordism and post-Marxism and all the other posts of our time, we might rebaptize this period "post-Haste."

This time pressure *reflects* global capital, of course, but that is not the only relation between the two terms. The word "reflects" misses the relative autonomy of the cultural from the economic — the possibility of economic damage translating, however unsatisfactorily, into some sort of cultural benefit, and even twisting back upon itself to offer purchase on or against global capital. In her book *The Time Bind*, Arlie Russell Hochschild observes that the cult of efficiency has been transferred from the office to the home, so that parents "increasingly find themselves in the role of 'time and motion' experts" (51). Yet it is also true, she concludes, that "many women are ... joining men in a flight from the 'inner city' of home to the 'suburbs' of the workplace" (247) and seeking at work the emotional satisfactions that had once seemed available to them only at home. For many women, blurring the lines between work and family is exhilarating, even something of a moral liberation. And what holds for the possibility of acting and bonding outside the family also holds for the possibility of acting and bonding outside the nation. This second possibility is discursively attached to the first and carried along with it by the fact that the family serves as common term in two parallel debates. Both the domain of work, on the one hand, and the domain of the international, on the other hand, are repeatedly defined against the family, which is asked to stand in for all the values that are supposedly sacrificed to their voracious demands. Dickens's Mrs Jellyby in *Bleak House*, who neglects her own children while devoting herself to a scheme for emigration to Africa, is the type (I've seen her quoted recently in two books of political theory) of an argument in which the family is mobilized against international commitments, its natural intimacy metaphorically bestowed on the vast anonymous populations of modern nation-states so as to claim correspondingly natural priority for those near and-dear to us at the expense of immigrants, foreign workers selling goods on American markets, and other non-nationals. From the viewpoint of the family, work is a foreign country.

But this equation can have unexpected results. Even the notorious conflict between the demands of work and family is a true dilemma in the sense that it cannot simply be resolved in favor of either side. Much will be said, will *have* to be said, on the side of work. And anything said on behalf of work will also resonate on behalf of the foreign. Think for example of Warren Beatty's film *Reds*, which made an uncharacteristically sympathetic case for American solidarity with the Bolshevik Revolution, and did so by framing its internationalist politics within a much more familiar narrative, a narrative about — of all things — the conflict between work and family, the strains of the two-career couple as lived by John Reed and Louise Bryant, Beatty and Diane Keaton. If work *is* a foreign country, as the film in effect suggests, if it is no more of a stretch to imagine someone giving her strongest feelings to work than to imagine someone giving her feelings to another nation's revolution, then what we've got here is something like the opposite of the anti-professional and anti-cosmopolitan logic Ishiguro seems to be laying out: making a case *for* work may mean making a case *for* internationalism. Or less ambitiously: if a case for cosmopolitanism *can* be made, meaning a case for some mode of global belonging that does not merely reflect global capital, but that will be necessary in order to *understand and act upon* global capital, such a case will perhaps only be made, or made real to us, within the shared vocabulary of everyday over-commitment, overload, harriedness.

In Ishiguro's penultimate and perhaps most extraordinary novel, *The Unconsoled* (1995), this "very busy just now" theme is both intensified and tied still more tightly to the domain of the international.[3] *The Unconsoled* seems to elevate harriedness into a sort of ontological principle, a description of Being itself. A famous musician, Ryder, arrives for the first time in a foreign city. In a citiscape of classical abstraction — no language specified, but no translation problems; no maps, street plans, or calendars; no ties to any identifiable locality — he finds himself moving at strangely varying speeds, sometimes breakneck, sometimes boring, through the seemingly choreographed but always confused schedule of his much-awaited visit. Asked again and again by near-strangers for awkward if not impossible favors, he is manifestly incapable of answering the many and wildly divergent claims on his time and attention. A globe-trotting father somewhat estranged from a stay-at-home family, Ryder finds he cannot do everything he has promised; he cannot practice for his performance, write his speech, act fast on a new house for his family, take care of the child who is or is not his. The novel's distortions of time and space become a metaphor for the harriedness of ordinary life, and the conflicting demands of home and work become a metaphor for the conflicting scales and rhythms of the foreign and the domestic. The two metaphors join in Ryder's memory of a recent conjugal argument:

"Look," I had been saying to her, my voice still calm, "the fact is, people need me. I arrive in a place and more often than not find terrible problems, and people are so grateful I've come."

Sophie's response to this rationale echoes de Waal's critique of humanitarian professionalism:

"But how much longer can you go on doing this for people? And for us. I mean for you and me and Boris, time's slipping away. Before you know it, Boris will be grown up. No one can expect you to keep on like this. And all these people, why can't they sort out their own problems? It might do them some good!"

To which Ryder answers:

"... Some of these places I visit, the people don't know a thing. They don't know the first thing about modern music and if you leave them to themselves, it's obvious, they'll just get deeper and deeper into trouble. I'm needed, why can't you see that? I'm needed out here! You don't know what you're talking about!" And it was then I had shouted at her: "Such a small world! You live in such a small world!" (37)

Critics of Ishiguro often point to a mysterious blockage of emotion between his characters. The frameworks usually chosen to describe this blockage are psychoanalytic and metaphysical. Despite his intriguingly anomalous status as a British writer with a Japanese name, critics have not leapt to interpret this theme of dammed-up emotion in the "small world" (that is, larger world) context of globalization. Yet the move seems worth trying out. In her book *The Overworked American*, Juliet Schor argues that it is not merely health and repose that are sacrificed to overwork: "People *will* work on their time off. They will work hard and long in what is formally designated as leisure time." But this work is not to be confused, Schor says, with a "quest for the second paycheck. Americans need time for unpaid work, for work they call their own. They need the time to give to others. Much of what will be done was the regular routine in the days when married women were full-time housewives. And it is largely caring work — caring for children, caring for sick relatives and friends, caring for the house. Today many haven't got the time to care" (160). Not having "the time to care" — the phrase links two of the most distinctive aspects of *The Unconsoled*, time deficit and the blockage of caring. If this is right, if the inability to care results from or is an aspect of the deficit of time, then stories about not having enough time, like *The Unconsoled*, acquire another interpretive dimension. The temporal limits on caring, which can be experienced without leaving the kitchen, become a way of confronting experientially the *geographical* limits on caring, the global borders of solicitude, which are harder to experience or to make into stories.

With this suggestion in mind, even *Remains of the Day* perhaps deserves another inspection. If a novelist as deep as Ishiguro seems to be saying something as superficial and uninteresting as "don't work too hard" or "overwork is bad for the family," perhaps the dullness is more in our reading than in his writing. We need not take at face value those easy, tried-and-true moral counters that Ishiguro seems to favor, like showing proper respect at the death of a parent and proper disrespect for Nazis, neither one of them a very controversial position. Perhaps this extreme moral obviousness is the sign of a mystery, an interpretive invitation.

In a "post-Haste" or "time bind" context, the title *The Remains of the Day* takes on a different irony. The mild pun on "remains" as both "time remaining in" and the "corpse of" the day would seem to underline the waste of the butler's life, a life evaded and distorted by means of professional rationalization and overwork. But it also suggests, less obviously, why readers should care about such a monstrous and unrepresentative creature. After all, even those of us who have not ignored a dying father in order to serve a pro-Nazi master also have reason to ask, along with the title, what remains of the day when the hours devoted to work are over. Or, more subversively: are we making a mistake when we think of "real" life as the remainder left over once work has been subtracted? At the risk of perversity, I'm tempted to suggest that Ishiguro makes use of the anachronism of the butler and the great English country house in part so as to offer an almost futuristic portrait of a *pure or absolute workplace* — a workplace which is also a residence for those who work there and which thus precludes the daily contest between work and family that would otherwise seem so inescapable. There is no familial life: we are left in the dark as to when and how Stevens *père* ever could have managed to sire Stevens *fils*. Yet one can perhaps detect a utopian tinge to this microcosm. When the titular metaphor displaces the work/family conflict from the scale of the day to the scale of the life, it conflates one's daily leisure, or "real" life, the locus of the family's claims, with one's retirement, hence also with one's mortality, thereby taking on a somewhat melancholy if not morbid coloring. Can we imagine that the sinking of the heart produced by this conflation of familial privacy with approaching death is part of an argument on Ishiguro's part, an argument *against* opposing work now to the endlessly postponed real life to come?

This would of course be counterintuitive, given the novel's enthusiastic satire of the butler's emotional frigidity and compulsive industriousness. But it dovetails nicely with a provocative reading by Renata Salecl. According to Salecl, professionalism in this novel is not set against love, as it might appear. "The masks of decency, professionalism, and a sexuality" that seem to block Stevens from his desire are actually what he desires. "It is useless to search in Stevens for some hidden love that could not come out because of the rigid ritual he engaged himself in — all of his love is in the rituals. Inasmuch as it can be said that he loves Miss Kenton, he loves her from the perspective of submission to the codes of their profession" (185).[4] What Salecl perceives in *Remains of the Day* is the historically emergent eroticizing of expertise and of the social bonds for which expertise stands. In other words, the erotically unconsummated affection between the butler and Miss Kenton, a relationship between colleagues that will not lead to marriage and children, exemplifies a characteristic professional affectivity, an affectivity that substitutes recruitment for reproduction and that has come to assume a larger and larger place in our lives, in our narratives, and not coincidentally in the fashioning of global or transnational subjects. The idea that the butler may have been right to love Miss Kenton in and for the working collegiality they shared, rather than wrong not to have followed her out of the workplace and into the founding of a normal heterosexual family, receives support from an unexpected quarter. Ishiguro does not deny the possibility that, historically speaking, Lord Darlington was right — that "a freezing of German reparation payments" in 1923, as he proposed at his conference, might indeed have stopped the Second World War from happening.[5] In terms of the novel's apparent moral clarity, this is a disturbing hypothesis, yet it was maintained in the 1920s by figures as respectable as John Maynard Keynes and by many subsequent historians. It is so disturbing that the film version avoids the idea entirely by pushing the conference forward into the 1930s, when the Nazis were already in power and there can no longer be any question that Lord Darlington is making a grave error. And if Darlington was *not* making an error, if the stakes at Darlington Hall in 1923 were indeed as large as the Second World War, then it is much harder to argue that the butler's extreme, almost inhuman devotion to his professional duty at this conference was a self-evident piece of self-delusion.[6] So both the anti-professionalism and the anti-cosmopolitanism of the novel are thrown into some doubt.

Here I switch back to *The Unconsoled*. As reviewers were quick to point out, there is a strong continuity between the butler of *The Remains of the Day* and *The Unconsoled*'s hotel porter, who appears on the novel's second page and introduces us to its characteristic play with time and space. Riding up in the elevator minutes after his arrival in this anonymous Central European city, Ryder innocently asks the elderly porter why he doesn't put the bags down. The porter, whose name turns out to be Gustav, responds to this as if it were a genuine question, launching into a leisurely, roundabout speech about the professional history and standards of hotel porters. Time passes. The ride takes on the feel of a casual evening among friends. It is suddenly difficult to distinguish the elevator from a living room (a new character is discovered standing in the corner). Pages and pages go by; all the while the elevator is still supposedly rising, and the porter is still holding the bags, and still speaking. Years before, Gustav says, he had overheard a chance remark to the effect that carrying bags would mean not having a care in the world. He has connected that remark to others (times and places of the remarks supplied in unnecessary detail) suggesting that being a porter is something that requires no special skill, something anyone could do. And he has concluded that porters must assert the dignity and difficulty of their vocation — for example, by never resting on the job. So, no, he won't put the bags down. The notion of professional standards as horrifyingly rigorous, and even ultimately fatal, even though they are also arbitrary and unnecessary, supports Pico Iyer's description of the porter as "Stevens the butler in a new disguise" (22).

One of a series of locals who obstruct the global hero's progress through his visit by politely demanding small but increasingly burdensome favors for themselves or their loved ones, Gustav wants Ryder to use his upcoming speech to say a word on behalf of porters. From Ryder's point of view, these demands become nightmarishly irritating. The porter who takes portering too seriously is clearly offered as a comic parallel to the over serious professionalism of Ryder himself, a musician who is so rarely at home that when he gets there it looks like just another stop — some of the faces and places vaguely familiar, others not — on his endless tour of concerts and lectures. The idea that this foreign city may after all *be* his home is one of the novel's darkest and longest-running jokes. Perhaps Gustav's daughter, with whom the porter asks him to undertake a sort of diplomatic mission, is actually his own wife? Surely he has seen her somewhere before? At the end of the novel Gustav's death will cement this side of the plot. It is immediately after his death — brought on, it is suggested, by voluntary overwork — that Ryder is expelled from his perhaps-family by his perhaps-wife. The expulsion is aimed both at his professionalism and at his cosmopolitanism. He is "outside of our grief," Sophie says, just as he was always "outside of our love." " 'Leave him be, Boris. Let him go around the world, giving out his expertise and wisdom' " (532).

Like Gustav, it seems, Ryder is killing himself for his job while not addressing either his own real emotional needs or those of his loved ones. As Iyer puts it: "in honoring little obligations, [he] has missed out on the biggest ones ... he has cheated himself out of a life" (22). Professionalism, or belief in the redemptive value of our work, is thus (to quote Michael Wood) one of "the stories we tell ourselves to keep other stories away" (18). It is a delusion, as we see again in the anticlimactic ending, where Ryder never gets either to lecture or even to play. When he finally gets on stage, after so many distractions and interruptions, there's no audience left, and even the seats have been removed from the auditorium. Yet the fact that he hasn't performed isn't even noticed by the community, which has somehow re-formed itself happily around the night's other, no doubt locally more significant, events. So all his sacrifice of the personal has been for nothing.

If so, the moral again seems disappointingly simplistic. Louis Menand writes that Ishiguro's "single insight into the human condition is that people need love but continually spoil their chances of getting it, a piece of wisdom slightly below the level of Dr. Joyce Brothers" (7). With respect to professionalism, this wisdom is worse than merely advice-column dumb. Contrasting the family's real emotional needs to the empty show of professional performance is a piece of ideological privatism that excludes from the real such things as the need for respect and connection to the larger community. It makes the real into the private, the public into the false. This moral seems strangely out of sync with a novel of such formidable scale and virtuosity. But I would suggest that it is in fact overturned by the very premise of metaphysical harriedness that is the novel's real center. Consider: if this *is* Ryder's home after all, then he is *right* to listen respectfully to the endless disquisition of Gustav on porters, if for no other reason than that this is not an anonymous porter he will never see again but his wife's father. If the man carrying your bags turns out to have a daughter who turns out possibly to be your wife, then any stranger may turn out to be a member of your family and should thus be treated as such. Any porter deserves the kind of patient, respectful, even utopian attention that hotel guests are not in the habit of extending to hotel personnel.

From this perspective, the novel's metaphysical fireworks take on an unexpected ethical dimension. Ryder's long-suffering desire to please, though interrupted by fits of hysterical petulance when he realizes he has no time to practice the piano or decide what he's going to say in his speech, would not be a reprehensible passivity, a professional deformation resulting from too much time on the road. Rather, it would belong to a stretching of the human sensibility to accommodate the unaccustomed rhythms and ranges of sympathy that are demanded of us all in the oft-described age of global flows. The traveler's strained, fragile politeness would be properly seen as a stressed-out, lugubrious version of what we all feel, travelers or not, to the extent that we are stretched and stressed by the larger and larger circles of our interdependence. It would be a figure for one phase in the long-term project of refashioning ethics to suit our transnational condition.

This may seem like too public and political a vocabulary for a novel so manifestly concerned with the bitter blockage of intimate feeling. Yet the pains Ishiguro takes to set the novel's pattern of emotional demands and withdrawals in a context of sanitized foreignness, a foreignness that specifies no nationalities and thus can offend no one, and indeed may not be foreign at all, yet around which the perhaps-visitor so persistently defines his role — all this assertion and withdrawal of foreignness suggests that work-related blockage of emotion in the intimacy of the family is also a figure for blockage of emotion on a transnational scale. Perhaps the most precise way to say this, borrowing a phrase from the dissertation-in-progress of Katherine Stanton, is to call *The Unconsoled* a "European Union" novel. Its hero wavers between cruel emotional withdrawal, especially at moments when consolation is called for, and helpless entrapment in nightmarish proximity to seemingly distant figures, like the porter who suddenly makes absurdly disproportionate claims on his time and attention. Both the claims and the wavering are characteristic of a moment when, with the borders of Europe in the long and sometimes bloody process of being redrawn, the usual guidelines have disappeared that once helped us separate (for better or worse) legitimate from illegitimate claims. We have become even less clear than we used to be as to who we must or must not let in, and on what grounds. We are unclear as to where the First World ends and the Third or (as in this novel) the Second begins. We are more confused than we have ever been as to when and where and whether to release our sympathy, or our bombers — when and where and whether a particular set of atrocities is close enough to demand so-called humanitarian intervention, or not.[7] It's the moment of Kosovo, which is to say the moment when we are equally unsure about what was done on our behalf in Kosovo and about what was not done in Chechnya, or in any number of other places. It's the moment when the exhaustion that comes of daily harriedness melts indistinguishably into what we have learned to call "compassion fatigue."

The phrase "compassion fatigue" could have served as Ishiguro's subtitle — less because he accepts this concept, I think, than because he obsessively questions it. Are we sure such a thing exists? In her recent book of that name, Susan Moeller argues that "Compassion fatigue is not an unavoidable consequence of covering the news," but only "an unavoidable consequence of the way the news is now covered" (2).[8] Her fatigue trope often seems to undercut this argument, suggesting an exhaustion that follows inevitably from the objective limits on disposable time, attention, and (perhaps) sympathy. Moeller writes: "we can't respond to every appeal. And so we've come to believe that we don't care" (9). "The big complaint that [newspapers] hear from readers is 'I don't have time' " (30). And yet the trope is undercut by the "oft-cited passage in Jonathan Kozol's book on poverty in urban America, *Amazing Grace*," where (as Moeller paraphrases) "a mother with AIDS is told about compassion fatigue among the well-to-do. She says to Kozol, 'I don't understand what they have done to get so tired.' "[9] When she quotes this passage, Moeller returns to her argument that without the flaws in media coverage, and with some better outlet in action, we would *not* be "so tired." If our tiredness is a relative rather than an absolute condition, then the harriedness in *The Unconsoled* could also be seen as a temporal metaphor representing a dilemma that is not itself wholly or even primarily temporal: the dilemma of conflicting and uncertain demands for sympathy and solidarity. The problem would not at bottom have to do with the scarcity of time. The feeling of overload that many of us experience in a temporal mode, as a fact about time and not having enough of it, would have as its real referent the uncertainty of borders and the social units and solidarities, the nations and the cities, they more or less roughly delineate.[10] The real problem would be a matter of the polis and its principles, the institutions and available modes of action by which we define or delimit our belonging.

The notion of a natural limit to compassion, an emotional exhaustion as absolutely predictable as the limits on the energy of human muscles or the 24-hour limit to the day, should I think be understood as one of the more successful ideological spin-offs of the myth of globalization. Globalization is a myth because, or to the extent that, it presents a real but partial and contingent phenomenon (capitalism's global integration is much more pronounced at the level of finance, for example, than in production or even trade) as if it were total, natural, and inevitable, beyond human intervention.[11] The slippage from capitalism to global capitalism is a way of slipping the actors responsible across the border into an unspecifiable elsewhere where their decision-making will no longer seem accessible to our powers of oversight and contestation, where they can no longer be held accountable. By the same logic, it seems useless to complain that there are only 24 hours in the day; we may wish it had more, but that's the way things are. And thus the problems of the planet will have to keep. For now, there's dinner to be cooked, bedtime stories to be read, the garbage to be taken out. The day itself becomes your enemy, and the fact that so little remains of it. The logic is so compelling that it's hard to remember that, as with globalization, we are dealing with a mixture of reality and trope.

By identifying Ryder with the global and Sophie and Boris with the local, one would be tempted to conclude that Ishiguro is denouncing the destructive effects of globalization (in the form of overwork) on the intimate sphere of the family. But such a reading would have to ignore all the ostentatious play with time and space, all the deliberate uncertainties that make the novel so distinctive — first and foremost, of course, the uncertainty as to whether the unnamed city is indeed foreign or on the contrary Ryder's home, which he now looks at as an alien. By intensifying the time bind to the breaking point, in other words, Ishiguro also gestures beyond it. All of the imaginative energy of the novel's premise does not, after all, go toward reinforcing our desperate sense of a zero-sum relation between one person's demands and another's, compassion here and compassion there. When Ishiguro messes with the objective limits of time and space, making them pliant to emotional moods, he also messes with the zero-sum game of everyday common sense: the family should not be sacrificed to overwork; known domestic needs should never be ignored in favor of the far-off, ultimately unknowable demands of people in other countries, where we have no real business getting involved. *The Unconsoled* creates the atmosphere of a prolonged anxiety dream, a hallucinatory exaggeration of the daily time bind. But it also jokes ambiguously about the plenitude of additional commitments that it would be possible to take on, and the importance one's works and days might then assume, if only the usual limits of time and space did not apply. It magnifies the *freedom* to overcommit oneself, to which we pay indirect tribute when we take someone's declaration of busy-ness not as a degrading confession of external constraint but as a boast. It allows us to ask what life would be like if, while taking care of a child (perhaps your own?), you could agree to be interviewed, leave the child in a café in front of some pastry for a few minutes, find yourself suddenly driving out in the country, interfering (however ignorantly) in the host nation's symbolic politics, play a concert that lightens the mood of an aged composer engaged in burying his beloved dog, and return to find the child still there in the corner, not angry, though the pastry is finished. Like the darkly funny premise that everyone in this unnamed city looks to music to determine what direction the city should take, so too the premise of time/space compression also includes a utopian foretaste of unearthly temporal abundance.[12]

The utopian glimmerings that shine intermittently through the novel's darkness are located in particular in two typically urban vehicles. The novel begins with a ride on an elevator, and it ends with a ride on a tram. As James Gleick shows in his book *Faster: The Acceleration of Just About Everything*, elevators have become an icon of modern impatience. "Anger at elevators rises within seconds, experience shows. A good waiting time is in the neighborhood of fifteen seconds. Sometime around forty seconds, people start to get visibly upset ... Once on board, our antsiness only intensifies as we wait for the door to close. How long? *Door dwell*, as the engineers call it, tends to be set at two to four seconds. For some, that is a long time. And not just Americans" (27).[13] People tend to exaggerate wildly the amount of time they spend waiting either for or in an elevator. A few extra seconds get translated as "I waited ten minutes" or "it seemed like hours." As Gleick says, in elevators we "abandon our basic ability to measure short intervals of time" (28). And yet this disturbance of our time sense is only the other side of the historical role of the elevator, which made possible the city's vertical expansion on a scale that might once have seemed limited to science-fiction, and with it a comparable multiplication of human possibilities for contact within the once inviolable limits of the 24-hour span. In effect, the elevator gave us more hours in the day. So the transcendence of the habitual limits of time in Ishiguro's opening elevator ride is not a simple sadistic joke on our professionalism and our impatience. It's also a way of refreshing our sense of the city's historical achievements and continuing utopian energy.[14]

The same utopian note is also struck, just as incongruously, in the final scene on the tram. The protagonist's perhaps-wife and child have just gotten off, abandoning him. It's early in the morning; he's in shock. But a fellow passenger speaks to him, reminding him that things are not so bad; at the other end of the car, a hearty breakfast is being served. He gets up, hungry and already imagining further rides. Eating bacon and eggs balanced on your knees among a crowd of people on their way to work may leave him, and us, unconsoled for the loss of a family, or even a perhaps-family. But there is something genuinely utopian, I think, about the way breakfast, the most intimate meal of the day, here spills out of its privacy into the public world of mass transit, sweetening thereby the shared submission to the rhythms of the commute and quite explicitly taking over some of the emotional functions of the family.[15]

If Ishiguro is indeed infusing the urban symbols of the tram and the elevator with something approaching consolation, then you might conclude that he's being nostalgic about an old and even perhaps outmoded image of the city. Perhaps, but his nostalgia is also critical in a complex and constructive sense: critical not just of modern overwork but also of any *critique* of overwork that would send us back to the family, to the suburbs, to privacy. Ishiguro's vision of the city would belong, in other words, to a necessary re-invention of the public at the level of personal experience. This effort to reinvent the public, undercutting the gendered divide between work and family, is equally necessary at the urban and transnational levels, and the two are not merely parallel to each other. Cynthia Enloe has famously remarked that the personal is the international. The pertinence of this remark to the personal dilemma of work versus family is what I take Ishiguro to have demonstrated by means of his strangely imagined local/global space, both urban and cosmopolitan, neither foreign nor domestic. I take him to be suggesting that in order to cohabit with less indecency in a world of immigrants, refugees, and strangers, the largely invisible world that carries our bags or hands us bags to carry, that mysteriously delivers the morning tea, coffee, chocolate, and sugar out of which we fashion the beginning of our day, we need a broader and more inclusive civility, and the civility of the city can be a daily model and training site for it.[16]

12

Concentricity, Teleology, and Reflexive Modernity in Edward Yang's *Yi Yi*

David Leiwei Li[1]

Among Hou Hsiao-hsien's aching yearning for the agrarian tradition, Ang Lee's comic rumination on filiation and affiliation, and Tsai Ming-liang's wrenching condemnation of angst and alienation, Edward Yang's films stand out as the most complex cinematic treatment of contemporary Taiwan, caught between an inertial Confucian structure of feeling and a vibrant if not violent domination of global capital. From *That Day on the Beach* (1983) to the most recent *Yi Yi* (2000), Yang's camera has tracked the meteoric rise of the island economic miracle with a clairvoyant eye on its social, cultural, and affective mutations.[2] His oeuvre has at least two main functions: first it serves as a representation of a particular East Asian instance of modernization and second it performs a general conversation with contemporary theories of globalization. As such, it captures on screen a phenomenon unique to developing and postcolonial nations in the last quarter of the twentieth century. That is, the radical condensation of historical experience within a single generation — the transition and transformation from the agrarian, to the industrial, to the postindustrial — what takes European and American societies centuries to accomplish. By capturing this distinctive condensation and dramatizing its radical consequences, Yang's cinema mounts a discursive challenge to the competing definitions of the modern at a time when capitalism seems to have saturated different corners of the world. It provides a critical lens to examine, on the one hand, the periodizing maneuvers in cultural theory, whether through an older binary of tradition and modernity or the newer coinages of "post," "multiple," "singular," "alternative" or "reflexive" modernities (Eisenstadt et al, Jameson 2002, Gaonkar et al, and

Beck et al). Moreover, the films' engagement with the various modes of anti-
or pro-developmental temporality also enters a productive dialogue with
arguments for the geocultural distinct forms of capitalism and opposition
against such marking of national and civilizational boundaries (Berger and
Hsiao, Ong, and Tu 2000).

Small wonder then that Yang's *Kongbu fenzi* (*Terrorizer* or *Terrorist* 1986)
should become a centerpiece in Frederic Jameson's delineation of "the
geopolitical aesthetic" to exemplify an "uneven-developmental language"
(1992/1995: 1). This uneven development is elsewhere defined as the co-
existence in late capitalism of the West's "more homogeneously modernized
condition" as opposed to the rest's "situation of incomplete modernization"
(1991:310).[3] Curiously enough, by equating Taipei with any "international
urban society of late capitalism," Jameson seems to have downplayed the
"pedagogical-formative" in Yang, redolent of early modernity, and
undermined his own thesis about the contemporary East Asian juxtaposition
of divergent historic moments (1992/1995 128, 130). Although the
disintegration of the family and the decentering of the self are everywhere
evident in his cinematic scope of vision, Yang does not appear to share the
postmodern sentiment of the deceased subject and displaced morality. In
effect, there is always this insistent probing by the film director into the
"rather old-fashioned commodities in the universal sway of positivism," this
"peculiarly inappropriate" "pedagogical-formative" (ibid., and 143–4). *Duli
shidai* or *Confucian Confusion* (1995), for example, is prefaced with an excerpt
from *The Analects*:

> Confucius travels to the state of Wei, riding on the carriage driven by Ran
> You. "This is really a populous country," Confucius comments. "With
> such a large population," Ran You queries, "what needs to be done?"
> "Enrich the people," Confucius replies. "And after that?" the disciple asks
> further. (142–3)

Curtailing Confucius's original reply, which is, "Educate them," Yang
instead inserts the following: "Two millenniums later, within the short span
of two decades, Taipei has become one of the world's wealthiest metropolis."[4]
In situating the film against the drastic condensation of Taiwanese
development, Yang has clearly foreshadowed the confusing collision of
changing social mores. In implying yet withholding the Confucian
prescription, Yang has simultaneously foregrounded his film narrative as a

substitute pedagogical formative, and literally endowed his filmmaking, beyond its apparent entertainment value, with educational authority and ethical agency.

Several issues immediately arise from this position, however. Given the historical incongruity between feudalistic China and late capitalist Taiwan, is the Confucian lesson, in spite of its various contemporary "neo" incarnations, relevant *In Our Time?*[5] To pose this question is to ask if Yang holds a contingent or transcendent view of ethics and how his cinematic pedagogical formative negotiates the question of responsibility and community amid Taiwan's mixed modes of production at a time of global informational, financial, and cultural flows. For this is the time of disorganized capitalism, of manufactured uncertainty, of plurality of fragmented systems, and of the decline of such collective structures as class, nation, and the nuclear family. It is a time when postmodernists affirm the attrition of grand narratives and the ascent of multiple language games just as reflexive modernists propose the preference of identity choice against the "heteronomous monitoring," or the externally imposed governance, of previous eras.[6] *Yi Yi*, while fully in tune with this time, is at odds with the postmodern resignation to the impossibility of truth claims and impatient with the sort of survivalist instrumental reason recognizable in theories of reflexive modernity. Yang appears to agree with Ulrich Beck et al. that reflexivity is at once structural and subjective, in which agents are called upon to reflect on the "rules" and "resources" of dysfunctional structures (ibid.). But to institute self-regulation, to make choice against chaos, the late modern subject will have to contemplate its place within historical time and social space precisely as such time-space has been, as David Harvey has it, "compressed" (240–2). If the population of schizophrenic characters in his previous works is symptomatic of such time-space compression, Yang refuses to submit similar characters in *Yi Yi* to the same sorry state of helplessness. This is not because the basic social condition has changed for his most recent film. Instead, the director seems determined to find alternatives of regaining temporal and spatial sanity, to write against a dominant discourse which forecloses forms of imagination that dare to contradict the logic of flexible capital. In this sense, *Yi Yi* has enacted a narrative possibility of embedding, or rather, reflexively re-embedding after the institutional forces of modernity have successfully "dis-embedded" one's attachment to land and lineage, just as the flows of late modernity have automatically discouraged one's fondness for interdependency and commensurability (Giddens 21).

I

The state of social attenuation is aptly named *Yi Yi*. A repetition of the identical Chinese character "Yi," which refers to the number "one," the smallest positive integer, *Yi Yi* means "One One" in literal English translation.[7] The Chinese usage is unmistakably outlandish, for as an adverbial phrase, "Yi Yi" or "one by one" is always succeeded by a verb, as in "Yiyi jieshao," to "introduce one by one." On the other hand, when used as an adjective phrase to modify two separate but the same type of nouns, as in "Yisheng yishi," or "[one's] whole life," it signifies the integrity of a complete unit. Once divorced from the noun and the verb, subject and agency, Yang's neologism "Yi Yi" lacks the sense of both temporal sequence and spatial completeness within the Chinese linguistic convention. As a pair of detached minimal whole numbers departing from the traditional usage, "Yi Yi" comes to betray the accelerated process of atomization in a global reflexive modernity when human beings are increasingly individualized and isolated. Intriguingly, the Chinese titular register of such disengaged individualism is balanced by Yang's choice of the English heading, *A One and a Two*, which, with characteristic jazzy incantation, bounces back on the schizophrenic state of *One One* only to indicate the potential for improvisation. The bilingual titles suggest that although subjects of reflexive modernity may be fragmented, they are still capable of reconstituting themselves in the field of disparate social forces.

The film opens with a wedding, sandwiches a birth in the middle, and ends with a funeral. It centers on a multigenerational middle-class family in Taipei, its kinship relations and extended social interactions with their neighbors, friends, schools, businesses, the local city space, and the global sphere of media and commerce. Narratively speaking, the birth of the baby in the middle of the film signifies Yang's idea of the individual not as a sovereign but an encumbered being born amid the course of humanity and the nexus of social relations. The cradle to grave story, on the other hand, demonstrates the bare simplicity of an individual life trajectory and its inevitably limited purchase on time. *Yi Yi*'s narrative structure seems premised on a human in-between-ness, relatedness, as well as transience in the historical scheme of things, demanding a way of living appropriate to and respectful of this conception.

Yang's cinematic mapping of Taipei in terms of a family's temporal and spatial circumferences and encumbrances partakes the recent debates in philosophy that wrestle with the pressing question of the social in a globalized world. Although unnecessarily in conversation with each other, there is a concurrent cosmopolitan model of "concentric circles" in neo-Confucian and neo-Stoic revivals. For the former, Tu Weiming writes about a Confucian perception of self-development, "based upon the dignity of the person, in terms of a series of concentric circles: self, family, community, society, nation, world, and cosmos" (1998: 302). For the latter, Martha Nussbaum reworks Hierocles to argue a local and global association similarly "surrounded by a series of concentric circles." "The first one encircles the self, the next takes in the immediate family," she explains, "then follows the extended family, then, in order, neighbors or local groups, fellow city dwellers, and fellow countrymen — and we can easily add to this list groupings based on ethnic, linguistic, historical, gender or sexual identities" (9). Both Tu and Nussbaum posit an ideal of social affinity through an image of spatial extension — from the individual and the local to the national and global, thereby promulgating a cosmopolitan citizenship against jingoist fever and nihilist abandon.[8]

While sharing this ideal of cosmopolitan concentricity, the director of *Yi Yi* understands its twofold problem, one concerning the solidity of the centre and the other the visibility and thus the availability of the model. Yang's artistic solution, to foreshadow what is yet to unfold, is couched in the film's central dialectic of blindness and insight — what the adults do not see and what the child Yangyang does see in the mutli-facet universe. Before unveiling the intricate possibilities of the concentric ideal, therefore, Yang bombards his audience with the mind-boggling imagery of the global urban that *Yi Yi*'s characters inhabit. He is emphatic it is this international urban, with its inherent complexity, volatility, and velocity, that has made murky the centre upon which the multiple circles are supposed to radiate. For in Taiwan's late or reflexive modernity, individuals are no longer centrally or singularly "interpellated" in the biological family (Althusser). Family is no longer the center of social, economic and cultural reproduction, the model of the Confucian state, neither does it serve as a significant and specific site for relatively stable subjectivities to emerge. In fact, with the apparent hegemony of global capitalism come the cultural logics of flexibility, which, according to Aihwa Ong, inform the new "regimes of the family, the state, and capital" worldwide (3). Instead of being "coerced or resisted," "flexibility, migration, and relocations have become practices to strive for rather than stability" (ibid., 19). Consummate masters of this cultural logic of flexibility, the select "Chinese cosmopolitans" of her study have come to "illuminate the practices of an elite transnationalism" and exemplify "the late modern subject" par excellence (ibid., 24, 3). What is for Yang the serious erosion of the stable familial center seems for Ong an opportunity to marshal and maximize mobility. Both zero in on the well-to-do Chinese subjects, their responses and strategies to reflexively organize their lives amid the decentering flows of global capital, but Yang refutes the absolute governance of an economic rationality based on flexible accumulation and strives for practices of concentric affiliation.[9] *Yi Yi* presents the scene of familial decline as a trope of social disintegration and ponders if a teleology of life, not the kind affirming a divine design but a form of affectivity heavily hinged on continuity and community, can still maintain their viability.

Yang frames the difficulty earlier on with the wedding pictures. First is the ideal composition of the big family photo: families and friends saunter over and gather under the lush canopy for a group picture that symbolizes the vitality of "the living tree" and its ever-expanding roots and branches (Tu 1991). The serenity of nature's green, however, is followed by the crimson red of the banquet hall that suggests less festivity than the intense heat of contention. The groom's old flame, Yunyun, literally bursts into the wedding party, vociferously accusing the bride of hijacking her man while frantically apologizing to the groom's mother for failing to become her daughter-in-law. Amid the commotion, the gigantic photo blow-up of the newly-weds, Adi and Xiaoyan, is misplaced. Heads down toward the floor, smiles turned into grimaces, it reverses optical logic just as the obvious pregnancy of the bride disrupts the old social sequence of marriage and child-bearing. No wonder Popo, the mother of the groom and grandmother of the family, feels ill and goes home. "This kind of thing is everywhere nowadays," remarks her daughter Minmin in defense of her sister-in-law's unseasonable gestation, "we are no longer that rigid." But Minmin's tolerance or ethical flexibility sits uneasily with her daughter's Tingting's moral innocence. "If Auntie Yunyun [the ex-girlfriend of Adi] is not a bad person," Tingting confronts her father NJ, "Auntie Xiaoyan [the bride] has got to have a problem." While NJ's diplomatic equivocation, "we hardly know her," sounds similarly acquiescent as his wife's to the emerging permissiveness, their daughter's disapproval echoes an ethical certitude befitting her Popo's age. NJ asks if grandma reproves the bride. "Not really," replies Tingting, "she just says she is old and I don't understand what she means."

Still 12.1   An upset social order

Popo never gets to tell what she means since a post-wedding stroke sends her into a coma from which she hardly awakens, except for a magical moment before her death when she communicates with Tingting in the speechless art of origami.[10] A sagacious matriarch of a bygone age and a retired teacher who cannot talk, let alone instruct, Popo is Edward Yang's object-correlative for the new built-in obsolescence of the old filial authority. Contrary to the grandma figures in Clara Law's *Autumn Moon* (1992) and *Floating World* (1996), or the grandpa figures in Ang Lee's *Pushing Hands* (1991) and Hou Hsiao-hsien's *Goodbye South, Goodbye* (1996), Popo does not have the residual capacity to command or cajole her offspring, however impotently, through guilt trips or shaming tactics. To be able to whip her descendants in line would imply the vitality of the generational line, thus the mutual generation of filial meaning, the essential closure of the clan, and thus the shared goals of life. When neither appears tangible in a Taipei of mobile freeways and tenuous cell phones, the social solidity of the family is virtually in splinter.

Yang pictures this state of disintegration as the breakdown of generational interlocution in a cluster of carefully crafted scenes at Popo's bed. The doctor prescribes that the family "talk with" grandma to stimulate her brain and enhance her chances of revival. What is meant as therapy for the ancestor on life support, however, turns out to be torture for the progeny. Son and groom Adi, the self-proclaimed champion talker, assures his mom that he is out of his money trouble but soon runs out of words to say. Daughter Minmin gets so depressed by the poverty of her daily routine and the perfunctory minutes by Popo's side she cannot help but weep. Only Tingting has the real urge and content to communicate. Sneaking out of her bedroom in the quiet of the night, she beseeches Popo's forgiveness like a penitent, blaming herself for the tragedy. "If you do not wake up," she whispers, "I can never fall soundly asleep." But the metaphoric priest of filial order remains reticent, refusing the comfort of moral certainty that the burgeoning adolescent desperately seeks.

Popo's comatose state and Tingting's bewilderment about her uncle's marriage represent not just the collapse of a pre-modern Chinese tradition on a late modern stage. The fragmentation of filial, and by extension, vertical and hierarchical authority also speaks of an attractive ascent of individual liberty. What Edward Yang cinematically exposes in terms of "the great transformation" in Taiwan (Marsh), or for that matter, the historically mixed and compressed modernity in East Asia, coincides with Alisdair MacIntyre's philosophical critique of the Enlightenment Project. They seem preoccupied with the consequences of the disappearance of both the density of social fiber and the teleological understanding of individual destiny. Though unquestionably liberating, the kind of instrumental rationality underlying the formation of the sovereign modern individual is for MacIntyre ultimately unsatisfactory because it is devoid of significant societal dimensions and detached from a "narrative" and thus a social conception of the good. Autonomy of this sort is wedded to anomie, and its remedy lies only in the recovery of an Aristotelian teleology:

> the key question for men is not about their own authorship; I can only answer the question 'What am I to do?' if I can answer the prior question 'Of what story or stories do I find myself a part?' We enter human society, that is, with one or more imputed characters — roles into which we have been drafted — and we have to learn what we are in order to be able to understand how others respond to us and how our responses to them are apt to be construed. (216)

While sympathetic with his insistence on the ascriptive condition of the self and its necessary imbrication with the social, Yang is hardly as prepared as MacIntyre to evoke the construction of Aristotelian traditions and "local forms of community" that are pre-modern in historical origin and relatively enclosed socially (ibid., 263).[11] The director of Yi Yi is not "after virtue" in abstraction. He wants to show how the "imputed characters" have necessarily become more complex after modernity, how the "local forms of community" are no longer bounded with their own centripetal energy in globality, and finally, how a purposive narrative against the tyrannical economism of our time could still be imagined.

II

The attenuation of filial linearity as the central motif of self-actualization coincides with the everyday dispersion of activities: individuals in reflexive modernity are living on multiple planes with ever-expanding social horizons. Arjun Appadurai best characterizes such horizons as a series of landscapes, of "ethnoscapes, mediascapes, technoscapes, fiancescapes, and ideoscapes" that shape international capital and its disjunctive cultural flows (33). Yang figures this perspectival construct of layered global formations first of all in the omnipresence of Taipei's techno-visual culture. The surveillance camera at the family's luxury high-rise apartment home frames Popo's return. The coming into being of Adi and Xiaoyan's unborn baby is heralded on the ultrasound monitor, and its birth witnessed later via the video viewfinder. The murder of the English teacher is broadcast on TV, whose mug shot accompanies the reportage that links the gratuitous violence of electronic games to its deliberate execution in the real world by the teenager, "Fatty." With this sequence, Yang initiates a visual dialectic of the interior and the exterior, or rather, the dissolution of such dialectic as the multiple landscapes of modern living converge. The technology-facilitated penetration of the residential and reproductive spaces comes to stand for the colonization of the private and the biological, while the enactment of media-prompted slaughter, the transgression of boundary between the existential and the fantastic. Not only does the infiltration of the historically mysterious or the sacred preoccupy the director but the hold of science on the lot of humanity as well.

In a refreshing juxtaposition of voice-over and image, the audience is surprised into recognition that what they took to be the nurse's line about the baby on the ultrasound screen is in fact the translator's explanation about the artificial intelligence of the computer. Ota, a Japanese computer wizard invited by NJ to rescue his company from its impending demise, is giving his presentation. "It has begun to acquire signs of human life," as the thumping of the baby's heart fades to the monotone of the translator:

> Besides thinking and calculating, it will mature into a living entity and become our most trusted companion. That is truly the limitless future of computer games. The reason we are unable at present to go beyond the games of fighting and killing has little to do with our limited grasp of the "electronic brain" [computers]; it has everything to do with our failure to understand us humans.

With this defamiliarization of the human-machine interface, both cinematically and thematically, Yang demonstrates the complex condition of reflexive modernity that N. Katherine Hayles calls "the posthuman" — where cognition and action increasingly take place in "information-rich and computationally embedded environments" (121). Contrary to the Enlightenment thinking of earlier modernity, Yang wants to impress upon us that scientific knowledge of the natural world may not necessarily enhance human control of the social world but engender other forms of uncertainty as well. The conflation of the voice-over and image thus dramatizes the convergence in reflexive modernity of formerly separate realms of agency, of science and the humanities, while betraying the director's secret preference for the latter's governance.

To supplement this motif of blurring boundaries, Yang makes ingenious use of abundant glass in metropolitan architecture, which, whether in Tokyo or in Taipei, is the transnational space his characters traverse. Unlike masonry walls, glass panes mark space without total delimitation, suggesting permeability, liquidity, and flexibility, qualities especially valorized under global capital. Yang foregrounds the visual prominence of the glass immediately before Ota's presentation when NJ and his colleagues ride in Dada's car, debating salvaging plans and exit strategies. One suggests searching for a copycat of Ota in Taipei while another banters about Dada's retirement to San Francisco. The characters appear one moment through the windshield and disappear the next in the curve of the auto-glass, as the reflection of office buildings in the uniform international box style rolls over, engulfing their visage. Yang conveys through the medium of glass the intertwined connectivity and intricate fluidity between global capital flow and the motion of business and people. But this double play of transparency and reflexivity also becomes a larger metaphor for the collapse of the older binaries Jameson describes as the "depth model," such as "essence and appearance," the "latent and the manifest," and "authenticity and inauthenticity" (1991: 12).

No wonder the close-up of the windshield, mirroring the sheer opacity of the office buildings in motion as driven by both capital expansion and individual ambition, is succeeded by a medium shot in still frame. This time, we see Adi and Yunyun, ex-boy and girlfriends, two of the most superficial characters in the film, having their rendezvous in Eslite Café. Barely visible on the screen, as the shifting reflection of street traffic, passing cars, motorcycles, and pedestrians, obscure and obstruct their contours, Adi and Yunyun appear to embody nothing save for the imprints of their environments, a glass-sutured subjectivity, if you will, in reflexive modernity. The only thing standing out is the talk of their stock holdings in AOL and Yahoo, the buzz of business revealing the boors they are.[12]

Although implicitly privileging the depth and composure of character more favored in the earlier modernity and capital of "inner direction," Yang shows that the "other direction" of reflexive subjectivity is by no means unique to Adi and Yunyun. Yang shares with David Riesman's analysis that the telos-driven self-discipline of "inner direction" appropriate to industrial societies is yielding to a peer-prompted and mass communication mediated "other direction" of consumer societies (Riesman 14–25). He seems specially sensitive to the sway of socialized other direction on his characters when Taiwanese society swings far more suddenly than American society did from a culture of relative scarcity to that of material abundance. In showing the speed and scale with which Taiwan is turned into a silicon island, Yang wants to illuminate the collective and crushing impact that the radical condensation of economic development has on individual subjectivity at large.

Not at all a superficial person like her brother Adi, Minmin is spotted repeatedly before the mirror as in the heart-wrenching scene — reminiscent of Tsai Ming-liang's closing shot for *Vive L'amour* — where she can no longer conceal her anguish about life's monotony and her inability to report to Popo things of interest. After an extraordinarily long take, the camera steers away from the sobbing Minmin, the mirror image of her back, and the semi-open venetian blinds filtering the intermittent light of car traffic below. Her husband NJ pauses, looking at his wife pensively, and turns his back to close their bedroom door and shield the children from the sorrow. The camera cuts to outside the apartment in a long shot, with street lamps in the distance, headlights rushing toward us, and the reflection of the house lights mixed together on the same plane of vision. The apartment next door is then illuminated at the upper corner of the screen, showing the silhouettes of lovers in a bitter squabble against the indifference of nocturnal city motion. The camera pans in toward the domestic sphere of Minmin as NJ paces toward the window, and slowly closes the venetian blinds as though to contain the troubles. We can no longer see the inside but we are overwhelmed by the outside: the windowpane-reflected urban panorama of pitch darkness is broken by dotted white lights, the neighbors' bickering now commingling with Minmin's whimpering.

Still 12.2   The domestic as determined by city traffic

Glass as a visual trope of dimensions that one can see through or dimensions that are overlaid with reflection and refraction thereby comes to denote horizontal "other direction" in reflexive modernity, a dialogical formation of subjectivity that displaces the centrality of teleological "inner direction" of old. Glass also figures the growing indistinguishability of the inside and outside that Michael Hardt and Antonio Negri characterize the generation of "imperial subjectivity." "The enclosures that used to define the limited space of the institutions have broken down," they argue, "so that the logic that once functioned primarily within the institutional walls now spreads across the entire social terrain" (196). The sequence on Minmin we have followed amply illustrates the invasion of the outside, or the internalization of the external that engenders much psychological and social instability. Husband and wife are scarcely the principal agents of their own ennui but subjects in conversation with other social forces in a much larger nexus of economic and emotional exchange. The transparency and reflexivity of the glass enables the camera's panning to establish visual simultaneity and spatial complementarity not only between the two apartments but also their relation to the city as an engine of social as well as individual change. Although the residents may entertain the illusion of their sovereign existence in separate units, Yang convinces us that they actually inhabit the same condominium of "the lonely crowd" without optimal escape routes (Riesman).

To drive this point home, the director frames Minmin before a mammoth window again, this time at her office. We see her at the beginning of the shot almost completely immersed in the gloom, standing motionless and staring blankly at the void, which as we recognize all too quickly is the reflection of the city below. In the distance is the reflection of the steady flash of a stop signal positioned precisely where Minmin's heart would be if we had X-ray vision. The audience is absorbed in the rhythmic beat of the red light at the intersection of a far away surface street, the perpetual swishing of the tires on the nearby freeway the only sound audible. The heart is where the light is, their separate pulses regulated by a parallel surge of synergy and a parallel arrest of stagnation. Similar to the previous juxtaposition of the baby's ultrasound image and the translator's soundtrack on the subject of computers, the human-machine interface is reconfigured here in this over-layering, a breath-taking image of the total interpenetration and interpellation of society and subjectivity, and of exteriority and interiority. "Haven't you gone back yet?" inquires Nancy after she steps into the office. After what feels a long-drawn-out moment, Minmin replies, "I have nowhere to go."

Still 12.3   The heart is where the light is

III

The sense everywhere of having nowhere to go is surely symptomatic of reflexive modernity, a global risk society whose predicament is defined by Ulrich Beck as "unintentional self-dissolution or self-endangerment" (Beck, Giddens, and Lash 176). As NJ puts it to the comatose Popo after Minmin has left home, "I am not sure about anything these days. Every morning, I wake up feeling uncertain." "If you were me," he asks Popo, "would you like to wake up?" The vanishing certainty about old social structures entails the use of a new decentralized expert system, according to Anthony Giddens, wherein the reflexivity and circularity of social know-how can help the subject change her condition of action (ibid., 187). Minmin's retreat to the Buddhist temple, a Chinese equivalent of the therapist's couch in the West, certainly indicates how the traditional folk or new age spirituality can reclaim authority alongside other burgeoning expert systems in late modernity. But this type of reflexive self-monitoring is also the subject of Yang's scathing satire. The master monk is later shown as a minstrel minister, for instance, coming down the mountains to recruit NJ but returning happily with his fat check. Besides exposing the material contamination in institutionalized religion, thus questioning the apparent objectivity of the reflexive apparatus, Yang also raises doubts about the moral legitimacy of the expert system. Though *Yi Yi* does not provide any explicit social alternative to the late capitalist system either, Yang seems discontent with the implications of Giddens that reflexivity is purely a matter of personal management and adaptation. For Yang, self-reflexivity will have to involve self-reflection, not reflection as the bouncing back and forth of images or the superficial suturing of subjectivity but as individual ethical engagement through apprehension of social totality.[13]

This reflective search for knowledge serves the film's principal pedagogical-formative, which is figured in the cinematic narrative as a dialectic of vision. As the boy protagonist Yangyang puts it to his father NJ, "I can only see what it is in front of me and not what's behind. Does it mean that we can only see half of the world?" Yangyang is evidently a junior alter ego of Director Yang. With all his intellectual precocity, Yangyang is concerned about vision and cognition in at least two different senses. One is the urge to transcend partial and peripheral for holistic vision, an attempt at grasping social and spatial interdependency and integrity. The other is the desire to recognize a temporality of sight, to couple the forward-looking eye/I with the history of its own immanence and the origin of its imminent becoming. If Yangyang pictures the rear of people's heads to enable their self-perception, the director of *Yi Yi* wants to locate the failure of constructing totality in the postmodern fracturing of time and space while recuperating its possibility.[14]

Ironically, the loss of holistic vision results from a contemporary suffusion of vision, a vision of life burdened with sensorial overload and its absolute satisfaction. "The relentless saturation of any remaining voids," as Jameson notes, "[exposes the postmodern body] to a perpetual barrage of immediacy from which all sheltering layers have been removed" (1988: 351). As "Fatty" sums it up for Tingting after their trip to the movies that the invention of cinema has considerably extended human life: "the experience we get through the movies at least doubles what we experience in real life." To illustrate, he cites the movie as a manual for murder. Only when "Fatty" is arrested for that crime does the audience realize the importance of cinematic foreshadowing. The boundary between fantasy and reality has been abolished while the pursuit of intensified virtual experience in actuality becomes Yang's apt allegory of moral collapse. The attempt at extending one's own experience endlessly has resulted in the curtailing of another's life, as "Fatty" comes to embody "the aesthetic way of life" in his "attempt to lose the self in the immediacy of present experience." "The paradigm of aesthetic expression is the romantic lover who is immersed in his own passion," writes MacIntyre in his reading of Kierkegaard, "[b]y contrast the paradigm of the ethical is marriage, a state of commitment and obligation through time, in which the present is bound by the past and to the future" (40). Not rejecting modern technologies and its enrichment of life, Yang encourages his audience to keep alive a teleological notion of time as well as the place of an other in the process of self-fulfillment.

If the audience has so far been frustrated by the random dispersal of families and friends on the cinematic scope of vision, they are enlightened by the sequence of frames that inter-cut NJ and "Sherry" with Tingting and "Fatty." On learning his business visit to Ota, his now married first love Sherry flies from Chicago to Tokyo to meet him. The camera captures both waiting at a Japanese commuter train station, catching up on old times and new stories. "I get jealous as my daughter is growing into a woman," NJ says, "knowing that she'll eventually be with someone else." Before his voice tails off, a passing train obscures NJ and Sherry and the film cuts to Tingting standing at the corner of a Taipei theater. As "Fatty" slowly walks into view, the clucking of the train fades into the din of city traffic. Tingting asks, "What's the time?" "Nine," replies "Fatty." "It's almost ten now. Eight a.m. Chicago time," Sherry's voice jumps in, just before the film cuts back to her. "Nine p.m. in Taipei," murmurs NJ as they saunter toward a railroad crossing. Time and space of transnational proportions are radically compressed into living immediacy to exemplify the arrival for some of the condition of a global village.[15] Sherry remarks on the crossing's resemblance to the one near their school, harking back in late modern Japan to a modernizing Taiwan three decades ago.[16] "That's long gone," NJ updates her, "but I remember the first time I held your hand there, before our going to the movies." We hear this as the camera cuts from the quiet night of the Japanese town to the hustle and bustle of the Taipei street crossing, where Tingting and "Fatty" are waiting for the pedestrian light, silently holding hands. "I'm holding your hand once again," continues NJ's voice, speaking to Sherry off screen, "only at a different place, at a different time, at a different age." The lens closes in on Tingting and "Fatty," hands clasped together, crossing the street, as Sherry's voice finishes NJ's sentence, "but the same sweaty palm."

In his cinematic correlation of romance in separate international time zones, different generations, and varied speeds of motion, Yang in fact rejects

Still 12.4

Still 12.5   The same sweaty palm across generations and geopolitical time zones

the dominant temporality of late capital which Manuel Castells labels "timeless time." Such time is said to depend on a "systemic perturbation in the sequential order," either taking the form of a "compress[ed]" "instantaneity" or "a random discontinuity" (494). While the series of intercutting we witness compress on screen the immediacy of concurrent events, it also crystallizes the obscured order of succession in generational distinction and identity. One may say that Yang has put Castells's time schemes into perspective when the dominant frame of "timeless time" — with its "virtual" temporality, "instant wars," and "split-second capital transactions" — is forced to confront "time discipline" with its "biological" boundaries and "socially determined sequencing" (ibid., 494, 495). By positioning his characters as participants of both timeless time and time discipline, Yang wishes to caution his audience not to be carried away by the former and to induce their reconciliation with the latter.

Timeless time is thus set against the unchanging cycle of the generations, of human procreation, of economic production, and of the origination of subjectivity. In this manner, Yang couples the space of flow inextricably with place bound time. While global capital's perpetual manufacturing of difference and engineering of sensation threatens to compact our sense of time into ephemeral pleasures, Yang wants us to see such simple beauty as the generational repetition and duration of locked hands and hearts. Against the contemporary dispersion of subjectivity in the multiple spheres of work and leisure, Yang tries to cultivate a new agency in globality that reckons with the limited human temporal purchase and thereby a willful teleological necessity of temporal continuity. *Yi Yi* is not content with merely stating the finitude of human life; it wants the recognition of this finitude to effectively counter timeless time's erosion of communal purpose and promotion of instantaneous individual gratification.

"Fatty's" formula of experiential expansionism in the episodic mode — recall his quest to double his experience within the finite span of life, migrating from one event to the next as he does one girlfriend to another — thus provides the backdrop against which NJ's deliberation resolutely rails. Indeed, NJ's interlude with Sherry in Japan is not fundamentally different from the flights of fancy that plague "Fatty" or his in-laws, neighbors, and friends, who all wish for the thrill of novel experience. There are no impeccable characters on Yang's late modern landscape immune to the passage from the industrializing society to a consumer one with their respective cultural logic, the "delay of gratification" for one and the "delay of payment" for the other (Bauman 1995: 5). However, some are less vulnerable and more capable than others to recall Yangyang's dialectical tale of hindsight and foresight, to weigh the excitement of the moment with the progression of a teleological trajectory.

After considerable reflection — in postures eminently evocative of Auguste Rodin's "The Thinker," one in a silhouette behind a Japanese screen and another on an embankment stretching out to the ocean — NJ turns down Sherry's proposal to start their life anew, and decides to go back to his Taipei family and company. NJ's seems as much a choice against the romantic notion of limitless self-invention as is against the late capitalist logic of endless "creative destruction" (Harvey 16). With Popo's death, Yang brings Minmin back from her Buddhist retreat and puts her with NJ in the same frame for the first time in the film:

> NJ: How was it up in the mountains?
>
> Minmin: It was OK. In fact, it was not that different. It was as if they [the monks] were talking to Mom, except our roles were reversed. They were like me and I was like my mother. They took turns talking to me about the same things, repeating them several times a day. I've come to realize that so much is in fact not complicated. But why did they ever appear so?
>
> NJ: Right. Could I say this? While you were away I had a chance to relive part of my youth. I thought that if I had had the opportunity to do it again, things would have turned out differently. They turned out pretty much the same. I suddenly realized that even given a second chance, I would not really need it. It is quite unnecessary.

If Minmin has emerged from the confusing complexity of reflexive modernity by grasping the kernel of simplicity underneath, NJ has refrained from the tantalizing prospect of a fresh start and an apparent alternative to his perceived rut. Having wandered lonely as a cloud in the lonely crowd, husband and wife have literally landed on their bed, an image of re-embedding after their disembedding ventures into the exhilarating unknown.[17]

The reconciliation of the couple hinges on a shared refusal of endless experiential experiments and a restoration of binaries, boundaries, and brakes (traffic lights and slow or stop signs abound in the film as cautions against reckless movements and unbridled mobility). For Minmin, the realization that appearance can be deceiving leads to her conviction of an inarticulate essence. For NJ, that essence is defined by his reconceived needs and

Still 12.6   Re-embedding after dis-embedding

obligations as opposed to his equally reticent and ultimately repressed wants. Both have embraced, through their individual routes of discovery, a sameness, an identity, an elemental simplicity that is tied to a prior commitment and projected to a certain future. The scene of the couple on their bed seems a moment of recovery when a secular form of teleological time, at once embodied in people and bound to place, re-emerges. Refuting the aesthete's indulgence in the infinite capaciousness of the moment for oneself alone, Minmin and NJ have come to reaffirm a generational cycle of perpetuity that entails a limitation of individual gratification and a recognition of fundamentals. The centrifugal forces of reflexive modernity that engender much confusion have finally occasioned the reflection necessary for self-regulation and re-organization to occur.

In many ways, *Yi Yi* has enacted the common contemporary narrative of people "in search of fundamentals," a narrative prompted by time-space compression and its disruptive consequences, and therefore must, argues Roland Robertson, be understood as a crucial aspect of globalization (166). This search for fundamentals often appears in terms of localized meaning, yet it is a diffused worldwide phenomenon. As reflexive structuring of preferences against "alienation, homelessness, [and] anomie," it tends to fall into "the nostalgic paradigm" and has, as is implied, conservative overtones (ibid., 169). However, differentiation seems in order as far as Yang's fundamental ideology and *Yi Yi's* pedagogical formative are concerned. Although the site of the biological family appears the cinematic center of this recuperation from and within radiating reflexive modernity, the film is not endorsing a model of patrilineal governance. An earlier coupling of Popo and Tingting's hands, the symbolic gesture of affection between maternal grandma and granddaughter, for instance, receives its visual encore in Tingting and NJ toward the movie's closing, suggesting an interruption of paternal heritage as well as a preservation of kindred sentiments.[18] A similar visual duet is at work in the film's successive frontal framing of Tingting and NJ, Yangyang and NJ, and Ota and NJ together behind the windshield, intimating a transgender, transgenerational, transracial and transnational solidarity of spirit. By contrast, Adi's ride with his brother-in-law NJ is shot from behind just as NJ is put in the passenger seat when Dada drives: neither seems NJ's true fellow-travelers nor shares with him his ideal universe. One cannot fail to observe that Yang has significantly revised the genealogical core of community in Tu Weiming and Martha Nussbaum's outline of concentric circles. Rather than bowing to the ascribed condition of filiation as the center of cosmopolitan sociality, Yang has made affiliation of ideals central in his mapping of global interrelatedness. His concentric vision of an egalitarian planetary community thus defies a blind submission to both blood and the market.

It is small wonder that those who seek short-term interests, either in the arena of emotional or economic transaction, fare much worse through Yang's lens than those who are committed to the durability of reciprocal benefits. If Adi's crass materialism is condemned in the rapid boom and bust of his fortune, Dada's chase of Ato, the copycat of Ota that cannot deliver, is a lesson against instant profits. The kind of instrumental reason that matches means to ends in exclusive economic terms turns out neither ethical nor efficient. Yang's mild melodramatic manichaeism is reminiscent of James and Balzac's unveiling of the "moral occult," a "domain of spiritual forces and imperatives that is not clearly visible" but "believe[d] to be operative" in a "desacralized" post-Enlightenment world (Brooks 15, 20–21). An exemplary film at the turn of a new millennium, *Yi Yi* provides a similar yet more radical dramatization of Taiwan's passage into another world of risk-ridden modernity. There, the providential is no longer viable, the filial and the local no longer stable, yet rediscovery of ethical imperatives remains fundamental. Edward Yang seems to have possessed an identical urge as the masters of early modernity to register into consciousness the power of the residual, to recover a weakened sense of historicity, a narrative conception of the self, and a teleology of the human species. Cultural capital properly belonging to a previous era yet not entirely eradicated in the mixed and compressed modernity of today seems to hold promise. Tingting, Yangyang, NJ, and Ota are emblems not of the past but of the potential of our future, for they have made evident the sham of a reigning cultural logic that the likes of Adi and Dada personify — maximum growth, instant profits, and flexible accumulation. That these are not the ultimate or sole objective of human actions constitutes *Yi Yi*'s primary pedagogical-formative.

"I'm sorry, Popo, It wasn't that I didn't want to talk to you. I thought whatever I told you, you would have already known," Yangyang says in tribute to Popo at her funeral. "I know so little, Popo. But you know what I'll do when I grow up? I will tell people what they do not know and show them what they cannot see." Reflexive modernity finally requires that social "knowledge spiral in and out of the universe of social life, reconstructing both itself and that universe as an integral part of that process" (Giddens 15–16). *Yi Yi* has shown us a world of jet travel, bullet trains, and instant electronic transfer of money, image, and information. But it has also illuminated the incontrovertible limits of nature on human life, Popo's death being the most striking sign, despite the scientific overcoming of space and time. Yangyang's remark thus implies that the ever-expanding circles of social knowledge, enabled by the liberating technologies of global modernity, must be appropriated with nature's limits and the preservation of the species in mind.

"Throughout human history," argues Zygmunt Bauman, "the work of culture consisted in sifting and sedimenting hard kernels of perpetuity out of transient human lives [and] actions, in conjuring up duration out of transience," and in "transcending thereby the limits imposed by human mortality by deploying mortal men and women in the service of the immortal human species." It is not incidental that Bauman deploys the past tense in his summary of that history, for "demand for this kind of work is," as he puts it, "shrinking" (2000: 126). Bauman's concern with the waning of such demand and the devaluation of immortality is Edward Yang's as well, for both are preoccupied with the decisive turning point in human history, when the sovereign and solipsistic self — the figure of "Yi," "the One" — is becoming the figure of hegemony in global modernity. No one can fully anticipate the consequences of globalization as a radical individualization of culture, but it is not premature to recall a cultural outlook that has sustained the divergent groups of humanity thus far. "I miss you, Popo, especially when I see my still nameless newborn cousin. I remember that you always say that you feel old. I'd like to tell my cousin," the boy Yangyang declares, "I feel old too." Childhood and age, and innocence and experience finally converge in this articulation of a continuous life narrative, and with it, a reiteration of an ethical imperative so often submerged in the fragments of late modernity. Unlike the pre-modern resignation to the biological and or a post-modern deferral of death in instant consumption, Yangyang's signification on Popo's silence suggests a collective triumph over atomic mortality, a cultural transcendence of individual earthly sojourn. The film *Yi Yi* has come to affirm a sense of purposeful time and a notion of spatial and social integrity, a version of neo-Confucian or neo-Stoic concentricity and teleology possibly, or rather the tenets of a cosmopolitan communitarianism regardless of civilizational origins.

Afterword:
Can We Judge the Humanities by Their Future as a Course of Study?

Paul A. Bové

> If we were moving in the right direction, where reality might fulfill our hopes, we shouldn't need any visionary ideals to beckon us. Events would open out before us congenially, and would call forth our innocent interest and delight, gradually, concretely, in ways odder and more numerous than we expected. Why, then, is this not so? Why does experience leave us so desolate, so puzzled, so tired, that like Plato and Plotinus and the Christian saints we must look to some imaginary heaven or some impossible utopia for encouragement and for peace? (Santayana 497)

US readers have made Michael Hardt and Antonio Negri's *Empire* a widely noticed academic bestseller. The book came into the market at a time when globalization was still a term on almost everyone's lips; it afforded a way for a subset of academic humanists to link their work to what they took to be an issue of deep socio-political, cultural, and economic consequence. *Empire* built itself from a great many terms and ways of talking already circulating in the university and media. Its familiarity made it easy for academic cultural studies scholars to engage with it. Its bold and universal account of what was going on in a long secular period of neo-liberal economics and state policy excited readers eager for some sort of radical explanation that could contest with official Hayekian accounts of post-Cold War change and so it afforded many chances to do more work, ways to tie the terms of especially US-based cultural studies to the world of (post)-state politics and economy — all in a way that showed how culturalist work mattered. Addressing the largest questions of the age, as this book and its adopters claimed to do, in itself legitimized work that followed from or indeed had made it possible by emphasizing the role of cultural politics and supra-state institutions. As part of a paradigm's normal academic development, the book and its adherents faced opposition, sometimes from a statist political right that despises Negri for his past politics just as it despises cultural criticism;[1] and sometimes from competitive ('left') academics who prefer other models or categories for humanistic and cultural work. In other words, the book fell into a normal pattern of market behavior.[2]

The events of September 11, 2001 have given us a new commonplace. "9/11 changed everything," we almost all say. Those former masters of the universe who attend the World Economic Forum tell us that terrorism, war, and the United States have moved globalization out of sight; everything that seemed real in the 1990s almost matters no more.[3] Globalization goes on, as it did during the late nineteenth and early twentieth centuries before the Cold War changed the relations of capital to space. But globalization as the phenomenon of the Clinton years has disappeared in the dust of collapsing towers, smart bombs, and dead bodies. As a result, as a topic for academic preoccupation, globalization has lost some of its charm to legitimate humanists' work and self-opinion.

All my debatable assertions matter less, however, than two other things: first, we now know that the Bush regime's strategic intellectuals planned something like a global war of preemption — with an initial focus on Iraq — long before the murders of the workers in the World Trade Towers [Kessler]; second, we now know that the US has an appetite for unilateral, preemptive, imperial,[4] and military adventures. Indeed, the war in Yugoslavia, with the bombing of Belgrade, taught that lesson during the 1990s.[5] Discussions of globalization assert the nation-state's decline, even when they acknowledge the particular role played by the US state-apparatus in nurturing the neo-liberal order of NAFTA, the WTO, and China's liberalization. These discussions valuably moved humanistic work out of the grasp of nation-state concepts and made possible new alignments, canon formations, and research projects — what we now call interdisciplinary hybridity.[6]

If 9/11 changed everything, then they have changed the relations between the humanities and globalization. How fundamental are these changes? Do they include a reconsideration of the figure of the 'weakened nation-state' troping upon the nation-state concepts of older cultural work? Do we wonder if "the politics of representation" belongs to the historical past? Do we accept any intellectual who asserts that the US has abandoned military adventurism?[7]

The humanities have no future unless they set out an ongoing process to describe and analyze the present time's main forces. Without this *Ansatzpunkt*, events whip-saw the humanities from place to place, topic to topic, vision to vision. Meanwhile, the humanistic professional establishment shrinks; and, although many defend its virtue, its social legitimacy is at least as bad as it has been in quite some time. Our ability to find virtue should not mislead us; we are dogged defenders of our basic ideals and expert interpreters in an age obsessed with subjectivity. A stronger profession would not need so many arguments to re-legitimate itself — even in opposition — nor would it invoke for so long so many objections to its own value. We must think what is meant that ours is an historical situation in which one story and practice of legitimation seems to follow another, or, all seem to coexist at once on a spectrum of legitimated positions. We have reached a place that professionals can only delusively justify as the liveliness of civil society, the conflict of interpretations, and the healthy vitality of cultural and political difference. One way to see this is to recognize some of the reasons why we might not. For example, the long history of American intellectual anti-professionalism, rooted in various class elements that abhorred compromises and advances, can draw our attention away from the historical specificity of a profession weakened to the point that its very best members, at the highest level, the very best of our readers, need to ward off its own critics as they ward off right-wing opportunists.[8] Most important, the humanities cannot answer the question, *cui bono*, but finds their own future solely within the reiterative value of keeping themselves alive, convinced of its inherent moral and political value.[9]

After 9/11 we can easily consider *Empire*'s wide circulation, treat it as the profession's symptom, and ask how else to explain the celebrity of a book that makes these claims:

> As a kind of historical shorthand, we could locate the end of the third and the beginning of the fourth regime of the U. S. Constitution in 1968. The Tet offensive [in the Vietnam War] in January marked the ***irreversible*** [emphasis added] military defeat of the U.S. imperialist adventures. More important, however, as is the case before each shift of constitutional regimes, the pressure for a return to republican principles and the original constitutional spirit was already prepared by the powerful internal social movements. Just when the United States was most deeply embroiled in an imperialist adventure abroad, when it had strayed farthest from its original constitutional project, that constituent spirit bloomed most strongly

at home — not only in the antiwar movements themselves, but also in
the civil rights movements, and eventually the second-wave feminist
movements. The emergence of the various components of the New Left
was an enormous and powerful affirmation of the principle of constituent
power and declaration of the reopening of social spaces. (Hardt and Negri,
179)

While the Bush regime's commitments to unilateralism, preemptive war,
and extra-legal action undermine a considerable part of *Empire*'s façade, what
matters most is the rushed judgment with which academic humanists accepted
such foundationally erroneous remarks.[10] Admirers predictably would defend
these statements by 'contextualizing' them as part of a 'larger argument' about
the cycles of US constitutionalism and society. None of this matters since
the text unambiguously announces that Tet "marked the ***irreversible*** military
defeat of the U. S. imperialist adventures" (Hardt and Negri 179, emphasis
added). The emphasis on irreversible and declarative nature of the sentences
pluralized object, 'adventures,' leaves no room for qualification. American
cultural humanists, in particular, have an historically self-interested desire
and predisposition to assent to these sentences' real symbolic and professional
content. Extraordinary social and cultural advances in democracy, in civil
and women's rights took place during the Vietnamese war to defeat American
imperialism. As Hardt and Negri recall all this in conjunction with Tet, what
appeals to the US cultural studies scholars is the authors' general praise for
new social movements. Especially post-theoretical, cultural studies humanists
have aligned their work with representational politics, which they often
link to new social movements. Facing defeat in the extra-academic national
political arena, cultural studies achieves persistent (moral) legitimacy in its
closed professional circles by asserting its alignment (real or imaginary),
with these often distant local and subaltern groups.

The US right-wing's "Southern strategy," based on Christian
fundamentalism, Straussian anti-democratic elitism, and a pseudo-Gramscian
march through the institutions, has ripped away so many of the victories of
'68 (Hall; Drury; Black; Lind) and the years after that we can understand
how so many American 'tenured radicals'[11] and their students have embraced
Empire. But this embrace is a sign of weakness in the intellectual community
precisely because *Empire* disguises historical error and categorical ignorance
in a cloak of seemingly transformative and irreversible political victory. In
an age of imperial defeat for most of those forces, it passes off an incredible

utopia as a basis for current action, hope, and belief — in short, a utopia arising when no one, except the desperate, should give it any assent.[12] Following all of Reagan's 'incursions,' the first Gulf War, and the US-led bombing of Belgrade (which proceeded without United Nations authorization), Hardt and Negri incredibly write that Tet "marked the irreversible military defeat of the U.S. imperialist adventures" (179). They ignore forms of especially state power not amenable to representational politics or the critique of representation. More important, they find assurance that such concerns with representation can continue, based on the supposed US constitutional transformation that, resulting from new social movements, both opened social spaces and seemingly made such events as (imperial) war and state politics of so little concern. Academic interest in this book can only come from an embrace of the utopian, vague vision of a future, of a way ahead, but no serious reader worried by the absurd claims that bring Tet and anti-racism and feminism together to end US imperial adventures, irreversibly, could trust these authors or their intentions. The fact that some find these authors' rhetoric 'useful' merely strengthens my claim that the internal desire of humanists to keep their work going, with some sense of 'world-historical' legitimacy, ironically rests upon careless reading,[13] a machinic model of intellectual work as repetition, a flight from the task of describing and analyzing the present, and the consequent requirement to produce new knowledges, new figures, and new theories that give the humanities a future from outside their academic and professionalized forms of practice.

Gopal Balakrishnan has done enough to discredit *Empire* in his essay in *NLR*.[14] He makes two essential points: that *Empire* is as neo-liberal a text as Thomas Friedman's *Lexus and the Olive Tree*; and that, in effect, *Empire* absolves America from any strenuous critique in the post-Cold War arrangements of capital. Indeed, in a manner strangely reminiscent of Chinese liberals (Bové 2002), Hardt and Negri cast accolades on the founding documents of the American republic, as if the long-standing violations of human and civil rights (struggled for the sixties and after) were not steadily eroded in the progress of the US right, culminating in the Supreme Court's decision on the 2000 presidential election in the US and in the USA Patriot Act drafted by John Ashcroft and passed by the US Congress. Balakrishnan bares how *Empire*, calling Europe 'old' in comparison with the US, praises the innovative US for its supersession of the past.

Welcoming *Empire* symbolically and typically denies the importance of intellectual, factual, and judgmental error among those cultural academics committed to the representational cultural politics that seemingly mark the victory Tet embodies over US and state adventures; as a result, despite their intentions, they find themselves on the side of those oppose. This point, made brilliantly and dramatically by Miyoshi in this volume, has profound repercussions. Unlike Hardt and Negri, Miyoshi draws readers into an intellectual regime defined as historical-temporal. His chapter structures historical loss — of passion, meaning, and purpose — in a contrast between two moments, separated by the effects of professionalization upon academic work. His style — lucid, dispassionate, unadorned — matter-of-factly pictures our political intellectual situation as what it is, a fact of history with the status of a fact of nature. This is how it is; we need to note it; we need to measure it; we should remove ourselves from worry over it. The facts are clear; the case is closed; the profession is of no interest. For many, this is a moment of political defeat.

Miyoshi's severe historical and intellectual judgments rest on an analysis of the current political, cultural climate and the inadequacy of academic cultural practice to new historical circumstances. Hardt and Negri's intellectual errors exemplify not only the carelessness Miyoshi finds everywhere but also the professional utopianism that concerns me. Cultural studies absorption of the academic humanities plays havoc with the value and importance of historical evidence. This leads many to harsh judgments. Not only right-wing ideological antagonists but 'left' social scientists often bemoan the lack of empirical information and precision in cultural studies work. Of course, there are familiar and powerful arguments available to defend against such charges. Nonetheless, even among intellectual allies, there must be honesty about imprecision. In this volume, for example, Radhakrishnan asks, "When was the last time that an American president showed concern or altered foreign trade policy in response to dire job losses in Mexico or in the Philippines?" The presumptive answer is 'never.' Yet even a close reader of newspapers knows this is not true. When the Bush regime came to power, one of its first acts was to end the Clinton-established policy that gave favored import treatment to Caribbean textiles. Radhakrishnan needs to correct his thinking because, as it were, 'the facts' do not bear out his case. Of course, Clinton was a capitalist modernizer interested in expanding markets and modernity through targeted means. So, his action was not 'state disinterested.' Nonetheless, an accurate presentation of the current situation would lead to theoretical modification, but more important to an entirely different intellectual political stance than that offered by CS — with its emotional attachment to 'resistance,' 'new social movements,' and a private language. Moreover, such assertion embodies poor judgment; it is repetitive: we 'know' that capitalist states do nothing like self-sacrifice. That cliché, however, obstructs the opportunity afforded by the lowering of trade barriers and then their raising. For example, in this one instance stands all the difference between hegemony and violence; between modernity and extraction; between knowledge and arrogance; and between slavery and liberal democracy. To occlude these demanding opportunities for analysis, argument, and persuasion establishes the solely internal legitimacy of cultural studies.

Balakrishnan describes *Empire* as "theoretical ecstasy," which, as such, substitutes for engagement with the "remorseless realities" of the present time. Ecstasy normally stands out, is 'out of place,' remarkable, but 'theoretical ecstasy' has, nowadays, become habitual and commonplace. We experience the rapid and involuted expression of difficult language as jargon. Ecstatics could be spiritual isolates, like John of the Cross or Teresa of Avila, but Balakrishnan uses the term insultingly, to refer to a morbid state, a sort of stupor or unconsciousness in which the mind is literally beside itself rather than 'adjacent' to the relentless reality that presses upon us. Theoretical ecstasy has become habitual stupor and whenever it appears rapture rather than thinking takes place. Of course, rapture can be banal as 'critics' speak in tongues, envisioning a utopian fantasy. So, theoretical rapture is belated, or, to use a more colloquial term, boring. Criticism should recover boredom as a judgmental category and apply it to those books and essays that add nothing to knowledge, even to well-intentioned essays that support repressed or resisting groups. Not everyone needs to say the same things about similar topics — no matter how legitimate they might seem. Boredom can be the category that allows criticism to advance against normal cultural work without giving comfort to the reactionaries whose ideological hatred for serious thinking and scholarship is deeper than their hatred for those tenured radicals whose work, I submit, indirectly supports their own.

This remarkable anthology gives us the strengths and weaknesses of cultural studies as an US-based export for the study of Asia-Pacific. There is some repetition; this is unavoidable in any disciplinary practice. But, as we learn from several of the chapters in this book, it matters in an imperial economy how something old in the US market it remains old even if its new market is Asia-Pacific.

Rob Wilson's chapter exposes conventional treatment of the recurrent problem, the relation between culture and economy, but far exceeds the limits of repetition. Dissatisfied with the politics of representation, he adds the dimension of state and international state politics to the mix of powers and realities critical imagination must confront in battling for the shape of Asia/Pacific. Wilson makes clear that the declared analytic liberatory goals of cultural studies cannot succeed without giving the imagination's pride of place over and against the dead hand of boredom: "It [this paper] tracks the dynamics of globalization and movements towards localization under which 'Asia-Pacific' is being constructed into a postcolonial, if not postnational, identity as a coherent region of teleological belonging." Wilson wants to suggest imagined alternatives to this process, to find the potentialities for life and agency implicit in the cultural workings of the forced emergent, Asia-Pacific: "The chapter invokes literary and cultural producers in order to force upon 'Asia/Pacific' a critical awareness of its own regional unevenness, alternative possibility, spatial contestation, and desublimated otherness. 'Asia/ Pacific' can thus become a critical signifier for a cultural and literary studies (inside APEC, as it were) in which opposition, location, indigeneity, and an alternative discursive framing of the region can be articulated." Unlike normative cultural studies' hostility to literature — an hostility that results in such markers as the listing of cultural studies books in social sciences' indices — Wilson's writing depends upon remembering both the twentieth century's preoccupation with language and the fundamental Vichian fact that institutions come from historical poiesis. So, for Wilson, 'Asia/Pacific' is a literary figure: "This trope of Asia yoked to Pacific is used to mobilize the cash-driven transfusion and to drive the megatrends of transnationalizing economies in the region, which, without such a user-friendly geopolitical signifier, does not yet exist in anything like a coherent geopolitical or cultural framework."

Wilson's chapter has an implied power of critique, not only of the capital constructors of 'Asia/Pacific,' but of those disciplinary rhetorics that reify the movement of troping in the repetition of the self-legitimating academic same. Within a chapter itself powerfully driven by anthropological interest in the unequal relation of power and freedom among genders, Jaggar, by contrast, nonetheless represents the intellectual legitimacy of professional closet talk. We must ask ourselves if we need to be told again that "The present organization of the global economy undermines democracy by rendering the sovereignty of poor nations increasingly meaningless and further excluding the poorest and most vulnerable people across the world. Many women, who are disproportionately represented among the poorest and most vulnerable of all, are effectively disenfranchised. The virtual absence even of privileged women from the decision-making processes of such bodies as the World Bank, the International Monetary Fund, and the World Trade Organization reflects the minimal influence exercised by women at the highest levels of global politics." This is an example of what post-Foucauldians should call 'normal knowledge.'[15]

Recovering boredom as a critical value allows friendly readers to say that normal discourse about horrifying abuse is more rather than less culpable. Setting aside sympathy for and active political work on behalf of the oppressed as the obvious justification for critics' writing requires an intellectual's attention to matters of critical thinking, lest that writing become self-sanctifying resting, for its own legitimacy, not upon the intellectual or imaginative struggles of the scholar/writer, but precisely upon the ease with which we add our voices to condemn (reveal? resist? subvert?) the repression of 'subaltern' groups. Wilson, the poet-critic, urges the critical mind not to be ecstatic, not to be beside him or herself, not to repeat, and to avoid imitating the mind-killing and maiming processes of the 'oppressors.' Wilson places the critic next to the world, ironically to some, by being firm about the importance of language. He calls for a poetics: "one of my contentions is that if there is to be an Asia-Pacific Cultural Studies worthy of its peoples, symbolic heritages, and cultures, then one of the tasks for such a poetics is to challenge and critique these economistic master formations and discourses of the Pacific region."

Among critics whose easy adoption of 'death of the state' rhetoric has been subtly and gently undermined by the actions of the Bush regime and the writings of its state-intellectuals, the easy repetition of certain cultural studies mantra, especially about globalization, should result in a temporary pull-back into modest silence, a practice that can do much to alleviate repetition and enhance poetic invention.[16] Balakrishnan writes that such claims, while implying the power of especially financial markets neo-liberally to destroy national sovereignty of a traditional European type (as in the Thai currency crisis), implicitly grant the US and other attached states (Japan, UK, Germany) imperial power to arrange markets and services in their own interests. The Reagan era's destruction of social services in the US, ending the resource-shifting made available by the progressive income tax and revenue-sharing with the US states — all these are examples of state action. Setting aside the entire historical and theoretical record of US ambitions to globalize neo-liberalism from the famous Open Door policy in China to the anti-union accomplishments of NAFTA, even during the height of Clintonian neo-liberalism, the ability of Malaysia (to some extent) and China (powerfully) to protect their domestic markets from neo-liberal predatory practices should cast the Friedman/Hardt-Negri consensus on weakening state power into question.

US cultural studies has a potential, no matter what the politics of its avowed critiques is, to maintain the status quo. We see this in two ways. As Balakrishnan makes clear, *Empire* is an Americanism. So too is Paul Jay writing in a long-historical manner that makes the recent neo-liberalizing regime nothing more than the nature of history, an inelegant but given status quo: "It seems to me that transnational literary studies, whether it presents itself as postcolonial or global, has to begin with a recognition that cultures have always traveled and changed, that the effects of globalization, dramatic as they are, only represent in an accelerated form something that has always taken place: the inexorable change that occurs through intercultural contact, as uneven as the forms it takes may be." This remark lacks what Radhakrishnan calls the "precision" needed for cultural studies critics to matter. Why not cast the time frame back to the migrations from Africa? In that time, US state practice seems insignificant, indeed.

Of course, US cultural studies critics not only have an aversion to the literary, but a defensive insistence on killing the fathers. Bruce Robbins' powerful reading of Ishiguro, for example, exemplifies an opportunity and a trouble for such cultural studies ambitions. Robbins is not afraid to adapt sometimes unfashionable terms and traditions for critical purposes. Rather than join in the anti-professionalism that was itself a near commodity in recent years, he modulates the category to open an entire line of thought — because the reality has not closed into a settled way of being or being thought: "professionalism would seem well suited to new trans-national demands for loyalty and solidarity at a distance, whether corporate or quasi-governmental. The question is whether this is any cause for celebration." Rather than dismiss vast oeuvres as passé, Robbins gives us critical history. History is taken seriously; it is left open as a process; and it affords space for complex judgments demanding imaginative presentations such as those found in literature. Chun and Cheng's chapter, in an entirely different mode, attempts to hold open the historical social spaces Internet modernization represents:

> The kind of globalization taking place here is perhaps consistent with what Lash and Urry calls "disorganized capitalism," following Claus Offe,

in the sense of being decentered. Lacking a regulative core, the kind of network space so engendered does not appear to be culturally hegemonic, thus does not seem prone to the homogenizing tendencies of an earlier modern world system. Discursive communities emerging in such a space would also appear to be spontaneous in a way that maximizes local autonomy. ... such disorganized flows of people, images, technology, capital and ideologies inevitably bring about incipient crises of identity. But in what sense do these crises directly engender changing public spaces, if at all?

The killing of the fathers (and mothers, let it be added), repetitive boredom, claims that appear in simple declarative sentences — mere assertions, 'justified' by theoretical reference or context — all these belong to an old pattern of intellectual life which, once upon a time, was called the treason of the clerks. Once Gramsci's influence on the question of intellectuals penetrated US-based academic life, it joined forces with the populist post-theory need for Reagan-era legitimacy to develop various arguments against the so-called 'elite' functions of the intellectual. This socio-historical fact, marked by a turning away from the near-idolatry of individual figures such as Paul de Man, Michel Foucault, and Edward W. Said among 'advanced' critics, toward more socially conscious New Historicist-based criticism legitimated by alignment with new social movements (especially on rights), itself demands greater reflection. Briefly, one noticeable side effect, in addition to those symptoms already touched upon here, is impatience with the skills of the traditional intellectual. It is as if the post-Gramscians have forgotten Gramsci's own formation as a traditional intellectual, as what Joseph Buttigieg authoritatively refers to as "a philologist." Ironically, Gramsci's great attachments to erudition, truth, and rigor have given way to a sort of ideological spontaneism of the sort he would have not recognized as intellectual at all. If each of us is an intellectual in our work wherever we are, it is because of the developed use of thinking in relation to circumstance — history, force, tradition, knowledge, as well as innovation. Ironically, especially US-based cultural studies generally prefers to reduce the specific abilities of the intellectual to the merely repetitive norms of an ordinary critical practice and discourse that, in a time of crisis, survives on its own echoes within the ever-narrowing and ineffectual chambers of ecstatic survival.

David Li's own interpretive and editorial purpose in this volume has been to overturn the problems I have tried to discuss. We can learn from his dramatic statement of how such efforts can transform the normal into the creatively persuasive. His own writing about Yang embodies the theoretical, critical, imaginative powers needed to fulfill Wilson's poetic ambition and to meet Robbins's sense of the demands an open-ended, undecided history makes upon intellectual life and society. Li persuades us that a proper utopianism sees and acts in the name of an inviting future — even in the most severely tried examples of critical dissatisfaction. He would have critics see that history is redeemable without merely relying on faith. His gracious conclusion is a strong warning, for the dangers he mentions can and do appear in criticism. They need to be cut out and thrown away in the name of that future Li finds history holding for us. The issue we engage is how we do more to enable that future we embrace, sure it is no fantasy of our present dire needs.

Li ends his introduction with a vision that is best fit to close the volume as a whole. It bears repetition:

> Yang's privileging of an ethic of relationality is resonant of Jaggar's conception of the "good," Miyoshi's "ideal of planetarianism," Robbins's notion of "inclusive civility," and Radhakrishnan's model of "reciprocal transcendence," just to name a few voices in this critical chorus on globalization and the humanities. Against the tyranny of the market and the violence of unilateral militarism, ours are among the voices of resistance that endeavor to open up dialogues on how we want to live together as a global community. It is my hope that this anthology will help us puzzle out, however minusculy, the predicament of our interdependent planetary culture. It shall help us garner the imaginative energy of writers, critics, artists and scholars to engender ways of thinking and means of creating conditions that will warrant the equal, just, and environmentally sound flourishing of our humanity.

Notes

INTRODUCTION

1. For phrase in quotation, see Bourdieu.
2. Perceptive in his mapping, Castells's heavy reliance on the "space of flows" nevertheless tends to mystify the glaring class disparity in the era of globalization to which this book is especially attentive (500–9).
3. I am grateful to all the contributors whose collective intellect makes this volume shine. I also want to thank Paul Bové for his critical assessment in the "Afterword" and Mina Kumar of Hong Kong University Press for bringing this book into fruition.

CHAPTER 1

1. Eric Hobsbawm and David Landes agree in estimating the gap in wealth among the nations to have been one digit until 1900 or later, when it widened to two digits, and then to three digits only in very recent years. The gap is far wider now between the richest and the poorest, both between nations and within nations, of which more later (Hobsbawm 15; Landes xx).
2. On February 7, *The New York Times* reported that an Indian generic drug manufacturer, Cipla Ltd. of Bombay, and companies in Brazil, Thailand, etc. are offering to sell their products at a far lower price to African countries. Of course, major patent-holders in the US, Britain, and Germany "can be expected to wage a hard fight against the distribution of generic versions of their drugs" (see McNeil).
3. One of the most concise and forceful arguments on the subject is found in Jeff Faux and Larry Mishel, "Inequality and the Global Economy."
4. Studies of neo-liberalism and globalization are by now numerous. Some of

the most helpful books are: David Held, et al., William Greider, John Gray, Juliet B. Schor and Douglas B. Holt.

CHAPTER 2

1. The collapse of the Soviet bloc has made the older terminology of First, Second and Third Worlds inapplicable, and it is now often replaced by talk about the global North and the global South. Roughly, the "global North" refers to the world's highly industrialized and wealthy states, most of which are located in the northern hemisphere — though Australia and New Zealand are exceptions. The "global South" refers to poorer states that depend mostly on agriculture and extractive industries and whose manufacturing industry, if it exists, is likely to be foreign-owned. Many (though far from all) of these states are located in the southern hemisphere, and their populations tend to be dark-skinned, whereas the indigenous populations of Northern states are mostly (though not exclusively) light-skinned. Northern states often have a history as colonizing nations, and Southern states often have been colonized. The binary opposition between global North and South is a useful shorthand, but, like all binaries (and like the older terminology of three Worlds), it is problematic if taken too seriously. Many states, such as Japan and Russia, do not fit neatly into it.

2. Domestic battery is the leading cause of injury for women in many nations of the world, but systemic violence against women has not been recognized internationally as genocide or a crime against humanity. Similarly, the customary rape of women in war has not been recognized as a war crime — it is simply something normal that soldiers do — just as the sexual abuse and torture of women in custody is something done normally by men in authority, including male guards in prisons in the US. The sale of women in marriage is often not recognized as slavery, and forced genital surgery on girls and women without their consent has not been seen as torture — even though the equivalent on boys would be holding them down and cutting off their penises. Women around the world are, as Charlotte Bunch writes, "routinely subject to torture, starvation, terrorism, humiliation, mutilation, and even murder simply because they are female. Crimes such as these against any group other than women would be recognized as a civil and political emergency as well as a gross violation of the victims' humanity" (496).

CHAPTER 3

1. See in particular *New Left Review* 238 (1999), and *The Nation*, 31 January 2000, 24 April 2000, and 8 May 2000.

2. For a succinct and insightful diagnosis of the pitfalls of postcolonial historiography, see Chakrabarty.

3. For a postcolonial critique of postmodernity, see my essay, "Postmodernism and the Rest of the World," in Afzal-Khan and Seshadri-Crooks, 37–70.

4. Slavoj Zizek has been relentless on his insistence on the importance of the big O in the project of reconceptualizing universalism. See *The Ticklish Subject* and "Cyberspace."

5. For the former, see "Traveling Theory," in *The World, the Text, the Critic*; for an articulation of "contrapuntal" reading strategies, see *Culture and Imperialism*.

6. For a brilliant co-articulation of the metropolitan with the postcolonial, see Spivak's "Reading *The Satanic Verses*," in *Outside in the Teaching Machine*, 217–41.

7. Theorists such as William Connolly and Giorgio Agamben, each in his own way, have been attempting in their work to articulate a transformative praxis between pure form and/or procedurality and the determinacy of specific ideological contents.

8. Rustom Bharucha's *In the Name of the Secular: Contemporary Cultural Activism* takes up the concept of *sarma dharma sama bhava* and provides a useful analysis of the relationship of humanity to itself through denominational variants.

9. For a provocative reading of the relationship of the "agonistic" to the "antagonistic" in the context of modern day democracy, see Mouffe. See also, Butler, Laclau, and Zizek, *Contingency, Hegemony, Universality: Contemporary Dialogues on the Left*.

10. For more on the nature of the ethical in the context of Lacan and Kant, see Zupancic and Critchley.

11. For more on the joys and perils of recognition, see "The Use and Abuse of Multiculturalism" in my forthcoming book, *Theory in an Uneven World*, where I discuss at great length the contributions of Charles Taylor and Nancy Fraser, among others, to the politics of multiculturalism.

12. "Theory in an Uneven World, " a chapter in my forthcoming book with the same title, is an attempt to come to grips, in the context of Gayatri Chakravorty Spivak's discussion of subaltern alienation, with the phenomenon of alienation. See also Beverley.

CHAPTER 4

1. See in particular the following works: Roland Robertson, *Globalization* (1992), Malcolm Waters, *Globalization* (1995), *Culture, Globalization and the World-*

System: Contemporary Conditions for the Representation of Identity edited by Anthony D. King (1997), Arjun Appadurai, *Modernity at Large: Cultural Dimensions of Globalization* (1996), Caren Kaplan, *Questions of Travel: Postmodern Discourses of Displacement* (1996), Frederick Buell, *National Culture and the New Global System* (1994), Robin Cohen, *Global Diasporas: An Introduction* (1997), Hannerz, Ulf, *Transnational Connections: Culture, People, Places* (1996), Frederic Jameson and Masao Miyoshi, editors, *The Cultures of Globalization* (1998), Susan Stanford Friedman, *Mappings: Feminism and the Cultural Geographies of Encounter* (1998), David Morley and Kevin Robins, *Spaces of Identity: Global Media, Electronic, Landscapes, and Cultural Boundaries* (1995).

2. For a variety of essays on globalization and literary studies see *Globalizing Literary Studies*, PMLA, January 2001.

3. For detailed studies of the history of literary studies in the US see Graff, Court, and Readings.

4. For similar critiques from more conservative critics see Delbanco and the recent study (issued in the summer of 2000) of fragmentation in English by the National Association of Scholars, "Losing the Big Picture: The Fragmentation of the English Major Since 1964."

5. This was particularly true of the British through the East India Company in India and the plantation system in the Caribbean.

6. For a careful discussion of this process see Waters, pp. 7–10 and chapter 6. See also Appadurai, Part One, *passim*.

7. For an extended discussion of globalization as a long historical process see Jay, "Beyond Discipline," pp. 34–36. See also Waters, pp. 1–4.

8. For a discussion of these historical phases see Loomba, chapter one. Her distinction here between pre-capitalist and capitalist forms of colonization is useful for analyzing the history of globalization as well.

9. For a counter-position, see Appadurai, who argues against the notion that globalization can simply be equated with homogenization and Westernization. He stresses how cultural forms exported from the West are often appropriated and transformed by local and diasporic populations in ways that can have positive effects.

10. On the complexity of this phenomenon see Appadurai's discussion of the "work of the imagination," pp. 5–11.

11. For extended discussion of this syncretism in the Caribbean see Benítez-Rojo and Gilroy.

12. See Appadurai's discussion of the role of the media in globalization, pp. 35–6 and *passim*. For a more extended discussion of this topic see Morley and Robbins.

13. Interview with Alex Wilber in *Plus, The Sunday Times,* October 19, 1997 online at http://www.lacnet.org/suntimes/971019/plus2.html.
14. For other extended treatments in the book of the debilitating effects of globalization see Roy's discussion of the fate of the Kathakali dancers, the transformation of the History House into a tourist hotel, and her use of the film, "The Sound of Music." On the History House as a tourist hotel, see pp. 119–20. See also pp. 52–54 on the relationship between the History House and colonialism. For Roy's extended treatment of "The Sound of Music," see pp. 90–107.
15. I want to thank my student, Abid Vali, for putting this timeline together.
16. See, for example, the episode concerning the British printer, Markline, who insists that Sanjay study Aristotle's *Poetics* in order that he might purge himself of all things Indian. "There is much in here," Markline says, jabbing Sanjay on the chest, "we need to get rid of, much stuff we need to scoop out and throw away ... . If you want to progress, you must cut yourself off from your past!" (298–9).

CHAPTER 5

1. Parts of this chapter are drawn from my essay published last year in *Revista Iberoamericana.*
2. John Muthalaya's recent essay offers a very thorough critique of literary Americanism, at least as it pertains to the way the field works in English. A similarly incisive approach to the Latin American and Latino sources he consults would have completed an important new mapping.
3. Many scholars have dealt with the "invention of America" theme as it relates to Latin America. Edmundo O'Gorman's book, first published in 1948, remains a point of departure and contention. See also José Rabasa's poststructural critique of that book and the theme in general.
4. For a detailed discussion of poststructuralism and contemporary Latin American literary criticism, see my *Latin Americanism.*
5. It seems clear that the combination of new theories and market forces has opened the way for women's voices, cultural studies, and new genres such as testimonio literature, through which various critiques of the modern Latin American identity are being articulated. One should emphasize, however, the disparate responses to such discourses in the United States and Latin America, even if these communities don't ever correspond to monolithic or opposite camps.
6. The recent anthology of essays *Mambo Montage: The Latinization of New York City,* edited by Agustín Lao-Montes and Arlene Dávila, breaks new ground in this regard.

7. The tug of war between postmodern and postcolonial approaches to Latin Americanism finds a symptomatic register in Santiago Colás's reading. As for the difficulties, and ambitions, of the subaltern turn, they are fully exemplified in *The Real Thing*, edited by Georg Gugelberger.

8. Latin Americanists working in the United States have absorbed, and to a large degree advanced, a dramatic change in the role of literature and criticism within the humanities, even if the deeper question of the United States as the historically correct model of the Americas often remains unquestioned, if not implicitly reaffirmed. In Latin America, on the other hand, literary and cultural criticism often preserve ontological, if not ideological, predicaments in which the aesthetic role of literature continues to figure prominently. To reduce these differences to nothing but a persistent remnant of Latin America's failed modernist ontology seems rather simplistic at this juncture.

9. I am referring in particular to two of Miguel Algarín's narrative poems, "Malo Dancing" and "Mongo Affair."

10. Latino groups continue to be studied and theorized by specialists in isolation from each other. Mexican Americans study Chicanos in the name of Latinos; Puerto Ricans and Cuban Americans follow analogous routes. Felix Padilla's study of Mexican Americans and Puerto Ricans in Chicago remains a highly valuable exception.

11. For an extended approach to this topic, see "Cuban-Latino Seams" in my *Cuba on My Mind: Journeys to a Severed Nation.*

12. Although an important text in many regards, it is not often observed that the often-cited *Life on the Hyphen* by Gustavo Pérez-Firmat comprises a deeply nostalgic look at the Cuban exile imaginary prior to the shift in 1980.

13. Mike Davis provides an important discussion of recent Latin migration to US metropolitan centers in *Magical Urbanism.*

14. Suzanne Oboler's *Ethnic Labels, Latino Lives* provides an excellent discussion on this topic.

15. Néstor García Canclini's work suggests various new lines of dialogue for postmodern social sciences and humanitistic disciplines.

16. The old paradigm of modern identity has also led to a state of mourning in many Latin American nations and metropolitan centers in the last decade or so. These communities now find themselves in the midst of de-modernization, as is the case in Argentina, or coping with a sense of trauma that comes with the disintegration of modern narratives in the absence of viable new ones. Idelber Avelar argues that the "state of mourning" perhaps constitutes the best understanding of Latin American postmodern literature today, although his model only deals with Southern Cone nations. It also remains unclear, in his otherwise valuable approach to the postdictatorship literary scene, how mourning will position itself, as cultural criticism, within the global capital hegemony.

17. To pretend that deconstruction is exempt from these contradictions, or that it absorbs them effortlessly, would be to fail to recognize its need to clarify its critical edge in the context of global capitalism, as Derrida, Negri and Hardt labor to show in different ways. Such a pretense would also mean ignoring the symptoms behind Harold Bloom's turn against deconstruction, or behind Richard Rorty's proposal to confine it to a North American postmodern aesthetic domain.

CHAPTER 6

1. On the resistance towards globalized "metalanguages" and the "postcolonial" turn towards more localization and the voicing of "a set of contested localized knowledges" within transnational cultural studies, see Stuart Hall, "Cultural Studies and Its Theoretical Legacies," in Lawrence Grossberg, Cary Nelson and Paula Treichler, eds., *Cultural Studies* (292). For a situated example of viewing physical and cultural geography in Asian/Pacific sites as an historical process of sub-national and transnational regionalization that links cores, peripheries, and "cultural counter-cores," see Karen Wigen.

2. Unlike many similar transnational organizations, APEC has a web page offering an open archive of their history, press releases, and policy statements that is maintained and updated daily in the "global city" of Singapore. See APEC homepage [http://ww.apecsec.org.sg]. (Tani Barlow has informed me that the headquarters of APEC may actually be located in a Seattle office on the University of Washington campus, but I have not been able to confirm this Pacific Northwest location.)

3. *Das Kapital* had been published in 1867 to map this globalized yet dispersed class struggle and spreading culture of the commodity-form, but in this interview Marx is theorizing about the suppression and misrepresentation of the Paris Commune by the British and world press.

4. During the November 14–16, 1997, meeting of APEC in Vancouver — at which point Russia, Chile and Vietnam were added to the expanding roster of APEC players in the Pacific despite the crisis of over-capitalization felt in South Korea, Thailand, and Japan — the indigenous peoples of the Pacific issued a "Pacific Peoples Declaration on APEC" (representing 12 nation states, 16 First Nations, and over 50 organizations) resisting and countering policies of "trade liberalization and other mechanisms for economic globalization" in the region as "undemocratic," disadvantaging to many, dislocating, and culturally and environmentally damaging. In short, the statement goes on to affirm, "APEC is not viable for Pacific Peoples."

5. See Leo Ching on imperialist and transnational forms of Asian-based regionalism as the ally of global capital: "In this sense mass cultural Asianism

mediates between the process of the globalization of capital and the anxiety over the erosion of the nation form" (255). Nevertheless, the ability of nation-states to set market policies, frame cultural hegemony, and handle the drastic social consequences of global capitalism cannot be denied, however "internationalist" or "post-national" the current moment appears. See Arjun Appadurai, *Modernity at Large*, chapter 8.

6. Portraying various versions of local and global regionality in the Pacific islands, Richard A. Herr notes the shift from decolonizing visions of Pacific Islands regionalism to those which are more transnationally driven: "The emerging international order is likely to propel the islands towards further engagement with the rest of the world, particularly the countries of the Pacific rim" (298).

7. Ackbar Abbas, "Cultural Studies in a Postculture," paper presented at the Second International Symposium on Cultural Criticism at The Chinese University of Hong Kong, January 4–6, 1996, on the telling global/local theme, "Cultural Politics of Cosmopolitanism: Critiques of Modernity in the Non-Western Context."

8. What counts as a "regional" unity of symbolic and material forces in Europe, America, and East Asia is up for disciplinary grabs, as postmodern US "area studies" now mutate into something palpably transnational and micropolitical in formation and aim; see Rafael.

9. As the "black" (meaning "people of color" in the UK), in its global coloration and multiple locations, is being put back into the Union Jack, and "the Black Atlantic" diaspora is reimagined as an historical event, the core of cultural identity and nationhood is being constructed and creolized in contexts of ethnic difference, from Birmingham and Melbourne, to the ex-British colony of Hong Kong, where a new cultural identity of "the local" has begun — against the apocalyptic odds of Milton Friedman and 1997 — to assert itself, as in the work of cultural critics like Stephen Chan and Akbar Abbas. For a critical and "queer" take on this Hong Kong diaspora, see Audre Yue.

10. On the formation of "Asia-Pacific" and "inter-Asia" networks of cultural-political solidarity wherein Britain and Europe are hardly as important as "East-West" binaries once implied, see Jon Stratton and Ien Ang (1995).

11. See Stephen Sumida's wide-ranging study of Bamboo Ridge culture, *The View From the Shore*, and my chapbook, *Pacific Postmodern*, as well as my book-length study *Reimagining the American Pacific: From "South Pacific" to Bamboo Ridge and Beyond*.

12. Wendt's talk is reprinted, in expanded form, in *Inside Out* (Hereniko and Wilson 1999). On the heteroglossic and multi-sited range of emergent literatures of decolonization and primordial indigeneity/hybridity inside the postmodern Pacific, see also Wendt, *Nuanua: Pacific Writing In English Since 1980* (1995).

13. Rafael is describing the cold war American's uncanny fascination with the "romance of Asia" as a predisposition ("call") to study, love, and work in sites in Asia/Pacific.

14. I could also invoke new literary journals like *Melimelo* in Kyoto and *Tinfish* and *Hybolics* in Honolulu, which are fusing an interest in Asian/Pacific-based aesthetics with more experimental modes of writing in literature and ethnography, something happening in *Hawai'i Review* as well, which appears to be forging a "post-local" view of Hawai'i beyond a Bamboo Ridge aesthetic of "the local." On these issues, tactics, and polemics, see Rob Wilson, *Pacific Postmodern* (2000).

CHAPTER 7

1. For some of the best work on diaspora, which does not succumb to this essentializing tendency, see Chow, Clifford, and Hall.

2. See the extensive bibliography in Gordon and Newfield. For some comparative work with predominantly European countries, see Dunne and Bonazzi, and Milich and Peck.

3. The revised version also notes, "The term multiethnic education was used in the title and throughout the first edition; in the revised edition, multicultural education is used. Today, multicultural education is the most frequently used term to refer to the issues and concerns discussed in this document. The term multiethnic education has almost faded from our lexicon."

4. For Trudeau's "national will, " see *Federalism*, especially "Federalism, Nationalism, and Reason" and *Meech Lake*, 45.

5. Gairdner has a PhD in French from Stanford.

6. For a balanced view of Rousseau and totalitarianism see Chapman and D'Entrèves.

7. Lowe so wants to show how the state subordinates racial, cultural and other differences to a "public culture" that she effaces Althusser's important distinction between state and ideological state apparatuses in describing the "state apparatuses — schooling, the communications media, the legal system" (144).

8. This helpful formulation comes from Lloyd and Thomas, who generate it only to disagree and insist on an Althusserian model.

CHAPTER 8

1. TCP/IP is an abbreviation for Transmission Control Protocol/Internet Protocol. For details, see RFC 1594.

2. NSFNET stands for National Science Foundation Network. USENET is a Unix-

based network that first linked systems at University of North Carolina and Duke University. CSNET is the Computer Science Network that was formed as a result of collaboration between computer scientists at University of Wisconsin, University of Delaware, Purdue University and the Rand Corporation. Lastly, BITNET evolved out of an IBM system that linked City University of New York to Yale.

3. For a detailed timetable of the major events in Internet's development, see Zakon (1997) and Leiner et al.

4. For a technical discussion of cyberspace, see the essays in Benedikt (1992).

5. See, for example, the definition of cyberspace interpretive community employed by Gourgey and Smith (1996). A more constructive definition of cyber-community is found in Jones (1994). Case examples are examined extensively in Smith and Kollock (2000).

6. As Baudrillard (1983) once put it, cyberspace does not eliminate social forms and relations so much as *simulate* them, i.e. by reproducing them as codes and structures of information.

7. MUD is also known as Multiple User Dimension and Multiple User Dungeon. Internet Relay Chat is a multiuser chat system that allows participants to engage in simultaneous dialogue by text input. In Taiwan, newsgroups and bulletin board systems are usually provided on network servers to enable participants to make inquiries and engage in interactive discussions. Gopher is an information system created in 1991 at the University of Minnesota that also provided links to netnews, ftp, hytelnet, BBS, archie and WAIS servers. The World Wide Web was also created in 1991 at CERN that took advantage of the TCP/IP protocol to enable data access to graphics sites.

8. For an overview of Taiwan's Internet development, see Table 8.4. For detailed information on TANet, see their website at http://www.ntu.edu.tw/TANet. Electronic mail is provided by the telnet protocol, which is an open remote login system that differs from closed email systems such as BITNET. FTP stands for file transfer protocol that enables transfer of files between servers as well as uploading and downloading to PCs. Archie is a server that provides access to public domain software and databases. WAIS is short for Wide Area Information Servers, developed by Thinking Machines Corporation in 1991.

9. The major gopher server in Taiwan is operated by the Information Engineering Department at National Chiao-tung University (gopher.csie.nctu.edu.tw).

10. For further information on the development of Taiwan's Internet, see the WWW website of the Taiwan Network Information Center at http://www.twnic.net.

11. A precise indication of the increasing volume of Taiwan's Internet activity on a worldwide scale is clearly reflected in Usenet statistics compiled by various service websites, the most useful being The Freenix Top 1000 List, http://www.freenix.fr/top1000, and The Feedinfo Newsfeed Statistics Gatherer, http:/

/www.paranoia.org/news. For instance, The Freenix Top 1000 List shows that, from January 1995 to September 1997, the number of Taiwan Usenet sites that have appeared among the 1000 most active sites has gradually grown from 3 to over 30. Over 75% of the Taiwan sites originate from academic nodes (edu.tw), and the most active of these sites tend to be computer hardware discussion groups.

12. See American Anthropological Association and Computing Research Association (1995: 14–16).

13. The newsgroup discussion groups listed on the Academia Sinica netserver also include links to discussion groups at National Chiao-tung University.

14. For a systematic, comprehensive discussion of governance, see Loader (1997).

15. For Habermas' reformulation in this regard, see Habermas (1989).

16. See Chun (1994) and Chun (1995).

CHAPTER **9**

1. Media censorship in China is conducted by the Propaganda Departments of the Communist Party at various levels, from the county to municipal, provincial, and national (the highest being the Central Committee's Propaganda Department). Significant domestic and international news, such as Sino-American relations, a serious plane crash, and so on, must be approved by the Central Committee's censorship group.

2. A web source on *Huayue luntan* (a US-based Chinese-language online forum/chat room) reveals that the National Endowment for Democracy (NED) in the US funds several dozens of Chinese political dissident groups, including the CND and *Hua Xia Wen Zhai*. The source charges that the CIA is actually the underwriter of the NED (though the evidence of this allegation is not yet verified). *Huayue luntan*, January 14, 2001, http://huayue.org.

3. For a story of the "beauty-baby authors" told from the American media perspective, see Craig Smith.

CHAPTER **10**

1. Ian Baucom develops a related notion of global form "a spoked wheel whose expanding rim spins ever more tightly around a glittering metropolitan hub." He goes on to argue that globalism must be apprehended as a simultaneous expansion and contraction (160).

2. As Fernando Coronil notes economic growth in the Third World has often occurred at the expense of a sense of national belonging. As the income disparities between the rich and the poor widen in both transnational and national contexts, globalization increasingly promotes the formation of a class of global labor within the bounds of the nation-state that owe their allegiance

to global rather than national culture and lifeways (362). A quasi-comic instance of this is provided by Mark Landler's report in the *New York Times* of the customer service units for US companies based in Bangalore where employees take on "fake" American identities to give the impression that they are based in the US, to erase their location and reinvent themselves as real immigrants ("Hi, I'm In Bangalore").

3. This is a phenomenon that sociologists Robertson, Pieterse, Friedman and Luke have termed "glocal" (*Global Modernities*). For an intriguing critique of what is invested in a term like globalization, see Victor Li's "What's in a Name" (12).

4. POI represent a recent census category created by the Indian government to further nuance the existing category of the NRI (Non-Resident Indian). This is seen as a step towards dual citizenship.

5. This nomenclature of Valley/Alley is itself indicative of the production of locality in information technology culture.

6. Koramangalam.com (accessed, 8 March 2001).

7. It is essential, especially in the light of the recent collapse of so many e-commerce sites, to stress the fact that cyberspace was not meant to take over everyday life but rather stretch the limits of the possible. It promised more rather than less, choices rather than substitutes. E-commerce realized at considerable cost that it could only become profitable by supplanting, rather than substituting, brick and mortar companies.

8. Immigrants/Migrants worldwide tend to be very "net-friendly." As scholars from different disciplines have observed displaced populations from different nationalities and ethnicities use the net to reinsert themselves in the nation left behind. Jon Anderson in "Cybarities" explores the Internet use patterns of the Middle Eastern Diaspora while Lynn A. Staeheli explores the formation of Mexican political communities in cyberspace and the ways in which they remotely intervened in the national elections.

9. This experience of space left behind as time past is itself an aspect of the Western modernity, which characterized the "other spaces" from where "Third-World" immigrants inevitably come as "backward." From the accounts of eighteenth-century travelers through the discourse of development and underdevelopment, modernity measures space via time.

10. Jean Starobinski enacts this precise move in using the language of border-crossing and immigration to speak the discourse of nostalgia (81).

11. Andrea Huyssens claims that in modernism, memory is always associated with some utopian space and time beyond what Benjamin called the "homogeneous time of the capitalist present" (8).

12. Cyberspace, after all, is the co-creation of US military and the folk from its exact ideological opposite, aging hippies.

13. In vocational terms, Indians in North America can be grouped as follows: professionals like doctors, academics and researchers; tradespeople ranging from convenience store and gas station owners through those in the hospitality industry; a largely urban group of taxi-drivers, janitors, etc. concentrated in the coasts; and finally, tech workers across all levels from "slave coders" on H-1B visas through star entrepreneurs. The more recent diaspora, owing to immigration policies dictated by industry needs, has been overwhelmingly in this last area. For more specific data and a historical and demographic analysis see Ronald Takaki, Karen Leonard and Vijay Prashad.

14. *Business India* and *Business Week.*

15. Ajit Balakrishnan, CEO of Rediff.com, arguably the most popular of these portals, expresses this when he says that in order to increase rediff.'s marketshare, the company would have to target "less net-savvy users" by making the site more easily navigable. But even as he discusses the prospects of rediff's e-commerce division, he acknowledges that inroads into the Indian market might be slow.

16. The immigrant, in a real sense, extricated herself from the homeland's economy, thus the concept of the "brain drain."

17. "Hindu Being/Hindu Buying: Hindutva Online and the Commodity Logic of Cultural Nationalism," forthcoming in *South Asian Review.*

18. Chaitime.com was a victim of the recent Internet crash. Though there is little evidence as to why it went under, one can speculate that the site, based in the US, experienced logistical difficulties and escalating costs in making the "home" present to the diaspora. Unlike rediff.com, it was not glocalized enough but rather sought to cater to a more traditional "immigrant" market based in the US.

CHAPTER 11

1. Several of the following paragraphs are taken from my discussion of *Remains of the Day* in "The Village of the Liberal Managerial Class." The present chapter extends the argument of the earlier one.

2. More recently Ulf Hannerz has made much the same connection in *Cultural Complexity: Studies in the Social Organization of Meaning,* 252–55.

3. The same is true of Ishiguro's *When We Were Orphans* (2000), which invites an extension of the present argument.

4. Salecl goes on: "For that reason, it would be a mistake to depict Stevens as the only culprit for the nonrealization of the love affair ... On the one hand [Miss Kenton] wants Stevens to change, to reveal his love for her, but on the other hand she loves him only for what he actually is — a functionary who tries by all available means to avoid his desire" (185).

5. This hypothesis is vigorously debated by Ferguson, who ultimately rejects the idea, pressed forcefully by figures like John Maynard Keynes, that "the burden of reparations on Germany doomed Europe to a new war" (439). For him, responsibility for the rise of Nazism falls more heavily on the Versailles treaty's assumption that "disarmament could suffice to eradicate militarism" and on its "invocation of the principle of 'self-determination'" (439). According to Ferguson, "Keynes was manipulated by his German friends" (408). He was "too trusting" (410). Still, the intriguing parallels between Keynes and Ishiguro's Lord Darlington clearly work in the latter's favor, especially considering how widespread Ferguson shows the reaction in Britain to be against the perceived harshness of the reparations (397).

6. As it happens, Keynes was also a proponent of professionalism in international affairs. The speech in which "Keynes's influence on the reparation issue reached its zenith," in August 1922, when he urged an abandonment of national revenge in the interest of world peace, also contained a prediction that "'the day of scientific, administrative and executive skill was at hand'" (Ferguson 405–6).

7. The situation of the putatively world-renowned musician and expert makes him a useful figure, at the level of manners where the novel is most comfortable, not just for Ishiguro's own book tours, but also for the vast differential in cultural and economic power separating metropolis and periphery, whether that periphery belongs to the Third World or (as here) the former Second. Of course, this is not just a fact about Europe, where Ishiguro's Britishness seems to echo Britain's peculiar reluctance to be either in or out. It's also characteristic of the 1990s troubles over humanitarian internationalism in what's been called the age of human rights.

8. Moeller: "The most insidious of the reasons for minimalist reporting is the constant restriction of time and space. The world cannot really be covered in the 21 or 22 minutes of news broadcast in the networks' evening programs or in the hundred odd pages of the newsweeklies or even in the thick wad of newsprint of the Sunday *New York Times.* Given newshole constraints, the stories most likely to disappear from news programs and newspapers are continuing international stories" (29).

9. Moeller comments: "They haven't *done* anything. But as they sit passively in front of their TV sets, they've been barraged with redundant images" (43).

10. What we experience as lack of time, like the expression "not having time for something," would be a sort of pragmatic euphemism (if I did have time I might be more open to it) for a rejection that really happens on principle.

11. In *The End of Capitalism (as we knew it): A Feminist Critique of Political Economy,* J. K. Gibson-Graham has seized on the "penetration" metaphor to illustrate the shortcomings of the globalization concept.

12. More might be said both about the professionalism of Ryder's music, the transnational expertise that gets him invited in the first place and that one might argue is never quite discredited by the subsequent events, and about the Porter's Dance — a dance in which the porters act out their heroic ability to keep bags in the air — as a local or national parallel to music, as a seemingly arbitrary and yet valuable community-forming genre of expertise. More might also have to be said about the death of Gustav, which seems to result from the Porter's Dance and is a sort of limit case for professionalism, much as the death of Stevens's butler father in *Remains of the Day* was a test or limit case for professionalism there. If professionalism uses competence as grounds for social inclusion, it reaches its limits at the moment of mortal incompetence, for example the moment when the professional becomes too old or infirm to perform his or her duties properly, when he or she no longer fits by virtue of competence but, if at all, according to some more capacious principle. The obvious examples from *Remains of the Day* are the moments when Stevens's father trips and drops a tray and can no longer stop a drop of snot from falling from his nose. But it should not simply be assumed that no more capacious principle is compatible with professionalism, which means being too "busy" to deal with moments and matters of ultimate importance, putting off ultimates in the name of an ultimate purposelessness. Death is also the test that Benedict Arnold applies to cosmopolitanism. According to Anderson, the success of nationalism results from its ability to offer the solace for death that religion once offered. In offering the individual a continuity of the self in time as well as space, it offers a practical form of immortality. The implication is that just as the professional cannot compete affectively with the family, so genuine consolation cannot be found beyond the nation, where feeling is less intense. But Anderson's own argument works against this conclusion. Anderson says the erotic form of American nationalism is the homosocial buddy plot. Anderson writes: "Rather than a national eroticism [as suggested by Leslie Fielder], it is, I suspect, an eroticized nationalism that is at work" (202–3 n32). But buddy plots are now both heterosexual and transnational. That is, they point, however provisionally, at professional bonding that is also transnational bonding.

13. Gleick continues: " 'If you travel in Asia at all, you will notice that the DOOR CLOSE button in elevators is the one with the paint worn off,' says [the director of technology at Otis Elevator]. 'It gets used more than any other button.' "

14. In his brilliant new novel *The Intuitionist,* the African-American novelist Colson Whitehead imagines a genius of elevator theory who, in a book entitled *Theoretical Elevators,* imagines an elevator that waits — for speech to happen, for the circuit of communication to be completed: You are standing on a train platform. A fear of missing the train, a slavery to time, has provided ten minutes

before the train leaves. There is so much you have never said to your companion and so little time to articulate it ... The conductor paces up and down the platform and wonders why you do not speak. You are a blight on his platform and timetable. Speak, find the words, the train is warming towards departure ... The train is always leaving and you have not found your words. Remember the train, and that thing between you and your words. An elevator is a train. The perfect train terminates in Heaven. The perfect elevator waits while its human freight tries to grab through the muck and find the words. (86–87)

15. There is an analogy here with the equally sudden addition to the butler's conversational repertoire of "banter," which mixes work and play, the responsible and the erotic, at the end of *Remains of the Day*.

16. This argument demands more attention to the feminist politics of time. If feminists can easily agree on the need for greater gender equality in the time spent on housekeeping and childrearing, the next step is less obvious. What about the absolute time the family puts into those tasks? Must it also be reduced? And if so, how? One solution — the one encouraged these days, and adopted by those who can afford it — is to commodify more and more tasks, paying others to do or produce, either inside or outside the home, what was once done or produced inside the home. A second, not incompatible, solution is more government-supported institutions like day care, which are often seen as more of an "intrusion" into the family than cash payment, though cash payment decreases the total time the family must invest in its maintenance only by increasing the need for earned income. A third solution is for both men and for women to wean themselves away from the work ethic and the assumption that work outside the home is more meaningful, thus freeing up a larger proportion of total time for the family. To this I have no objection (on the contrary), but I add the observation that it would entail transforming not just the workplace but also the family. Indeed, it would transform the family so drastically as to blur the line between the family and the workplace, with its (relative) sexual equality, its increasing open-endedness of sexual roles, and its ambiguous mixture of intimacy and distance. Consider for example Judith Stacey's account of the "postmodern family": "a truly democratic gender and kinship order, one that does not favor male authority, heterosexuality, a particular division of labor, or a singular household or parenting arrangement [has become] thinkable for the first time in history" (258). In other words, such a family might be said to aim at something very like the erotic collegiality that, according to Renata Salecl, draws the butler and housekeeper together in *Remains of the Day*.

   At any rate, it would have to aim in a different direction than that of E.P. Thompson's classic essay "Time, Work-Discipline and Industrial Capitalism."

In that essay Thompson describes women's work "with the children and in the home" as "necessary and inevitable, rather than . . . an external position. This remains true to this day," he goes on, "and, despite school times and television times, the rhythms of women's work in the home are not wholly attuned to the measurement of the clock. The mother of young children has an imperfect sense of time and attends to other human tides. She has not yet altogether moved out of the conventions of 'pre-industrial' society." As Carol Watts points out (15), this is nothing worth returning to. Indeed, it comes very close to justifying Ryder's complaint about Sophie's "small world" view of both space and time.

CHAPTER **12**

1. I would like to thank Julia Lesage and Leah Middlebrook for their perceptive readings of an earlier version of this chapter.
2. For an informative Chinese-language study of Yang's film career up to *A Confucian Confusion*, see Huang. I thank Chris Berry for this reference.
3. I agree in principle with this characterization. However, to treat Western societies as free from "non-simultaneities and non-synchronicities" of the modern seems to disregard the fact that globalization of economy and culture has in effect produced within all existing nation-states the co-existence of First World and Third World.
4. Yang anticipates his dual audience, Chinese and non-Chinese via a deliberate play of bilingualism and biculturalism. Just as he omits Confucius's answer in the citation, he does not literally translate *Duli Shidai* as *Age of Independence* but prefers *Confucian Confusion*. Not at all a contradiction in terms, the Chinese and the English titles have epitomized the film's exposition of the liberties and bewilderment in late capitalist Taiwan. The quotation of Confucius is from Chapter 13 "Zi Lu" of *The Analects* (translation mine).
5. See Berger and Hsiao, and Tu as examples of Neo-Confucianism. *In Our Time* is the English title of the collaborative cinematic project, *Guangyin de gusi* (literally, *The Story of Time*) that marks Yang's film debut in 1982.
6. Lyotard typifies the postmodernist I have in mind while Beck, Giddens, and Lash (115–6) stand for the reflexive modernists. Both groups share the diagnosis that the organized capitalism of earlier industrialization is over and contemporary societies are characterized by heterogeneity of life-worlds.
7. I am using the DVD version of *Yi Yi* (2001). All English citations in the text are based on this edition's subtitles and my own translation.
8. While it is not the focus of this chapter, to read the Nussbaum volume on cosmopolitanism and patriotism together with de Barry and Tu's edition on Confucianism and human rights yield unexpected insights on the question of membership, of rights and responsibilities in globalization.

9. It behooves us to recall Pierre Bourdieu in this context: "It is perhaps no accident that so many people of my generation have moved from a Marxist fatalism to a neoliberal fatalism: in both cases, economism forbids responsibility and mobilization by canceling out politics. ... What is surprising is that this fatalistic doctrine gives itself the air of a message of liberation, through a whole series of lexical tricks round the idea of freedom, liberation, deregulation, etc." (50).

10. The figure she made is a butterfly, which, in the context of "Zhuang Zhou Meng Die" when the Taoist master becomes the butterfly in his dream, has at least two dimensions of significance, first, as a self-referential commentary on fantasy and reality, and second, as a metaphor for the radical unpredictability of life, this time, in contemporary Taipei or in global modernity.

11. See Horton and Mendus's collection on MacIntyre's corpus in general, and Haldane's critique of his Roman Catholicism and Thomistic Aristotelianism in particular.

12. The other character whose presence is ushered by his noise is Meiguo, literally translated to mean "America," a translation the English transliteration of the DVD does not provide.

13. Giddens, and to some degree, Ong, are more interested in the possibilities of successfully coping with disorganized capitalism by highlighting individual and institutional agency and flexibility than in contemplating on fundamental structural alternatives and resistances. What is absent in their theories is an ethical critique of late capitalism that Yang insists on.

14. It is not accidental that Yangyang gave Adi a photo of his head from the back, helping his uncle to see what he cannot, a point as lost on Adi as it is on the schoolmaster, who trashes the entire stack of Yangyang's photos as "expensive," "useless," "avant-garde art." Both men, intriguingly, are featured with thick glasses, spectacles of myopia standing for the fragmented state of the self.

15. Of related interest is Tsai Min-liang's treatment of the simultaneity of France and Taiwan in *Ni neibian jidian* (*What Time is it There?* 2001).

16. It is important to observe Yang's positioning of Japan as an idyllic country, a nostalgic retreat from the metropolitan and cosmopolitan rush of Taipei, contrary to Wong Kar-wai's more standard use of less developed nation-states (e.g. Argentina and Cambodia) as escapes from Hong Kong. I don't have space here to pursue this significance further, however.

17. For the theme of re-embedding in the mainland cinematic allegory on globalization, *Ermo*, see my essay, "What Will Become of Us if We Don't Stop?". It is worth noting that Edward Yang's resolution of tempting affairs in *Yi Yi* is identical to Wong Kai-wai's in *In the Mood for Love* (2001). Both have favored an inhibition of individual desire, an aesthetic and ethic alternative very much against the cultural grain of late modernity.

18. NJ is practically married into Minmin's family since Popo is his mother-in-law. The alternative scenario of Tinging and Nainai, or her paternal grandma, holding hands would suggest some sort of straight patrilineal descent, but it is not in the film proper.

AFTERWORD

1. See Alexander Stille, "Apocalypse Soon." *The New York Review of Books.* 7 November 2002. Cf. <http://www.nybooks.com/articles/15801>

2. It is completely normal for any academic humanistic or cultural book to be attacked by a certain set of right-wing ideological hound-dogs who immediately sniff out and cover with mud anything that even erroneously might seem to open up a space for thinking outside the box of right-wing censorship. It is not surprising then that Alan Wolfe, chief anti-intellectual hunter in *The New Republic*, in an essay wonderfully entitled "The Snake," so conveniently and neatly ties up the features of *Empire* that amuse me: "Still, Empire has become something of a publishing sensation. The *Times* has pronounced that it has 'buzz,' the most enviable epithet of all. It has sold out in bookstores around the country; it is being translated into at least ten languages; and it has been featured in gushing media accounts, including [Emily] Eakin's uninformed account in the *Times*. (For the *Times'* reporter on "Arts and Ideas," testimony from tired Marxists such as Stanley Aronowitz or Fredric Jameson is taken as proof that *Empire* may be the next big thing among other equally washed-out Marxists.)"

3. Sir Howard Stringer, the President of SONY America, told the *Times* "The global economy, he said, remains on the ropes, while the preparations for war in Iraq have transformed the conference, once a showcase for the high-technology ambitions of companies like Sony and Microsoft, into a forum for criticism of the United States and its foreign policy. 'How do you separate the protesters outside from the hostility inside?' said Sir Howard, who is a repeat visitor to the conference. 'For the first time, the demonstrations seem peculiarly redundant.'" Scott McNealey, the chief executive of Sun Microsystems, said: "I suppose you could ask, `What good is it to have Web browser access when your building falls down?'" (*New York Times*; Titans)

4. There is evidence that the Bush regime embraces the term as well as the practice of imperialism in the fact that the work of a British Foreign Office intellectual influences several figures in the American State (Cooper; Young).

5. There were and are a number of arguments that might claim the Belgrade bombing was not a US military adventure. Chief among such apologists would be Habermas. Habermas makes clear his defense of state realism in defending the US bombing of Belgrade and casts this defense in terms of civil rights:

"Naturally the United States and the member states of the European Union, who carry the burden of political responsibility, start from a unified position. After the collapse of the talks at Rambouillet the threatened military strikes against Yugoslavia are being carried out with the expressed intention of pushing through a liberal solution for the autonomy of Kosovo within Serbia. Within the framework of traditional international law this action would have counted as an interference in the internal affairs of a sovereign state, i.e. a violation of the principle of non-intervention. Under the premise of human rights policy, this intervention is now to be seen as an armed peace-creating mission, which is authorised by the association of nations (admittedly without a UN mandate). According to this Western interpretation the Kosovo war could turn into a leap from the classical conception of international law for sovereign states towards the cosmopolitan law of a world civil society." The Clinton administration's use of civil rights talk as legitimation of American neo-liberalism has been the object of critique (Bové). It would be an error, characteristic of the mindset of *Empire*'s authors, not to see how the Habermasian or Clintonian defense of US-led military and economic action within globalization, even when masked as a human rights appeal, also legitimates US hegemony backed, as became clear in Belgrade, by overwhelming diplomatic, political, and military state power. Not to understand the bombing of Belgrade as an act of US military adventurism is willfully naïve.

6. This volume contains a number of important examples of cultural political work consequent upon the development of extra-state or supra-state institutions, such the International Monetary Fund, the Internet, the EU, APEC, and so on, each of which can be interpreted as a partial surrender of sovereignty and, along with such phenomena as border-crossing, migration, and diaspora make possible post-statist forms of critical discussion to explicate their importance. These chapters also show that discussing these post-state or porous state phenomena depends upon the inventiveness of cultural studies. See the chapters by Jaggar, Wilson, Jay, and de la Campa, among others, for the results of such work.

7. The strategic planners in the US government do not agree with Hardt and Negri (or many others) about the declining power of the state, especially the US State. In the "The National Security Strategy of the United States," George W. Bush asserts "It is time to reaffirm the essential role of American military strength. We must build and maintain our defenses beyond challenge" (Bush).

8. The very best commentator on the value inherent within professionalism and, at its best, cosmopolitanism is Bruce Robbins. In an important series of essays that includes the one collected in this volume, "Very Busy Just Now: Globalization and Harriedness in Ishiguro's *The Unconsoled*," Robbins closely

reads through novels specifying the representative value of literature to our social discussions and the complex interactions that modern and postmodern professionalization and cosmopolitanism present to our judgments. For example, writing of Ishiguro Robbins asks: "professionalism would seem well suited to new trans-national demands for loyalty and solidarity at a distance, whether corporate or quasi-governmental. The question is whether this is any cause for celebration."

9. It is worth recalling here some of Stanley Fish's arguments in defense of professionalization as they have developed from his debates with Edward W. Said in the pages of *Critical Inquiry* (Fish; Said).

10. See, for example, Munck, which opens describing *Empire* as "opportune ... influential ... bold ... striking ... radicalized. ... with a vision of a 'postmodernised global economy,' Hardt and Negri do not believe that any nation-state, even the US, can act as a centre for an imperialist project today."

11. Kimball's book is a carefully plotted ideological assault by a political writer with a reactionary bias whose aim is to drive anti-conservative scholars and teachers from the university as part of the right-wing's patient and thorough effort to control American institutions. Many came to embrace his definition of a generation and cadre committed to justice and learning.

12. For some sense of how common this aspiration is among both the anonymous academic workers and their professional and ideological leaders or paradigmatic points of reference, see Bové (1999).

13. Rowe makes the strongest case that "Behind the demand for 'close' and 'careful' reading there is also a profoundly conservative impulse to keep us focused on familiar texts recognized as 'difficult' and 'serious' " (112).

14. "But while they downplay the mailed fist of the US in the global arena, they grant America a more gratifying centrality as a laboratory of domestic political innovation. As they see it, both the apogee and the antithesis of Empire lie in the inclusive, expansive republicanism of the US Constitution, which long ago shed the European fetish of a homogeneous nation. In this spirit, Hegel is cited — "America is the country of the future, and its world historical importance has yet to be revealed in the ages which lie ahead ... It is the land of desire for all those who are weary of the historical arsenal of old Europe" — and Tocqueville congratulated for deepening him, with an exemplary understanding of the significance of American mass democracy. There is an echo of old illusions here. *Empire* bravely upholds the possibility of a utopian manifesto for these times, in which the desire for another world buried or scattered in social experience could find an authentic language and point of concentration. But to be politically effective, any such reclamation must take stock of the remorseless realities of this one, without recourse to theoretical ecstasy" (Balakrishnan).

15. "The same may be said for complaints that cultural studies relies on formulaic or predictable considerations of race, class, gender, and sexual orientation. These categories are important precisely because they help map so many social fields and because so many people have something to say about them." Rowe's commitments to social democracy could not be more evident. But where are the intellectuals in the class "so many people"? Does the permission to say ever cross the border into professional (that is, elite) repetition and intellectual irresponsibility? (Rowe, 111)

16. Paul Jay writes the following: "However, the rise of the multi-national corporation, and later, the internet, has transformed Wallerstein's world system by decentering the role of the nation-state. Indeed, more and more, Wallerstein's world system, tied as it is to the dominance of the modern nation-state, looks like the last phase of an age in eclipse, since under globalization the nation-state is being undermined by transnational forces that threaten its traditional power to regulate subjectivity and determine what constitutes cultural belonging."

Works Cited

INTRODUCTION

Abramson, Jeffrey B., F. Christopher Arterton and Gary R. Orren eds. *The Electronic Commonwealth: The Impact of New Media Technologies on Democratic Politics.* New York: Basic Books, 1988.

Beck, Ulrich, Anthony Giddens and Scott Lash. *Reflexive Modernization: Politics, Tradition and Aesthetics in the Modern Social Order.* Stanford: Stanford University Press, 1994.

Bourdieu, Piérre. Trans. Richard Rice. *Acts of Resistance: Against the Tyranny of the Market.* New York: The New Press, 1998.

Buell, Frederick. *National Culture and the New Global System.* Baltimore: Johns Hopkins University Press, 1994.

Castells, Manuel. *The Rise of the Network Society.* Malden, MA: Blackwell, 1996.

Cheah, Pheng and Bruce Robbins eds. *Cosmopolitics: Thinking and Feeling beyond the Nation.* Minneapolis, MN: University of Minnesota Press, 1998.

Eisenstadt, S. N. ed. *Daedalus: "Multiple Modernities, A Special Issue."* 129.1 (Winter 2000).

Gaonkar, Dilip Paramwshwar ed. *Alternative Modernities.* Durham, NC: Duke University Press, 2001.

Giddens, Anthony. *The Consequences of Modernity.* Stanford: Stanford University Press, 1990.

Gilroy, Paul. *Against Race: Imagining Political Culture Beyond the Color Line.* Cambridge, MA: Harvard University Press, 2000.

Hardt, Michael and Antonio Negri. *Empire.* Cambridge, MA: Harvard University Press, 2000.

Harvey, David. *The Condition of Postmodernity: An Enquiry into the Origins of Social Change.* Cambridge: Blackwell Publishers, 1990.

Held, David, Anthony McGrew, David Goldblatt and Johnathan Perraton eds. *Global Transformations: Politics, Economics and Culture.* Stanford: Stanford University Press, 1999.

Jameson, Fredric. *A Singular Modernity: Essay on the Ontology of the Present.* New York: Verso, 2002.

Jameson, Fredric and Masao Miyoshi eds. *The Cultures of Globalization.* Durham, NC: Duke University Press, 1998.

Nussbaum, Martha and Joshua Cohen eds. *For the Love of Country: Debating the Limits of Patriotism.* Boston: Beacon Press, 1996.

Okin, Susan Moller, Joshua Cohen, Matthew Howard, and Martha Nussbaum eds. *Is Multiculturalism Bad for Women?* Princeton: Princeton University Press, 1999.

Poster, Mark. "Digital Networks and Citizenship." *PMLA: Mobile Citizens, Media States.* 117.1 (January 2002): 98–103.

Readings, Bill. *The University in Ruins.* Cambridge, MA: Harvard University Press, 1996.

Sen, Amartya. *Development as Freedom.* New York: Anchor Books, 1999.

Wilson, Rob and Wimal Dissanayake eds. *Global/Local: Cultural Production and the Transnational Imaginary.* Durham, NC: Duke University Press, 1996.

CHAPTER **1**

Appiah, K. Anthony. "Battle of the Bien-Pensant." *The New York Review of Books* 27 April 2000: 42–44.

Auerback, Nina. "Acrimony." *The London Review of Books* 6 July 2000: 6–8.

Barthes, Roland. *Writing Degree Zero.* Trans. Annette Lavers and Colin Smith. New York: Hill and Wang, 1967.

Castells, Manuel. "Information Technology and Global Capitalism." *Global Capitalism.* Eds. Will Hutton and Anthony Giddens. New York: The New Press, 2000. 52–74.

Chartier, Roger. *The Cultural Uses of Print in Early Modern France.* Trans. Lydia G. Cochrane. Princeton: Princeton University Press, 1987.

Derrida, Jacques. *Of Grammatology.* Trans. Gayatri Chakravorty Spivak. Baltimore: Johns Hopkins University Press, 1976.

The Economist Pocket World in Figures, 2000. London: Profile Books, Ltd., 2000.

Faux, Jeff and Larry Mishel. "Inequality and the Global Economy." *Global Capitalism.* Eds. Will Hutton and Anthony Giddens. New York: The New Press, 2000. 93–111.

Frank, Thomas. *One Market Under God.* New York: Doubleday, 2000.

Goody, Jack and Ian Watt. "The Consequences of Literacy." *Literacy in Traditional Societies.* Ed. Jack Goody. Cambridge: Cambridge University Press, 1968. 27–68.

Gray, John. *False Dawn.* New York: The New Press, 1998.

Greider, William. *One World, Ready or Not: The Manic Logic of Global Capitalism.* New York: Simon and Schuster, 1997.

Held, David, et al. *Global Transformations.* Stanford: Stanford University Press, 1999.

Hobsbawm, Eric. *The Age of Empire, 1875–1914.* New York: Pantheon Books, 1987.

Landes, David S. *The Wealth and Poverty of Nations: Why Some Are So Rich And Some So Poor.* New York: W. W. Norton, 1998.

Levi-Strauss, Claude. "A Writing Lesson." *Tristes Tropiques.* Trans. John Russell. New York: Atheneum, 1972. 286–97.

McNeil, Donald G., Jr. "Indian Company Offers to Supply AIDS Drugs at Low Cost in Africa." *New York Times* 7 February 2000: A1.

Miyoshi, Masao. "A Borderless World? From Colonialism to Transnationalism and the Decline of the Nation-State." *Critical Inquiry* 19 (1993): 726–51.

———. "Against the Native Grain: Reading the Japanese Novel in America." *Critical Issues in East Asian Literature: Report on an International Conference on East Asian Literature, 13–20 June 1983.* Seoul, Korea: International Cultural Society of Korea, 1983. 221–48.

———. *As We Saw Them: The First Japanese Embassy to the United States (1860).* Berkeley: University of California Press, 1979.

———. "Ivory Tower in Escrow." *boundary 2* 27.1 (2000): 7–50.

Ong, Walter. *Orality and Literacy: The Technologizing of the Word.* London: Methuen, 1982.

Phillips, Kevin. "The Wealth Effect." *Los Angeles Times* 16 April 2000: M1.

Said, Edward. *Orientalism.* New York: Pantheon, 1978.

Schor, Juliet B. and Douglas B. Holt. *The Consumer Society Reader.* New York: W. W. Norton, 2000.

Street, Brian. *Literacy in Theory and Practice.* Cambridge: Cambridge University Press, 1984.

Vogel, Ezra F. *Japan as Number One: Lessons for America.* Cambridge, MA: Harvard University Press, 1979.

CHAPTER 2

Bunch, Charlotte. "Women's Rights Are Human Rights: Toward a Re-Vision of Human Rights." *Human Rights Quarterly* 12 (1990): 486–98.

CHAPTER 3

Afzal-Khan, Fauzia and Kalpana Seshadri-Crooks, eds. *The Pre-Occupation of Postcolonial Studies.* Durham, NC: Duke University Press, 2000.

Amin, Samir. *Eurocentrism.* Trans. Russell Moore. New York: Monthly Review Press, 1989.

Agamben, Giorgio. *Means Without End.* Trans. Vincenzo Binetti and Cesare Casarini. Minneapolis, MN: University of Minnesota Press, 2000.

Anzaldua, Gloria. *Borderlands/La Frontera: The New Mestiza.* San Francisco: Aunt lute, 1987.

Appadurai, Arjun. *Modernity at Large.* Minneapolis and London: University of Minnesota Press, 1996.

Bakhtin, Mikhail. *The Dialogic Imagination.* Trans. Caryl Emerson and Michael Holquist. Austin: University of Texas Press, 1981.

Balibar, Etienne and Immanuel Wallerstein. *Race, Nation, Class: Ambiguous Identities.* London and New York: Verso, 1991.

Beverley, John. *Subalternity and Representation.* Durham, NC: Duke University Press, 1999.

Bharucha, Rustom. *In the Name of the Secular: Contemporary Cultural Activism in India.* Delhi: Oxford University Press, 1998.

Bidwai, Praul and Achin Vinaik. *New Nukes: India, Pakistan, and Global Disarmament.* Northampton, MA: Interlink Books, 2000.

Butler, Judith, Ernesto Laclau, and Slavoj Zizek. *Contingency, Hegemony, Universality.* London and New York: Verso, 2000.

Canclini, Nestor Garcia. *Hybrid Cultures: Strategies for Entering and Leaving Modernity.* Trans. Christopher L. Chiappari and Silvia L. Lopez. Minneapolis and London: University of Minnesota Press, 1995.

Chakrabarty, Dipesh. "Postcoloniality and the Artifice of History: Who Speaks for 'Indian' Pasts." *Representations* 37 (1992): 1–26.

Chatterjee, Partha. *Nationalist Thought and the Colonial World: A Derivative Discourse?* Minneapolis and London: University of Minnesota Press, 1993.

Chomsky, Noam. "Free Trade and the Free Market: Pretense and Practice." *The Cultures of Globalization.* Ed. Fredric Jameson and Masao Miyoshi. Durham, NC: Duke University Press, 1998. 356–70.

———. "Talking 'Anarchy' with Chomsky." *The Nation,* 24 April 2000: 28–30.

Connolly, William. *Why I am not a Secularist?* Minneapolis, MN: University of Minnesota Press, 1999.

Critchley, Simon. *Ethics, Politics, Subjectivity.* London and New York: Verso, 1999.

Das, Veena. "Subaltern as Perspective." *Subaltern Studies, Vol. VI.* Ed. Ranajit Guha. Delhi: Oxford University Press, 1989. 310–24.

Ellison, Ralph. *Invisible Man.* New York: Vintage, 1972.

Ghosh, Amitav. *The Shadow Lines.* London: Bloomsbury, 1988.

Guinier, Lani. *The Tyranny of the Majority.* New York: Macmillan Free Press, 1994.

Gupta, Akhil. *Postcolonial Developments.* Durham, NC: Duke University Press, 1998.

Hardt, Michael and Antonio Negri. *Empire.* Cambridge, MA: Harvard University Press, 2000.

Hooks, Bell. "Eating the Other." *Black Looks: Race and Representation*. Boston: South End Press, 1992. 21–39.

Jameson, Fredric. "Notes on Globalization as a Philosophical Issue." *The Cultures of Globalization*. Ed. Fredric Jameson and Miyoshi Masao. Durham, NC: Duke University Press, 1998. 54–77.

Lacan, Jacques. *Ecrits: A Selection*. Trans. Alan Sheridan. London and New York: Norton, 1977.

Madan, T. N. *Pathways: Approaches to the Study of Society in India*. Delhi: Oxford, 1994.

Minh-ha, Trinh T. *Woman, Native, Other*. Bloomington, IN: Indiana University Press, 1989.

Mouffe, Chantal. *The Democratic Paradox*. London and New York: Verso, 2000.

Nandy, Ashis. *The Intimate Enemy*. Delhi: Oxford University Press, 1983.

———. *Traditions, Tyranny, and Utopias: Essays in the Politics of Awareness*. Delhi: Oxford University Press, 1992.

New Left Review 1/238 (November/December 1999), and 2/4 (July/August 2000).

Radhakrishnan, R. *Diasporic Mediations*. Minneapolis and London: University of Minnesota Press, 1996.

———. *Theory in an Uneven World*. Forthcoming, Blackwell , August 2003.

Said, Edward W. *Culture and Imperialism*. New York: Alfred Knopf, 1993.

———. *The World, the Text, the Critic*. Cambridge, MA: Harvard University Press, 1983.

Sen, Amartya. *Development as Freedom*. New York: Alfred Knopf, 1999.

Spivak, Gayatri Chakravorty. *Outside in the Teaching Machine*. New York and London: Routledge, 1993.

The Nation 270.4, 270.16, and 270.18 (31 January, 24 April, and 8 May 2000).

Yegenoglu, Meyda. *Colonial Fantasies: Towards a Feminist Reading of Orientalism*. Cambridge: Cambridge University Press, 1998.

Zizek, Slavoj. "Cyberspace, or How to Traverse the Fantasy in the Age of the Retreat of the Big O." *Public Culture* 10.3 (1998): 483–513.

———. *The Ticklish Subject*. London and New York: Verso, 1999.

Zupancic, Alenka. *Ethics of the Real: Kant, Lacan*. London and New York: Verso, 2000.

CHAPTER 4

Appadurai, Arjun. *Modernity at Large: Cultural Dimensions of Globalization*. Minneapolis, MN: University of Minnesota Press, 1996.

King, Anthony D., ed. *Culture, Globalization and the World-System: Contemporary Conditions for the Representation of Identity*. Minneapolis, MN: University of Minnesota Press, 1997.

Benítez-Rojo, Antonio, *The Repeating Island: The Caribbean and the Postmodern Perspective*. Trans. James Maraniss. Durham, NC: Duke University Press, 1997.

Buell, Frederick. *National Culture and the New Global System*. Baltimore: The Johns Hopkins University Press, 1994.

Chandra, Vikram. *Red Earth and Pouring Rain*. New York: Little, Brown & Co., 1995.

Cohen, Robin. *Global Diasporas: An Introduction*. Seattle: University of Washington Press, 1997.

Court, Franklin E. *Institutionalizing English Literature: The Culture and Politics of Literary Study, 1750–1900*. Stanford: Stanford University Press, 1992.

Cvetkovich, Ann and Douglas Kellner. *Articulating the Global and the Local: Globalization and Cultural Studies*. Boulder: Westview Press, 1997.

Friedman, Susan Stanford. *Mappings: Feminism and the Cultural Geographies of Encounter*. Princeton: Princeton University Press, 1998.

Friedman, Thomas L. *The Lexus and the Olive Tree: Understanding Globalization*. New York: Farrar Straus & Giroux, 2000.

Gilroy, Paul. *The Black Atlantic: Modernity and Double Consciousness*. Cambridge, MA: Harvard University Press, 1993.

Graff, Gerald. Professing Literature: An Institutional History. Chicago: University of Chicago Press, 1987.

Gunn, Giles, ed. *Globalizing Literary Studies*. PMLA 116 (January 2000). New York MLA, 2001.

Hamid, Mohsin. *Moth Smoke*. New York: Farrar Straus & Giroux, 2000.

Hannerz, Ulf. *Transnational Connections: Culture, People, Places*. London: Routledge, 1996.

Harvey, David. *The Condition of Postmodernity*. Cambridge, MA: Basil Blackwell, 1990.

Jameson, Frederic, and Masao Miyoshi, eds. *The Cultures of Globalization*. Durham, NC: Duke University Press, 1998.

Jay, Paul. "Beyond Discipline? Globalization and the Future of English." *PMLA* 116 (January 2000): 32–47.

Kaplan, Caren. *Questions of Travel: Postmodern Discourses of Displacement*. Durham, NC: Duke University Press, 1996.

Loomba, Ania. *Colonialism/Postcolonialism*. London: Routledge, 1998.

Morley, David and Kevin Robins. *Spaces of Identity: Global Media, Electronic, Landscapes, and Cultural Boundaries*. London: Routledge, 1995.

Readings, Bill. *The University in Ruins*. Cambridge, MA: Harvard University Press, 1996.

Robertson, Roland. *Globalization*. London: Sage Publications, 1992.

Roy, Arundhati. *The God of Small Things*. New York: Random House, 1997.

Rushdie, Salman. *The Ground Beneath Her Feet*. New York: Picador, 2000.

Said, Edward. "Globalizing Literary Study." *PMLA* 116 (January 2000): 64–68.

Smith, Zadie. *White Teeth.* New York: Random House, 2000.

Syal, Meera. *Anita and Me.* New York: New Press, 1977.

———. *Life Isn't All Ha Ha Hee Hee.* New York: New Press, 2000.

Wallerstein, Immanuel. *The Modern World System II.* New York: Academic Press, 1974.

Waters, Malcolm. *Globalization.* London: Routledge, 1995.

CHAPTER 5

Algarín, Miguel and Miguel Piñero. *Nuyorican Poetry: An Anthology of Puerto Rican Words and Feelings.* New York, Morrow, 1975.

Avelar, Idelber. *The Untimely Present: Postdictatorial Latin American Fiction and the Task of Mourning.* Durham and London: Duke University Press, 1999. 1–22.

Bloom, Harold. *The Western Canon: The Books and School of the Ages,* New York: Harcourt Brace, 1994.

Colás, Santiago. "Of Creole Symptoms, Cuban Fantasies, and Other Latin American Postcolonial Ideologies." *PMLA* 110. 3 (1995): 75–81.

Davis, Mike. *Magical Urbanism: Latinos Reinvent the U.S. Big City.* London: Verso, 2000.

De la Campa, Román. *Cuba on My Mind: Journeys to a Severed Nation.* London: Verso, 2000.

———. "Norteamérica y sus mundos Latinos: Ontologías, Globalización, Diásporas." *Revista Iberoamericana* 193 (2000): 753–69.

———. *Latin Americanism.* Minneapolis, MN: Minnesota University Press, 1999.

———. "Latin Lessons: Do Latinos Share a World … or a Word?" *Transition* 63 (1994): 68–76.

Derrida, Jaques. *Specters of Marx.* London: Routledge, 1994.

Flores, Juan. *From Bomba to Hip-Hop.* New York: Columbia University Press, 2000.

Flores, Juan and George Yúdice. "Living Borders/Buscando a Amica." *Social Text* 24 (1999): 57–80.

García Canclini, Néstor. *Consumidores y Ciudadanos.* Mexico: Grijaldo, 1995.

Gugelberger, Georg M., ed. *The Real Thing: Testimonial Discourse and Latin America.* Raleigh: Duke University Press, 1996.

Hardt, Michael and Antonio Negri. *Empire.* Cambridge, MA: Harvard University Press, 2000.

Lao-Montes, Agustín and Arlene Dávila. *Mambo Montage: The Latinization of New York City.* New York: Columbia University Press, 2001.

Martí, José. "Our America." *The America of José Martí: Selected Writings.* Trans. Juan de Onís. New York: Funk and Wagnalls, 1954.

Muthyala, John. "Reworlding America: The Globalization of American Studies." *Cultural Critique* 47 (2001): 91–119.

Oboler, Suzanne. *Ethnic Labels, Latino Lives: Identity and the Politics of (Re)Presentation in the United States.* Minneapolis, MN: Minnesota University Press, 1995.

O'Gorman, Edmundo. *The Invention of America: An Inquiry into the Historical Nature of the New World and the Meaning of Its History.* 1948. Bloomington: Greenwood Press, 1961.

Omi, Michael and Howard Winant. *Racial Formation in the United States: From the 1960s to the 1980s.* New York: Routledge & Kegan Paul, 1986.

Padilla, Felix. *Latino Ethnic Consciousness: The Case of Mexican Americans and Puerto Ricans in Chicago.* Indianapolis: Notre Dame University Press, 1985.

Paz, Octavio. *The Labyrinth of Solitude.* Mexico: Fondo de Cultura Económica, 1959.

Pérez-Firmat, Gustavo. *Life on the Hyphen: The Cuban-American Way.* Austin, TX: Texas University Press, 1974.

Rabasa, José. *Inventing America: Spanish Historiography and the Formation of Eurocentrism.* Norman: Oklahoma University Press, 1993.

Rodó, José Enrique. *Ariel.* Trans. Margaret Sayers Peden. Austin, TX: Texas University Press, 1988.

Rodriguez, Richard. *Hunger of Memory.* New York: Bantam, 1983.

Rodriguez, Richard. *Days of Obligation.* New York: Viking Penguin, 1992.

Rodriguez, Richard. *Brown.* New York: Viking, 2002.

Rorty, Richard. *Objectivity, Relativism, and Truth.* Cambridge: Cambridge University Press, 1991. 197–292.

Saldívar, José David. *The Dialectics of Our America.* Durham, NC: Duke University Press, 1991.

Spielmann, Ellen, ed. *Las Relaciones Culturales entre América Latina y Estados Unidos después de la Guerra Fría.* Berlin: Wissenschaftlicher Verlag, 2000.

CHAPTER **6**

Appadurai, Arjun. "Patriotism and Its Futures." *Modernity At Large: Cultural Dimensions of Globalization.* Minneapolis, MN: University of Minnesota Press, 1998.

Ching, Leo. "Globalizing the Regional, Regionalizing the Global: Mass Culture and Asianism in the Age of Late Capital." *Public Culture* 12 (2000): 233–57.

Cumings, Bruce. "Rimspeak; or, The Discourse of the 'Pacific Rim.'" *What Is In a Rim?: Critical Perspectives on the Pacific Region Idea.* Ed. Arif Dirlik. Boulder, CO: Westview, 1993.

Dirlik, Arif, ed., "Introduction: Pacific Contradictions." *What Is in a Rim? Critical*

Perspectives on the Pacific Region Idea. Boulder, CO: Rowman and Littlefield Press, 1998.

Duras, Marguerite. *The Lover.* Trans. Barbara Bray. New York: Harper, 1992.

Grossberg, Lawrence, Cary Nelson and Paula Treichler, eds. *Cultural Studies.* New York: Routledge, 1992.

Hall, Stuart. "The Local and the Global: Globalization and Ethnicity." *Culture, Globalization and the World-System.* Ed. Anthony D. King. Binghampton: State University of New York, Department of Art and Art History, 1991. 19–39.

Hau'ofa, Epeli. "Our Sea of Islands." *Asia/Pacific as Space of Cultural Production.* Ed. Rob Wilson and Arif Dirlik. Durham, NC: Duke University Press, 1995. 86–98.

Hereniko, Vilsoni and Rob Wilson, ed. *Inside Out: Literature, Cultural Politics and Identity in the New Pacific.* Boulder, CO: Rowman and Littlefield Press, 1999.

Herr, Richard A. "Regionalism and Nationalism." *Tides of History: The Pacific Islands in the Twentieth Century.* Ed. K. R. Howe, Robert C. Kiste, and Brij V. Lal. Honolulu: University of Hawai'i Press, 1994. 283–99.

Honolulu Advertiser. "Pentagon focus shifts to Asia — as do risks." 5 June 2000: A8.

Jameson, Fredric. "On 'Cultural Studies.' " *Social Text* 34 (1993): 17–52.

Korea Herald. "U.S. sees critical role for APEC in post-crisis Asia." 5 August 1999: 1.

Marx, Karl. Interviewed by R. Landor for *New York World,* 18 July 1871. *The Norton Book of Interviews.* Ed. Christopher Silvester. New York: W. W. Norton, 1996. 59.

Miyoshi, Masao. "Sites of Resistance in the Global System." *boundary 2* 22 (1995): 61–84.

Naisbitt, John. *Global Paradox: The Bigger the World Economy, the More Powerful Its Smallest Players.* New York: Avon, 1994.

Oe, Kenzaburo. "The Myth of My Own Village." Interview with Rob Wilson, Joel Cohn, and Steve Bradbury. *Manoa* 6 (1994): 135–44.

Ohmae, Kenichi. "Putting Global Logic First." *Harvard Business Review* 73 (1995): 125–37.

Rafael, Vincente L. "AHR Forum: Regionalism, Area Studies, and the Accidents of Agency." *The American Historical Review* 104 (1999): 1208–20.

Ross, Kristin. "The World Literature and Cultural Studies Program." *Critical Inquiry* 19 (1993): 666–76.

Stratton, Jon and Ien Ang. "On the Impossibility of a Global Cultural Studies: 'British' Cultural Studies in an 'International' Frame." *Critical Dialogues: Cultural Studies, Marxism, and Postmodernism in the Writings of Stuart Hall.* Eds. Kuan-Hsing Chen and David Morley. London and New York: Routledge, 1995. 361–91.

Sumida, Stephen. *The View From the Shore.* Seattle: Washington University Press, 1991.

Trask, Haunani Kay. *From a Native Daughter: Colonialism and Sovereignty in Hawai'i.* Monroe, ME: Common Courage Press, 1993.

Walker, Richard. "California Rages Against the Dying of the Light." *New Left Review* 209 (1995): 42–74.

Wendt, Albert, ed. *Nuanua: Pacific Writing In English Since 1980.* Honolulu: University of Hawai'i Press, 1995.

Wigen, Karen. "Culture, Power, and Place: The New Landscapes of East Asian Regionalism." *The American Historical Review* 104 (1999): 1183–201.

Wilson, Rob. *Pacific Postmodern: From the Sublime to the Devious, Writing the Experimental/Local Pacific.* Honolulu: Tinfish Works, 2000.

———. *Reimagining the American Pacific: From 'South Pacific' to Bamboo Ridge and Beyond.* Durham, NC: Duke University Press, 2000.

Yeung, Yue-man, ed. *Pacific Asia in the 21st Century: Geographical and Developmental Perspectives.* Hong Kong: Chinese University Press, 1993.

Yue, Audre. "What's So Queer About *Happy Together?*" *Inter-Asia Cultural Studies* 1 (2000): 251–64.

CHAPTER **7**

Allen, Chadwick. "Postcolonial Theory and the Discourse of Treaties." *American Quarterly* 52 (2000): 59–89.

Althusser, Louis. "Ideology and Ideological State Apparatuses (Notes Toward and Investigation)." *Lenin and Philosophy, and Other Essays.* New York: Monthly Review Press, 1971. 127–86.

Appadurai, Arjun. "Disjuncture and Difference in the Global Cultural Economy." *Public Culture* 2 (1990): 1–23.

Attwood, Bain, ed. *In the Age of Mabo: History, Aborigines and Australia.* St. Leonards, NSW: Allen & Unwin, 1996.

Auerbach, Erich. "Philology and *Weltliteratur.*" Trans. Marie and Edward Said, *Centennial Review* 13 (1969): 15–32.

Balibar, Étienne. "Is There a 'Neo-Racism'?" In *Race, Nation, Class: Ambiguous Identities.* Étienne Balibar and Immanuel Wallerstein. London: Verso, 1991. 17–28.

Bauman, Zygmunt. *Globalization: The Human Consequences.* Cambridge: Polity Press, 1998.

Bell, Claudia. *Inventing New Zealand: Everyday Myths of Pakeha Identity.* Auckland: Penguin, 1996.

Berlin, Isiah. BBC Broadcast, *Freedom and Its Betrayal.* 5 November 1952.

Bhabba, Homi K. *The Location of Culture.* London: Routledge, 1994.

Bryce, James. *The American Commonwealth.* New York: Macmillan, 1888.

California State Board of Education. *History and Social Science Framework for California Public Schools Kindergarten through Grade Twelve.* Sacramento, CA: California State Department of Education, 1988.

Carty, Linda and Dionne Brand. "Visible Minority Women: A Creation of the Canadian State." In *Returning the Gaze: Essays on Racism, Feminism, and Politics.* Ed. H. Bannerji. Toronto: Sister Vision, 1993. 169–86.

Chapman, John William. *Rousseau — Totalitarian or Liberal?* New York: Columbia University Press, 1956.

Cheah, Pheng and Bruce Robbins, eds. *Cosmopolitics: Thinking Freely Beyond the Nation.* Minneapolis, MN: University of Minnesota Press, 1998.

Cherokee Nation v. Georgia. 5 *Peters* 1 (US 1831).

Chow, Rey. *Writing Diaspora: Tactics of Intervention in Contemporary Cultural Studies.* Bloomington: Indiana University Press, 1992.

Clarke, George Elliott. "White Like Canada." *Transition* 73 (1998): 98–109.

Clifford, James. *Routes: Travel and Translation in the Late Twentieth Century.* Cambridge, MA: Harvard University Press, 1997.

Davidson, Alistair. *From Subjects to Citizens: Australian Citizenship in the Twentieth Century.* Sydney: Cambridge, 1997.

D'Entrèves, Alexander Passerin. *The Notion of the State: An Introduction to Political Theory.* Oxford: Clarendon Press, 1967.

Dixson, Miriam. *The Imaginary Australian: Anglo-Celts an Identity: 1788- to the Present.* Sydney, NSW: University of New South Wales Press, 1999.

Dunne, Michael and Tiziano Bonazzi, eds. *Citizenship Rights in Multicultural Societies.* Keele, Staffordshire: Keele University Press, 1995.

Fleras, Augie. "Monoculturalism, Multiculturalism, and Biculturalism: The Politics of Maori Policy in New Zealand." *Plural Societies* 15 (1984): 52–75.

Gairdner, William D. *The Trouble with Canada.* Toronto: Stoddart, 1990.

———. *Constitutional Crack-Up: Canada and the Coming Showdown with Quebec.* Toronto: Stoddart, 1994.

Gordon, Avery and Christopher Newfield, eds. *Mapping Multiculturalism.* Minneapolis, MN: University of Minnesota Press, 1996.

Gunew, Sneja. "Multiple Multiplicities: Canada, US, Australia." In *Social Pluralism and Literary History: The Literature of the Italian Emigration.* Ed. F. Loriggio. Ottawa: Guernica, 1996.

Hall, Stuart. "Cultural Identity and Diaspora." In *Identity, Community, Culture, Difference.* Ed. Rutherford, James. London: Lawrence and Wishart, 1990. 222–37.

Hill, Mike, ed. *Whiteness: A Critical Reader.* New York: New York University Press, 1997.

Holston, James and Arjun Appaduarai, eds. "Cities and Citizensip." Special issue of *Public Culture* 8 (1996).

Hughes, Robert. *The Fatal Shore: A History of the Transportation of Convicts to Australia.* London: Collins Havill, 1987.

Huntington, Samuel. *The Clash of Civilizations? The Debate.* New York: Foreign Affairs, 1993.

———. "The West Is Unique, Not Universal." *Foreign Affairs* 75 (1996): 28–46.

Ignatiev, Noel. *How the Irish Became White.* New York: Routledge, 1995.

Jay, Gregory. "The End of American Literature: Toward a Multicultural Practice." *College English* 53 (1991): 264–81.

Jusdanis, Gregory. *The Necessary Nation.* Princeton: Princeton University Press, 2001.

Kallen, Horace. *Culture and Democracy in the United States.* New York: Arno Press, 1970 rpt. (1924).

Kawaharu, I. H. *Waitangi: Maori and Pakeha Perspectives on the Treaty of Waitangi.* Auckland: Oxford University Press, 1989.

Keneally, Thomas. *The Great Shame: and the Triumph of the Irish in the English-Speaking World.* New York: N. A. Talese, 1999.

Kymlicka, Will. *Multicultural Citizenship: A Liberal Theory of Minority Rights.* Oxford: Clarendon Press, 1995.

Lloyd, David and Paul Thomas. *Culture and the State.* New York: Routledge, 1998.

Lopez, Ian F. Hanny. *White by Law: The Legal Construction of Race.* New York: New York University Press, 1996.

Lowe, Lisa. *Immigrant Acts: On Asian American Cultural Politics.* Durham, NC: Duke University Press, 1996.

Lowell, A. Lawrence. "The Theory of the Social Compact." *Atlantic Monthly* 59 (1887): 750–67.

McHugh, Paul. *The Maori Magna Charta: New Zealand Law and the Treaty of Waitangi.* Auckland: Oxford University Press, 1991.

Michaels, Walter Benn. *Our America: Nativism, Modernism, and Pluralism.* Durham, NC: Duke University Press, 1995.

Michaelsen, Scott. *The Limits of Multiculturalism: Interrogating the Origins of American Anthropology.* Minneapolis, MN: University of Minnesota Press, 1999.

National Council for the Social Studies. "Position Statement: Curriculum Guidelines for Multicultural Education." <http://ww.ncss.org/standards/positon/multicultural.html>

Neumann, Klaus, Nicholas Thomas, and Hilary Ericksen, eds. *Quicksands: Foundational Histories in Australia and Aotearoa New Zealand.* Sydney: University of New South Wales Press, 1999.

New York State Social Studies Review and Development Committee. *One Nation, Many Peoples: A Declaration of Cultural Interdependence.* 1991.

Omi, Michael and Howard Winant. *Racial Formation in the United States: From the 1960s to the 1990s.* New York: Routledge, 1994.

Orange, Claudia. *The Treaty of Waitangi.* Wellington: Allen & Unwin. 1987.

Pearson, David. "Crossing Ethnic Thresholds: Multiculturalisms in Comparative Perspective." In *Nga Patai: Racism and Ethnic Relation in Aotearoa/New Zealand.* Palmerstone North: Dunmore.247–70.

Pease, Donald E. *Visionary Compacts: American Renaissance Writings in Cultural Context.* Madison: University of Wisconsin Press, 1987.

Pocock, J. G. A. "British History: A Plea for a New Subject." *Journal of Modern History*, 47 (1975): 601–21. First published in *New Zealand Journal of History* 8 (1974).

Prosad, Rajen. "Annual Report of the Race Conciliator for the Year Ending 30 June 1996." *Human Rights Law and Practice* 2 (1997): 211–7.

Reynolds, Henry. *Aboriginal Sovereignty: Reflections on Race, State and Nation.* St Leonards, NSW: Allen & Unwin, 1996.

Roediger, David. *The Wages of Whiteness: Race and the Making of the American Working Class.* London: Verso, 1991.

Schlesinger, Arthur M., Jr. *The Disuniting of America: Reflections on a Multicultural Society.* New York: Norton, 1992.

Sharp, Andrew. *Justice and the Maori: Maori Claims in New Zealand Political Argument in the 1980s.* Auckland: Oxford University Press, 1990.

Theophanous, Andrew C. *Understanding Multiculturalism and Australian Identity.* Melbourne: Elika Bks., 1995.

Trudeau, Pierre Elliott. *Federalism and the French Canadians.* Toronto: Macmillan, 1968.

———. *Pierre Trudeau Speaks Out On Meech Lake.* Toronto: General Paperbacks, 1990.

Young, Iris Marion. "Polity and Group Difference: A Critique of the Ideal of Universal Citizenship." *Ethics* 99 (1989): 250–74.

Zizek, Slavoj. "Multiculturalism, or, the Cultural Logic of Multinational Capitalism." *New Left Review* 225 (1997): 28–51.

CHAPTER **8**

American Anthropological Association and Computing Research Association. "Culture, Society and Advanced Information Technology. Social Aspects Report of a Workshop held on June 1–2." Washington: Computing Research Association and Arlington: American Anthropological Association, 1995: 14–16.

Appadurai, Arjun. "Disjuncture and Difference in the Global Cultural Economy."
   Public Culture 2.2 (1990): 1–24.

Baudrillard, Jean. *Simulations*. New York: Semiotext(e), 1983.

Benedikt, Michael ed. *Cyberspace: First Steps*. Cambridge, MA: MIT Press, 1992.

Bogard, William. "Simmel in Cyberspace: Distance and Strangeness in Postmodern
   Communications." *Space and Culture* 4–5 (2000): 23–46.

Castells, Manuel. *Rise of the Network Society*. 2nd ed. Oxford: Blackwell, 2000.

Chun, Allen. "From Nationalism to Nationalizing: Cultural Imagination and State
   Formation in Postwar Taiwan." *The Australian Journal of Chinese Affairs* 31
   (1994): 1–31.

——. "An Oriental Orientalism: The Paradox of Tradition and Modernity in
   Nationalist Taiwan." *History and Anthropology* 9.1 (1995): 27–56.

Escobar, Arturo. "Welcome to Cyberia: Notes on the Anthropology of Cyberculture."
   Current Anthropology 35.3 (1994): 211–31.

Featherstone, Mike and Roger Burrows eds. *Cyberspace, Cyberbodies, Cyberpunk:
   Cultures of Technological Embodiment*. Beverly Hills: Sage, 1995.

Gourgey, Hannah and Edward B. Smith. "'Consensual Hallucination': Cyberspace
   and the Creation of an Interpretive Community." *Text and Performance
   Quarterly* 16.3 (1996): 233–47.

Gunkel, David J. and Ann H. Gunkel. "Virtual Geographies: The New Worlds of
   Cyberspace." *Critical Studies in Mass Communication* 14.2 (1997): 123–37.

Habermas, Jurgen. *The Structural Transformation of the Public Sphere: An Inquiry
   into a Category of Bourgeois Society* Cambridge, MA: MIT Press, 1989.

Hardt, Michael and Antonio Negri. *Empire*. Cambridge, MA: Harvard University
   Press, 2000.

Jones, Steven G. ed. *Cybersociety: Computer Mediated Communication and
   Community*. Beverly Hills: Sage, 1994.

Kling, Rob. "Being Read in Cyberspace: Boutique, Mass Media Markets,
   Intermediation and the Costs of Online Services." *Communication Review*
   1.3 (1996): 297–314.

Kroker, Arthur and Michael A.Weinstein. "The Political Economy of Virtual Reality."
   Canadian Journal of Political and Social Theory 17.1–2 (1994): 1–31.

Lash, Scott and John Urry. *The End of Organized Capitalism*. Madison: University
   of Wisconsin Press, 1987.

Leiner, Barry M. et al. "A Brief History of the Internet." <http://www.isoc.org/internet-
   history/brief.html>

Loader, Brian D. ed. *The Governance of Cyberspace: Politics, Technology and Global
   Restructuring*. London: Routledge, 1997.

Mitchell, William J. *City of Bits: Space, Place and the Infobahn*. Cambridge, MA:
   MIT Press, 1995.

Reid, Elizabeth M. *Electropolis: Communication and Community on Internet Relay
   Chat*. BA thesis, University of Melbourne, 1991.

RFC 1594. "FYI on Questions and Answers: Answers to Commonly Asked 'New Internet User' Questions." <http://www.faqs.org/rfcs/rfc1594.html>

Rheingold, Howard. *The Virtual Community: Homesteading on the Electronic Frontier.* Reading: Addison-Wesley, 1993.

Shields, Rob. "Virtual Spaces, Real Histories and Living Bodies." *The Cultures of Internet.* Ed. Rob Shields. Beverly Hills: Sage, 1996.

Slouka, Mark. *War of the Worlds: Cyberspace and the High-Tech Assault on Reality.* New York: Basic Books, 1995.

Smith, Marc A. and Peter Kollock eds. *Communities in Cyberspace.* London: Routledge, 2000.

Stoll, Clifford. *Silicon Snake Oil: Second Thoughts on the Information Highway.* New York: Doubleday, 1995.

Stone, Allucquere Rosanne. *The War of Desire and Technology at the Close of the Mechanical Age.* Cambridge, MA: MIT Press, 1995.

Turkle, Sherry. *Life on the Screen: Identity in the Age of Internet.* New York: Simon and Schuster, 1995.

Volokh, Eugene. "Cheap Speech and What It Will Do." *Communication Review* 1.3 (1996): 271–89.

Virilio, Paul and Patrice Riemens. "Speed and Information — Cyberspace Alarm!" *Canadian Journal of Political and Social Theory.* 18.1–3 (1995): 82–89.

Winston, Brian. "There's No Such Thing as Cheap Speech." *Communication Review.* 1.3 (1996): 291–5.

Zakon, Robert H. "Hobbes' Internet Timeline v.3.1." 1997. <http://info.isoc.org/guest/zakon/Internet/History/HIT.html>

CHAPTER 9

"Bejing Residents and International News" (Beijing shimin yu guoji xinwen). *Beijing Youth Daily (Beijing qingnian bao),* 12 April 1999.

Associate Press (AP). "China to Tighten Web Regulation." *The New York Times,* 5 December 2000.

Bo Xiong. "The Making of 'China News Digest." In CND special issue, "CND Enters 10th Year of Internet Publishing, March 6, 1998." <http://www.cnd.org/CNDhistory.html>

Chan, Eliza and Steyn, Peter. "China Takes Prize for World's Second Largest At Home Internet Population as Numbers Reach 56.6 Million." Nielson Net Rating Survey, 22 April 2002. <http://www.nielson.netratings.com>

The China Press (Qiaobao). "The Case of 'people.com.cn': Observing the News Websites in China" (Cong renmin wang kan dalu xinwen wangzhan zouxiang). Special Report. 11 December 2000. B12.

China Youth Daily (Zhongguo qingnian bao). "A Profile of the Newer, New Humanity." 2 February 2001.

Chinese News Network (Duowei xinwen wang). "Mainland China Visions and Thoughts Website Forced to Shut Down" (Zhongguo dalu sixiang de jingjie beipo guanbi). 14 October 2000. <http://www.chinesenewsnet.com>

Cohen, Jean and Arato, Andrew. *Civil Society and Political Theory.* Cambridge, MA: MIT Press, 1992.

Ding Xueliang. "Law and Order in Transitional Societies — the Russian Phenomenon" ("Zhuanxing shehui de fa yu zhixu — eluosi xianxiang"). *Tsinghua Review of Sociology (Tsinghua shehuixue pinlun),* No. 2, 2000.

Ding Xueliang. *The Decline of Communism in China: Legitimacy Crisis, 1978–1989.* Cambridge: Cambridge University Press, 1994.

Ehrenberg, John. *Civil Society: The Critical History of an Idea.* New York: New York University Press, 1999.

FlorCruz, Jaime A. "Chinese Media in Flux." *Media Studies Journal,* Special Issue: *Covering China,* Vol. 13, No. 1 (Winter 1999): 32–48.

Herman, Edward and McChesney, Robert. *The Global Media: The New Missionaries of Global Capitalism.* London: Cassell, 1977.

Li Xiguang. "Future to the New Humanity and Online Journalists" (Weilai shuyu xin renlei he wangluo jizhe). In Li Xiguang ed., *Online Journalists* (Wangluo jizhe). Beijing: Zhongguo sanxia chubanshe, 2000. 298.

Li Yonggang. "To Friends of My Website Again" (Zai zhi gewei guanxin benzhan de pengyou). 14 October 2000. <http://www.sixiang.com>

Nye, Joseph. "Hard Power, Soft Power," *Boston Globe,* 6 August 1999; "The Power We Must Not Squander," *The New York Times,* 3 January 2000.

People's Liberation Army (PLA) Daily (Jiefangjun bao). "Noting the Phenomenon of Information Colonialism" (Guanzhu xinxi zhiminzhuyi xianxiang), editorial. 8 February 2000.

Pew Research Center. "The People and Press Poll on New Media Trends." April–May, 2000. <http://www. people-press.org>

Sina.com News. "The Internet Literature's Standard-bearer Bum Cai Will Have His First Intimate Touch with the Mainland" (Wangluo wenxue qishou Pizi Cai jiang diyici qinmi jiechu zuguo dalu). 25 September 2000. < 00/9/25" http://edu.sina.com.cn/news2000/9/25.html>

Smith, Craig. "Sex, Lust, Drugs: Her Novel's too Much for China." *New York Times.* 11 May 2000.

The New York Times. "Internet: A Double-Edged Sword in China." 23 December 1999.

Under the Banyan (Rongshuxia). "*Literature Gazette* Holds the Conference on Internet Literature" (Wenxue bao juban wangluo wenxue yantaohui). 23 January 2000. <http://www.rongshu.com>.

Xu Rongsheng ed. *Internet media* (Wangluo meiti). Beijing: Wuzhou chuanbo chubanshe, 1999. 7–11.

Ye Niu (Boar). "The New Humanity — the Mainstream in Modernized China" (Xin renlei — Zhongguo qiangdahou de zhuliu shehui). China University Campus Network — Newer, New Humanity (Zhongguo xiaoyuan wang — xin xin renlei), 12 December 2000. <http://www.54youth.com.cn/gb/paper107/zt/xyzt>

Zhou Xincheng and Chen Xiaokui. "Remaining Vigilant Against Western Antagonistic Forces' Infiltration in Ideological and Cultural Domains" (Jingti xifang didui shili de sixiang wenhua shentou). Strong Power Forum, *People's Daily*, 12 December 2000. <http://202.99.23.237.cgi.bbs>

CHAPTER 10

"About the Company." 3 March 2001.
<http://www.wipro.com/archiv/~news.htm>

Anderson, Jon. "Cybarities, Knowledge Workers and New Creoles on the Superhighway." *Anthropology Today* 2.4 (1995): 13–15.

Appadurai, Arjun. "Disjuncture and Difference in the Global Cultural Economy." *GlobalCulture: Natonalism, Globalization and Modernity*. Ed. M. Featherstone. London: Sage, 1990. 295–310.

———. "Global Etnoscapes: Notes and Queries for a Transnational Anthropology." *Recapturing Anthropology: Working in The Present*. Ed. R.G. Fox. Santa Fe: School of American Research Press, 1991. 191–210.

———. *Modernity at Large: Cultural Dimensions of Globalization*. Minneapolis, MN: University of Minnesota, 1996.

Baucom, Ian. "Globalit, Inc.: or, The Cultural Logic of Global Literary Studies." *PMLA* 116.1 (2001): 158–72.

Bhabha, Home. *The Location of Culture*. New York: Routledge, 1994.

———. "Minority Culture and Creative Anxiety." 21 July 2001.
<http://www.britishcouncil.org/studies/reinventing_britain/bhabha_1.htm>

Boym, Svetlana. *The Future of Nostalgia*. Basic Books, 2001.

Coronil, Fernando. "Towards a Critique of Globalcentrism: Speculations on Capitalism's Nature." *Public Culture* 12.2 (2000): 351–74.

Das, Gurcharan. *India Unbound*. New York: Knopf, 2001.

Denby, David. "The Speed of Light." *New Yorker* 27 November 2000: 139–40.

Dhawan, Radhika and Roopa Pai. "The Master of the Marketplace." 22 October 1999.
<http://www.businesstoday.com/archiv.htm)

Featherstone, Michael, Scott Lash and Roland Roberston, eds. *Global Modernities*. London: Sage, 1995.

Hall, Stuart. "The Postcolonial Question." *Common Skies: Divided Horizons*. Eds. Iain Chambers and Linda Curti. London: Routledge, 1996

Hardt, Michael and Antonio Negri. *Empire.* Cambridge, MA: Harvard University Press, 2000.

Huyssen, Andreas. *Twilight Memories: Marking Time in a Culture of Amnesia.* New York: Routledge, 1995.

Jameson, Frederic. *Postmodernism, Or, The Cultural Logic of Late Capitalism.* Durham, NC: Duke University Press, 1992.

Landler, Mark. "Hi, I'm in Bangalore (but I can't say so)." *New York Times,* 21 March 2001.

Leonard, Karen. *The South-Asian Americans.* Greenwood, 1998.

Lewis, Michael. *The New New Thing: A Silicon Valley Story.* New York: Penguin, 2001.

Li, Victor. "What's In a Name: Questioning Globalization." *Cultural Critique* 45 (2000): 1–39.

Luke, Timothy. "New World Order or Neo-World Orders: Power, Politics and Ideology in Informationalizing Glocalities." *Global Modernities.* Eds. Michael Featherstone, Scott Lash and Roland Robertson. London: Sage, 1996. 91–107.

Mauss, Marcel. *The Gift: The Form and Reason for Exchange in Archaic Societies.* Trans. W. D. Halls. New York: Norton, 1990.

Prashad, Vijay. *The Karma of Brown Folk.* Minneapolis, MN: University of Minnesota Press, 2000.

Sassen, Saskia. "Spatialities and Temporalities of the Global: Elements of a Theorization." *Public Culture* 12.2 (2000): 215–32.

Sen, Bish. "O Brave New World: The Indian in the Valley." *The Telegraph, Calcutta,* 15 January 2001.

Staeheli, Linda. "Transnational Migration, Information Technology and the Spaces of Citizenship." 11 April 2001. <http://human.ntu.ac.uk/im/im2.html>

Starobinski, Jean. "The Idea of Nostalgia." *Diogenes* 54 (1966): 81–103.

Stewart, Susan. *On Longing.* Baltimore: Johns Hopkins University Press, 1985.

Takaki. Ronald T. *A Different Mirror: A History of Multicultural America.* New York: Little Brown, 1994.

Turkle, Sherry. *Life on the Screen: Identity in the Age of the Internet.* Touchstone Books, 1997.

Vertovec, Steven. "Three Meanings of Diaspora exemplified Among South-Asian Religions." *Diaspora* 6.3 (1997). 3 June 2001. <http://www.utpress.utoronto.ca/journal/Diaspora/dias_6_3htm>

Wetzler, Brad. "Boomgalore." 11 March 2001. <http://www.wired.com/wired/archiv/8.03/bangalore.html>

Zisek, Slavoj. *The Plague of Fantasies.* London: Verso, 1997.

CHAPTER **11**

Anderson, Benedict. *Imagined Communities: Reflections on the Origin and Spread of Nationalism.* 1983. London and New York: Verso, 1991.

de Waal, Alex. *Famine Crimes: Politics and the Disaster Relief Industry in Africa.* Oxford and Bloomington: James Currey and Indiana University Press, 1997.

Ehrenreich, John and Barbara Ehrenreich. "The Professional-Managerial Class." In *Between Labor and Capital.* Ed. Pat Walker. Boston: South End Press, 1979. 5–45.

Ferguson, Niall. *The Pity of War: Explaining World War I.* New York: Basic Books, 1999.

Gibson-Graham, J. K. *The End of Capitalism (as We Knew It): A Feminist Critique of Political Economy.* Malden, MA, and Oxford: Blackwell, 1996.

Gleick, James. *Faster: The Acceleration of Just About Everything.* New York: Pantheon, 1999.

Gouldner, Alvin W. *The Future of Intellectuals and the Rise of the New Class.* New York: Continuum, 1979.

Hannerz, Ulf. *Cultural Complexity: Studies in the Social Organization of Meaning.* New York: Columbia University Press, 1992.

Hochschild, Arlie Russell. *The Time Bind.* New York: Metropolitan Books, 1997.

Ishiguro, Kazuo. *The Remains of the Day.* New York: Vintage International, 1989.

———. *The Unconsoled.* London: Faber and Faber, 1995.

———. *When We Were Orphans.* London: Faber and Faber, 2000.

Iyer, Pico. "The Butler Didn't Do It, Again." *Times Literary Supplement* 28 April 1995: 22.

Menand, Louis. "Anxious in Dreamland." *New York Times Book Review* 15 October 1995.

Moeller, Susan D. *Compassion Fatigue: How the Media Sell Disease, Famine, War and Death.* New York and London: Routledge, 1999.

Reich, Robert B. *The Work of Nations: Preparing Ourselves for Twenty-first Century Capitalism.* New York: Vintage, 1992.

Robbins, Bruce. "The Village of the Liberal Managerial Class." *Cosmopolitan Geographies: New Locations in Literature and Culture.* Ed. Vinay Dharwadkar. New York: Routledge, 2001. 15–32.

Salecl, Renata. "I Can't Love You Unless I Give You Up." *Gaze and Voice as Love Objects.* Ed. Renata Salecl and Slavoj Zizek. Durham and London: Duke University Press, 1996. 179–207.

Schor, Juliet B. *The Overworked American: The Unexpected Decline of Leisure.* New York: Basic Books, 1992.

Stacey, Judith. *Brave New Families: Stories of Domestic Upheaval in Late-Twentieth-Century America.* 1990. Berkeley: University of California, 1998.

Stanton, Katherine. Dissertation-in-progress. "Cosmopolitan Fictions." Department of English, Rutgers University.

Watts, Carol. "Time and the Working Mother: Kristeva's 'Women's Time' Revisited." *Radical Philosophy* 91 (1998): 6–17.

Whitehead, Colson. *The Intuitionist.* New York: Anchor, 1999.

Williams, Raymond. *Politics and Letters: Interviews with New Left Review.* London: Verso, 1979.

Wood, Michael. "Sleepless Nights." *New York Review of Books* 21 December 1995: 17–18.

CHAPTER 12

Appadurai, Arjun. *Modernity at Large: Cultural Dimensions of Globalization.* Minneapolis, MN: University of Minnesota Press, 1999.

Ulrich Beck, Anthony Giddens and Scott Lash, *Reflexive Modernization: Politics, Tradition and Aesthetics in the Modern Social Order.* Stanford: Stanford University Press, 1994.

Bauman, Zygmunt. *Life in Fragments: Essays in Postmodern Morality.* Oxford: Polity Press, 1995.

———. *Liquid Modernity.* Cambridge: Polity Press, 2000.

Berger, Peter, and Hsin-huang Michael Hsiao ed. *In Search of an East Asian Development Model.* New Brunswick, NJ: Transaction Books, 1988.

Bourdieu, Piérre. Trans. Richard Rice. *Acts of Resistance: Against the Tyranny of the Market.* New York: The New Press, 1998.

Brooks, Peter. *The Melodramatic Imagination: Balzac, Henry James, Melodrama, and the Mode of Excess.* New Haven, CT: Yale University Press, 1976/1995.

Castells, Manuel. *The Rise of the Network Society.* Malden, MA: Blackwell, 1996.

Confucius. *The Analects.* Taipei: Taiwan Xinshen News, 1984.

Eisenstadt, S. N. ed. *Daedalus: "Multiple Modernities, A Special Issue".* 129.1 (Winter 2000).

Gaonkar, Dilip Parameshwar ed. *Alternative Modernities.* Durham, NC: Duke University Press, 2001.

Giddens, Anthony. *The Consequences of Modernity.* Stanford: Stanford University Press, 1990.

Haldane, John. "MacIntyre's Thomist Revival: What Next?" In *After MacIntyre: Critical Perspectives on the Work of Alisdair MacIntyre.* Ed. John Horton and Susan Mendus. Notre Dame, IN: University of Notre Dame Press, 1994: 91–107.

Hardt, Michael, and Antonio Negri, *Empire.* Cambridge, MA: Harvard University Press, 2000.

Harvey, David. *The Condition of Postmodernity: An Enquiry into the Origins of Social Change.* Cambridge: Blackwell Publishers, 1990.

Hayles, M, Katherine. "The Complexities of Seriation." *PMLA: Mobile Citizens, Media States, A Special Issue*. 117.1 (January 2002): 117–21.

Huang, Jianye, *A Study of Yang Dechang's Films* (Yang Dechang Dianying Yanjiu). Taipei: Yuanliu, 1995.

Jameson, Fredrick. "Cognitive Mapping" in *Marxism and the Interpretation of Culture*. ed. Cary Nelson and Lawrence Grossberg. Urbana and Chicago: University of Illinois Press, 1988: 347–57.

———. *Postmodernism, or, The Cultural Logic of Late Capitalism*. Durham, NC: Duke University Press, 1991.

———. *The Geopolitical Aesthetic: Cinema and Space in the World System* Bloomington: Indiana University Press, 1992/1995.

———. *A Singular Modernity: Essay on the Ontology of the Present*. London: Verso, 2002.

Li, David Leiwei. "What Will Become of Us if We Don't Stop? *Ermo*'s China and the End of Globalization," *Comparative Literature* 53.4 (2001): 442–61.

Lyotard, Jean-François. *The Postmodern Condition: A report on Knowledge*. Trans. Geoff Bennington and Brian Massumi. Minneapolis, MN: University of Minnesota Press, 1984/1997.

MacIntyre, Alisdair. *After Virtue: A Study in Moral Theory*. Notre Dame, IN: University of Notre Dame Press, 1984.

Marsh, Robert M. *The Great Transformation: Social Change in Taipei Taiwan Since the 1960s*. Armonk: M. E. Sharpe, 1996.

Nussbaum, Martha C. "Patriotism and Cosmopolitanism." In *For the Love of Country*. Ed. Martha Nussbaum and Joshua Cohen. Boston: Beacon, 1996: 2–17.

Ong, Aihwa. *Flexible Citizenship: The Cultural Logics of Transnationality*. Durham, NC: Duke University Press, 1999.

Riesman, David. *The Lonely Crowd: A study of the Changing American Character*. New Haven, CT: Yale University Press, 1961.

Robertson, Roland. *Globalization: Social Theory and Global Culture*. London: Sage, 1992/1998.

Tu, Weiming ed., *Dædalus: "The Living Tree: The Changing Meaning of Being Chinese Today, A Special Issue."* 120. 2 (1991).

Tu Weiming, "Human Rights as a Confucian Moral Discourse." In *Confucianism and Human Rights*. Ed. Wm. Theodore de Barry and Tu Weiming. New York: Columbia University Press, 1998: 297–307.

———. "Multiple Modernities: A Preliminary Inquiry into the Implications of East Asian Modernity." *Culture Matters: How Values Shape Human Progress*. Eds. Lawrence E. Harrison and Samuel P. Huntington. New York: Basic Books, 2000. 256–67.

Yang, Edward Dechang. *Yi Yi: A One and A Two*. New York: Windstar TV and Video, 2001.

AFTERWORD

Balakrishnan, Gopal. "Hardt and Negri's *Empire*." *New Left Review* 5 (2000). September October 2000. <http://www.newleftreview.net/NLR23909.shtml>

Black, Earl and Merle Black. *The Rise of Southern Republicans.* Cambridge, MA: Harvard University Press, 2002.

Bové, Paul A. "Rights Discourse in the Era of US/China Trade." *New Literary History: A Journal of Theory and Interpretation* 33 (2002): 171–87.

Bové, Paul A. "Chauvinism und Neoliberalismus: Fortschritt bei Richard Rorty." Trans. Tilman Reitz. *Das Argument: Zeitschrift für Philosophie und Sozialwissenschaftern* 41 (1999): 383–95.

Bush, George W. "The National Security Strategy of the United States." *New York Times on the Web.* 20 September 2002. <http://www.nytimes.com/2002/09/20/international/20STEXT_FULL.html>

Buttigieg, Joseph. Introduction. *Antonio Gramsci: Prison Notebooks.* Vol. 1. By Antonio Gramsci. New York: Columbia University Press, 1992. 1–64.

Cooper, Robert. "The New Liberal Imperialism." *Observer Worldview* 7 April 2002; 25 April 2002. <http://www.observer.co.uk/worldview/story/0,11581,680095,00.html>

Drury, Shadia B. *Leo Strauss and the American Right.* New York: St. Martin's Press, 1999.

Fish, Stanley. "Profession Despise Thyself: Fear and Self-Loathing in Literary Studies." *Critical Inquiry* 10 (1983): 349–373.

Friedman, Thomas. *The Lexus and the Olive Tree: Understanding Globalization.* New York: Anchor Books, 2000.

Hall, Stuart. *The Hard Road to Renewal: Thatcherism and the Crisis of the Left.* London: Verso Books, 1988.

Hardt, Michael, and Antonio Negri. *Empire.* Cambridge, MA: Harvard University Press, 2000.

Habermas, Jürgen. "*Bestialität und Humanität.*" *Die Zeit* 54 (1999): 1–8. Trans. Franz Solms-Laubach. <http://www.theglobalsite.ac.uk/press/011habermas.htm>

Kessler, Glenn. "U.S. Decision on Iraq Has Puzzling Past Opponents of War Wonder When, How Policy Was Set." *The Washington Post* 12 January 2003: A01.

Kimball, Roger. *Tenured Radicals: How Politics Has Corrupted Our Higher Education.* Rev. ed. New York: Ivan R Dee Inc., 1998.

Lind, Michael. *Made in Texas.* New York: Basic Books, 2003.

Munck, Ronaldo. "Review." *Cultural Logic: An Electronic Journal of Marxist Theory and Practice* 3.2 (2000). <http://eserver.org/clogic/3-1&2/munck.html>

Rowe, John Carlos. "The Resistance to Cultural Studies." *Aesthetics in a Multicultural Age.* Ed. Emory Elliott et al. New York: Oxford University Press, 2002. 105–17.

Said, Edward. "Response to Stanley Fish." *Critical Inquiry* 10 (1983): 349–73.

Santayana, George. *The Last Puritan: A Memoir in the Form of a Novel.* Ed. William G. Holzberger and Herman J. Saatkanp, Jr. *The Works of George Santayana, Volume 5.* Cambridge, MA: MIT Press, 1994; 1995.

Stille, Alexander. "Apocalypse Soon." *The New York Review of Books.* 7 November 2002. Cf. <http://www.nybooks.com/articles/15801>

"Titans Still Gather at Davos, Shorn of Profits and Bravado." *The New York Times on the Web.* 27 September 2003. <http:/www.nytimes.com/2003/01/27/business/worldbusiness/27FUNK.html>

Wolfe, Alan. "The Snake." *The New Republic Online.* 27 September 2001; 1 October 2001. <http://www.tnr.com/100101/wolfe100101_print.html>

Young, Hugo. "A New Imperialism Cooked Up Over A Texan Barbecue: Sovereignty Is Being Redefined, So Why Has Nobody Noticed?" 2 April 2002; 25 April 2002. <http://www.guardian.co.uk/comment/story/0,3604,677315,00.html>

Contributors

Paul A. Bové is Professor of English at the University of Pittsburgh and editor of *boundary* 2. The author and/or editor of more than a dozen books, including *Intellectuals in Power* (Columbia University Press, 1988), he is writing a book on Henry Adams and recent US cultural politics.

Román de la Campa is Professor of Latin American and Comparative Literature and Chair of Department of Hispanic Languages and Literature at State University of New York, Stony Brook. His most current books include *Cuba On My Mind: Journeys to a Severed Nation* (Verso, 2000) and *Latin Americanism* (Minnesota University Press, 1999).

Jia-lu Cheng is a PhD candidate in the Centre for Cultural Studies, Goldsmiths College, University of London.

Allen Chun is Research Fellow at the Institute of Ethnology, Academia Sinica, Taiwan. He is the author of *Unstructuring Chinese Society: The Fictions of Colonial Practice and the Changing Realities of 'Land' in the New Territories of Hong Kong* (Harwood Academic Press, 2000).

Sangita Gopal is Assistant Professor of English at Old Dominion University. She has written articles on sexuality, nationalism and the global novel, and is completing a book-length project, entitled *World Citizen: The Elusive Subject of Globalization*.

Alison M. Jaggar is Professor of Philosophy and Women's Studies at the University of Colorado at Boulder. She is author of *Living with Contradictions: Controversies in Feminist Ethics* (Westview, 1994), and editor with Paula Rothenberg of *Feminist Frameworks* (McGraw Hill, 1993) and with Iris M. Young of *The Blackwell Companion to Feminist Philosophy* (Blackwell, 1998).

Paul Jay is Professor of English at Loyola University, Chicago. His books include *Being in the Text: Self Representation from Wordsworth to Roland Barthes* (Cornell University Press, 1984), *The Selected Correspondence of Kenneth Burke and Malcolm Cowley* (Viking, 1988), and *Contingency Blues: The Search for Foundations in American Criticism* (University of Wisconsin Press, 1997).

Liu Kang is Professor of Chinese and Cultural Studies at Duke University. His books include *Aesthetics and Marxism* (Duke University Press, 2000), *Globalization and Cultural Trends in China* (University of Hawaii Press, 2003), and *Demonizing China* (Chinese Academy of Social Sciences Press, 1996).

David Leiwei Li is Collins Professor of the Humanities at the English Department of University of Oregon. He is the author of *Imagining the Nation: Asian American Literature and Cultural Consent* (Stanford University Press, 1998).

Masao Miyoshi is Hajime Mori Professor of Literature at the University of California, San Diego. His recent works include *Off Center: Power and Culture Relations Between Japan and the United States* (Harvard University Press, 1991), *The Culture of Globalization*, co-edited with Fredric Jameson (Duke University Press, 1997), and *Learning Places: the Afterlives of Area Studies*, co-edited with H. D. Harootunian (Duke University Press, 2002).

Rajagopalan Radhakrishnan is Professor of English at the University of Massachusetts, Amherst. He is the author of *Diasporic Mediations: Between Home and Location* (University of Minnesota Press, 1996) and *Theory in an Uneven World* (Blackwell, 2003).

Bruce Robbins is Professor of English at Columbia University. His most recent book is *Feeling Global: Internationalism in Distress* (New York University Press, 1999).

Brook Thomas teaches in the Department of English and Comparative Literature at the University of California, Irvine. His most recent books and editions are *The New Historicism and Other Old-Fashioned Topics* (Princeton University Press, 1991) and *American Literary Realism and the Failed Promise of Contract* (California University Press, 1997), *Plessy v. Ferguson* (Bedford, 1997), *Literature and the Nation* (Gunter Narr, 1998), and *Law and Literature* (Gunter Narr, 2002).

Rob Wilson is Professor and Graduate Chair of the Literature Department, University of California at Santa Cruz. His recent books include *Reimagining the American Pacific: From 'South Pacific' to Bamboo Ridge* (Duke University Press, 2000) and *Inside Out: Literature, Cultural Politics and Identity in the New Pacific*, co-edited with Vilsoni Hereniko (Rowman and Littlefield, 1999).

Index